Sunday Year C • Weekday Year I

A book of prayer for each day of the liturgical year.

John Thomas Lane, SSS

Nihil Obstat
Reverend Mr. Daniel G. Welter
Vicar for Canonical Services
Archdiocese of Chicago
March 19, 2018

Imprimatur
Very Reverend Ronald A. Hicks
Vicar General
Archdiocese of Chicago
March 19, 2018

The *Nihil Obstat* and *Imprimatur* are declarations that the material is free from doctrinal or moral error, and thus is granted permission to publish in accordance with c. 827. No legal responsibility is assumed by the grant of this permission. No implications is contained herein that those who have granted the *Nihil Obstat* and *Imprimatur* agree with the content, opinions, or statements expressed.

Daily Prayer is based in part on the pattern established in *Children's Daily Prayer*, by Elizabeth McMahon Jeep. This book was edited by Mary Fox. Víctor Pérez was the production editor. Kari Nicholls was the designer and production artist.

Printed in the United States of America

ISBN: 978-1-61671-389-8

DP19

Table of Contents

Introduction iv

Advent
December 2 through December 24, 2018 1

Christmas Time
December 25 through January 13, 2019 24

Ordinary Time
January 14 through March 5, 2019 44

Lent
March 6 through April 17, 2019 95

Sacred Paschal Triduum
April 18 through April 21, 2019 138

Easter Time
April 22 through June 9, 2019 142

Ordinary Time
June 10 through November 30, 2019 191

Advent
December 1 through December 24, 2019 365

Christmas Time
December 25 through December 31, 2019 389

Psalter 396

Introduction

Rejoice always.
Pray without ceasing.
In all circumstances give thanks,
for this is the will of God for
you in Christ Jesus.

1 Thessalonians 5:16–18

Welcome to *Daily Prayer 2019,* Sunday Year C and Weekday Year I! This edition of the well-loved prayer book provides a familiar order of prayer for each day of the liturgical year, from the First Sunday of Advent, December 2, 2018, through December 31, 2019. Readings from the daily Mass are provided, and the prayer texts and reflections are connected to the liturgical time, solemnities, feasts of the Lord, and the memorials of the saints. The prayers on these pages will inspire and bring you to a deeper appreciation for the Word that is proclaimed and for Eucharist that is shared in the liturgical life of the Church.

The Order of Prayer

Daily Prayer 2019 follows a simple order of prayer: it begins with an opening verse with the Sign of the Cross, followed by a psalm, a reading from the daily Mass, a brief reflection, the Prayer of the Faithful, the Lord's Prayer, a closing prayer, and a closing verse with the Sign of the Cross. This order remains consistent for each day of the liturgical year, allowing its repetition to become part of your daily rhythm and routine.

Daily Prayer 2019 is organized by liturgical time, and the Psalter is located in the back of the book (pages 396–421). Everything you need is conveniently contained in this resource. Refer to the table of contents for easy reference.

DAILY HEADING

Daily Prayer 2019 is easy to use. A heading is provided for each day of prayer so you will always know where you are and what you should pray. The heading includes the date and the name of the liturgical observance. Typically, optional memorials are not celebrated in this edition of *Daily Prayer 2019*; however, if celebrated, the optional memorial will be noted in the heading. The liturgical observances are those according to the norms prescribed by the Secretariat of Divine Worship.

OPENING AND CLOSING VERSICLE WITH SIGN OF THE CROSS

The order of prayer begins each day with the Sign of the Cross and a versicle, or opening verse. The versicles are taken from the refrains proper to the Responsorial Psalms from the Mass; antiphons from *The Liturgy of the Hours* and *The Roman Missal*; verses from the Acclamation before the Gospel (*Lectionary for Mass*); and lines from Scripture, especially the psalms.

PSALMODY

The psalms are an important part of Catholic prayer. As poetic readings from Sacred Scripture, the psalms reflect upon God's saving work in various ways —praise, thanksgiving, and lamentation. The psalms in *Daily Prayer 2019* have been selected for their liturgical significance. Psalms for Advent implore God's return; psalms for Christmas

Time shout for joy; psalms for Lent evoke the need for God's mercy and forgiveness; psalms for Easter Time give praise for his glory and salvation; and psalms for Ordinary Time give thanks for all that is good. For many of the Marian solemnities and feasts, the psalm has been replaced by the Canticle of Mary. This canticle is included on page 420.

READING

Each day of prayer includes a reading from the daily Mass. This enables further reflection upon the Word of God proclaimed during the Eucharistic celebration (Mass)—the source and summit of our faith. On some days, excerpts, not the full text, from the Scripture passage have been selected. The Gospel is used for each Sunday, solemnity, and feast of the Lord.

REFLECTION

The author for this year has provided insights for meditation and reflection. These reflections guide the reader to a deeper relationship with God, neighbor, and self.

UNIVERSAL PRAYER

Universal Prayer, sometimes referred to as the Prayer of the Faithful, is a prayer of the baptized who, through Christ, voice their concerns to God regarding the Church, the world, the oppressed, local needs, and other concerns. Thus, the prayers in this book connect the individual and small faith groups to the universal Church and those in most need of God's love and mercy. Although specific prayers are provided in this resource, others may be added.

THE LORD'S PRAYER

Jesus taught us how to pray. It is fitting to follow the Universal Prayer with the Lord's Prayer, for it encapsulates the humility and reverence we give to our God—and neighbor—while asking for his mercy and forgiveness.

CLOSING PRAYER

The closing prayer follows the form of the traditional Collect. This prayer "is usually addressed to God the Father, through Christ, in the Holy Spirit" (*General Instruction of the Roman Missal*, 54). Essentially, this prayer "collects" our daily prayer, the prayers found in this book, and those of our hearts and minds, those as individuals or groups, into one Trinitarian prayer, concluding with our assent of faith in the response "Amen."

Using the Book

This resource may be used by individuals, families, or prayer groups; on retreats; to begin meetings or catechetical sessions, formational and youth ministry events; or as prayer with the aged, sick, and homebound. The prayers may be used at any time during the day, and given this book's convenient size, it is easily transported to meet various prayer needs and situations.

The order of prayer may be prayed silently or, especially for group prayer, prayed aloud. If used for prayer gatherings, it might be helpful to designate someone to open the prayer, lead the Prayer of the Faithful, begin the Lord's Prayer, and to conclude the prayer. Select an additional volunteer to proclaim the reading. Allow the faithful to read the psalm together either as an entire group, or divide the stanzas among the faithful with alternating recitation.

Feel free to adapt these prayers for specific needs—intercessions (or petitions) may be added, music may begin and conclude the service, and the psalm response to the Universal Prayer and the Lord's Prayer may be chanted or sung.

Other Uses for Daily Prayer

Daily Prayer 2019 also may be used in other situations or for various needs.

- Use the Prayer of the Faithful during the Mass. The prayers have been written in accordance with paragraphs 69 and 70 of the *General Instruction of the Roman Missal*. Since this book contains prayers for each day of the liturgical year, you may use the intercessions for every day of the year for Mass.
- Use the included reflections as homily sparkers and catechetical tools.

Customer Feedback

Daily Prayer 2019 is the seventeenth edition of an annual publication; *Daily Prayer 2020* is already being prepared. Because it is an annual, it can be changed from year to year to become a better tool for your daily prayer. As you use this book and adapt it for yourself, you may have ideas about how it can be made more useful for your prayer. Feel free to email us at DailyPrayer@LTP.org.

About the Author

Fr. John Thomas Lane, sss, is the pastor of his home parish, St. Paschal Baylon Catholic Church, Highland Heights, Ohio. The Blessed Sacrament priest writes on liturgy for *Emmanuel Magazine*. He is the author of *Guide for Celebrating® Worship of the Eucharist Outside of Mass* (Chicago: Liturgy Training Publications, 2015) and has contributed to *Sourcebook for Sundays, Seasons and Weekdays* 2012, 2013, and 2017 (LTP). He leads parish missions and gives workshops on liturgy, music, and the catechumenate.

Prior to serving at St. Paschal Baylon, Fr. Lane was a pastor at a parish in Albuquerque, New Mexico, vocation director for his order in Houston, Texas, and director of liturgy for the Diocese of Salt Lake City.

Besides degrees in music and education, he received a master of divinity with word and worship specialization from Catholic Theological Union, Chicago, and a master of arts in theology/liturgical studies from the University of Notre Dame.

Sunday, December 2, 2018
First Sunday of Advent

✝ To you, O Lord, I lift my soul.

Psalm 25

page 399

Reading

Luke 21:25–28

Jesus said to his disciples: "There will be signs in the sun, the moon, and the stars, and on earth nations will be in dismay, perplexed by the roaring of the sea and the waves. People will die of fright in anticipation of what is coming upon the world, for the powers of the heavens will be shaken. And then they will see the Son of Man coming in a cloud with power and great glory. But when these signs begin to happen, stand erect and raise your heads because your redemption is at hand."

Reflection

As the liturgical year begins, we hear of the need to be alert to the coming of the Lord. The Gospel depicts a time when people are so filled with terror that some die of fright. In our time, we may be fearful because of crime, natural disasters, or a family crisis. We have the choice to act from these emotions or from the hope that God brings. We can be among those causing panic among family and friends or we can spread the hope that we have received from the Gospel. When our actions are inspired by the Gospel, we read the signs of the times as opportunities for Jesus to be born anew in our communities. Through us, Jesus can provide comfort and joy to those we meet.

Prayers

others may be added

Recognizing that all paths lead to the Lord, we pray:

◆ Lord, hear our prayer.

Encourage our leaders in the Church to continue working for peace with zeal, we pray: ◆ Help citizens to courageously live Gospel joy and hope, we pray: ◆ Present options to those who suffer from fear and anxiety, we pray: ◆ Deliver safety and protection to those in danger, we pray: ◆ Comfort and sustain those who await healing care, we pray: ◆ Bring those who have died to the heavenly banquet, we pray: ◆

Our Father . . .

O God,
each day you offer us peace.
Help us to know of your
constant presence
and renew our efforts
to give strength, protection, and hope
to those most in need.
Grant this through Christ our Lord.
Amen.

✝ To you, O Lord, I lift my soul.

Monday, December 3, 2018
Memorial of St. Francis Xavier, Priest

☩ Let us go rejoicing to the house of the Lord.

Psalm 122 *page 416*

Reading *Isaiah 2:1–5*

This is what Isaiah, son of Amoz, saw concerning Judah and Jerusalem.

In days to come, / The mountain of the LORD's house / shall be established as the highest mountain / and raised above the hills. / All nations shall stream toward it / many peoples shall come and say: / "Come, let us climb the LORD's mountain, / to the house of the God of Jacob, / That he may instruct us in his ways, / and we may walk in his paths." / For from Zion shall go forth instruction, / and the word of the LORD from Jerusalem. / He shall judge between the nations, / and impose terms on many peoples. / They shall beat their swords into plowshares / and their spears into pruning hooks / One nation shall not raise the sword against another, / nor shall they train for war again.

O house of Jacob, come, / let us walk in the light of the LORD!

Reflection

In this reading, Isaiah presents a vision of hope. People of every nation stream toward the house of God, where they will receive instruction so that they can walk in his path. On our journey to God, we rely on the way that Christ has shown us. We travel with the light that Christ has provided, and as disciples, seek to share that light with others on the journey.

Prayers *others may be added*

With faith lighting our journey and adventures in life, we pray:

◆ Hear us, gracious Lord.

Light the way of justice for Church leaders, we pray: ◆ Strengthen the bonds of unity among elected officials to enable them to work for the common good, we pray: ◆ Help us to provide food and shelter to those who are hungry and homeless, we pray: ◆ Assist us as we seek to comfort the imprisoned, we pray: ◆ Call women and men to be like St. Francis and serve the Church as missionaries, we pray: ◆ Console those who miss and mourn their loved ones, we pray: ◆

Our Father . . .

Lord God,
you sent us your Son
to teach us peace.
May we always strive to share
the light of faith
with our brothers and sisters.
Through Christ our Lord.
Amen.

☩ Let us go rejoicing to the house of the Lord.

Tuesday, December 4, 2018
Advent Weekday

✝ Justice shall flourish in his time,
and fullness of peace for ever.

Psalm 25

page 399

Reading

Isaiah 11:1–6

On that day, / A shoot shall sprout from the stump of Jesse, / and from his roots a bud shall blossom. / The Spirit of the LORD shall rest upon him: / a Spirit of wisdom and of understanding, / A Spirit of counsel and of strength, / a Spirit of knowledge and of fear of the LORD, / and his delight shall be the fear of the LORD / Not by appearance shall he judge, / nor by hearsay shall he decide, / But he shall judge the poor with justice, / and decide aright for the land's afflicted. / He shall strike the ruthless with the rod of his mouth, / and with the breath of his lips he shall slay the wicked. / Justice shall be the band around his waist, / and faithfulness a belt upon his hips.

Then the wolf shall be a guest of the lamb, / and the leopard shall lie down with the kid; / The calf and the young lion shall browse together, / with a little child to guide them.

Reflection

Isaiah sees a future of hope, reconciliation, and peace. This vision holds unprecedented harmony among animals. A peaceful kingdom has been established in which prey and predator, children and fierce animals live side by side. We are to live in hope for the reign of God to take hold among us.

Prayers

others may be added

To our Lord, who sends the Spirit,
we pray:

◆ Come, Lord Jesus.

Assist parishes as they seek to tend to the needs in the modern world, we pray: ◆ Encourage legislators to support laws that will protect all life from conception until natural death, we pray: ◆ Help those who need to forgive, who hold hatred and burdens of woe, we pray: ◆ Console the sick, we pray: ◆ Guide us as we look to the Lord's return, we pray: ◆ Bring to the heavenly banquet our beloved who have died, we pray: ◆

Our Father . . .

O God,
you sent your Son to us
filled with the gifts of the Spirit.
Support us as we seek
to turn our hearts to you this Advent
and to build communities
with love and justice at their core.
Through Christ our Lord.
Amen.

✝ Justice shall flourish in his time,
and fullness of peace for ever.

Wednesday, December 5, 2018

Advent Weekday

☩ I shall live in the house of the Lord
all the days of my life.

Psalm 23

page 398

Reading

Isaiah 25:6–9

On this mountain the LORD of hosts / will provide for all peoples / A feast of rich food and choice wines. / On this mountain he will destroy / the veil that veils all peoples. / The web that is woven over all nations; / he will destroy death forever. / The LORD God will wipe away / the tears from every face; / The reproach of his people he will remove / from the whole earth; for the LORD has spoken.

On that day it will be said: / "Behold our God, to whom we looked to save us!" This is the LORD for whom we looked / let us rejoice and be glad that he has saved us!"

Reflection

This reading lays out the goodness that God provides. Not only does the divine offer us the food and drink that we need to survive but "rich food and choice wines." On the mountain where the feast awaits, people will not only be happy but tears will be wiped from every face. After a life of following the will of the Lord, our journey will be complete at the great feast. Now, we plan, prepare, wait, and climb, all while God nourishes and sustains our journey. We are comforted knowing that God is with us. How have you seen God in the events of the day?

Prayers

others may be added

Continuing to prepare for the coming of the Lord, we pray:

◆ Lord, hear our prayer.

Assist church leaders in their evangelization efforts, we pray: ◆ Keep police, firefighters, and others who protect us free from harm, we pray: ◆ Guide researchers as they seek to find cures for diseases, we pray: ◆ Support those in hospice facilities, we pray: ◆ Set the poor and afflicted free from burdens, we pray: ◆ Bring those who have died to the perfection in heaven, we pray: ◆

Our Father . . .

O God,
you travel with and guide us,
to comfort those who labor and
are burdened.
Nourish our faith,
free us from worries,
and hear our prayers for strength
as we look forward to your coming.
Through Christ our Lord.
Amen.

☩ I shall live in the house of the Lord
all the days of my life.

Thursday, December 6, 2018
Optional Memorial of St. Nicholas, Bishop

✝ Blessed is he who comes in the name of the Lord.

Psalm 118 *page 414*

Reading *Isaiah 26:1–6*

On that day they will sing this song in the land of Judah: / "A strong city have we; / he sets up walls and ramparts to protect us. / Open up the gates to let in a nation that is just, one that keeps faith. / A nation of firm purpose you keep in peace; / in peace, for its trust in you."

Trust in the LORD forever! / For the LORD is an eternal Rock. / He humbles those in high places, / and the lofty city he brings down; / He tumbles it to the ground, levels it with the dust. / It is trampled underfoot by the needy, / by the footsteps of the poor.

Reflection

Isaiah presents two types of nations. Judah, who trusts in the Lord, is at peace and secure. The country that is not just will be brought down and trampled by the poor. Isaiah's tune of hope is of a world fulfilled in God, a world that God protects. Today, we honor St. Nicholas, who is remembered for the ways in which he looked out for the welfare of others. According to legend, he spared three daughters from prostitution by throwing bags of gold coins into their home. How have you helped another through your trust in the Lord?

Prayers *others may be added*

In Advent hope, we pray:

◆ Lord, hear our prayer.

Assist the Church to proclaim a message of harmony, we pray: ◆ Help elected officials seek ways to end divisions, we pray: ◆ Support peacekeeping efforts, we pray: ◆ Through the intercession of St. Nicholas, guide gift-giving efforts this season, we pray: ◆ Heal the depressed, we pray: ◆ Raise up all who have fallen asleep, we pray: ◆

Our Father . . .

Almighty God,
you raise up the lowly
and tumble the wicked.
Build us up in your strong love
and send out your justice
that gives hope to all peoples.
Through Christ our Lord.
Amen.

✝ Blessed is he who comes in the name of the Lord.

Friday, December 7, 2018

Memorial of St. Ambrose, Bishop and Doctor of the Church

☩ The Lord is my light and my salvation.

Psalm 27

page 399

Reading

Isaiah 29:17–21

Thus says the Lord GOD:
But a very little while,
and Lebanon shall be changed
into an orchard,
and the orchard be regarded as
a forest!
On that day the deaf shall hear
the words of a book;
And out of gloom and darkness,
the eyes of the blind shall see.
The lowly will ever find joy in
the LORD,
and the poor rejoice in the Holy
One of Israel.
For the tyrant will be no more
and the arrogant will have gone;
All who are alert to do evil will be
cut off,
those whose mere word
condemns a man,
Who ensnare his defender at the gate,
and leave the just man with an
empty claim.

Reflection

Isaiah provides a vision of the world during the reign of God. At this time, the blind shall see and the tyrant will disappear. Any of us can be a little deaf, blind, and mute sometimes. Advent reminds us that we are awaiting the Lord but also a coming into our own. We are called to humbly share our sight, wisdom, words, and ways so that all may hear of the glory of God. We are to shed light on the elements of faith that bring about a blossoming forest and life in God for all to see.

Prayers

others may be added

To our Lord, who makes the deaf hear and the blind see, we pray:

◆ Lord, hear our prayer.

Assist Church leaders as they seek wisdom, we pray: ◆ Encourage dialogue among civic authorities, we pray: ◆ Support estranged families as they seek to work through crises, we pray: ◆ Guide young people to discern their future paths, we pray: ◆ Comfort the sick, we pray: ◆ Wipe away the tears from all who mourn a loss, we pray: ◆

Our Father . . .

Ever-faithful God,
you call your people
to open their ears and eyes
to see the wonder of your justice and care.
Teach us to be people
of hope and encouragement
so that we may bring all
to knowledge of your compassion.
Through Christ our Lord.
Amen.

☩ The Lord is my light and my salvation.

Saturday, December 8, 2018
Solemnity of the Immaculate Conception of the Blessed Virgin Mary

✝ Sing to the Lord a new song,
for he has done marvelous deeds.

Canticle of Mary *page 423*

Reading *Ephesians 1:3–6, 11–12*

Brothers and sisters: Blessed be the God and Father of our Lord Jesus Christ, who has blessed us in Christ with every spiritual blessing in the heavens, as he chose us in him, before the foundation of the world, to be holy and without blemish before him. In love he destined us for adoption to himself through Jesus Christ, in accord with the favor of his will, for the praise of the glory of his grace that he granted us in the beloved.

In him we were also chosen, destined in accord with the purpose of the One who accomplishes all things according to the intention of his will, so that we might exist for the praise of his glory, we who first hoped in Christ.

Reflection

Today we contemplate not only how God loved Mary into being but that God also chose us "before the foundation of the world." He has provided us with the grace "to be holy and without blemish." Our lives, too, can be a song that praises the Lord, acclaiming his greatness and the blessings bestowed on us. Looking to Mary as our example, may we accept our call to holiness.

Prayers *others may be added*

To our Lord, who deserves our praise, we pray:

◆ Come, Lord Jesus.

Protect the pope as he seeks to bring people to Christ, we pray: ◆ Guide legislators to work for justice, we pray: ◆ Call men and women to serve the Church through the consecrated life, we pray: ◆ Support married couples as they discern how to serve you as a family, we pray: ◆ Assist the sick and suffering, we pray: ◆ Strengthen those who have lost a child, we pray: ◆

Our Father . . .

O God,
you chose us to be holy.
May we look to Mary
as an example of one
who trusted in your will.
May we seek to praise
you each day
for the blessing
of our lives
and aim to stay away
from the darkness of sin.
Through Christ our Lord.
Amen.

✝ Sing to the Lord a new song,
for he has done marvelous deeds.

Sunday, December 9, 2018

Second Sunday of Advent

✝ The Lord has done great things for us; we are filled with joy.

Psalm 126 *page 417*

Reading *Luke 3:1–6*

In the fifteenth year of the reign of Tiberius Caesar, when Pontius Pilate was governor of Judea, and Herod was tetrach of Galilee, and his brother Philip tetrach of the region of Ituraea and Trachonitis . . . the word of God came to John in the desert. John went throughout the whole region of the Jordan, proclaiming a baptism of repentance for the forgiveness of sins, as it is written in the book of the words of the prophet Isaiah: / *A voice of one crying out in the desert: / "Prepare the way of the Lord, / make straight his paths. / Every valley shall be filled / and every mountain and hill shall be made low. / The winding roads shall be made straight, / and the rough ways made smooth, / and all flesh shall see the salvation of God."*

Reflection

As Luke names the leaders of the nation and region and gives the year of Caesar's reign, he provides readers with the setting for the work of John the Baptist. God situated John in the desert during a certain time. Situated in a certain country, state, and region in the twenty-first century, we are called to do God's work. Through us, God can bring justice and righteousness to the world. We cannot disregard our time and place as worthy to prepare for the coming of the Lord.

Prayers *others may be added*

To the Lord, who calls us to prepare for him, we pray:

◆ Lord, hear us.

For the Church, that she seek to evangelize the lost, we pray: ◆ For world leaders to always be instruments of peace, we pray: ◆ For the strength to assist victims of violence, war, and natural disasters, we pray: ◆ For our parish to grow in holiness during this Advent, we pray: ◆ For all the sick to feel comfort and joy, we pray: ◆ For those who have died, may they see the glory of God's mercy, we pray: ◆

Our Father . . .

Lord God,
you led John the Baptist
to the desert
so that he could call people
to prepare their lives for your coming.
May we work during our time
to spread the Good News of salvation.
Through Christ our Lord.
Amen.

✝ The Lord has done great things for us; we are filled with joy.

Monday, December 10, 2018
Advent Weekday

† Our God will come to save us!

Psalm 85
page 407

Reading
Isaiah 35:1–6

The desert and the parched land will exult; / the steppe will rejoice and bloom. / They will bloom with abundant flowers, / and rejoice with joyful song. / The glory of Lebanon will be given to them, / the splendor of Carmel and Sharon; / They will see the glory of the LORD, / the splendor of our God. Strengthen the hands that are feeble, / make firm the knees that are weak, / Say to those whose hearts are frightened: / Be strong, fear not! / Here is your God, / he comes with vindication; / With divine recompense / he comes to save you. / Then will the eyes of the blind be opened, / the ears of the deaf be cleared; / then will the lame leap like a stag, / Then the tongue of the mute will sing.

Reflection

Isaiah presents a vision in which even the desert rejoices in the glory of God and all are made whole. With the splendor of God made known, the weak are made strong, the eyes of the blind are opened, and the mute sing. In this second week of Advent, you might want to spend time considering what you would like to be healed in your life. Is there something that prevents you from seeing the beauty of the way God works in your life? Or does your heart hold back on singing of God's glory?

Prayers
others may be added

To our Lord, who protects us, we pray:

◆ Come, Lord Jesus.

For faith communities, that they act as a beacon of hope, we pray: ◆ For world leaders, that they awaken hope in their citizens, we pray: ◆ For those who are spiritually blind and deaf, that they see and hear God's blessings in their lives, we pray: ◆ For those recovering from natural disasters, we pray: ◆ For healing for the sick, we pray: ◆ For those who have died, that they rejoice in the new and eternal Jerusalem, we pray: ◆

Our Father . . .

God of glory and majesty,
you guide our steps
and reverse the ills of this world
to bring hope and renewal.
Strengthen us
to be firm in hope and faith
so that we may radiate your goodness.
Through Christ our Lord.
Amen.

† Our God will come to save us!

Tuesday, December 11, 2018
Advent Weekday

✝ The Lord our God comes with power.

Psalm 96 *page 409*

Reading *Isaiah 40:1–5*

Comfort, give comfort to my people, / says your God. / Speak tenderly to Jerusalem, and proclaim to her / that her service is at an end, / her guilt is expiated; / Indeed, she has received from the hand of the LORD / double for all her sins.

A voice cries out: / In the desert prepare the way of the LORD! / Make straight in the wasteland a highway for our God! / Every valley shall be filled in, / every mountain and hill shall be made low; / The rugged land shall be made a plain, / the rough country, a broad valley. / Then the glory of the LORD shall be revealed, / and all people shall see it together; / for the mouth of the LORD has spoken.

Reflection

The prophet pleas that tenderness and comfort be brought to the Lord's people. Those who are lowly need our gentle, humble response to them. Isaiah's words encourage us to shelter and care for others so that through the experience, they will feel the Lord's presence. As we prepare the way of the Lord, the straightening of paths may rely on the tenderness we provide to those we meet. When such care is given and received, the glory of the Lord is revealed.

Prayers *others may be added*

To our just Lord, we pray:

◆ Lord, hear our prayer.

For the health and well-being of all who serve in leadership in the Church, we pray: ◆ For legislators and governors, that they provide for the needs of those who are marginalized, we pray: ◆ For nurses and other caregivers, that they stay strong and healthy, we pray: ◆ For teachers stressed about end-of-the-year projects, we pray: ◆ For the sick and those who care for them, we pray: ◆ For those who have died estranged from family, we pray: ◆

Our Father . . .

Compassionate God,
through your prophets
you taught us to comfort each other.
Continue to shepherd us
with your gentle ways
and help us teach others of your love.
Through Christ our Lord.
Amen.

✝ The Lord our God comes with power.

Wednesday, December 12, 2018

Feast of Our Lady of Guadalupe

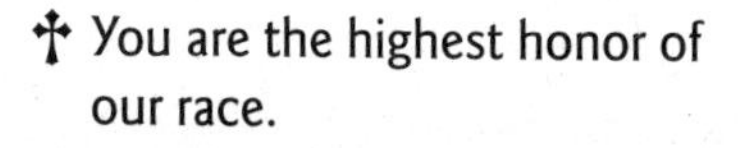

✝ You are the highest honor of our race.

Psalm 96

page 409

Reading

Zechariah 2:14–17

Sing and rejoice, O daughter Zion! See, I am coming to dwell among you, says the LORD. Many nations shall join themselves to the LORD on that day, and they shall be his people, and he will dwell among you, and you shall know that the LORD of hosts has sent me to you. The LORD will possess Judah as his portion in the holy land, and he will again choose Jerusalem. Silence, all mankind, in the presence of the LORD! For he stirs forth from his holy dwelling.

Reflection

During this time of preparing for the coming of the Lord, we celebrate Our Lady of Guadalupe, who came to Tepeyac as a pregnant indigenous woman. This feast day in the Americas reminds us of God's desire to not only be present to all people but to dwell among them. Our Lady of Guadalupe points to God, who has so many possibilities for us and desires for us to see the glory of God here, now, and in the future. The prophet Zechariah presented God as both with his people and coming in the future. Today, with prayer, song, and dance, we rejoice that God hears the cry of his people and dwells among them.

Prayers

others may be added

Believing and trusting in God's presence, we pray:

◆ Lord, in your mercy, hear our prayer.

For the Church, as mother, that she always exemplify compassion and love, we pray: ◆ For nations, that they seek to care for their citizens, we pray: ◆ For those who protect us, that they may be kept safe from harm, we pray: ◆ For couples who struggle to find joy in their marriage, we pray: ◆ For those in hospice and their families, we pray: ◆ For the beloved dead, that they be brought to dwell in heaven, we pray: ◆

Our Father . . .

God of ages past and present,
you sent Our Lady of Guadalupe
to give hope to your people.
May we always be open
to your dwelling among us
and with tenderness bring
the Good News of salvation
to all who need to hear it.
Through Christ our Lord.
Amen.

✝ You are the highest honor of our race.

Thursday, December 13, 2018

Memorial of St. Lucy, Virgin and Martyr

✝ The Lord is gracious and merciful;
slow to anger, and of great kindness.

Psalm 145

page 421

Reading

Isaiah 41:13–16

I am the LORD, your God, / who grasp your right hand; / It is I who say to you, "Fear not, / I will help you." / Fear not, O worm Jacob, / O maggot Israel; / I will help you, says the LORD; / your redeemer is the Holy One of Israel. / I will make of you a threshing sledge, / sharp, new, and double-edged, / To thresh the mountains and crush them, / to make the hills like chaff. / When you winnow them, the wind shall carry them off / and the storm shall scatter them. / But you shall rejoice in the LORD and glory in the Holy One of Israel.

Reflection

Just as the Lord God brought the commands and law to the people through the prophet Moses, Isaiah shows that the Lord brings care and compassion to us. Today, too, we need to hear "fear not," for some will seek to frighten to persuade people to change their minds. No matter the reaction that others seek, we need to remember that God is present and will always provide. St. Lucy, whom we honor today, was not afraid to devote her life to God, no matter the threat to her life.

Prayers

others may be added

To the Lord, our cause for rejoicing, we pray:

◆ God of mercy, hear our prayer.

For charitable agencies, that they overcome obstacles to continue their mission, we pray: ◆ For nations, that they uphold human rights, we pray: ◆ For educational programs that assist in the healing of divisions in communities, we pray: ◆ For the visually impaired, that through the intercession of St. Lucy, they may be healed, we pray: ◆ For the critically wounded, that they heal quickly, we pray: ◆ For the dying, that they be led to eternal glory, we pray: ◆

Our Father . . .

God of all ages,
you guide your people
through the trials and tribulations of life
to enter into peace with you.
Help us abandon fear and anxiety
as we seek to build your reign.
Through Christ our Lord.
Amen.

✝ The Lord is gracious and merciful;
slow to anger, and of great kindness.

Friday, December 14, 2018
Memorial of St. John of the Cross,
Priest and Doctor of the Church

✝ Those who follow you, Lord,
will have the light of life.

Psalm 96 *page 409*

Reading *Isaiah 48:17–19*

Thus says the LORD, your redeemer, / the Holy One of Israel: / I , the LORD, your God, / teach you what is for your good, / and lead you on the way you should go. / If you would hearken to my commandments, / your prosperity would be like a river, / and your vindication like the waves of the sea; / Your descendants would be like the sand, / and those born of your stock like its grains, / their name never cut off or blotted out from my presence.

Reflection

The statement from Isaiah may remind us of the wisdom elders tried to impart during our youth. They, too, tried to show us the way to prosperity through righteousness. Sometimes these lessons were heeded, and at other times, we may have turned away from them. As we prepare for the Lord's return, we know that good comes our way when we trust God. We can be assured that God will guide us in goodness and keep us growing along that path.

Prayers *others may be added*

Trusting in God's care, we pray:

◆ Lord, graciously hear us.

For the renewal of hearts of all who have fallen away from the Church, we pray: ◆ For laws that seek to build the common good in our nation, we pray: ◆ For all who are seeking meaningful employment, we pray: ◆ For patience for merchants as customers shop for gifts, we pray: ◆ For theologians, writers, and philosophers who share the wisdom of God through the intercession of St. John, we pray: ◆ For our beloved deceased, we pray: ◆

Our Father . . .

Lord God,
you guide us with your wisdom,
always seeking what is good for us.
Grant that we may willingly
follow where you lead
so that we may come to know you
and live in your kingdom.
Through Christ our Lord.
Amen.

✝ Those who follow you, Lord,
will have the light of life.

Saturday, December 15, 2018
Advent Weekday

✝ Lord, make us turn to you;
let us see your face and we shall
be saved.

Psalm 147 *page 422*

Reading *Sirach 48:1–4, 9–11*

In those days, / like a fire there appeared the prophet Elijah / whose words were as a flaming furnace. / Their staff of bread he shattered, / in his zeal he reduced them to straits; / By the Lord's word he shut up the heavens / and three times brought down fire. / How awesome are you, Elijah, in your wondrous deeds! / Whose glory is equal to yours? / You were taken aloft in a whirlwind of fire, / in a chariot with fiery horses. / You were destined, it is written, in time to come / to put an end to wrath before the day of the LORD, / To turn back the hearts of fathers toward their sons, / and to re-establish the tribes of Jacob. / Blessed is he who shall have seen you / and who falls asleep in your friendship.

Reflection

In this passage, we read of the deeds of Elijah, the greatest of the prophets. Israel held him in high esteem because of his zeal for fighting God's enemies as well as his preaching and miracles. While our story is still being written, we should take time to contemplate how we are leaving our mark on the world. Will others recall our zeal for the faith? Do your closest family and friends even know of your prayer life, or do you keep that a secret? Let your family know of your love for the Lord and how you direct your life to follow his ways.

Prayers *others may be added*

Aware of the goodness of God,
we pray:

◆ Lord, hear our prayer.

For the pope, that his writings inspire the faithful as he tells of the glories of God, we pray: ◆ For legislators, that they work zealously for the common good, we pray: ◆ For those preparing for final exams, we pray: ◆ For vocations to the consecrated life, we pray: ◆ For the sick, that they recover, we pray: ◆ For the dying, that they enter eternal life, we pray: ◆

Our Father . . .

Mighty God,
you inspire our hearts
to share your marvelous ways.
Guide our actions
to proclaim your goodness
so that others will know of your wonders.
Through Christ our Lord.
Amen.

✝ Lord, make us turn to you;
let us see your face and we shall
be saved.

Sunday, December 16, 2018
Third Sunday of Advent

† Cry out with joy and gladness:
for among you is the great and Holy One of Israel!

Psalm 98 *page 410*

Reading *Luke 3:10–14*

The crowds asked John the Baptist, "What should we do?" He said to them in reply, "Whoever has two cloaks should share with the person who has none. And whoever has food should do likewise." Even tax collectors came to be baptized and they said to him, "Teacher, what should we do?" He answered them, "Stop collecting more than what is prescribed." Soldiers also asked him, "And what is it that we should do?" He told them, "Do not practice extortion, do not falsely accuse anyone, and be satisfied with your wages."

Reflection

A series of people—the crowds, tax collectors, and soldiers—ask the question: "What should we do?" Are they hoping for a minimal approach to life or are they serious about their conversion? We do not know their intent, only ours. Today, on Gaudete Sunday, the Entrance Antiphon tells us that we are "to rejoice in the Lord always." If we do that, we will spread joy and hope to those we encounter.

Prayers *others may be added*

To our Lord, our reason for joy,
we pray:

◆ Lord, hear our prayer.

That leaders in the Church always be witnesses of joy and hope, we pray: ◆ That newly elected officials be open to the many ways they can help others, we pray: ◆ That bigotry and fear may end, we pray: ◆ That catechumens witness joy in their parishes, we pray: ◆ That the sick be strengthened through the Sacrament of Anointing, we pray: ◆ That those who have died be welcomed to the banquet in heaven, we pray: ◆

Our Father . . .

O God,
you sent John the Baptist to us
to show the way to you.
Help us to determine
what we are to do
to spread the Gospel
so that others may possess
the same joy that you have given us.
Through Christ our Lord.
Amen.

† Cry out with joy and gladness:
for among you is the great and Holy One of Israel!

Monday, December 17, 2018
Advent Weekday

✝ Justice shall flourish in his time,
and fullness of peace for ever.

Psalm 72
page 406

Reading
Genesis 49:2, 8, 10

Jacob called his sons and said to them:
"Assemble and listen, sons of Jacob,
listen to Israel, your father.

"You, Judah, shall your
brothers praise
—your hand on the neck of
your enemies;
the sons of your father shall bow
down to you. . . .
The scepter shall never depart
from Judah,
or the mace from between his legs,
While tribute is brought to him,
and he receives the people's
homage."

Reflection

During the last week of Advent, we prepare more intensely for the coming of Christ as we hear our story of faith from the Old Testament readings. In today's reading, Jacob gathers his sons and tells of what is ahead for the family. Their story is our story, and we listen to it and tell others of how God came to make his home among us. This story of faith reminds us of the great promise and care God has for us. What is your family's story of living the faith and how does it fit into the larger story. Evangelize by telling that story.

Prayers
others may be added

With confidence that God is with us,
we pray:

◆ Lord, hear our prayer.

That those entrusted with the art and environment in our parishes have patience in their work, we pray: ◆ That elected officials see the power that has been entrusted to them as a special gift to be used cautiously, we pray: ◆ That more men come forward, with the support of their wives, to become deacons, we pray: ◆ That the peace God brings does not become overshadowed by holiday preparations, we pray: ◆ That those seeking a transplant may find peace in their waiting, we pray: ◆ That the dying enter eternal life, we pray: ◆

Our Father . . .

Lord God,
you have blessed us
through generations.
Help us to be faithful to our heritage
and mindful of the gifts
you have bestowed on us.
Through Christ our Lord.
Amen.

✝ Justice shall flourish in his time,
and fullness of peace for ever.

Tuesday, December 18, 2018
Advent Weekday

✝ Justice shall flourish in his time,
and fullness of peace for ever.

Psalm 72

page 406

Reading

Jeremiah 23:5–8

Behold, the days are coming, says the LORD, / when I will raise up a righteous shoot to David; / As king he shall reign and govern wisely, / he shall do what is just and right in the land. / In his days Judah shall be saved, / Israel shall dwell in security. / This is the name they give him: / "The LORD our justice."

Therefore, the days will come, says the LORD, when they shall no longer say, "As the LORD lives, who brought the children of Israel out of the land of Egypt"; but rather, "As the LORD lives, who brought the descendants of the house of Israel up from the land of the north"—and from all the lands to which I banished them; they shall again live on their own land.

Reflection

This reading looks to the day when God's reign is complete and justice and peace will flourish. At that time, the king will do only what is just and right. As we anticipate the Second Coming, we look to the time when all will dwell in security. We recognize that as we pray the "O" Antiphon: "O Leader of the House of Israel, giver of the Law to Moses on Sinai: come to rescue us with your mighty power."

Prayers

others may be added

Turning to God with our concerns,
we pray:

◆ Gracious Lord, hear our prayer.

That the Church lift up those struggling with many burdens, we pray: ◆ That world leaders embrace their role as peacekeepers, we pray: ◆ That social workers who assist so many in need during this season may have strength and confidence in their mission, we pray: ◆ That travelers reach their destinations safely, we pray: ◆ That all who are ill may find strength and healing, we pray: ◆ That those we miss and mourn be welcomed at the heavenly banquet, we pray: ◆

Our Father . . .

Righteous, loving God,
you provide our strength.
Assist us as we seek to make straight
the paths to justice and mercy
in our communities
so that all may grow in holiness.
with our sisters and brothers.
Through Christ our Lord.
Amen.

✝ Justice shall flourish in his time,
and fullness of peace for ever.

Wednesday, December 19, 2018

Advent Weekday

✝ My mouth shall be filled with your praise, and I will sing your glory!

Psalm 98

page 410

Reading

Judges 13:2–5, 24–25a

There was a certain man from Zorah, of the clan of the Danites, whose name was Manoah. His wife was barren. . . . An angel of the LORD appeared to the woman and said to her: "Though you are barren and have had no children, yet you will conceive and bear a son. . . . Be careful to take no wine . . . and to eat nothing unclean. As for the son you will conceive and bear, no razor shall touch his head, for this boy is to be consecrated to God from the womb. It is he who will begin the deliverance of Israel from the power of the Philistines."

The woman bore a son and named him Samson. The boy grew up . . . and the Spirit of the LORD stirred him.

Reflection

In today's Scripture, we hear of another barren woman who is to give birth to a child who will play an important role for Israel. Samson, the son of the wife of Manoah, would deliver Israel from the Philistines. During these last days of Advent, contemplate how God fulfills the dreams of the faithful. Is there something in your life that seems to have gone barren? Pray to God to make that part of your life fruitful.

Prayers

others may be added

To our Lord God, who makes the barren fertile, we pray:

◆ Lord, hear our prayer.

That the Spirit guide our parish leaders, we pray: ◆ That our governor and state officials serve the needs of the marginalized, we pray: ◆ That families hoping for a child may conceive or adopt, we pray: ◆ That those whose faith is lost may have hope, we pray: ◆ That those in hospice may be comforted, we pray: ◆ That those who have lost a child may find healing and strength, we pray: ◆

Our Father . . .

Good and gracious God,
you make the barren fertile,
uplifting the lowly.
As you brought Manoah, his wife,
and Samson
to do great things in your name,
guide our words and actions
to give you praise and honor
so that all may know of your goodness.
Through Christ our Lord.
Amen.

✝ My mouth shall be filled with your praise, and I will sing your glory!

Thursday, December 20, 2018
Advent Weekday

✝ Let the Lord enter; he is the king of glory.

Psalm 98

page 410

Reading

Isaiah 7:10–14

The LORD spoke to Ahaz: Ask for a sign from the LORD, your God; let it be deep as the nether world, or high as the sky! But Ahaz answered, "I will not ask! I will not tempt the LORD!" Then Isaiah said: Listen, O house of David! Is it not enough for you to weary men, must you also weary my God? Therefore the Lord himself will give you this sign: the virgin shall conceive and bear a son, and shall name him Emmanuel.

Reflection

How blessed are we that the Lord provides signs that he is with us! Though Ahaz refused to request a sign, God would provide one. The impossible would come to be and a virgin would bear a son. That son would be named Emmanuel or "God is with us." We go on a journey with this mystery, just as we do with the other mysteries that life presents. When tragedy occurs, some wonder where God is. For faith to endure, it is important to be attentive to the signs God provides.

Prayers

others may be added

Turning to our faithful God, we pray:

◆ Come, Lord Jesus.

That leaders in the Church always act as a sign of Christ's love, we pray: ◆ That legislators seek to help those who are marginalized, we pray: ◆ That an end be put to violence, we pray: ◆ That those who await the miracle of a child do so with awe, we pray: ◆ That the sick recover quickly, we pray: ◆ That those who have lost a child receive comfort from family and friends, we pray: ◆

Our Father . . .

Radiant God,
you give us signs and wonders
that announce your presence.
May we appreciate
your goodness and help others
to see the marvels
you provide.
Through Christ our Lord.
Amen.

✝ Let the Lord enter; he is the king of glory.

Friday, December 21, 2018
Advent Weekday

☩ Exult, you just, in the Lord!
Sing to him a new song.

Psalm 98
page 410

Reading
Zephaniah 3:14–18a

Shout for joy, O daughter Zion! / Sing joyfully, O Israel! / Be glad and exult with all your heart, / O daughter Jerusalem! / The LORD has removed the judgment against you, / he has turned away your enemies; / The King of Israel, the LORD, is in your midst, / you have no further misfortune to fear. / On that day, it shall be said to Jerusalem: / Fear not, O Zion, be not discouraged! / The LORD, your God, is in your midst, / a mighty savior; / He will rejoice over you with gladness, and renew you in his love, / He will sing joyfully because of you, / as one sings at festivals.

Reflection
In the days before Christmas, we may feel more angst than joy as we seek to take care of the details of the season. Today's readings remind us not to fear and worry about details that do not go as smoothly as we would like. Though it is easy to get caught up in consumer culture, we are called to rest in the Lord and rejoice over our relationship with him. The Lord is in our midst. By our patience during these days, may we help others know of the presence of God.

Prayers
others may be added

To our Lord God, who rejoices with us, we pray:

◆ Gracious Lord, hear our prayer.

That the Church continue to be a sign of hope and compassion, we pray: ◆ That our world leaders turn away from evil desires and focus on the good of all, we pray: ◆ That those who have suffered the effects of an abortion heal and grow in the power of God's forgiveness, we pray: ◆ That the holidays be a time of joy for those who dread them, we pray: ◆ That the sick regain their health, we pray: ◆ That the dead rest in the new and eternal Jerusalem, we pray: ◆

Our Father . . .

Eternal God of joy,
you call us to trust
and be renewed during Advent.
Help us to be people of joy
as we await the coming of your Son.
Through Christ our Lord.
Amen.

☩ Exult, you just, in the Lord!
Sing to him a new song.

Saturday, December 22, 2018
Advent Weekday

✝ My heart exults in the Lord,
my Savior.

Psalm 96 *page 409*

Reading *1 Samuel 1:24–28*

In those days, Hannah brought Samuel with her, along with a three-year-old bull, an ephah of flour, and a skin of wine, and presented him at the temple of the LORD in Shiloh. After the boy's father had sacrificed the young bull, Hannah, his mother, approached Eli and said: "Pardon, my lord! As you live, my lord, I am the woman who stood near you here, praying to the LORD. I prayed for this child, and the LORD granted my request. Now I, in turn, give him to the LORD; as long as he lives, he shall be dedicated to the LORD." She left Samuel there.

Reflection

When Hannah leaves her only child at the temple, she fulfills her promise to the Lord. Barren, Hannah had prayed to God that if her request for a child was granted, she would give him to the Lord. Hannah recognizes that this child and all else comes from God. Knowing that he is a gift, she returns him to God. How do you regard the gifts God has bestowed on you? We are to make an offering of our lives. What sacrifice do you make to the Lord?

Prayers *others may be added*

To our Lord, who has given us all we have, we pray:

◆ Come, Lord Jesus.

That Church authorities remain unwavering in their service, we pray: ◆ That people of every nation seek to care for the earth's resources, we pray: ◆ That homes be found for orphans, we pray: ◆ That foster parents receive strength to care for the children in their care, we pray: ◆ That those recovering from illness return to excellent health, we pray: ◆ That those who have died be welcomed into heaven, we pray: ◆

Our Father . . .

God of compassion,
you gave Hannah the faith
to dedicate her trial to you.
Grant that we may trust you enough
to dedicate our lives to you each day
so that we may honor you and praise you
through lives of service.
Through Christ our Lord.
Amen.

✝ My heart exults in the Lord,
my Savior.

Sunday, December 23, 2018

Fourth Sunday of Advent

✝ Lord, make us turn to you;
let us see your face and we shall
be saved.

Psalm 100

page 410

Reading

Luke 1:39–45

Mary set out and traveled to the hill country in haste to a town of Judah, where she entered the house of Zechariah and greeted Elizabeth. When Elizabeth heard Mary's greeting, the infant leaped in her womb, and Elizabeth, filled with the Holy Spirit, cried out in a loud voice and said, "Blessed are you among women, and blessed is the fruit of your womb. And how does this happen to me, that the mother of my Lord should come to me? For at the moment the sound of your greeting reached my ears, the infant in my womb leaped for joy. Blessed are you who believed that what was spoken to you by the Lord would be fulfilled."

Reflection

The Visitation is a scene of joy and humility. Upon Mary's arrival, Elizabeth proclaims the blessedness of her visitor and the child in her womb. She then humbly asks how Mary could be coming to her. We then hear that Mary's faith is at the root of the blessing. Amid the preparations of these days, do you allow yourself to feel blessed by the coming of the Lord? Do you see the Lord in the midst of your guests? With love, we recognize it is Jesus we welcome to each event in our lives.

Prayers

others may be added

To our Lord, who blesses us with faith,
we pray:

◆ Come, Lord Jesus.

May the Church be a welcome place
for returning believers, we pray: ◆
May nations open their arms to migrants,
we pray: ◆ May the cries of women
for equal pay be heeded, we pray: ◆
May all travelers find welcome, we pray: ◆
May the sick regain their health, we pray: ◆
May the dead be welcomed to their
eternal home, we pray: ◆

Our Father . . .

God of compassion,
you blessed Mary and Elizabeth
with the faith that is open
to the possibilities you offer.
Relieve our worries and fears
and help us to greet the joys of your Son,
who lives and reigns with you in the unity
of the Holy Spirit,
one God, for ever and ever.
Amen.

✝ Lord, make us turn to you;
let us see your face and we shall
be saved.

Monday, December 24, 2018
Advent Weekday

✝ Forever I will sing the goodness of the Lord.

Psalm 89 *page 407*

Reading *2 Samuel 7:1–5, 8b–12, 14a, 16*

When King David was settled in his palace, and the LORD had given him rest from his enemies on every side, he said to Nathan the prophet, "Here I am living in a house of cedar, while the ark of God dwells in a tent!" Nathan answered the king, "Go, do whatever you have in mind, for the LORD is with you." But that night the LORD spoke to Nathan and said: "Go, tell my servant David, 'Thus says the LORD: Should you build me a house to dwell in?

"'It was I who took you from the pasture and from the care of the flock to be commander of my people Israel. I have been with you wherever you went, and I have destroyed all your enemies before you. And I will make you famous like the great ones of the earth. I will fix a place for my people Israel; I will plant them so that they may dwell in their place without further disturbance. Neither shall the wicked continue to afflict them as they did of old, since the time I first appointed judges over my people Israel. I will give you rest from all your enemies. The LORD also reveals to you that he will establish a house for you. And when your time comes and you rest with your ancestors, I will raise up your heir. . . . I will be a father to him, and he shall be a son to me. Your house and your Kingdom shall endure forever before me; your throne shall stand firm forever.'"

Reflection

David wishes to build a grand house for God's dwelling. The Lord, however, rebukes him for this. Eventually, a stable is a dwelling for the Son of God, for there was no room in an inn or a tent. The irony is that there is no containing God, who wishes to dwell and be seen in us. Our happiness reminds us that God came to give us abundant life. We grow from a child into a transformative body, where we bring to birth again God's spirit in our tent.

Prayers *others may be added*

To our Lord, who makes a home in our hearts, we pray:

◆ Come, Lord Jesus.

May the Church be a safe haven for those seeking refuge, we pray: ◆ May states make education of all a priority, we pray: ◆ May those who work for peace be strengthened, we pray: ◆ May travelers and safety enforcers be kept free from harm, we pray: ◆ May those who are ill be lifted up and healed, we pray: ◆ May those who have died see their hope in heaven, we pray: ◆

Our Father . . .

All-powerful God,
each day you give us
refuge and hope.
Strengthen our resolve to serve you
and let others know
of your love and goodness.
Through Christ our Lord.
Amen.

✝ Forever I will sing the goodness of the Lord.

Tuesday, December 25, 2018

Solemnity of the Nativity of our Lord

☩ Today is born our Savior, Christ the Lord.

Psalm 96

page 409

Reading

Luke 2:8–14

Now there were shepherds in that region living in the fields and keeping the night watch over their flock. The angel of the Lord appeared to them and the glory of the Lord shone around them, and they were struck with great fear. The angel said to them, "Do not be afraid; for behold, I proclaim to you good news of great joy that will be for all the people. For today in the city of David a savior has been born for you who is Christ and Lord. And this will be a sign for you: you will find an infant wrapped in swaddling clothes and lying in a manger." And suddenly there was a multitude of the heavenly host with the angel, praising God and saying: / "Glory to God in the highest / and on earth peace to those on whom his favor rests."

Reflection

The joy the angels proclaimed to the shepherds continues in us today as we celebrate the birth of the Savior. For Mary and Joseph, who would put their newborn in a manger, this was a night of trusting in God. For the shepherds, this was a night to seek the sign of the Messiah. For the angels, there was great rejoicing. How do you celebrate the birth of the Lord?

Prayers

others may be added

To our God, who sent us our Savior, we pray:

◆ Lord, hear our prayer.

May our Church always nurture joy, we pray: ◆ May legislators recall the season's spirit as they serve their constituents, we pray: ◆ May sales clerks enjoy well-deserved rest, we pray: ◆ May those who work with us know of our gratitude, we pray: ◆ May the sick recover quickly, we pray: ◆ May those we miss and mourn enjoy the fruits of their labors in heaven, we pray: ◆

Our Father . . .

Lord Jesus,
from your birth in a lowly stable,
you brought joy to the whole world.
Renew our resolve
to spread your love
so that all will know
of the love that God sent
to dwell on earth.
Through Christ our Lord.
Amen.

☩ Today is born our Savior, Christ the Lord.

Wednesday, December 26, 2018

Feast of St. Stephen, the First Martyr

☩ Into your hands, O Lord, I commend my spirit.

Psalm 31

page 400

Reading

Acts 6:8–10; 7:54–59

Stephen, filled with grace and power, was working great wonders and signs among the people. Certain members of the so-called Synagogue of Freedmen, Cyrenians, and Alexandrians, and people from Cilicia and Asia, came forward and debated with Stephen, but they could not withstand the wisdom and the spirit with which he spoke.

When they heard this, they were infuriated, and they ground their teeth at him. But he, filled with the Holy Spirit, looked up intently to heaven and saw the glory of God and Jesus standing at the right hand of God, and he said, "Behold, I see the heavens opened and the Son of Man standing at the right hand of God." But they cried out in a loud voice, covered their ears, and rushed upon him together. They threw him out of the city, and began to stone him. . . . As they were stoning Stephen, he called out "Lord Jesus, receive my spirit."

Reflection

The Feast of St. Stephen recalls his martyrdom and his complete trust in God. Since the birth of Christ points to his passion, death, and Resurrection, it makes sense to honor the first martyr the day after Christmas. Stephen was touched by the Paschal Mystery, and so was filled with the Holy Spirit. Christ continues to transform the world when we open ourselves to the Spirit and witness in wisdom to the Spirit working among us.

Prayers

others may be added

Turning to Christ, who guides us,
we pray:

◆ God of mercy, hear our prayer.

May missionaries be kept free from harm, we pray: ◆ May all who work on behalf of human rights find hope in God's justice, we pray: ◆ May more people seek to become catechists, we pray: ◆ May the unemployed and underemployed quickly find work, we pray: ◆ May the sick find comfort and relief from their suffering, we pray: ◆ May those martyred for the faith today join with Stephen in reaching the glory of heaven, we pray: ◆

Our Father . . .

Lord God,
you filled St. Stephen with grace.
Grant that we may imitate
this martyr's trust in you
and never fear
the consequences
of witnessing to Christ,
who lives and reigns with you
in the unity of the Holy Spirit,
one God, for ever and ever.
Amen.

☩ Into your hands, O Lord, I commend my spirit.

Thursday, December 27, 2018

Feast of St. John, Apostle and Evangelist

✝ Rejoice in the Lord, you just!

Psalm 98

page 410

Reading

1 John 1:1–4

Beloved:
What was from the beginning, / what we have heard, / what we have seen with our eyes, / what we looked upon / and touched with our hands / concerns the Word of life— / for the life was made visible; / we have seen it and testify to it / and proclaim to you the eternal life / that was with the Father and was made visible to us— / what we have seen and heard / we proclaim now to you, / so that you too may have fellowship with us; / for our fellowship is with the Father / and with his Son, Jesus Christ. / We are writing this so that our joy may be complete.

Reflection

Writing and receiving letters, especially those filled with messages of joy and love, are rare today. Most people share a quick email or text about a task or meeting. This feast day of John inspires us, especially through this letter, to hear the transmission of the faith, of God's love that touched the heart of the author and our call to share our joy. We continue the writing of Christ's story with his faithful by the way we live our faith and transmit it to the next generation.

Prayers

others may be added

Open to the will of God, we pray:

◆ Lord, hear our prayer.

May the People of God joyfully support the mission of the Church, we pray: ◆ May hope guide the work of all elected leaders, we pray: ◆ May all believers understand their actions as rooted in faith, we pray: ◆ May parishioners be supportive of the catechumens, we pray: ◆ May those affected by natural disasters experience relief quickly, we pray: ◆ May the saints and angels joyfully greet those who have died, we pray: ◆

Our Father . . .

Lord God,
you gave John
the ability to evangelize
through letters.
Grant that we continue to share
your love through the communications
of our day.
Inspire in us words and actions
to share the joys of your life
and proclaim the mysteries
of our faith.
Through Christ our Lord.
Amen.

✝ Rejoice in the Lord, you just!

Friday, December 28, 2018
Feast of the Holy Innocents, Martyrs

✝ Our soul has been rescued like a bird from the fowler's snare.

Psalm 124 *page 417*

Reading *1 John 1:5—2:2*

Beloved: This is the message that we have heard from Jesus Christ and proclaim to you: God is light, and in him there is no darkness at all. If we say, "We have fellowship with him," while we continue to walk in darkness, we lie and do not act in truth. But if we walk in the light as he is in the light, then we have fellowship with one another, and the Blood of his Son Jesus cleanses us from all sin. If we say, "We are without sin," we deceive ourselves, and the truth is not in us. If we acknowledge our sins, he is faithful and just and will forgive our sins and cleanse us from every wrongdoing. If we say, "We have not sinned," we make him a liar, and his word is not in us.

My children, I am writing this to you so that you may not commit sin. But if anyone does sin, we have an Advocate with the Father, Jesus Christ the righteous one. He is expiation for our sins, and not for our sins only but for those of the whole world.

Reflection

As members of the Body of Christ, we share a special fellowship and are called to live in Christ's light. The Feast of the Holy Innocents reminds us of evil leaders who fail to join in God's vision and choose the darkness of sin, killing young children and the unborn. Our role as Christ's faithful disciples is to continuously live and share the message of truth and act in the life, love, and light of God so that innocent blood is not shed.

Prayers *others may be added*

Looking to our God of love, we pray:

◆ Lord, hear our prayer.

May the Church consistently proclaim respect for all life, from conception to natural death, we pray: ◆ May legislators protect the most vulnerable in our societies, we pray: ◆ May those who have had an abortion and confessed their wrong continue to heal and feel God's mercy and reconciliation, we pray: ◆ May the seeds of the martyrs' blood continue to inspire others to join in the Christian tradition, we pray: ◆ May the sick be comforted, we pray: ◆ May the dearly departed reach the glory of the heavenly kingdom, we pray: ◆

Our Father . . .

Each day, O Lord God,
you call us to be children of the light
and follow your Son.
Assist us in our actions
to be people who respect all human life
and seek to show forth the grace
that reflects your love.
Through Christ our Lord.
Amen.

✝ Our soul has been rescued like a bird from the fowler's snare.

Saturday, December 29, 2018

Fifth Day within the Octave of the Nativity of the Lord

✝ Let the heavens be glad and the earth rejoice!

Psalm 96

page 409

Reading

I John 2:3–11

Beloved: The way we may be sure that we know Jesus is to keep his commandments. Whoever says, "I know him," but does not keep his commandments is a liar, and the truth is not in him. But whoever keeeps his word, the love of God is perfected in him. This is the way we are to know we are in union with him: whoever claims to abide in him ought to walk just as he walked.

Beloved, I am writing no new commandment to you but an old commandment that you had from the beginning. The old commandment is the word that you have heard. . . . Whoever says he is in the light, yet hates his brother, is still in the darkness. Whoever loves his brother remains in the light, and there is nothing in him to cause a fall. Whoever hates his brother is in darkness; he walks in darkness and does not know where he is going because the darkness has blinded his eyes.

Reflection

These strong words from the First Letter of John remind us of our call to be authentic followers of Christ. We are called to true love. No one wants to be considered "a liar." Our challenge is to live as people of the light. We might ask ourselves whether we seek to walk as Jesus walked.

Prayers

others may be added

To our faithful God, we pray:

◆ Lord, hear our prayer.

May the Church seek to be a model of love, we pray: ◆ May world leaders witness to concern for the common good, we pray: ◆ May families grow in love and courage to strengthen one another, we pray: ◆ May travelers be kept safe, we pray: ◆ May those who have suffered trauma be relieved of fear and anxiety, we pray: ◆ May those who have died see the loving face of God, we pray: ◆

Our Father . . .

O God,
caring for all your children in love,
you bring us to the light of truth.
Transform our lives
so that we may share your gifts
and renew others in the hope of
your light,
freed from the corruption of sin.
Through Christ our Lord.
Amen.

✝ Let the heavens be glad and the earth rejoice!

Sunday, December 30, 2018
Feast of the Holy Family of Jesus, Mary, and Joseph

☩ Blessed are they who dwell in your house, O Lord.

Psalm 84
page 406

Reading
Luke 2:43–51

After three days [Jesus' parents] found him in the temple, sitting in the midst of the teachers, listening to them and asking them questions, and all who heard him were astounded at his understanding and his answers. When his parents saw him, they were astonished, and his mother said to him, "Son, why have you done this to us? Your father and I have been looking for you with great anxiety." And he said to them, "Why were you looking for me? Did you not know that I must be in my Father's house?" But they did not understand what he said to them. He went down with them and came to Nazareth, and was obedient to them; and his mother kept all these things in her heart.

Reflection

At a young age, Jesus took the opportunity to explore the faith by seeking out leaders that he could question and listen to so he could grow deeper in knowledge. We should not be content with the catechism of our youth but find ways to study our faith. Do you take your faith for granted, or do you seek to become more engaged in it through reading and faith formation sessions in the parish?

Prayers
others may be added

To the Lord, who seeks to dwell within us, we pray:

◆ Lord, hear our prayer.

Support Church leaders as they seek to be people of prayer, we pray: ◆ Help us secure the freedom to worship for people all around the world, we pray: ◆ Guide families to find quality time to be together, we pray: ◆ Allow couples who desire a child to conceive or adopt, we pray: ◆ Heal the ill and injured, we pray: ◆ Lead to your heavenly glory those who have died, we pray: ◆

Our Father . . .

O God,
through the travels and trials of life,
you guard and protect us
to grow together as your people.
Continue to show us the way
and lead us safely to discern your will
until we arrive in our heavenly home.
Through Christ our Lord.
Amen.

☩ Blessed are they who dwell in your house, O Lord.

Monday, December 31, 2018

Seventh Day within the Octave of the Nativity of the Lord

✝ Let the heavens be glad and the earth rejoice!

Psalm 96

page 409

Reading

1 John 2:18–21

Children, it is the last hour; and just as you heard that the antichrist was coming, so now many antichrists have appeared. Thus we know this is the last hour. They went out from us, but they were not really of our number; if they had been, they would have remained with us. Their desertion shows that none of them was of our number. But you have the anointing that comes from the Holy One, and you all have knowledge. I write to you not because you do not know the truth but because you do, and because every lie is alien to the truth.

Reflection

During Baptism, Christians were anointed to be "priest, prophet and king." Our Baptism calls us to live the truth of our faith and share it with others. The first Christians were concerned that Christ was coming soon. As we celebrate this last day of the secular calendar year, let us be vigilant for the Holy One in our midst. Let us, too, acknowledge our lifelong pilgrimage to show Christ to others.

Prayers

others may be added

Longing for the coming of the kingdom, we pray:

◆ God of mercy, hear our prayer.

Grant that the pope continue to nurture a listening heart, we pray: ◆ Guide leaders to care for our planet, we pray: ◆ Protect those welcoming in the new year, we pray: ◆ Support those longing for warmth and shelter from the cold, we pray: ◆ Heal those in need of health care, we pray: ◆ Guide those who have died to the everlasting glory of heaven, we pray: ◆

Our Father . . .

O God,
in your loving kindness,
you guide the times, places, and seasons,
renewing our lives in hope.
Support our efforts
to preach and live the truth
and be faithful to serve you
with hearts fixed on your glory.
Through Christ our Lord.
Amen.

✝ Let the heavens be glad and the earth rejoice!

Tuesday, January 1, 2019
Solemnity of Mary, the Holy Mother of God

✝ May God bless us in his mercy.

Canticle of Mary

page 423

Reading

Luke 2:16–20

The shepherds went in haste to Bethlehem and found Mary and Joseph, and the infant lying in the manger. When they saw this, they made known the message that had been told them about this child. All who heard it were amazed by what had been told them by the shepherds. And Mary kept all these things, reflecting on them in her heart. Then the shepherds returned, glorifying and praising God for all they had heard and seen, just as it had been told to them.

Reflection

When feeding a child in her arms, a mother takes time to ponder. On the eighth day of the Octave of the Nativity of the Lord, the Church reflects on Mary, the mother of the Church. Mary is presented as one who models reflection, peace, and care for others. We imitate her as we pray for peace on this World Day for Peace. By striving to nourish others and centering our lives on the Eucharist, we give witness to the glory of God just as the angels and shepherds did.

Prayers

others may be added

Open to God's ways, we pray:

◆ Lord, hear our prayer.

Assist the Church as she seeks new ways to evangelize this year, we pray: ◆ Watch over newly appointed government workers, we pray: ◆ Satisfy the longings of those hoping for justice, we pray: ◆ Support peacekeepers in their mission, we pray: ◆ Renew the strength of those who are sick and suffering, we pray: ◆ Welcome the faithfully departed to the joys of heaven, we pray: ◆

Our Father . . .

O God,
you gave us Mary to be a witness
of faith, truth, and your Light.
Help us to contemplate your mysteries
and share our blessings
with our sisters and brothers
to renew our Church and world
in this year of grace and hope.
Through Christ our Lord.
Amen.

✝ May God bless us in his mercy.

Wednesday, January 2, 2019

Memorial of Sts. Basil the Great and Gregory Nazianzen, Bishops and Doctors of the Church

✝ All the ends of the earth have seen the saving power of God.

Psalm 98 *page 410*

Reading *John 1:19–23*

This is the testimony of John. When the Jews from Jerusalem sent priests and Levites to him to ask him, "Who are you?" he admitted and did not deny it, but admitted, "I am not the Christ." So they asked him, "What are you, then? Are you Elijah?" And he said, "I am not." "Are you the Prophet?" He answered, "No." So they said to him, "Who are you, so we can give an answer to those who sent us? What do you have to say for yourself?" He said: / "I am *the voice of one crying out in the desert, / 'Make straight the way of the Lord,'* / as Isaiah the prophet said."

Reflection

Like Sts. Basil and Gregory, we are called to testify to Christ. Our lives are to be ones of truth and witness that point to our Savior. As we spread the Word of God's love for us, we live out our baptismal call. Our words may not be as blatant as John's but we should act with his humility to make God's ways straight and known. How will you tell others today of what Christ has done in your life?

Prayers *others may be added*

To our God, who has instilled us with faith, we pray:

◆ Lord, hear our prayer.

Inspire the leaders of our Church to lead lives of mercy, we pray: ◆ Enlighten the faithful to their call of service, we pray: ◆ Bless newly elected civic leaders, we pray: ◆ Calm the fears of those awaiting surgery, we pray: ◆ Transform the hearts of enemies to seek good will, we pray: ◆ Awaken the dead to the glory and hope of eternal life, we pray: ◆

Our Father . . .

O God,
enkindle in our hearts
a willingness
to be your faithful witnesses.
Through our Baptism,
you make us a part of your family.
Support our efforts
to alert others to your love.
Through Christ our Lord.
Amen.

✝ All the ends of the earth have seen the saving power of God.

Thursday, January 3, 2019
Optional Memorial of the Holy Name of Jesus

✝ All the ends of the earth have seen the saving power of God.

Psalm 98
page 410

Reading
John 1:29–34

John the Baptist saw Jesus coming toward him and said, "Behold, the Lamb of God, who takes away the sin of the world. He is the one of whom I said, 'A man is coming after me who ranks ahead of me because he existed before me.' I did not know him, but the reason why I came baptizing with water was that he might be made known to Israel." John testified further, saying, "I saw the Spirit come down like a dove from heaven and remain upon him. I did not know him, but the one who sent me to baptize with water told me, 'On whomever you see the Spirit come down and remain, he is the one who will baptize with the Holy Spirit.' Now I have seen and testified that he is the Son of God."

Reflection

Each Mass reminds us of the key reality in our lives: Jesus Christ, the Lamb of God, became human to be present among us. We celebrate that the Lamb of God is with us now. This first testimony of John the Baptist leads us to testify to the Spirit living in our midst. We have seen and experienced the Christ and are called continuously to point out that he has changed our lives. When we do so, others may seek him to transform their lives.

Prayers
others may be added

Turning to our Lord, who calls us to him, we pray:

◆ Gracious Lord, hear us.

Strengthen leaders of the Church to promote the good works of Christ, we pray: ◆ Protect the vulnerable, especially the unborn, we pray: ◆ Assist world leaders to act as agents of peace, we pray: ◆ Renew families in their mission to care for each other, we pray: ◆ Help the sick to recover quickly, we pray: ◆ Lead those who have died to the joys of heaven, we pray: ◆

Our Father . . .

Dear God,
you allowed John the Baptist
to see the Spirit
so that he might
witness the Messiah
in the world.
Help us as we seek
to communicate the Good News
and share the signs of joy and love
that you have sent to us.
May we always praise and proclaim
your Son's Holy Name.
Through Christ our Lord.
Amen.

✝ All the ends of the earth have seen the saving power of God.

Friday, January 4, 2019
Memorial of St. Elizabeth Ann Seton, Religious

✝ All the ends of the earth have seen the saving power of God.

Psalm 98 *page 410*

Reading *John 1:35–42*

John was standing with two of his disciples, and as he watched Jesus walk by, he said, "Behold, the Lamb of God." The two disciples heard what he said and followed Jesus. Jesus turned and saw them following him and said to them, "What are you looking for?" They said to him, "Rabbi"—which translated means Teacher—, "where are you staying?" He said to them, "Come, and you will see." So they went and saw where he was staying, and they stayed with him that day. It was about four in the afternoon. Andrew, the brother of Simon Peter, was one of the two who heard John and followed Jesus. He first found his own brother Simon and told him, "We have found the Messiah"—which is translated Christ. Then he brought him to Jesus. Jesus looked at him and said, "You are Simon the son of John; you will be called Cephas"—which is translated Peter.

Reflection

John's disciples heard Jesus say, "Come," and they followed Jesus. St. Elizabeth Ann Seton was open to God's will and discerned in her heart what God wanted her to do, and she followed. With a generous, hospitable heart, Elizabeth Ann founded the order now known as the Sisters of Charity. The order cared for children, establishing schools and teaching in orphanages. As this new year begins, may we seek to discover how God is deepening our call to serve others.

Prayers *others may be added*

In solidarity with those in need,
we pray:

◆ Lord, hear our prayer.

Strengthen the Church through her care for the poor, we pray: ◆ Awaken young women to work as a Sister of Charity, we pray: ◆ Unite world leaders in harmony and peace, we pray: ◆ Support those affected by inclement weather, we pray: ◆ Protect the sick and suffering from doubt and fears, we pray: ◆ Welcome those who have died to the glory of eternal life, we pray: ◆

Our Father . . .

O God,
you call each of us by name
to come and follow you.
Lead us to love you more deeply
and nurture our commitment
to your ways.
Through Christ our Lord.
Amen.

✝ All the ends of the earth have seen the saving power of God.

Saturday, January 5, 2019
Memorial of St. John Neumann, Bishop

☩ All the ends of the earth have seen the saving power of God.

Psalm 98 *page 410*

Reading *John 1:45–51*

Philip found Nathanael and told him, "We have found the one about whom Moses wrote in the law, and also the prophets, Jesus son of Joseph, from Nazareth." But Nathanael said to him, "Can anything good come from Nazareth?" Philip said to him, "Come and see." Jesus saw Nathanael coming toward him and said of him, "Here is a true child of Israel. There is no duplicity in him." Nathanael said to him, "How do you know me?" Jesus answered and said to him, "Before Philip called you, I saw you under the fig tree." Nathanael answered him, "Rabbi, you are the Son of God; you are the King of Israel."

Reflection

We can imagine that St. John Neumann was guided in his voyage to the United States by Jesus' words: "You will see greater things than this." St. John Neumann came to the United States to assist immigrants in establishing a better life for themselves. He guided immigrants as he built churches and schools to support their call as disciples. Many of these immigrants surely heard remarks such as, "Can anything good come from . . ." In this new year, we seek to trust where God is leading us on our journey of faith. Our call summons us to do both small and great things.

Prayers *others may be added*

To the Lord of life, we pray:

◆ Lord, hear our prayer.

Assist our pastor as he seeks to serve the many needs of the parish, we pray: ◆ Help civic authorities to be aware of their constituents' needs, we pray: ◆ Support those seeking a better future in new countries and lands, we pray: ◆ Aid young people discerning a call to the religious life, we pray: ◆ Through the intercession of St. John Neumann, help Catholic education be available to all who seek it, we pray: ◆ Heal the sick, we pray: ◆

Our Father . . .

O God,
awaken in us
a sense of your call
so that as we begin this new year
we may trust in the path
that you provide.
We ask this through Christ our Lord.
Amen.

☩ All the ends of the earth have seen the saving power of God.

Sunday, January 6, 2019

Solemnity of the Epiphany of the Lord

✝ Every nation on earth will adore you, Lord.

Psalm 72 *page 406*

Reading *Matthew 2:1–2, 9–12*

When Jesus was born in Bethlehem of Judea, in the days of King Herod, behold, magi from the east arrived in Jerusalem, saying, "Where is the newborn king of the Jews? We saw his star at its rising and have come to do him homage." . . . After their audience with the king they set out. And behold, the star that they had seen at its rising preceded them, until it came and stopped over the place where the child was. They were overjoyed at seeing the star, and on entering the house they saw the child with Mary his mother. They prostrated themselves and did him homage. Then they opened their treasures and offered him gifts of gold, frankincense, and myrrh. And having been warned in a dream not to return to Herod, they departed for their country by another way.

Reflection

God guided the path of the Magi so that they would arrive in Bethlehem looking for "the newborn king of the Jews." God seeks to show us the way also. We need to trust God and journey on the road he shows us. With every new *Star Wars* movie, fans have seen how the "force" has guided and awakened talent from each new Jedi. After sacrifice and the offering of their gifts, these characters discover the power of good within them. We need to find our gifts and strengths, too. Sometimes fears and worries may cause us to be conflicted, but we must not let anxiety hold us back from following the route God has for us.

Prayers *others may be added*

Trusting the guidance of God, we offer our prayers:

◆ Lord, hear our prayer.

That the pope may bring joy and hope to those who see him during his travels, we pray: ◆ For members of Congress, that they seek to serve the needs of the most vulnerable, we pray: ◆ For unity and growth within the Orthodox Church, we pray: ◆ For those seeking new work and meaningful employment, we pray: ◆ For those suffering with cancer, we pray: ◆ For those we miss and mourn, we pray: ◆

Our Father . . .

Led by the guidance of a star, Lord God,
you guided the Magi to see your Son
and present their precious gifts.
Help us trust your path for us
so that we may always share the gifts
you have given us
for the betterment of the world.
Through Christ our Lord.
Amen.

✝ Every nation on earth will adore you, Lord.

Monday, January 7, 2019
Christmas Weekday

† I will give you all the nations for your heritage.

Psalm 72 *page 406*

Reading *1 John 4:1–3a, 6*

Beloved, do not trust every spirit but test the spirits to see whether they belong to God, because many false prophets have gone out into the world. This is how you can know the Spirit of God: every spirit that acknowledges Jesus Christ come in the flesh belongs to God, and every spirit that does not acknowledge Jesus does not belong to God. We belong to God, and anyone who knows God listens to us, while anyone who does not belong to God refuses to hear us. This is how we know the spirit of truth and the spirit of deceit.

Reflection

We belong to God! This mantra can be said over and over in the face of temptations and worry. When beset with negative feelings, you may want to remind yourself that your Baptism made you a child of God. What could be better than knowing that you belong to God? As you go about your day, the assurance of God's love should provide confidence to follow the path of the spirit of truth.

Prayers *others may be added*

Confident that the Lord listens to our pleas, we pray:

◆ Lord, hear our prayer.

For the Church, as she seeks to build God's kingdom in love, we pray: ◆ For our newly elected leaders, that they seek a vision of care for the marginalized, we pray: ◆ For those challenged by natural disasters, we pray: ◆ For married couples struggling with their relationship, we pray: ◆ For the well-being and health of all who are suffering, we pray: ◆ For eternal rest to all the beloved dead, we pray: ◆

Our Father . . .

O God,
you lift us up
and help us cling to your love.
Hear the prayers of your people
and lead us from temptations and
self-doubt
to the knowledge of your support
and care.
Through Christ our Lord.
Amen.

† I will give you all the nations for your heritage.

Tuesday, January 8, 2019

Christmas Weekday

✝ Every nation on earth will adore you, Lord.

Psalm 72 *page 406*

Reading *I John 4:7–10*

Beloved, let us love one another, because love is of God; everyone who loves is begotten by God and knows God. Whoever is without love does not know God, for God is love. In this way the love of God was revealed to us: God sent his only Son into the world so that we might have life through him. In this is love: not that we have loved God, but that he loved us and sent his Son as expiation for our sins.

Reflection

As a wise spiritual director brought his aggravation for his religious brother to God, he had an insight. He realized that God loves the person he considered a "jerk" as much as God loves him. God, he understood, loves every "jerk." God created every "jerk," and loved them into being, he thought. So he realized that if God is able to love them, then he should also. As we show others love, we realize that we are blessed to be loved. During this week, seek to realize and share the life we have through the love of God.

Prayers *others may be added*

With hearts devoted to God's people, we pray:

◆ Lord, hear our prayer.

For those who find the hierarchical structure of the Church difficult, we pray: ◆ For all world leaders to work to remove prejudices, we pray: ◆ For lay organizations to grow in membership with others who will love and support their services, we pray: ◆ For renewed interest in service, we pray: ◆ For the sick, may they be healed, we pray: ◆ For the blessing and strength of all those who mourn, we pray: ◆

Our Father . . .

All-powerful God,
you teach your people to love
and nourish them with your gifts.
Lead us through the challenges
of caring and compassion
to bring your message and witness
of radiant joy to others.
Through Christ our Lord.
Amen.

✝ Every nation on earth will adore you, Lord.

Wednesday, January 9, 2019
Christmas Weekday

☩ Every nation on earth will adore you, Lord.

Psalm 97

page 409

Reading

Mark 6:45–51

After the five thousand had eaten and were satisfied, Jesus made his disciples get into the boat and precede him to the other side toward Bethsaida, while he dismissed the crowd. And when he had taken leave of them, he went off to the mountain to pray. When it was evening, the boat was far out on the sea and he was alone on shore. Then he saw that they were tossed about while rowing, for the wind was against them. About the fourth watch of the night, he came toward them walking on the sea. He meant to pass by them. But when they saw him walking on the sea, they thought it was a ghost and cried out. They had all seen him and were terrified. But at once he spoke with them, "Take courage, it is I, do not be afraid!" He got into the boat with them and the wind died down. They were completely astounded.

Reflection

After being tossed by the waves, the disciples may have been too afraid to recognize Jesus walking on the water. Giving in to the fear, they may have let their hearts become crusty. That may sometimes be our reality with the Eucharist. Sometimes we celebrate the liturgy and receive Communion but have not been open to a change in our hearts. In this new year, may our attitude be shaken and expanded as we go forth with hopeful hearts that do not give in to fear.

Prayers

others may be added

To our Lord, who feeds us, we pray:

◆ Gracious Lord, hear our prayer.

For all Christian leaders, that they may seek unity, we pray: ◆ For our civic authorities, that they recognize the dignity of all human life, we pray: ◆ For all who protect us, that they be kept free from harm, we pray: ◆ For those who suffer from addictions, we pray: ◆ For those whose hearts need special openness and love, we pray: ◆ For those who have died, that they know the joys of heaven, we pray: ◆

Our Father . . .

O God,
in kindness and truth
gently lead us from our fears.
Continue to nourish and sustain us in your love,
that trusting in you,
we may proclaim your goodness to all.
Through Christ our Lord.
Amen.

☩ Every nation on earth will adore you, Lord.

Thursday, January 10, 2019
Christmas Weekday

✝ Every nation on earth will adore you, Lord.

Psalm 97 *page 409*

Reading *1 John 4:19–21*

Beloved, we love God because he first loved us. If anyone says, "I love God," but hates his brother, he is a liar; for whoever does not love a brother whom he has seen cannot love God whom he has not seen. This is the commandment we have from him: Whoever loves God must also love his brother.

Reflection

Different theories exist about how many times we hear something before we grasp it. Some say we need to hear a message three, others twenty-three times. This letter of John is clear: love others as you love God or you are a liar. How long will it take for us to understand this? Will that take a lifetime? We have a lifetime on earth to show the love that God has for us and to continue to help others believe that God loves them. This love can flow from our joy at being loved. Through such loving, we will live the Christmas message.

Prayers *others may be added*

To our compassionate God, we pray:

◆ Lord, hear our prayer.

For the continued strength of our Church leaders to witness God's love, we pray: ◆ For nations to end their arms race and devote their resources to helping the poor, we pray: ◆ For young people discerning their vocation, we pray: ◆ For families to come to a greater appreciation and love for one another, we pray: ◆ For release of pain and suffering for all who are ill, we pray: ◆ For our departed sisters and brothers, that they rest in the love of God, we pray: ◆

Our Father . . .

O God,
in your constant love and care,
you summon us to experience
a bond with you so tight
that it can never be broken.
Help us see all human relationships
with your eyes
so that we will love others as we do you.
Through Christ our Lord.
Amen.

✝ Every nation on earth will adore you, Lord.

Friday, January 11, 2019
Christmas Weekday

✝ Praise the Lord, Jerusalem!

Psalm 97
page 409

Reading
1 John 5:5–9, 13

Beloved: Who indeed is the victor over the world but the one who believes that Jesus is the Son of God?

This is the one who came through water and Blood, Jesus Christ, not by water alone, but by water and Blood. The Spirit is the one who testifies, and the Spirit is truth. So there are three that testify, the Spirit, the water, and the Blood, and the three are of one accord. If we accept human testimony, the testimony of God is surely greater. Now the testimony of God is this, that he has testified on behalf of his Son.

I write these things to you so that you may know that you have eternal life, you who believe in the name of the Son of God.

Reflection

"I write these things to you that you may know that you have eternal life." These words from John focus on what is important. John's letter reminds us that we need not search for so many things that we are tempted to think are important. Our relationship with the Lord is cemented in Christ, the Son of God. John's letter assures us that we need to focus on the blessing of our Baptism and the life in Christ that we are given. Consider what you have searched for and whether it compares to eternal life.

Prayers
others may be added

To our Lord, who offers us eternal life, we pray:

◆ Hear us, gracious Lord.

For our Church, that her members take time to understand the message the pope gave January 1 on the World Day of Peace, we pray: ◆ For patience with civic leaders whose views differ from ours, we pray: ◆ For students preparing for testing, we pray: ◆ For couples hoping to adopt a child, we pray: ◆ For the lonely and abandoned, that they be comforted, we pray: ◆ For those who have died, that they be welcomed into eternal life, we pray: ◆

Our Father . . .

Heavenly God,
you offer us eternal life through your Son.
Support us as we seek
to remain faithful to you
and to serve you in our every act.
Through Christ our Lord.
Amen.

✝ Praise the Lord, Jerusalem!

Saturday, January 12, 2019
Christmas Weekday

☩ The Lord takes delight in all people.

Psalm 72 *page 406*

Reading *I John 5:14–16, 19–20*

Beloved: We have this confidence in him that if we ask anything according to his will, he hears us. And if we know that he hears us in regard to whatever we ask, we know that what we have asked him for is ours. If anyone sees his brother sinning, if the sin is not deadly, he should pray to God and he will give him life. This is only for those whose sin is not deadly.

We know that we belong to God, and the whole world is under the power of the Evil One. We also know that the Son of God has come and has given us discernment to know the one who is true. And we are in the one who is true, in his Son Jesus Christ. He is the true God and eternal life.

Reflection

Today's passage from the First Letter of John counsels "to pray to God" when we see another committing a sin that is not deadly. When a sin is deadly, one needs to approach the individual. Through the lenses of love and dialogue, we are encouraged to support one another. Although we are all sinners, we can uphold and grow together when we communicate love fraternally in ways that build up one another.

Prayers *others may be added*

To the Lord, who sent his Son to us, we pray:

◆ Lord, hear our prayer.

For our parish priests, that they lead with compassion, we pray: ◆ For civic leaders, that they serve with integrity, we pray: ◆ For organizations discerning new board members, we pray: ◆ For those rebuilding their lives after natural disasters, we pray: ◆ For scientists researching cures for diseases, we pray: ◆ For our beloved dead, we pray: ◆

Our Father . . .

Gracious God,
you love us so much
that you forgive our sins.
May we strive to forgive friends
and family
as we seek to grow in compassion.
Through Christ our Lord.
Amen.

☩ The Lord takes delight in all people.

Sunday, January 13, 2019
Feast of the Baptism of the Lord

✝ O bless the Lord, my soul!

Psalm 104

page 411

Reading

Luke 3:15–16, 21–22

The people were filled with expectation, and all were asking in their hearts whether John might be the Christ. John answered them all, saying, "I am baptizing you with water, but one mightier than I is coming. I am not worthy to loosen the thongs of his sandals. He will baptize you with the Holy Spirit and fire."

After all the people had been baptized and Jesus also had been baptized and was praying, heaven was opened and the Holy Spirit descended upon him in bodily form like a dove. And a voice came from heaven, "You are my beloved Son; with you I am well pleased."

Reflection

The manifestations of Christ that we celebrate during Christmas Time culminate in the baptism of the Lord. On the last day of the Christmas season, may we think of how we will be open to allow Christ to be manifested in our lives. Let us resolve to consciously choose to follow Christ more closely and take seriously our baptismal call to live as disciples.

Prayers

others may be added

To our faithful Lord, we pray:

◆ Lord, hear our prayer.

May all members of the Church strive to be faithful to their Baptism and grow in discipleship, we pray: ◆ May world leaders share their gifts to build God's vision, we pray: ◆ May young people hear the call to serve the Church and build up the Body of Christ, we pray: ◆ May those preparing to have a child have a safe and healthy pregnancy, we pray: ◆ May others turn to Christ and support those in the catechumenate, we pray: ◆ May the sick recover, we pray: ◆

Our Father . . .

O God,
you called Jesus your beloved Son
at his baptism in the Jordan.
At our Baptism, you adopted us.
Sustain us as we seek to follow Christ.
In our discipleship,
may we be faithful to you
and serve the needs of all.
Through Christ our Lord.
Amen.

✝ O bless the Lord, my soul!

Monday, January 14, 2019
Weekday

✝ Let all the angels worship God!

Psalm 104 *page 411*

Reading *Mark 1:14–20*

After John had been arrested, Jesus came to Galilee proclaiming the gospel of God: "This is the time of fulfillment. The Kingdom of God is at hand. Repent, and believe in the Gospel."

As he passed by the Sea of Galilee, he saw Simon and his brother Andrew casting their nets into the sea; they were fishermen. Jesus said to them, "Come after me, and I will make you fishers of men." Then they left their nets and followed him. He walked along a little farther and saw James, the son of Zebedee, and his brother John. They too were in a boat mending their nets. Then he called them. So they left their father Zebedee in the boat along with the hired men and followed him.

Reflection

Today's Gospel shows Jesus calling Simon, Andrew, James, and John. The encounters are quick: Jesus beckons and the men follow. Christ proclaimed a time of fulfillment, repentance, and belief in the Gospel, as he called the fishers and expected a rapid response. We see Jesus move quickly from person to person and realize that we must keep pace to follow the Christian way toward a new reality.

Prayers *others may be added*

To the Lord, who seeks for us to follow, we pray:

◆ Lord, hear our prayer.

May Church leaders always make proclaiming the Good News a priority, we pray: ◆ May Congress support those who seek to further their education, we pray: ◆ May women and men be open to the consecrated life, we pray: ◆ May parishioners answer the call to share their gifts in liturgical ministry, we pray: ◆ May the sick regain their health, we pray: ◆ May those who have died find eternal happiness in heaven, we pray: ◆

Our Father . . .

Good and gracious God,
you call us to come and follow
and make known your reign.
Give us courage and strength
in times of doubt and fear
so that we may not back away
from spreading the Good News
of salvation.
Through Christ our Lord.
Amen.

✝ Let all the angels worship God!

Tuesday, January 15, 2019
Weekday

✝ You have given your Son rule over the works of your hands.

Psalm 104

page 411

Reading

Mark 1:21–28

Jesus came to Capernaum with his followers, and on the sabbath entered the synagogue and taught. The people were astonished at his teaching, for he taught them as one having authority and not as the scribes. In their synagogue was a man with an unclean spirit; he cried out, "What have you to do with us, Jesus of Nazareth? Have you come to destroy us? I know who you are—the Holy One of God!" Jesus rebuked him and said, "Quiet! Come out of him!" The unclean spirit convulsed him and with a loud cry came out of him. All were amazed and asked one another, "What is this? A new teaching with authority. He commands even the unclean spirits and they obey him." His fame spread everywhere throughout the whole region of Galilee.

Reflection

When Jesus taught at Capernaum, it was with an authority that we will not possess no matter how much we study. However, we can lead simply, in the spirit of humility and openness and with complete trust in God. When our service to others flows from the spirit God has given us, we will be seen as Christ's disciples. As we teach with our lives, the Lord will work marvels through us.

Prayers

others may be added

To our faithful God, we pray:

◆ Lord, hear our prayer.

May Church leaders serve with wisdom, we pray: ◆ May elected officials guide their constituents with compassion, we pray: ◆ May married couples be strengthened in holiness, we pray: ◆ May those persecuted and in prison find hope, we pray: ◆ May the suffering find comfort and healing, we pray: ◆ May those who have died be raised to glory, we pray: ◆

Our Father . . .

O God,
you spoke with authority
and cast out demons.
Guide us as we speak
in your name
and seek to spread news of your glory
to all we meet.
May we lift the spirits of others
so that they may hear the Good News,
that all are healed and made one
with you.
Through Christ our Lord.
Amen.

✝ You have given your Son rule over the works of your hands.

Wednesday, January 16, 2019
Weekday

✝ The Lord remembers the covenant for ever.

Psalm 104 *page 411*

Reading *Mark 1:29–39*

On leaving the synagogue Jesus entered the house of Simon and Andrew with James and John. Simon's mother-in-law lay sick with a fever. They immediately told him about her. He approached, grasped her hand, and helped her up. Then the fever left her and she waited on them.

When it was evening, after sunset, they brought to him all who were ill or possessed by demons. The whole town was gathered at the door. He cured many who were sick with various diseases, and he drove out many demons, not permitting them to speak because they knew him.

Rising very early before dawn, he left and went off to a deserted place, where he prayed. Simon and those who were with him pursued him and on finding him said, "Everyone is looking for you." He told them, "Let us go on to the nearby villages that I may preach there also. For this purpose have I come." So he went into their synagogues, preaching and driving out demons throughout the whole of Galilee.

Reflection

We may not have the power to perform miraculous cures, but we can offer a healing touch to others. Visiting the sick and the shut-in brings joy to those who are isolated. In these simple gestures, we can show Christ's love to those struggling with illness. May we remember the power of Christ in a smile, hug, and message of caring to those who are ill.

Prayers *others may be added*

To our Lord, who heals the sick,
we pray:

◆ Lord, hear our prayer.

May parishes see the value of offering the Sacrament of the Anointing of the Sick, we pray: ◆ May government leaders ensure proper health care for all, we pray: ◆ May all in the healing professions be given the gift of patience, we pray: ◆ May those awaiting transplants receive them, we pray: ◆ May the sick be healed, we pray: ◆ May those who mourn the loss of a loved one find comfort, we pray: ◆

Our Father . . .

O God,
you healed Simon's mother-in-law
with just a grasp of the hand.
Renew our efforts
to bring your healing love
through our concern for others.
May the compassion we offer
bring people to acknowledge
your presence to them.
Through Christ our Lord.
Amen.

✝ The Lord remembers the covenant for ever.

Thursday, January 17, 2019
Memorial of St. Anthony, Abbot

✝ If today you hear God's voice,
harden not your hearts.

Psalm 104 *page 411*

Reading *Mark 1:40–45*

A leper came to [Jesus] and kneeling down begged him and said, "If you wish, you can make me clean." Moved with pity, he stretched out his hand, touched him, and said to him, "I do will it. Be made clean." The leprosy left him immediately, and he was made clean. Then, warning him sternly, he dismissed him at once. Then he said to him, "See that you tell no one anything, but go, show yourself to the priest and offer for your cleansing what Moses prescribed; that will be proof for them." The man went away and began to publicize the whole matter.

Reflection

This Gospel may cause us to reflect on the leprosy that is within our lives. From what do you need healing? The leper who humbly knelt before the Lord for physical healing offers the posture we should take as we ask to be cleansed of a fault or weakness. As we honor St. Anthony, who sought solitude to pray, we might think of a quiet place where we can seek healing from God. In that sacred place, we can bring our brokenness to the Lord.

Prayers *others may be added*

Confident in the compassion of God,
we pray:

◆ Lord, graciously hear us.

May parishes make available the Sacraments of Anointing of the Sick and Reconciliation, we pray: ◆ May monks and hermits, through the intercession of St. Anthony, find strength and solace in their vocation, we pray: ◆ May those in the single life be strengthened in their vocation, we pray: ◆ May efforts to renew the earth's resources continue, we pray: ◆ May true healing come to the sick, we pray: ◆ May peace and comfort surround the dying, we pray: ◆

Our Father . . .

O God,
you call your people
to be renewed
by your healing touch.
Accept our plea
to be made clean
so that we will have the grace
to follow you more closely.
Through Christ our Lord.
Amen.

✝ If today you hear God's voice,
harden not your hearts.

Friday, January 18, 2019
Weekday

✝ Do not forget the works of the Lord.

Psalm 104 *page 411*

Reading *Mark 2:1–5, 11–12*

When Jesus returned to Capernaum after some days, it became known that he was at home. Many gathered together so that there was no longer room for them, not even around the door, and he preached the word to them. They came bringing to him a paralytic carried by four men. Unable to get near Jesus because of the crowd, they opened up the roof above him. After they had broken through, they let down the mat on which the paralytic was lying. When Jesus saw their faith, he said to him, "Child, your sins are forgiven." . . . [Jesus] said to the paralytic, "I say to you, rise, pick up your mat, and go home." He rose, picked up his mat at once, and went away in the sight of everyone. They were all astounded and glorified God, saying, "We have never seen anything like this."

Reflection

Friday is considered a penitential day in which we remember the passion and death of Jesus. Although Church law does not restrict the eating of meat on Fridays, individuals are still to do penance that day. Some still continue the devotion of the Way of the Cross, and in their meditation, ponder Jesus' forgiving those who hanged him. In today's reading, Jesus forgives as he heals. How has forgiveness healed you?

Prayers *others may be added*

To our Lord, who offers forgiveness and healing, we pray:

◆ **Lord, graciously hear us.**

May efforts at forgiveness be renewed through reception of the sacraments, we pray: ◆ May leaders at the United Nations be instruments of healing, we pray: ◆ May health care workers never lose hope, we pray: ◆ May ecumenical efforts deepen in communities, we pray: ◆ May those who care for the sick never lose their sense of compassion, we pray: ◆ May those who have died be led to eternal glory, we pray: ◆

Our Father . . .

Ever-faithful God,
you lead your people
to open their hearts and minister
to those in need.
Guide us to share
your mercy and love
and bring compassion
to those awaiting your healing presence.
Through Christ our Lord.
Amen.

✝ Do not forget the works of the Lord.

Saturday, January 19, 2019
Weekday

✝ *Your words, Lord, are Spirit and life.*

Psalm 104
page 411

Reading
Mark 2:13–17

Jesus went out along the sea. All the crowd came to him and he taught them. As he passed by, he saw Levi, son of Alphaeus, sitting at the customs post. Jesus said to him, "Follow me." And he got up and followed Jesus. While he was at table in his house, many tax collectors and sinners sat with Jesus and his disciples; for there were many who followed him. Some scribes who were Pharisees saw that Jesus was eating with sinners and tax collectors and said to his disciples, "Why does he eat with tax collectors and sinners?" Jesus heard this and said to them, "Those who are well do not need a physician, but the sick do. I did not come to call the righteous but sinners."

Reflection
"Follow me." Jesus used two words to invite the tax collector Levi to participate in his mission. In every generation, Christ continues to call people to life in him. That life may bring us to dine with sinners just as Christ did, for we do his work in the world. May we be more focused on the marginalized than the righteous and may we know the virtue of eating with sinners. Such humility may reveal Christ to our dining companions.

Prayers
others may be added

With confidence in God's redeeming power, we pray:

◆ Lord, hear our prayer.

May the Church continue its efforts to unite Christians, we pray: ◆ May all those who protect us be kept free from harm, we pray: ◆ May the moral framework of our society be built on compassion not fear, we pray: ◆ May men and women join communities of vowed religious, we pray: ◆ May all who are ill be lifted up by God's healing touch, we pray: ◆ May those who have died rejoice with the saints, we pray: ◆

Our Father . . .

O God,
you call us to your service,
and invite us to feast
with the sinners and saints
who share in your bountiful love.
Grant that we may renew our resolve
to help your Church
be a witness of your love.
Through Christ our Lord.
Amen.

✝ *Your words, Lord, are Spirit and life.*

Sunday, January 20, 2019
Second Sunday in Ordinary Time

✝ Proclaim God's marvelous deeds to all the nations.

Psalm 96 *page 409*

Reading *John 2:1–8, 10*

There was a wedding in Cana in Galilee, and the mother of Jesus was there. Jesus and his disciples were also invited to the wedding. When the wine ran short, the mother of Jesus said to him, "They have no wine." And Jesus said to her, "Woman, how does your concern affect me? My hour has not yet come." His mother said to the servers, "Do whatever he tells you." Now there were six stone water jars there for Jewish ceremonial washings, each holding twenty to thirty gallons. Jesus told them, "Fill the jars with water." So they filled them to the brim. Then he told them, "Draw some out now and take it to the headwaiter." So they took it. . . . The headwaiter called the bridegroom and said to him, "Everyone serves good wine first, and then when people have drunk freely, an inferior one; but you have kept the good wine until now."

Reflection

This first sign of Christ's glory in John's Gospel account reminds us that the best is yet to come. We may have moments of panic when we are concerned about what will occur next, but this reading provides assurance that God will provide. Just as at this banquet, God gives us more than we will ever need.

Prayers *others may be added*

To our Lord, whose kindness is bountiful, we pray:

◆ Lord, hear our prayer.

May Church leaders always trust in the Holy Spirit to guide the Church, we pray: ◆ May the Week of Prayer for Christian Unity bring hope, we pray: ◆ May those who suffer from the cold find shelter and warmth, we pray: ◆ May all be provided with affordable housing, we pray: ◆ May the sick be renewed in health, we pray: ◆ May those who have died join with the saints in heaven, we pray: ◆

Our Father . . .

O God,
you quench the thirst of all
who yearn for your presence.
May we always trust
that our concerns
affect you and will be met
with your abundant goodness.
Through Christ our Lord.
Amen.

✝ Proclaim God's marvelous deeds to all the nations.

Monday, January 21, 2019

Memorial of St. Agnes, Virgin and Martryr

✝ You are a priest for ever, in the line of Melchizedek.

Psalm 96

page 409

Reading

Mark 2:18–22

The disciples of John and of the Pharisees were accustomed to fast. People came to him and objected, "Why do the disciples of John and the disciples of the Pharisees fast, but your disciples do not fast?" Jesus answered them, "Can the wedding guests fast while the bridegroom is with them? As long as they have the bridegroom with them they cannot fast. But the days will come when the bridegroom is taken away from them, and then they will fast on that day. No one sews a piece of unshrunken cloth on an old cloak. If he does, its fullness pulls away, the new from the old, and the tear gets worse. Likewise, no one pours new wine into old wineskins. Otherwise, the wine will burst the skins, and both the wine and the skins are ruined. Rather, new wine is poured into fresh wineskins."

Reflection

Jesus gives reason for his followers to act differently than others' disciples. His disciples have the bridegroom among them so they will not act according to the old ways. Jesus tells of a new wine that cannot be poured into old wineskins. He invites us to his feast. Life in him offers to stretch us in ways that will offer new growth. St. Agnes, who is honored today, gave witness to Christ with her life.

Prayers

others may be added

With hopes and dreams for a brighter future, we pray:

◆ Lord, hear our prayer.

May the Church continue to strive to heal divisions, we pray: ◆ May our country seek justice for all, we pray: ◆ May efforts at ecumenism foster dialogue with other Christians, we pray: ◆ May peacekeepers be renewed in their work, we pray: ◆ May the sick find comfort and strength, we pray: ◆ May those who have died see the glory of the Lord, we pray: ◆

Our Father . . .

O God,
you offer us a new way of living.
Grant that we grow in faith daily
as we give witness to your glory.
Encourage us to look
to St. Agnes
to strengthen our resolve for virtue.
May our world be enriched
as we seek for the Body of Christ
to be united in harmony.
Through Christ our Lord.
Amen.

✝ You are a priest for ever, in the line of Melchizedek.

Tuesday, January 22, 2019

Day of Prayer for the Legal Protection of Unborn Children

✝ The Lord will remember his covenant for ever.

Psalm 96

page 409

Reading

Mark 2:23–28

As Jesus was passing through a field of grain on the sabbath, his disciples began to make a path while picking the heads of grain. At this the Pharisees said to him, "Look, why are they doing what is unlawful on the sabbath?" He said to them, "Have you never read what David did when he was in need and he and his companions were hungry? How he went into the house of God when Abiathar was high priest and ate the bread of offering that only the priests could lawfully eat, and shared it with his companions?" Then he said to them, "The sabbath was made for man, not man for the sabbath. That is why the Son of Man is lord even of the sabbath."

Reflection

When the Pharisees see the disciples picking food, Jesus notes that the Sabbath is to serve our needs. People have a need for rest and worship and so Christians have put aside Sunday as a day for renewal and praising God. Unfortunately, Sunday has become much like any other day in which people serve themselves. Since we were created to serve and worship God, we should seek to protect Sunday as we would a gift.

Prayers

others may be added

Confident that the Lord will guide us, we pray:

◆ Lord, hear our prayer.

May the Church be a tireless advocate for the preservation of human life, we pray: ◆ May countries enact laws that protect the unborn, we pray: ◆ May religious liberty be respected so all may freely worship, we pray: ◆ May all be protected from inclement weather, we pray: ◆ May the sick find healing and comfort, we pray: ◆ May those who have died enter into eternal life, we pray: ◆

Our Father . . .

Lord God,
you form all people into your likeness
and call us to be stewards of
your creation.
Lead those struggling
with difficult decisions
to always choose the gift of life.
Through Christ our Lord.
Amen.

✝ The Lord will remember his covenant for ever.

Wednesday, January 23, 2019
Optional Memorial of St. Vincent, Deacon and Martyr

✝ You are a priest for ever, in the line of Melchizedek.

Psalm 96 *page 409*

Reading *Mark 3:1–6*

Jesus entered the synagogue. There was a man there who had a withered hand. They watched Jesus closely to see if he would cure him on the sabbath so that they might accuse him. He said to the man with the withered hand, "Come up here before us." Then he said to them, "Is it lawful to do good on the sabbath rather than to do evil, to save life rather than to destroy it?" But they remained silent. Looking around at them with anger and grieved at their hardness of heart, he said to the man, "Stretch out your hand." He stretched it out and his hand was restored. The Pharisees went out and immediately took counsel with the Herodians against him to put him to death.

Reflection

Is choosing to do the right thing simple? Recognizing certain realities, we may realize that the correct action may not always be clear-cut but may conflict with a regulation. Jesus seeks to help onlookers understand that rules do not have the last say. He advocates choosing to "do good," or to do what brings life. May we challenge the Pharisee within us to bring us to a new order and heal what keeps us from being true to God's call.

Prayers *others may be added*

Trusting in God, who brings healing and wholeness, we pray:

◆ Lord, hear our prayer.

May the caregivers who work in the Church be renewed in their efforts to bring healing, we pray: ◆ May community health centers always be places of welcome and concern, we pray: ◆ May deacons, under the inspiration of St. Vincent, be renewed in their service to the Church, we pray: ◆ May we respect the need for sabbath rest within our lives, we pray: ◆ May the sick experience quick recoveries, we pray: ◆ May those who have died be led to the glories of eternity, we pray: ◆

Our Father . . .

Gracious God of healing and renewal,
you help and guide us along life's paths.
Strengthen our efforts
to be open to your law of love
and bring compassion and guidance
to all in need.
Through Christ our Lord.
Amen.

✝ You are a priest for ever, in the line of Melchizedek.

Thursday, January 24, 2019

Memorial of St. Francis de Sales,
Bishop and Doctor of the Church

✝ Here am I, Lord; I come to do your will.

Psalm 96

page 409

Reading

Mark 3:7–12

Jesus withdrew toward the sea with his disciples. A large number of people followed from Galilee and from Judea. Hearing what he was doing, a large number of people came to him also from Jerusalem, from Idumea, from beyond the Jordan, and from the neighborhood of Tyre and Sidon. He told his disciples to have a boat ready for him because of the crowd, so that they would not crush him. He had cured many and, as a result, those who had diseases were pressing upon him to touch him. And whenever unclean spirits saw him they would fall down before him and shout "You are the Son of God." He warned them sternly not to make him known.

Reflection

After confronting the rules of the Sabbath with the Pharisees, Jesus takes time away to pray. His prayer, though, is interrupted by people looking for change and healing in their lives. Sometimes interruptions disturb us, for we fear they keep us from completing our tasks. However, interruptions can be seen as opportunities from God. St. Francis would say, "Do everything quietly and in a calm spirit. Do not lose your inner peace for anything whatsoever, even if your whole world seems upset." May we pass along peace as we bring healing to those in need.

Prayers

others may be added

To God, who welcomes our pleas, we pray:

◆ Lord, hear our prayer.

May the Church extend healing to all who approach her, we pray: ◆ May our president and legislators always seek the common good, we pray: ◆ May victims of abuse find healing and strength, we pray: ◆ May more men discern a calling to serve as deacons, we pray: ◆ May the Spirit guide all in need of healing and care, we pray: ◆ May those who have died be granted eternal life, we pray: ◆

Our Father . . .

O God,
you care for our health and our souls,
graciously call us to your
  healing presence
to listen, rest, and learn your ways.
Help us to be people of wisdom
who trust in your Spirit and seek
to radiate joy and gentleness to the world.
Through Christ our Lord.
Amen.

✝ Here am I, Lord; I come to do your will.

Friday, January 25, 2019

Feast of the Conversion of St. Paul the Apostle

✝ Go out to all the world and tell the Good News.

Psalm 117

page 413

Reading

Mark 16:15–18

Jesus appeared to the Eleven and said to them: "Go into the whole world and proclaim the Gospel to every creature. Whoever believes and is baptized will be saved; whoever does not believe will be condemned. These signs will accompany those who believe: in my name they will drive out demons, they will speak new languages. They will pick up serpents with their hands, and if they drink any deadly thing, it will not harm them. They will lay hands on the sick, and they will recover."

Reflection

With his conversion, St. Paul the Apostle took to heart the command to "proclaim the Gospel to every creature." The fruits of the labor of Paul and the Eleven continue to this today as Christians own the mandate from Jesus. With a talent for writing and preaching, Paul spread the news of Christ with zeal. No Christian should shirk from their duty to spread the Good News, thinking themselves not worthy or good enough. God has given each follower gifts to share the faith.

Prayers

others may be added

Confident that the Holy Spirit guides and leads the Church, we pray:

◆ Hear us, O Lord.

May the Church's efforts at ecumenism continue to bring unity, we pray: ◆ May world religions witness peace and harmony, we pray: ◆ May legislators work for the health and well-being of all, we pray: ◆ May missionaries be supported as they face persecution and strife, we pray: ◆ May the ill be healed, we pray: ◆ May all who have died be led to the Father's glory, we pray: ◆

Our Father . . .

O God,
through the conversion,
contemplation, writing,
and preaching of St. Paul,
you lead your people
to the knowledge of salvation.
May our faith burn brightly
so that we may give witness
to the truth of your Son
and those we meet
may come to believe
that Jesus Christ is Lord
and reigns with you in unity
with the Holy Spirit, for ever and ever.
Amen.

✝ Go out to all the world and tell the Good News.

Saturday, January 26, 2019

Memorial of Sts. Timothy and Titus, Bishops

✝ Proclaim God's marvelous deeds to all the nations.

Psalm 96

page 409

Reading

2 Timothy 1:1–8

Paul, an Apostle of Christ Jesus by the will of God for the promise of life in Christ Jesus, to Timothy, my dear child: grace, mercy, and peace from God the Father and Christ Jesus our Lord.

I am grateful to God, whom I worship with a clear conscience as my ancestors did, as I remember you constantly in my prayers, night and day. I yearn to see you again, recalling your tears, so that I may be filled with joy, as I recall your sincere faith that first lived in your grandmother Lois and in your mother Eunice and that I am confident lives also in you.

For this reason, I remind you to stir into flame the gift of God that you have through the imposition of my hands. For God did not give us a spirit of cowardice but rather of power and love and self-control. So do not be ashamed of your testimony to our Lord, nor of me, a prisoner for his sake; but bear your share of hardship for the Gospel with the strength that comes from God.

Reflection

Paul's letter expresses gratitude to God for the gift of faith Timothy has received. Reading this, we should consider how we support one another in ministry. Share with others how God gives them strength to bear their "hardship for the Gospel." Disappointment and discouragement may come our way as we work to spread the Good News, but we can be inspired by the faith of those who came before us just as Timothy's mother and grandmother inspired him. Such inspiration will help us as we "stir into flame the gift of God."

Prayers

others may be added

To our Lord, who does marvelous things, we pray:

◆ Lord, hear our prayer.

May our parish staff never shirk from sharing the Gospel, we pray: ◆ May world leaders confidently act as witnesses for peace and justice, we pray: ◆ May people be kept safe during harsh winter weather, we pray: ◆ May athletes be kept free from harm, we pray: ◆ May the sick be open to receiving the Sacrament of the Anointing of the Sick, we pray: ◆ May bereavement groups find strength to encourage those with loss, we pray: ◆

Our Father . . .

Lord God,
you gave us Sts. Timothy and Titus
as witnesses of the apostolic life.
Help us to reach out to others and
encourage their faith.
May we find strength in you
to bear hardships for the Gospel.
Through Christ our Lord.
Amen.

✝ Proclaim God's marvelous deeds to all the nations.

Sunday, January 27, 2019
Third Sunday in Ordinary Time

✝ Your words, Lord, are spirit and life.

Psalm 19

page 397

Reading

Luke 4:17b–19

[Jesus] unrolled the scroll and found the passage where it was written: / *The Spirit of the Lord is upon me, / because he has anointed me / to bring glad tidings to the poor. / He has sent me to proclaim liberty to captives / and recovery of sight to the blind, / to let the oppressed go free, / and to proclaim a year acceptable to the Lord.*

Reflection

During the anointing at Baptism, the new Christian is told of their status as "a member of Christ who is Priest, Prophet, and King." We have been anointed to bring the good news of salvation to all, but especially the poor. As you begin another week, consider the ways you may fulfill this Scripture passage. How can you bring sight to the blind, freedom to the oppressed, and release to captives? Sealed with the Spirit, we have a mission to help others see the Lord in their life.

Prayers

others may be added

To our Lord, who forms us into the Body of Christ, we pray:

◆ Lord, hear our prayer.

For N., our bishop, that he continue to witness to the Good News of Christ, we pray: ◆ That our governor seek to assist those in need, we pray: ◆ For a successful Catholic Schools Week, we pray: ◆ For vocations to the Ursuline Sisters, we pray: ◆ For the chronically ill, we pray: ◆ For our loved ones who have recently died, we pray: ◆

Our Father . . .

O God,
your encouragement and strength
guide us in our baptismal covenant.
May your Spirit always guide
our actions and words
so that we may raise others up
to know of your reign.
Through Christ our Lord.
Amen.

✝ Your words, Lord, are spirit and life.

Monday, January 28, 2019
Memorial of St. Thomas Aquinas, Priest and Doctor of the Church

† Sing to the Lord a new song, for he has done marvelous deeds.

Psalm 19
page 397

Reading
Mark 3:22–30

The scribes who had come from Jerusalem said, "[Jesus] is possessed by Beelzebul," and "By the prince of demons he drives out demons."

Summoning them, [Jesus] began to speak to them in parables, "How can Satan drive out Satan? If a kingdom is divided against itself, that kingdom cannot stand. And if a house is divided against itself, that house will not be able to stand. And if Satan has risen up against himself and is divided, he cannot stand; that is the end of him. But no one can enter a strong man's house to plunder his property unless he first ties up the strong man. Then he can plunder his house. Amen, I say to you, all sins and all blasphemies that people utter will be forgiven them. But whoever blasphemes against the Holy Spirit will never have forgiveness, but is guilty of an everlasting sin."

Reflection
In today's Gospel, Jesus warns against blaspheming against the Holy Spirit. Such blasphemy would tear against the Church. Our tongues should be used for the glory of God and to offer forgiveness to one another. Thomas Aquinas, whom we honor today, had a gift for language. He helped people understand our relationship with God through his writings. Most Catholics, though, may be more familiar with this theologian and philosopher's Eucharistic hymns. The Dominican priest composed "Pange lingua," "Tantum ergo," and "Panis Angelicus."

Prayers
others may be added

In confidence and love, we pray:

◆ Hear us, O Lord.

For the Church, that she act as a symbol of unity, we pray: ◆ For world leaders, that they seek to protect human rights for all peoples, we pray: ◆ For vocations to the Dominican order, we pray: ◆ For the oppressed, we pray: ◆ For quick relief for those who are sick, we pray: ◆ For those who have died, that they be granted eternal rest, we pray: ◆

Our Father . . .

Lord God,
in times of trouble or despair
you call us to trust in you and your Spirit.
Shape our minds and hearts to continue
to stand against the forces of evil
that seek to obscure your grace and love.
Through Christ our Lord.
Amen.

† Sing to the Lord a new song, for he has done marvelous deeds.

Tuesday, January 29, 2019
Weekday

✝ Here am I Lord; I come to do your will.

Psalm 19

page 397

Reading

Mark 3:31–35

[The mother of Jesus] and his brothers arrived. Standing outside they sent word to him and called him. A crowd seated around him told him, "Your mother and your brothers and your sisters are outside asking for you." But he said to them in reply, "Who are my mother and my brothers?" And looking around at those seated in the circle he said, "Here are my mother and my brothers. For whoever does the will of God is my brother and sister and mother."

Reflection

Jesus does not limit his family to relatives. He links his family to those who have done the will of God. Mary fulfilled the will of God, yet why is she outside of the gathering? Perhaps we can consider that she was asking for him so that God's will would be fulfilled. In this passage, Jesus is able to proclaim an inclusive God who shows no favor to those with a certain status. All who seek God's will have a place around the master.

Prayers

others may be added

To our Lord, who embraces all in the family of God, we pray:

◆ **Lord, hear our prayer.**

For our Church, may she seek to be welcoming and inclusive, we pray: ◆ For nations to extend care to all who migrate, we pray: ◆ For victims of abuse, may they know kindness, we pray: ◆ For those who seek meaningful employment, we pray: ◆ For those who are sick, we pray: ◆ For those who have died, that they be granted eternal life, we pray: ◆

Our Father . . .

Gracious God,
your mercy extends
to all who seek you
with a sincere heart.
Turn our minds to your ways of mercy
that we may seek to fulfill your will
and encourage others to manifest
your desires.
Through Christ our Lord.
Amen.

✝ Here am I Lord; I come to do your will.

Wednesday, January 30, 2019
Weekday

✝ You are a priest for ever.

Psalm 19 *page 397*

Reading *Mark 4:1–9*

On another occasion Jesus began to teach by the sea. A very large crowd gathered around him so that he got into a boat on the sea and sat down. And the whole crowd was beside the sea on land. And he taught them at length in parables, and in the course of his instruction he said to them, "Hear this! A sower went out to sow. And as he sowed, some seed fell on the path, and the birds came and ate it up. Other seed fell on rocky ground where it had little soil. It sprang up at once because the soil was not deep. And when the sun rose, it was scorched and it withered for lack of roots. Some seed fell among thorns, and the thorns grew up and choked it and it produced no grain. And some seed fell on rich soil and produced fruit. It came up and grew and yielded thirty, sixty, and a hundredfold." He added, "Whoever has ears to hear ought to hear."

Reflection

The parable of the sower helps us realize that God continues to invite us to bear good fruit throughout our lives. No matter our age, we are to hear God's invitation to build the kingdom. What will we let blossom in our life so that others can know the Lord? Each day we have another chance to be seeds of love and grow in God.

Prayers *others may be added*

Attentive to God's Word growing in and around us, we pray:

◆ Graciously hear us, O Lord.

For the Church, that she continue to show the face of God in the world, we pray: ◆ For our nation's leaders, that they sow seeds of peace, we pray: ◆ For our parishioners, that they act as instruments of grace, we pray: ◆ For Catholic schools, that they continue to nurture faith, we pray: ◆ For those who suffer bitterness, that they heal, we pray: ◆ For those who have died, that they know the joys of heaven, we pray: ◆

Our Father . . .

Bountiful God,
you cultivate your truth within us.
Grant us the grace to seek
to be nourished by your Word
and sacrament
so that your kingdom
will grow wherever we live.
Through Christ our Lord.
Amen.

✝ You are a priest for ever.

Thursday, January 31, 2019
Memorial of St. John Bosco, Priest

✝ O, bless the Lord, my soul!

Psalm 19 *page 397*

Reading *Mark 4:21–25*

Jesus said to his disciples, "Is a lamp brought in to be placed under a bushel basket or under a bed, and not to be placed on a lampstand? For there is nothing hidden except to be made visible; nothing is secret except to come to light. Anyone who has ears to hear ought to hear." He also told them, "Take care what you hear. The measure with which you measure will be measured out to you, and still more will be given to you. To the one who has, more will be given; from the one who has not, even what he has will be taken away."

Reflection

Jesus gives his disciples images to help understand how we are to act as disciples. We are to let our light shine, to share the Gospel, and to hear attentively. All our senses are engaged through our actions, assuring that our whole person is given in total gift. As faithful stewards, we give our time, talent, and treasure to build the Body of Christ. "A lot" is measured out to us, for we are given much. By our selfless giving, may we encourage others to give and never hold back so that we do not lose our precious treasure.

Prayers *others may be added*

To our God, who gives us the light of faith, we pray:

◆ Lord, hear our prayer.

For leaders in the Church, that they illumine the world with faith, we pray: ◆ For world leaders, that they give hope to those in need, we pray: ◆ For Catholic schools, that they encourage students to grow in faith and wisdom, we pray: ◆ For the sick, that they see the face of God in their caregivers, we pray: ◆ For those who have died, that they experience the brilliant light of God, we pray: ◆

Our Father . . .

Radiant God,
you call us to trust in your grace and light
and serve you with hearts
that illumine the darkness in our world.
Sustain our trust
as we seek your grace and mercy.
Through Christ our Lord.
Amen.

✝ O, bless the Lord, my soul!

Friday, February 1, 2019
Weekday

☩ The salvation of the just comes from the Lord.

Psalm 19 *page 397*

Reading *Mark 4:26–34*

Jesus said to the crowds: "This is how it is with the Kingdom of God; it is as if a man were to scatter seed on the land and would sleep and rise night and day and the seed would sprout and grow, he knows not how. Of its own accord the land yields fruit, first the blade, then the ear, then the full grain in the ear. And when the grain is ripe, he wields the sickle at once, for the harvest has come."

He said, "To what shall we compare the Kingdom of God, or what parable can we use for it? It is like a mustard seed that, when it is sown in the ground is the smallest of all the seeds on the earth. But once it is sown, it springs up and becomes the largest of plants and puts forth large branches, so that the birds of the sky can dwell in its shade." With many such parables he spoke the word to them as they were able to understand it. Without parables he did not speak to them, but to his own disciples he explained everything in private.

Reflection

To what would you compare the Kingdom of God today? Jesus spoke of the mustard seed, the smallest seed that grew to shelter birds. Do you think of the Kingdom of God growing in your Catholic school and parish, especially as Catholic Schools Week ends? Do you think of the Kingdom growing in your workplace or home? The parable continues to be lived as we take the seed of our faith and make it come alive in our school, workplace, home, church, and community. Wherever we are, we can bloom and grow, radiating our Baptism in Christ Jesus.

Prayers *others may be added*

As we look to the Lord as the
Kingdom is built in our midst,
we pray:

◆ Hear us, Lord.

For encouragement in times of trial, we pray: ◆ For farmers as they prepare their crops, we pray: ◆ For students learning the ways of God and life, we pray: ◆ For those who work with orphans, we pray: ◆ For those suffering the effects of harsh weather and illness, we pray: ◆ For those seeking refuge and passage to God, we pray: ◆

Our Father . . .

Almighty and ever-loving God,
you revealed your truths and mysteries
to those who hear.
Direct our hearts and actions
to always be of service
and bring your works to fulfillment.
Through Christ our Lord.
Amen.

☩ The salvation of the just comes from the Lord.

Saturday, February 2, 2019

Feast of the Presentation of the Lord

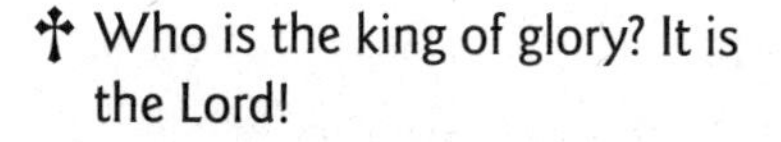

✝ Who is the king of glory? It is the Lord!

Psalm 98

page 410

Reading

Luke 2:25–32

Now there was a man in Jerusalem whose name was Simeon. This man was righteous and devout, awaiting the consolation of Israel, and the Holy Spirit was upon him. It had been revealed to him by the Holy Spirit that he should not see death before he had seen the Christ of the Lord. He came in the Spirit into the temple; and when the parents brought in the child Jesus to perform the custom of the law in regard to him, he took him into his arms and blessed God, saying: / "Now, Master, you may let your servant go / in peace, according to your word, / for my eyes have seen your salvation, / which you prepared in sight of all the peoples, / a light for revelation to the Gentiles, / and glory for your people Israel."

Reflection

In his prophecy Simeon both tells of the "light of revelation" and the sword that will pierce Mary's heart (verse 35). We know that Christ's death will not overshadow the brightness of his light. We live the eternal spring—the new life that is Christ. Through his light, we can help dispel the darkness in this world.

Prayers

others may be added

Presenting our prayers to God, who brings us light, we pray:

◆ Lord, hear our prayer.

Teach us to do our Father's will, we pray: ◆ Comfort those who dwell in darkness, we pray: ◆ Help us to obey the law of love in serving the least, we pray: ◆ Inspire us to proclaim Christ's words and acts, we pray: ◆ Provide Christ's healing power to the ill, we pray: ◆ Welcome our brothers and sisters who have died to the light of heaven, we pray: ◆

Our Father . . .

Father of all,
you allowed Simeon
to see the light of salvation.
May our hearts glow with your love.
Through your light,
may the darkness of sin and death be cast out.
May those who are fearful be free of anxiety and suffering.
Through Christ our Lord.
Amen.

✝ Who is the king of glory? It is the Lord!

Sunday, February 3, 2019
Fourth Sunday in Ordinary Time

✝ If today you hear God's voice,
harden not your heart!

Psalm 95 *page 408*

Reading *Luke 4:24–30*

[Jesus said:] "Amen, I say to you, no prophet is accepted in his own native place. Indeed, I tell you, there were many widows in Israel in the days of Elijah when the sky was closed for three and a half years and a severe famine spread over the entire land. It was to none of these that Elijah was sent, but only to a widow in Zarephath in the land of Sidon. Again, there were many lepers in Israel during the time of Elisha the prophet; yet not one of them was cleansed, but only Naaman the Syrian." When the people in the synagogue heard this, they were all filled with fury. They rose up, drove him out of the town, and led him to the brow of the hill on which their town had been built, to hurl him down headlong. But he passed through the midst of them and went away.

Reflection

Most of us would not be comfortable being called a prophet or considering ourselves an authority for Christ. However, in our Baptism, we were made a member of Christ, and we took on the roles of priest, prophet, and king. As today's prophets, we share the Good News that God is with us, providing healing and sharing in our life. This is the Good News that fishers found with Jesus. Sharing this message is prophetic today.

Prayers *others may be added*

To our Lord, who gives us the
authority to speak in his name,
we pray:

◆ Lord, hear our prayer.

For those seeking knowledge, that they may come to know the wealth of wisdom in the Church, we pray: ◆ For teachers, that they continue to be the presence of Christ to their students, we pray: ◆ For those living consecrated vows, we pray: ◆ For young people, that they hear their call to serve the Church, we pray: ◆ For the sick, that they feel the healing power of Christ, we pray: ◆ For those who have died, that they be welcomed to the heavenly banquet, we pray: ◆

Our Father . . .

Ever-faithful God,
you sent the prophets
to guide your people.
Give us the courage
to be your prophetic voice today
Through Christ our Lord.
Amen.

✝ If today you hear God's voice,
harden not your heart!

Monday, February 4, 2019
Weekday

✝ Let your hearts take comfort, all who hope in the Lord.

Psalm 95

page 408

Reading

Mark 5:1–10

Jesus and his disciples came to the other side of the sea, to the territory of the Gerasenes. When he got out of the boat, at once a man from the tombs who had an unclean spirit met him. The man had been dwelling among the tombs, and no one could restrain him any longer, even with a chain. In fact, he had frequently been bound with shackles and chains, but the chains had been pulled apart by him and the shackles smashed, and no one was strong enough to subdue him. Night and day among the tombs and on the hillsides he was always crying out and bruising himself with stones. Catching sight of Jesus from a distance, he ran up and prostrated himself before him, crying out in a loud voice, "What have you to do with me, Jesus, Son of the Most High God? I adjure you by God, do not torment me!" (He had been saying to him, "Unclean spirit, come out of the man!") He asked him, "What is your name?" He replied, "Legion is my name. There are many of us." And he pleaded earnestly with him not to drive them away from that territory.

Reflection

How many of us have felt like the man dwelling in the tomb? Feeling that God has abandoned us, left us alone in our suffering? Yet, in faith, we know that Christ holds us close, heals and strengthens us, and has pity on us. As Pope Francis has said, through the tears of suffering we can see clearer that God comforts and upholds those who suffer. God places caretakers around us. Let us remember that it is in the service of other people that God is able to heal us.

Prayers

others may be added

God has visited his people and so we pray:

◆ **Lord, hear our prayer.**

For those who suffer with terminal illness, we pray: ◆ For the strengthening of caretakers, we pray: ◆ For the courage to be peacemakers, we pray: ◆ For healing of wounds and memories, we pray: ◆ For couples preparing for marriage, we pray: ◆ For the forgiveness of the sins of those who have died, we pray: ◆

Our Father . . .

Loving God,
you drive out the darkness
that clouds our sight
and heal the brokenhearted.
Care for your people in need
and show pity on your servants
seeking wisdom, patience, and strength.
Through Christ our Lord.
Amen.

✝ Let your hearts take comfort, all who hope in the Lord.

Tuesday, February 5, 2019

Memorial of St. Agatha, Virgin and Martyr

☩ They will pray to you Lord, who long for you.

Psalm 95

page 408

Reading

Mark 5:25–29

There was a woman afflicted with hemorrhages for twelve years. She had suffered greatly at the hands of many doctors and had spent all that she had. Yet she was not helped but only grew worse. She had heard about Jesus and came up behind him in the crowd and touched his cloak. She said, "If I but touch his clothes, I shall be cured." Immediately her flow of blood dried up. She felt in her body that she was healed of her affliction.

Reflection

Today's Gospel from Mark recounts not only this woman who sought to be cured but the account of the healing of the daughter of Jairus. Both the woman and Jairus had their eyes fixed on Jesus, whom today's reading from Hebrews (12:1–4) calls "the leader and perfecter of faith." With faith, we are able to keep focused on Jesus and the belief that he can heal us—no matter our struggles. May we endure the crosses in our lives with the help of others, confident that as we keep our eyes toward Christ, we will be strengthened and healed.

Prayers

others may be added

Fixing our gaze on God, we pray:

◆ Lord, hear our prayer.

For the Church's outreach ministries, we pray: ◆ For affordable and available health care for all, we pray: ◆ For community leaders, that they act as instruments of peace, we pray: ◆ For those who suffer with incurable diseases, we pray: ◆ For those suffering from breast cancer, that they may seek solace in St. Agatha, the patron of those with breast cancer, we pray: ◆ For those who have died, we pray: ◆

Our Father . . .

Gentle God,
the compassion of your Son recalls
your care for us.
May we rid ourselves
of the burdens and sins
that hold us back from true healing
so that we may reach our destination
with the cloud of witnesses.
Through our Lord Jesus Christ, your Son,
who lives and reigns with you in union
with the Holy Spirit,
one God, for ever and ever.
Amen.

☩ They will pray to you Lord, who long for you.

Wednesday, February 6, 2019

Memorial of St. Paul Miki and Companions, Martyrs

☩ The Lord's kindness is everlasting to those who fear him.

Psalm 95

page 408

Reading

Mark 6:1–6

Jesus departed from there and came to his native place, accompanied by his disciples. When the sabbath came he began to teach in the synagogue, and many who heard him were astonished. They said, "Where did this man get all this? What kind of wisdom has been given him? What mighty deeds are wrought by his hands! Is he not the carpenter, the son of Mary, and the brother of James and Joseph and Judas and Simon? And are not his sisters here with us?" And they took offense at him. Jesus said to them, "A prophet is not without honor except in his native place and among his own kin and in his own house." So he was not able to perform any mighty deed there, apart from curing a few sick people by laying his hands on them. He was amazed at their lack of faith.

Reflection

We are reminded today that nothing is to stand in the way of our relationship to Christ and promoting his message. Christ came to share wisdom, a wisdom that was not easily accepted but necessary for salvation. Jesuit priest Paul Miki (†1597) was one of the twenty-six martyrs of Japan who held fast to sharing the faith and did so in creative ways. Though they knew they would be persecuted, they never ceased proclaiming the truth that Jesus Christ is Lord and healer of our souls.

Prayers

others may be added

To our faithful God, we pray:

◆ Hear us, gracious Lord.

For the Church's missionaries as they spread the message of Christ today, we pray: ◆ For leaders of nations, that they allow freedom for all to practice their faith, we pray: ◆ For renewed efforts of ecumenism, we pray: ◆ For the ill, that their health be restored, we pray: ◆ For peace in troubled regions, we pray: ◆ For those who have died, that they see the glory of God, we pray: ◆

Our Father . . .

Lord God,
as we see your glory in our midst,
may we renew our efforts
to share your wisdom
in our words and actions.
Help us to never waver in our faith
and trust in your goodness and care for us.
Through Christ our Lord.
Amen.

☩ The Lord's kindness is everlasting to those who fear him.

Thursday, February 7, 2019

Weekday

✝ O God, we ponder your mercy within your temple.

Psalm 95

page 408

Reading

Mark 6:7–13

Jesus summoned the Twelve and began to send them out two by two and gave them authority over unclean spirits. He instructed them to take nothing for the journey but a walking stick—no food, no sack, no money in their belts. They were, however, to wear sandals but not a second tunic. He said to them, "Wherever you enter a house, stay there until you leave from there. Whatever place does not welcome you or listen to you, leave there and shake the dust off your feet in testimony against them." So they went off and preached repentance. The Twelve drove out many demons, and they anointed with oil many who were sick and cured them.

Reflection

Today's Gospel reading relates that the disciples had such trust that they willingly traveled with no provisions. With just a walking stick, they went to preach repentance. They trusted that God would provide the hospitality they needed to carry out their ministry. What is your level of trust in others and in the providence of God? What do you feel you need in order to tell your story of faith? Since Christ has touched us, how can we hold back from sharing the message?

Prayers

others may be added

To our Lord, who provides for us, we pray:

◆ Lord, hear our prayer.

For missionaries around the globe, that they be strengthened in their ministry, we pray: ◆ For deeper wisdom to bring creative ways of Christian living to our countries, we pray: ◆ For hope for those who are distressed, we pray: ◆ For married couples, that they be renewed in their love, we pray: ◆ For the sick, that they experience healing, we pray: ◆ For those who have died, that they be granted eternal life, we pray: ◆

Our Father . . .

Good and gracious Lord,
you call us to serve your Word
and share your message of healing.
Grant us the trust and courage
to announce the Good News
and confidently live your message.
Through Christ our Lord.
Amen.

✝ O God, we ponder your mercy within your temple.

Friday, February 8, 2019
Weekday

✝ The Lord is my light and my salvation.

Psalm 95
page 408

Reading
Hebrews 13:1–8

Let brotherly love continue. Do not neglect hospitality, for through it some have unknowingly entertained angels. Be mindful of prisoners as if sharing their imprisonment, and of the ill-treated as of yourselves, for you also are in the body. Let marriage be honored among all and the marriage bed be kept undefiled, for God will judge the immoral and adulterers. Let your life be free from love of money but be content with what you have, for he has said, *I will never forsake you or abandon you.* Thus we may say with confidence: *The Lord is my helper, / and I will not be afraid. / What can anyone do to me? /*

Remember your leaders who spoke the word of God to you. Consider the outcome of their way of life and imitate their faith. Jesus Christ is the same yesterday, today, and forever. Let brotherly love continue.

Reflection
It is interesting that this reading follows yesterday's Gospel in which the Apostles were to rely on the hospitality of strangers. Not only do the two readings focus on the value of hospitality but of trust in the Lord. Yesterday, we heard that the disciples traveled without money, and today that the Christian is to be "free of love of money," for the Lord will provide. Trust is essential.

Prayers
others may be added

To our Lord, who knows our every need, we pray:

◆ Hear us, gracious Lord.

For the growth of charitable agencies in the Church, we pray: ◆ For social service organizations, that they reach those in need, we pray: ◆ For strength, courage, and hope for social workers, we pray: ◆ For pastors, confessors, and spiritual companions, we pray: ◆ For those who care for the sick, we pray: ◆ For bereavement ministers, we pray: ◆

Our Father . . .

God of compassion and goodness,
you raise up all who need your
loving kindness.
May we ever seek to serve you
and the needs of those
desperate for love and companionship
so that through our gentle care,
they may know that you live and reign
with your Son, our Lord Jesus Christ, in
the unity of the Holy Spirit,
one God, for ever and ever.
Amen.

✝ The Lord is my light and my salvation.

Saturday, February 9, 2019
Weekday

✝ The Lord is my shepherd; there is nothing I shall want.

Psalm 95

page 408

Reading

Mark 6:30–34

The Apostles gathered together with Jesus and reported all they had done and taught. He said to them, "Come away by yourselves to a deserted place and rest a while." People were coming and going in great numbers, and they had no opportunity even to eat. So they went off in the boat by themselves to a deserted place. People saw them leaving and many came to know about it. They hastened there on foot from all the towns and arrived at the place before them.

When Jesus disembarked and saw the vast crowd, his heart was moved with pity for them, for they were like sheep without a shepherd; and he began to teach them many things.

Reflection

With the many responsibilities in our lives, we often forget that Jesus and his disciples took time off to rest. To be good at whatever we do, including ministry, we cannot neglect times of rest and renewal. Work will always be there. Part of a life of sacrifice and praise includes taking regular moments to enjoy the peace of God and let the Good Shepherd care for us.

Prayers

others may be added

Looking to God, who cares for our needs, we pray:

◆ Lord, hear our prayer.

For just laws to ensure workers have rest, we pray: ◆ For those who work for peace and justice, we pray: ◆ For those who need encouragement, we pray: ◆ For a joyous Lord's Day, we pray: ◆ For those who care for the sick, we pray: ◆ For those who have died, that they be in the care of the angels, we pray: ◆

Our Father . . .

O God,
you nourish and refresh us.
May we trust in your providence enough
that we take time to be free from work
and worries and rest in you.
Through our Lord Jesus Christ, your Son,
who lives and reigns with you in the unity
of the Holy Spirit,
one God, for ever and ever.
Amen.

✝ The Lord is my shepherd; there is nothing I shall want.

Sunday, February 10, 2019

Fifth Sunday in Ordinary Time

✝ Praise the Lord, my soul!

Psalm 145

page 421

Reading

Luke 5:4–10

[Jesus] said to Simon, "Put out into deep water and lower your nets for a catch." Simon said in reply, "Master, we have worked hard all night and have caught nothing, but at your command I will lower the nets." When they had done this, they caught a great number of fish and their nets were tearing. They signaled to their partners in the other boat to come to help them. They came and filled both boats so that the boats were in danger of sinking. When Simon Peter saw this, he fell at the knees of Jesus and said, "Depart from me, Lord, for I am a sinful man." For astonishment at the catch of fish they had made seized him and all those with him, and likewise James and John, the sons of Zebedee, who were partners of Simon. Jesus said to Simon, "Do not be afraid; from now on you will be catching men."

Reflection

Simon did not know what he was getting into when he let Jesus into his boat and then lowered his nets at one command. Simon's hope for a catch was answered beyond all measure and followed with an invitation to another life. Through our Baptism, we have been called to discipleship. That sometimes means leaving our comfort zones and old patterns to take on a new life in the Lord.

Prayers

others may be added

Relying on God's grace, we pray:

◆ Lord, hear our prayer.

For leaders in the Church, that they be able to inspire through their preaching, we pray: ◆ For civic officials, that they respect the dignity of all, we pray: ◆ For outreach ministries in parishes, that they find those most in need, we pray: ◆ For inspiration to know how to help those who complain, we pray: ◆ For the sick, that they be healed and made whole, we pray: ◆ For those who have died and those who grieve, we pray: ◆

Our Father . . .

Loving God,
you raise up those who are lowly and lost.
May all see your loving grace and plan
guiding them to your Kingdom,
where you live and reign with our Lord
Jesus Christ in the unity of the
Holy Spirit,
one God, for ever and ever.
Amen.

✝ Praise the Lord, my soul!

Monday, February 11, 2019

Optional Memorial of Our Lady of Lourdes

✝ Praise the Lord, my soul!

Psalm 145

page 421

Reading

John 2:1–8, 10

There was a wedding in Cana in Galilee, and the mother of Jesus was there. Jesus and his disciples were also invited to the wedding. When the wine ran short, the mother of Jesus said to him, "They have no wine." And Jesus said to her, "Woman, how does your concern affect me? My hour has not yet come." His mother said to the servers, "Do whatever he tells you." Now there were six stone water jars there for Jewish ceremonial washings, each holding twenty to thirty gallons. Jesus told them, "Fill the jars with water." So they filled them to the brim. Then he told them, "Draw some out now and take it to the headwaiter." So they took it. . . . The headwaiter called the bridegroom and said to him, "Everyone serves good wine first, and then when people have drunk freely, an inferior one; but you have kept the good wine until now."

Reflection

The Optional Memorial of Our Lady of Lourdes celebrates Mary's ongoing concern for us. Even greater than her care for us was her absolute trust in God. She knew that the Word would bring compassion to those in need. As we celebrate this memorial, we are in communion with those who are sick. Especially keep in prayer today the ill of your parish.

Prayers

others may be added

To our God who heals, we pray:

◆ Lord, hear our prayer.

That God show compassion on the terminally ill, we pray: ◆ That researchers find cures for diseases, we pray: ◆ That civic leaders work for affordable care for all, we pray: ◆ That peace come to war-torn regions, we pray: ◆ That justice come to those suffering, we pray: ◆ That healing come to those who grieve, we pray: ◆

Our Father . . .

Merciful God,
your people have received your gifts
of healing
to bring Good News to the afflicted.
Comfort, bless, and heal those most in
need of strength
so that all may know the supreme
sacrament of grace, Jesus Christ,
who lives and reigns with you in the unity
of the Holy Spirit,
one God, for ever and ever.
Amen.

✝ Praise the Lord, my soul!

Tuesday, February 12, 2019
Weekday

☩ O God, how wonderful your name in all the earth!

Psalm 145

page 421

Reading

Genesis 1:20–25

God said, "Let the water teem with an abundance of living creatures, and on the earth let birds fly beneath the dome of the sky." And so it happened: God created the great sea monsters and all kinds of swimming creatures with which the water teems, and all kinds of winged birds. God saw how good it was, and God blessed them, saying, "Be fertile, multiply, and fill the water of the seas; and let the birds multiply on the earth." Evening came, and morning followed—the fifth day.

Then God said, "Let the earth bring forth all kinds of living creatures: cattle, creeping things, and wild animals of all kinds." And so it happened: God made all kinds of wild animals, all kinds of cattle, and all kinds of creeping things of the earth. God saw how good it was.

Reflection

The story of creation culminates with the making of man and woman in the image of God. They are given the responsibility of caring for creation. We are in a partnership with God. Today is an opportunity to look at our values as God's stewards and how we use the many blessings we have been given. Spend time examining your appreciation for creation and whether you are a good steward of the earth. Most of us have room for improvement.

Prayers

others may be added

To God, who abundantly blesses us, we pray:

◆ Graciously hear us, Lord.

For our parish, that we may find new ways to recycle and reuse, we pray: ◆ For our president, that he may be mindful of the dignity of all, we pray: ◆ For prisoners, that they know of our care, we pray: ◆ For those who protect and serve us, we pray: ◆ For the sick, that they be free from disease, we pray: ◆ For those who have died, that they enter the glory of God's house, we pray: ◆

Our Father . . .

God of all creation,
your beauty manifests itself throughout the world.
May we truly be your faithful stewards,
zealously caring for the earth
and providing a future full of hope
Through Christ our Lord.
Amen.

☩ O God, how wonderful your name in all the earth!

Wednesday, February 13, 2019
Weekday

✝ O, bless the Lord, my soul!

Psalm 145
page 421

Reading
Genesis 2:8–9, 15–17

[T]he LORD God planted a garden in Eden, in the east, and he placed there the man whom he had formed. Out of the ground the LORD God made various trees grow that were delightful to look at and good for food, with the tree of life in the middle of the garden and the tree of the knowledge of good and evil.

The LORD God then took the man and settled him in the garden of Eden to cultivate and care for it. The LORD God gave man this order: "You are free to eat from any of the trees of the garden except the tree of the knowledge of good and evil. From that tree you shall not eat; the moment you eat from it you are surely doomed to die."

Reflection
The Lord is clear that death will ensue should fruit be eaten from the tree of knowledge of good and evil. Still, Adam and Eve gave in to temptation. We also know that death comes when we turn our backs on God. Why do we set out to doom ourselves? Will we ever learn to trust that God has a better plan and knows what is best for us? We can make a first step today toward trusting God by changing our attitude to one of trust.

Prayers
others may be added

Turning to our all-knowing God,
we pray:

◆ Hear us, Lord.

May the Church grow in wisdom, we pray: ◆ May leaders renew efforts of peace and prosperity for all, we pray: ◆ May projects for renewing the environment grow stronger, we pray: ◆ May young people discover their gifts and vocation, we pray: ◆ May the sick be healed and strengthened, we pray: ◆ May those who have died rejoice with the saints, we pray: ◆

Our Father . . .

Almighty God of heaven and earth,
you reach out in goodness
to guide your people.
Help us to be good stewards
of the world you have created
and grow in appreciation
of the blessings we enjoy daily.
Through our Lord Jesus Christ, your Son,
who lives and reigns with you in the unity
of the Holy Spirit,
one God, for ever and ever.
Amen.

✝ O, bless the Lord, my soul!

Thursday, February 14, 2019

Memorial of Sts. Cyril, Monk, and Methodius, Bishop

✝ Blessed are those who fear the Lord.

Psalm 145

page 421

Reading

Genesis 2:18–23

The LORD God said: "It is not good for the man to be alone. I will make a suitable partner for him." So the LORD God formed out of the ground various wild animals and various birds of the air, and he brought them to the man to see what he would call them; whatever the man called each of them would be its name. The man gave names to all the cattle, all the birds of the air, and all the wild animals; but none proved to be the suitable partner for the man.

So the LORD God cast a deep sleep on the man, and while he was asleep, he took out one of his ribs and closed up its place with flesh. The LORD God then built up into a woman the rib that he had taken from the man. When he brought her to the man, the man said: / "This one, at last is bone of my bones / and flesh of my flesh; / this one shall be called 'woman,' / for out of 'her man' this one has been taken."

Reflection

Before sin entered the world, we were pure. Once jealousies, envy, and other vices that destroy relationships with God and others entered the world, life changed. Perhaps this second creation story is a reminder that we need to strip down to our bare bones to be vulnerable before God and one another. When that is done, there is no want or gain, only us—the beloved created.

Prayers

others may be added

With the saints, we pray:

◆ Lord, hear our prayer.

For ecumenism to grow in communities, we pray: ◆ For couples, that they desire to renew their love and dedication, we pray: ◆ For civic leaders, that they act transparently, we pray: ◆ For the healing of divisions among cultures, we pray: ◆ For the sick, we pray: ◆ For blessed peace for the deceased, we pray: ◆

Our Father . . .

Loving God,
you inspired Sts. Cyril and Methodius
to bring your message of Good News
and love.
Free us from worries and concerns
that keep us bound to human distress
and open us to your creation.
Through Christ our Lord.
Amen.

✝ Blessed are those who fear the Lord.

Friday, February 15, 2019
Weekday

✝ Blessed are those whose sins are forgiven.

Psalm 145 *page 421*

Reading *Genesis 3:1–8*

Now the serpent was the most cunning of all the animals that the LORD God had made. The serpent asked the woman, "Did God really tell you not to eat from any of the trees in the garden?" The woman answered the serpent: "We may eat of the fruit of the trees in the garden; it is only about the fruit of the tree in the middle of the garden that God said, 'You shall not eat it or even touch it, lest you die.'" But the serpent said to the woman: "You certainly will not die! No, God knows well that the moment you eat of it your eyes will be opened and you will be like gods who know what is good and what is evil." The woman saw that the tree was good for food, pleasing to the eyes, and desirable for gaining wisdom. So she took some of its fruit and ate it; and she also gave some to her husband, who was with her, and he ate it. Then the eyes of both of them were opened, and they realized that they were naked; so they sewed fig leaves together and made loincloths for themselves.

When they heard the sound of the LORD God moving about in the garden at the breezy time of the day, the man and his wife hid themselves from the LORD God among the trees of the garden.

Reflection

Regularly we hide from God by taking a break from our prayer life. We allow other "serpents" to get in the path of listening to God and God's plan for us. We make our own plans and desires first, and then return to the realization that all is God's and we were foolish to do it alone. May we resolve today to be aware of how we have been blessed and seek God's direction for our lives.

Prayers *others may be added*

To our Lord, who desires the best for us, we pray:

◆ Lord, hear our prayer.

For all leaders, that they seek to understand God's presence in their lives, we pray: ◆ For the Church, that she strive to allow the Holy Spirit to direct mission efforts, we pray: ◆ For all of us to be open to new ways God is calling us to listen, we pray: ◆ For the caregivers who support deaf ministries, we pray: ◆ For the healing of the impaired, we pray: ◆ For those who have died, that they be joined with the Creator, we pray: ◆

Our Father . . .

Creator God,
you call us to be
in relationship with you
and enjoy your generous plan.
May we stay open to your will
and continuously seek to please you.
Through Christ our Lord.
Amen.

✝ Blessed are those whose sins are forgiven.

Saturday, February 16, 2019
Weekday

✝ In every age, O Lord, you have been our refuge.

Psalm 145

page 421

Reading

Mark 8:2–9

[Jesus said], "My heart is moved with pity for the crowd, because they have been with me now for three days and have nothing to eat. If I send them away hungry to their homes, they will collapse on the way, and some of them have come a great distance." His disciples answered him, "Where can anyone get enough bread to satisfy them here in this deserted place?" Still he asked them, "How many loaves do you have?" "Seven," they replied. He ordered the crowd to sit down on the ground. Then, taking the seven loaves he gave thanks, broke them, and gave them to his disciples to distribute, and they distributed them to the crowd. They also had a few fish. He said the blessing over them and ordered them distributed also. They ate and were satisfied. They picked up the fragments left over—seven baskets. There were about four thousand people.

Reflection

Jesus demonstrates compassion in feeding four thousand people who came to listen to him. He continues to feed us in the Eucharist. In our daily lives, we can see God taking what we have and multiplying the goodness it provides others. When we trust and share our blessings, God is manifested. May we appreciate our blessings and generously share them with others, trusting always in God.

Prayers

others may be added

To our compassionate Lord, we pray:

◆ Lord, hear our prayer.

For Church leaders, that they continue reaching out to the needy through charitable programs, we pray: ◆ For world leaders, that they recognize the blessings and gifts of their countries and distribute them among the marginalized, we pray: ◆ For renewed efforts in expanding water and food services, we pray: ◆ For farmers preparing to sow crops, we pray: ◆ For the sick, that they see their gifts in their trials, we pray: ◆ For those who have died, that the angels and saints welcome them in paradise, we pray: ◆

Our Father . . .

God of our ancestors,
we worship your glory
and marvel at our blessings.
Teach us to share our many gifts
for the good of all
in service to the Body of Christ.
Through our Lord Jesus Christ, your Son,
who lives and reigns with you in the unity
of the Holy Spirit,
one God, for ever and ever.
Amen.

✝ In every age, O Lord, you have been our refuge.

Sunday, February 17, 2019

Sixth Sunday in Ordinary Time

✝ Happy are they who hope in the Lord.

Psalm 95 *page 408*

Reading *Luke 6:20–26*

Raising his eyes toward his disciples [Jesus] said: / "Blessed are you who are poor, / for the kingdom of God is yours. / Blessed are you who are now hungry, / for you will be satisfied. / Blessed are you who are now weeping, / for you will laugh. / Blessed are you when people hate you, / and when they exclude and insult you, / and denounce your name as evil on account of the Son of Man. / Rejoice and leap for joy on that day! Behold, your reward will be great in heaven. For their ancestors treated the prophets in the same way. / But woe to you who are rich, / for you have received your consolation. / Woe to you who are filled now, / for you will be hungry. / Woe to you who laugh now, / for you will grieve and weep. / Woe to you when all speak well of you, / for their ancestors treated the false prophets in this way."

Reflection

In the Sermon on the Mount, Jesus showed his union with those who are poor, who are hungry, and who weep. In saying that they are "blessed," he pointed them toward heaven. Too often we think of the here and now. It is helpful to be reminded that we long and hope for heaven. Our time on earth, during which we may be hated for doing what is right, is just a station along the way. We may have sorrows now, but we can look forward to blessings in heaven.

Prayers *others may be added*

To our compassionate Lord, we pray:

◆ Lord, hear our prayer.

For more research funding for incurable diseases, we pray: ◆ For doctors, nurses, and all caregivers, we pray: ◆ For the Church, that she find new ways to reach out to the young, we pray: ◆ For benefactors of Catholic charitable agencies, we pray: ◆ For those preparing for high school and college, we pray: ◆ For those who have died, that they be welcomed into eternal life, we pray: ◆

Our Father . . .

Loving God,
we crave for your hand
to lead us to our heavenly home.
May we know that our present life is only
a glimpse
of the beautiful reality that awaits us
with our ancestors in faith.
Through Christ our Lord.
Amen.

✝ Happy are they who hope in the Lord.

Monday, February 18, 2019
Weekday

✝ Offer to God a sacrifice of praise.

Psalm 95

page 408

Reading

Mark 8:11–13

The Pharisees came forward and began to argue with Jesus, seeking from him a sign from heaven to test him. He sighed from the depth of his spirit and said, "Why does this generation seek a sign? Amen, I say to you, no sign will be given to this generation." Then he left them, got into the boat again, and went off to the other shore.

Reflection

Jesus provides a model of conflict resolution. Listen, barely comment, and then walk away. How often do we find people challenging and asking for more proof? Amid the questioning, may we see that we need to pay close attention to Christ's plan and recognize that we will never please everyone. Please God and the rest will come along—eventually following us to the other shore.

Prayers

others may be added

To our Lord, who provides for us,
we pray:

◆ Lord, hear our prayer.

Renew efforts of conflict resolution in our Church, we pray: ◆ Encourage leaders to strive for peace among nations, we pray: ◆ Encourage your followers to lovingly accept those unlike them, we pray: ◆ Challenge deception and conceit, we pray: ◆ Heal the ill, we pray: ◆ Raise those who have died to the realms of glory, we pray: ◆

Our Father . . .

Source of eternal glory,
you help us on our journey
to find ways to share your Word.
May we always recognize our purpose
to witness to your healing presence.
Through our Lord Jesus Christ, your Son,
who lives and reigns with you in the unity
of the Holy Spirit,
one God, for ever and ever.
Amen.

✝ Offer to God a sacrifice of praise.

Tuesday, February 19, 2019
Weekday

✝ The Lord will bless the people with peace.

Psalm 95
page 408

Reading
Mark 8:14–21

The disciples had forgotten to bring bread, and they had only one loaf with them in the boat. Jesus enjoined them, "Watch out, guard against the leaven of the Pharisees and the leaven of Herod." They concluded among themselves that it was because they had no bread. When he became aware of this he said to them, "Why do you conclude that it is because you have no bread? Do you not yet understand or comprehend? Are your hearts hardened? Do you have eyes and not see, ears and not hear? And do you not remember, when I broke the five loaves for the five thousand, how many wicker baskets full of fragments you picked up?" They answered him, "Twelve." "When I broke the seven loaves for the four thousand, how many full baskets of fragments did you pick up?" They answered him, "Seven." He said to them, "Do you still not understand?"

Reflection
Yes, we still do not understand. No matter the bountiful blessings God has bestowed on us, we fail to trust that God will continue to provide. When we trust in God, our narrow vision will be broadened and our ears will be opened. Just as the disciples focused on the bread, we worry about minute things. God helps us see the bigger picture. What is the bigger picture that you need to see right now? What is there within your heart that keeps you from opening up to God's love? We need to take time to be open to the works that God is doing in our lives.

Prayers
others may be added

To our faithful God, we pray:

◆ Lord, hear our prayer.

Inspire in us new ways of thinking and living in our Church, we pray: ◆ Grant our legislators a vision that respects all life, we pray: ◆ Encourage coworkers to learn new opportunities for collaboration, we pray: ◆ Assist those who minister to the sick and disheartened, we pray: ◆ Help families develop cooperative ways of relating, we pray: ◆ Bring those who have died to eternal life, we pray: ◆

Our Father . . .

Eternal God,
you help us grow in wisdom
and knowledge,
to work together for the common good.
Encourage us to seek your ways
and truths
so that we may love you above all else.
Through Christ our Lord.
Amen.

✝ The Lord will bless the people with peace.

Wednesday, February 20, 2019

Weekday

☩ To you, Lord, I will offer a sacrifice of praise.

Psalm 95

page 408

Reading

Mark 8:22–26

When Jesus and his disciples arrived at Bethsaida, people brought to him a blind man and begged him to touch him. He took the blind man by the hand and led him outside the village. Putting spittle on his eyes he laid his hands on him and asked, "Do you see anything?" Looking up he replied, "I see people looking like trees and walking." Then he laid hands on his eyes a second time and he saw clearly; his sight was restored and he could see everything distinctly. Then he sent him home and said, "Do not even go into the village."

Reflection

Jesus laid his hands on the blind man twice before he saw clearly. Is it possible that Jesus purposely took his time in healing the blind man? Does this process of healing remind you of times when you gradually began to see and understand something clearly? Especially when things go wrong in our lives, we want to grasp the meaning of the event quickly. It takes a while to view God's plan. Often, we just need to trust. This Gospel reminds us that restoration is a process and that we need to take our time with it.

Prayers

others may be added

To our Lord, who gives us sight, we pray:

◆ Hear us, O Lord.

For the grace to see the guidance of the Holy Spirit in the Church, we pray: ◆ For world leaders, that they have a renewed vision for their people, we pray: ◆ For tranquility and peace among enemies, we pray: ◆ For the blind, that they may access services they need, we pray: ◆ For those who are sick, that their health be restored, we pray: ◆ For the deceased, that they may take their place at the heavenly banquet, we pray: ◆

Our Father . . .

Ever-present God,
you restore our sight
and bring us your love.
Help us to renew our efforts
to believe and trust
the vision you set before us.
Give us the patience and wisdom
to grow in your goodness.
Through Christ our Lord.
Amen.

☩ To you, Lord, I will offer a sacrifice of praise.

Thursday, February 21, 2019
Weekday

✝ From heaven the Lord looks down on the earth.

Psalm 95 *page 408*

Reading *Mark 8:27–33*

Jesus and his disciples set out for the villages of Caesarea Philippi. Along the way he asked his disciples, "Who do people say that I am?" They said in reply, "John the Baptist, others Elijah, still others one of the prophets." And he asked them, "But who do you say that I am?" Peter said to him in reply, "You are the Christ." Then he warned them not to tell anyone about him.

He began to teach them that the Son of Man must suffer greatly and be rejected by the elders, the chief priests, and the scribes, and be killed, and rise after three days. He spoke this openly. Then Peter took him aside and began to rebuke him. At this he turned around and, looking at his disciples, rebuked Peter and said, "Get behind me, Satan. You are thinking not as God does, but as human beings do."

Reflection

Like Peter, we often do not think as God does. We are on the way, still growing in discovering how to live as true followers. Our whole lives are a journey seeking to image God. It is easy to become distracted with paths other than God's and lose our focus. May we continue to strive to stay on the path that God has set before us, picking up and carrying our cross and making God's will ours.

Prayers *others may be added*

To our God who blesses us each day, we pray:

◆ Lord, hear our prayer.

For community leaders, that they be mindful of the need to care for the earth, we pray: ◆ For scientists, that they make discoveries that lead to healthier lives, we pray: ◆ For world leaders, that they work for peace, we pray: ◆ For more missionaries to spread the message of Christ, we pray: ◆ For the healing of the sick, we pray: ◆ For the dead to be raised to God's glory, we pray: ◆

Our Father . . .

Loving God,
help our minds and hearts
to follow you more closely.
May we witness your ways
and be your true disciples,
sharing our many gifts
to help others know Christ,
who lives and reigns with you in the unity
of the Holy Spirit,
one God, for ever and ever.
Amen.

✝ From heaven the Lord looks down on the earth.

Friday, February 22, 2019

Feast of the Chair of St. Peter the Apostle

☩ The Lord is my shepherd there is nothing I shall want.

Psalm 23 *page 398*

Reading *Matthew 16:13–19*

When Jesus went into the region of Caesarea Philippi he asked his disciples, "Who do people say that the Son of Man is?" They replied, "Some say John the Baptist, others Elijah, still others Jeremiah or one of the prophets." He said to them, "But who do you say that I am?" Simon Peter said in reply, "You are the Christ, the Son of the living God." Jesus said to him in reply, "Blessed are you, Simon son of Jonah. For flesh and blood has not revealed this to you, but my heavenly Father. And so I say to you, you are Peter, and upon this rock I will build my Church, and the gates of the netherworld shall not prevail against it. I will give you the keys to the Kingdom of heaven. Whatever you bind on earth shall be bound in heaven; and whatever you loose on earth shall be loosed in heaven."

Reflection

In today's Gospel, we have essentially the same exchange between Jesus and the disciples as yesterday but from a different evangelist. As Jesus travels this region, he knows that there are statues of gods that are distracting his disciples' journey. He asks for faith statements in this setting. We are reminded that no matter what obscures our vision, we need to seek to continue to witness to Christ. Each day, we are to turn away from distractions and live as disciples.

Prayers *others may be added*

To our Lord, who sent the Christ to us, we pray:

◆ **Lord, hear our prayer.**

For the successor of Peter, that he continue to shepherd his flock with care, we pray: ◆ For leaders of nations, that they focus on peace, we pray: ◆ For our parishes, that they act as keystones to Christ, we pray: ◆ For vocations to the vowed religious and ordained life, we pray: ◆ For the sick, that they be comforted, we pray: ◆ For those who have died, that they be welcomed to eternal life, we pray: ◆

Our Father . . .

O God of the ages,
you shepherd your people
with tender mercy.
Lead us over the challenges of life
to the restful water that refreshes and
leads us to Christ,
who lives and reigns with you in the unity
of the Holy Spirit,
one God, for ever and ever.
Amen.

☩ The Lord is my shepherd there is nothing I shall want.

Saturday, February 23, 2019

Memorial of St. Polycarp, Bishop and Martyr

✝ I will praise your name for ever, Lord.

Psalm 95

page 408

Reading

Mark 9:2–9

Jesus took Peter, James, and John and led them up a high mountain apart by themselves. And he was transfigured before them, and his clothes became dazzling white, such as no fuller on earth could bleach them. Then Elijah appeared to them along with Moses, and they were conversing with Jesus. Then Peter said to Jesus in reply, "Rabbi, it is good that we are here! Let us make three tents: one for you, one for Moses, and one for Elijah." . . . Then a cloud came, casting a shadow over them; from the cloud came a voice, "This is my beloved Son. Listen to him." Suddenly, looking around, they no longer saw anyone but Jesus alone with them.

As they were coming down from the mountain, he charged them not to relate what they had seen to anyone, except when the Son of Man had risen from the dead.

Reflection

The narrative of the Transfiguration will be proclaimed five times at Mass during this liturgical year. Three times we hear from Mark's account: "This is my beloved Son. Listen to him." These words should stir in us the importance of listening to Christ. Sometimes, we need to be quiet to hear. Take some time to be on the mountain to rest in the silence of Christ. Try to say nothing for a few minutes and just be in the presence of the Christ.

Prayers

others may be added

Walking in faith, we pray:

◆ Lord, hear our prayer.

Help pastors find moments for reflection and prayer, we pray: ◆ Guide leaders to trust in the hope that Christ brings, we pray: ◆ Renew efforts for awareness of the environment, we pray: ◆ Encourage your followers to seek you in the quiet, we pray: ◆ Inspire legislators to work for better health care for those most in need, we pray: ◆ Bring the dying to the banquet table in heaven, we pray: ◆

Our Father . . .

Lord God,
you show us your goodness in
many ways.
May we recognize your presence
in the many moments
and wonders of our day.
May we look forward
to the eternal glory
promised us in Christ,
who lives and reigns with you in the unity
of the Holy Spirit,
one God, for ever and ever.
Amen.

✝ I will praise your name for ever, Lord.

Sunday, February 24, 2019
Seventh Sunday in Ordinary Time

✝ The Lord is kind and merciful.

Psalm 34 *page 401*

Reading *Luke 6:27–31, 35*

Jesus said to his disciples: "To you who hear I say, love your enemies, do good to those who hate you, bless those who curse you, pray for those who mistreat you. To the person who strikes you on one cheek, offer the other one as well, and from the person who takes your cloak, do not withhold even your tunic. Give to everyone who asks of you, and from the one who takes what is yours do not demand it back. Do to others as you would have them do to you . . . love your enemies and do good to them, and lend expecting nothing back; then your reward will be great and you will be children of the Most High, for he himself is kind to the ungrateful and the wicked."

Reflection

The directives Jesus gives today are difficult ones. Why would anyone want to do good to the person who hates? Why wouldn't we expect that what was borrowed would be returned? It may sometimes seem that it is getting harder to love. We might walk or even run away from conflict and never take the opportunity to repair relationships. Still, we say we are Christian. We are to be powerful in our love of others. Trusting in the Lord, we can fulfill our mandate to be Christian.

Prayers *others may be added*

To our loving God, we pray:

◆ Lord, hear our prayer.

Help us keep Sunday and every day holy, we pray: ◆ Teach us to do your will in a humble spirit, we pray: ◆ Give all the opportunity to join around the table of your Word, we pray: ◆ Open our hearts to love our enemies, we pray: ◆ Heal the broken spirits that despair, we pray: ◆ Welcome the dying to the glory of heaven, we pray: ◆

Our Father . . .

Reconciling God,
you show us your wisdom.
Mold us into your likeness
so that we may be imitators of your love.
Through our Lord Jesus Christ, your Son,
who lives and reigns with you in the unity
of the Holy Spirit,
one God, for ever and ever.
Amen.

✝ The Lord is kind and merciful.

Monday, February 25, 2019
Weekday

☩ The Lord is king; robed in majesty.

Psalm 34 *page 401*

Reading *Mark 9:19–29*

[Jesus] said to [the crowd and the scribes] in reply, "O faithless generation, how long will I be with you? How long will I endure you? Bring him to me." They brought the boy to him. And when he saw him, the spirit immediately threw the boy into convulsions. As he fell to the ground, he began to roll around and foam at the mouth. Then he questioned his father, "How long has this been happening to him?" He replied, "Since childhood. It has often thrown him into fire and into water to kill him. But if you can do anything, have compassion on us and help us." Jesus said to him, " 'If you can!' Everything is possible to one who has faith." Then the boy's father cried out, "I do believe, help my unbelief!" Jesus, on seeing a crowd rapidly gathering, rebuked the unclean spirit and said to it, "Mute and deaf spirit, I command you: come out of him and never enter him again!" Shouting and throwing the boy into convulsions, it came out. He became like a corpse, which caused many to say, "He is dead!" But Jesus took him by the hand, raised him, and he stood up. When he entered the house, his disciples asked him in private, "Why could we not drive it out?" He said to them, "This kind can only come out through prayer."

Reflection

"This kind can only come out through prayer." In our parishes, the healing power of prayer is used in compassionate outreach during Communion to the sick and the Sacrament of Anointing of the Sick. Prayer is always at the heart of ministry, since the good that is done comes from God.

Prayers *others may be added*

To our faithful God, we pray:

◆ Lord, hear our prayer.

Grant pastoral staff peace in their day's work, we pray: ◆ Inspire us to direct our actions to show Christ to others, we pray: ◆ Assist world leaders to work in harmony to quell conflict in troubled regions, we pray: ◆ Open hearts to answer the call to parish ministries, we pray: ◆ Heal those with incurable diseases, we pray: ◆ Show compassion on the departed faithful, we pray: ◆

Our Father . . .

Redeeming God,
may everything we say and do
begin with your inspiration and help.
Grant that our ministry find its origin in
your grace.
May we look forward to the
heavenly Kingdom,
where you live and reign with our Lord
Jesus Christ, your Son, in the unity of
the Holy Spirit,
one God, for ever and ever.
Amen.

☩ The Lord is king; robed in majesty.

Tuesday, February 26, 2019
Weekday

✝ **Commit your life to the Lord and you will be helped.**

Psalm 34

page 401

Reading

Mark 9:31–35

[Jesus] was teaching his disciples and telling them, "The Son of Man is to be handed over to men and they will kill him, and three days after his death he will rise." But they did not understand the saying, and they were afraid to question him.

They came to Capernaum and, once inside the house, he began to ask them, "What were you arguing about on the way?" But they remained silent. They had been discussing among themselves on the way who was the greatest. Then he sat down, called the Twelve, and said to them, "If anyone wishes to be first, he shall be the last of all and the servant of all."

Reflection

It is in our human nature to be competitive and place emphasis on placing first. From Adam and Eve until now, God is patient with us as we argue and distract ourselves from the purity of what we are meant to be. In today's Gospel, Jesus is asking the disciples to see their life in him differently. Following him does not mean glory but service. Their leadership will be one of servanthood.

Prayers

others may be added

Turning to God with joy, we pray:

◆ **Lord, hear our prayer.**

Inspire us to be of continual service, we pray: ◆ Help us keep your commandment of love, we pray: ◆ Guide civic leaders in wisdom, we pray: ◆ Help coworkers heal divisions, we pray: ◆ Assist friends in working through rifts caused by jealousy, we pray: ◆ Welcome those who have died into your kingdom, we pray: ◆

Our Father . . .

God of all peoples,
you comfort the fearful and anxious.
Assist us as we seek to heal divisions
so that the Body of Christ will be unified.
Through our Lord Jesus Christ, your Son,
who lives and reigns with you in the unity
of the Holy Spirit,
one God, for ever and ever.
Amen.

✝ **Commit your life to the Lord and you will be helped.**

Wednesday, February 27, 2019
Weekday

☩ O Lord, great peace have they who love your law.

Psalm 34
page 401

Reading
Mark 9:38–40

John said to Jesus, "Teacher, we saw someone driving out demons in your name, and we tried to prevent him because he does not follow us." Jesus replied, "Do not prevent him. There is no one who performs a mighty deed in my name who can at the same time speak ill of me. For whoever is not against us is for us."

Reflection
When we hear this Gospel, do we think about the many ways that people who do God's work are sometimes gossiped about and criticized? We need to take care to build up the people who preach the Gospel and minister in our parishes. Be cautious with your speech and also encourage others not to be judgmental about people who seek to do God's will. Work against the demonic but affirm disciples working for the kingdom.

Prayers
others may be added

To God, who strengthens us, we pray:

◆ Hear us, O Lord.

Humble the hearts of the proud, we pray: ◆ Strengthen those who are persecuted, we pray: ◆ Assist those who act on God's Word, we pray: ◆ Encourage people to affirm others, we pray: ◆ Heal the sick, we pray: ◆ Show the vision of your face to the departed, we pray: ◆

Our Father . . .

O God,
you shower us with goodness.
Assist us as we seek to do your will.
Grant that we always turn to you
and avoid evil ways.
May our hearts be open
to those who follow you.
Through Christ our Lord.
Amen.

☩ O Lord, great peace have they who love your law.

Thursday, February 28, 2019
Weekday

† Blessed are they who hope in the Lord.

Psalm 34 *page 401*

Reading *Mark 9:42–50*

[Jesus said to his disciples]: "Anyone who gives you a cup of water to drink because you belong to Christ, amen, I say to you, will surely not lose his reward.

"Whoever causes one of these little ones who believe in me to sin, it would be better for him if a great millstone were put around his neck and he were thrown into the sea. If your hand causes you to sin, cut it off. It is better for you to enter into life maimed than with two hands to go into Gehenna, into the unquenchable fire. And if your foot causes you to sin, cut if off. It is better for you to enter into life crippled than with two feet to be thrown into Gehenna. And if your eye causes you to sin, pluck it out. Better for you to enter into the Kingdom of God with one eye than with two eyes to be thrown into Gehenna, where *their worm does not die, and the fire is not quenched.*

"Everyone will be salted with fire. Salt is good, but if salt becomes insipid, with what will you restore its flavor? Keep salt in yourselves and you will have peace with one another."

Reflection

As salt of the world and light for all people, we are to add the flavor of discipleship to the world. We have been baptized to be a spark, and in that spark build up the peace and reign of God. We are challenged to live goodness and justice and do God's will. As Sirach says in today's First Reading (5:18): "Rely not on your wealth." We rely on God, using the gifts we have been given to bear much fruit, for the Kingdom of God is at hand when we add the flavor that we have been entrusted to share.

Prayers *others may be added*

Relying on the help of God, we pray:

◆ Lord, hear our prayer.

Fill us with light and wisdom throughout this day, we pray: ◆ Help us bear hardships with courage, we pray: ◆ Direct our feelings, thoughts, and actions, we pray: ◆ Call men to serve as your ordained leaders, we pray: ◆ Affirm the vocation of women to consecrated life, we pray: ◆ May the dead rest in eternal peace, we pray: ◆

Our Father . . .

Gracious God of our ancestors,
you lead us in the law of love.
In the challenges of this day,
encourage us
to be your light, salt, and truth
in a world hungering for you.
Through Christ our Lord.
Amen.

† Blessed are they who hope in the Lord.

Friday, March 1, 2019
Weekday

✝ Guide me, Lord, in the way of your commands.

Psalm 34 *page 401*

Reading *Mark 10:2–8*

The Pharisees approached [Jesus] and asked, "Is it lawful for a husband to divorce his wife?" They were testing him. He said to them in reply, "What did Moses command you?" They replied, "Moses permitted a husband to write a bill of divorce and dismiss her." But Jesus told them, "Because of the hardness of your hearts he wrote you this commandment. But from the beginning of creation, *God made them male and female. For this reason a man shall leave his father and mother and be joined to his wife, and the two shall become one flesh.* So they are no longer two but one flesh. Therefore what God has joined together, no human being must separate."

Reflection

Jesus' teaching on marriage and divorce is a difficult pastoral challenge for us, for every family is touched in some way by this reality. We know couples that grew apart and let the sacrament die, and we know of abuse in many forms. But we also know of couples who witness their love to their family, friends, and community. All need to be encouraged to see that God calls them to love and that their love should not be separated from God. Both love and God are necessary for living the vocation of marriage.

Prayers *others may be added*

To our faithful God, we pray:

◆ Lord, hear our prayer.

May couples be strengthened in their marriage, we pray: ◆ Help those struggling with divorce, we pray: ◆ Assist families in rearing children to a vocation of loving service in marriage, we pray: ◆ Unite those who long for collaborative work, we pray: ◆ Guide those who bear the cross of illness, we pray: ◆ Bring our friends who have died to eternal life, we pray: ◆

Our Father . . .

God of love,
you give us the law to guide our ways.
Strengthen those called to your service
to participate in the communion of love
and unity for the glory of the Body
of Christ.
Through our Lord Jesus Christ, your Son,
who lives and reigns with you in the unity
of the Holy Spirit,
one God, for ever and ever.
Amen.

✝ Guide me, Lord, in the way of your commands.

Saturday, March 2, 2019
Weekday

✝ The Lord's kindness is everlasting to those who fear.

Psalm 34 *page 401*

Reading *Mark 10:13–16*

People were bringing children to [Jesus] that he might touch them, but the disciples rebuked them. When Jesus saw this he became indignant and said to them, "Let the children come to me; do not prevent them, for the kingdom of God belongs to such as these. Amen, I say to you, whoever does not accept the kingdom of God like a child will not enter it." Then he embraced [the children] and blessed them, placing his hands on them.

Reflection

In today's passage, Jesus reminds us to come to him, to be touched, to be welcomed, and to feel the embrace of love. We can pass on this love as we treat others with respect and care. As disciples, we are cautious to overlook fear-mongering and place our trust in God. With such trust, we follow the ways that Jesus showed us, and will be welcomed into the Kingdom of God.

Prayers *others may be added*

With childlike trust, we turn to God in prayer:

◆ Lord, hear our prayer.

Heal those abused as children, we pray: ◆ Provide leaders with the gift of your vision, we pray: ◆ Enable us to see God's image in all, we pray: ◆ Help those in prison, we pray: ◆ Comfort the sick and those who care for them, we pray: ◆ Invite the departed to be among the saints, we pray: ◆

Our Father . . .

God of knowledge and goodness,
your covenant is everlasting.
Embrace the needs of all your people,
and help us to grow in trust
to build the kingdom of love and peace.
Through Christ our Lord.
Amen.

✝ The Lord's kindness is everlasting to those who fear.

Sunday, March 3, 2019

Eighth Sunday in Ordinary Time

✝ Lord, it is good to give thanks to you.

Psalm 34

page 401

Reading

Luke 6:39–42

Jesus told his disciples a parable: "Can a blind person guide a blind person? Will not both fall into a pit? No disciple is superior to the teacher; but when fully trained, every disciple will be like his teacher. Why do you notice the splinter in your brother's eye, but do not perceive the wooden beam in your own? How can you say to your brother, 'Brother, let me remove that splinter in your eye,' when you do not even notice the wooden beam in your own eye? You hypocrite! Remove the wooden beam from your eye first; then you will see clearly to remove the splinter in your brother's eye."

Reflection

It is much easier to discern another's faults and gifts than ours. Often what we find disturbing in another is a trait that we carry. Sometimes, too, jealousy and anxiety can blind us to the treasures God has gifted to those around us. The reading advises us to try to see ourselves and others appropriately. Our mouths are to emit positive words and comments to build up the Body of Christ.

Prayers

others may be added

Trusting that God will reveal goodness, we pray:

◆ Hear us, O Lord.

May the Church embrace the gifts of all believers, we pray: ◆ May the Sisters of the Blessed Sacrament receive new members as they recall their founder, St. Katharine Drexel, we pray: ◆ May all those waiting for transplants be afforded new life, we pray: ◆ May the blind and others with disabilities be healed, we pray: ◆ May we share our compliments with others, we pray: ◆ May the grieving be comforted, we pray: ◆

Our Father . . .

O God,
we give thanks to you
for your goodness and bounty.
May we treasure the riches of
your people,
praise others in love,
and bear burdens with grace.
Through Christ our Lord.
Amen.

✝ Lord, it is good to give thanks to you.

Monday, March 4, 2019
Weekday

✝ Let the just exult and rejoice in the Lord.

Psalm 34 *page 401*

Reading *Sirach 17:20–21*

To the penitent God provides a way back, / he encourages those who are losing hope / and has chosen for them the lot of truth. / Return to him and give up sin, / pray to the LORD and make your offenses few. / Turn again to the Most High and away from your sin, / hate intensely what he loathes, / and know the justice and judgments of God, / Stand firm in the way set before you, / in prayer to the Most High God.

Reflection

Days before Lent begins, this is a fitting reading to prepare us for the season. It recalls the wisdom of living a life in God: we are to be people who hope, seek forgiveness, stand firm in prayer, and demonstrate mercy. Such a life may seem hard to achieve, but remember that God is always assisting us. Focus the time before Lent on how you might live out an aspect of the reading so that you might love God and others better. You will become a better servant then of the Most High.

Prayers *others may be added*

To our merciful Lord, we pray:

◆ Lord, hear our prayer.

May our Church continue to witness virtues, we pray: ◆ May our leaders proclaim peace with fortitude, we pray: ◆ May our engineers design with care for the earth, we pray: ◆ May we affirm young people who seek to serve as consecrated religious, we pray: ◆ May research funds support cures for diseases, we pray: ◆ May the Most High draw all who have died to the banquet feast, we pray: ◆

Our Father . . .

Good and gracious God,
our prayers add nothing to your greatness
but help us return to witness your truths.
Guide us along the ways of goodness,
deepen our need for your justice
and support us with your loving mercy.
Through Christ our Lord.
Amen.

✝ Let the just exult and rejoice in the Lord.

Tuesday, March 5, 2019
Weekday

✝ To the upright I will show the saving power of God.

Psalm 34
page 401

Reading
Mark 10:28–31

Peter began to say to Jesus, "We have given up everything and followed you." Jesus said, "Amen, I say to you, there is no one who has given up house or brothers or sisters or mother or father or children or lands for my sake and for the sake of the Gospel who will not receive a hundred times more now in this present age: houses and brothers and sisters and mothers and children and lands, with persecutions, and eternal life in the age to come. But many that are first will be last, and the last will be first."

Reflection

We may sometimes be dramatic and feel we have given up everything to follow God. As we prepare for Lent, recognize that this season comes at a good time. We are invited to be "first" in allowing our life to be motivated by the cross of Christ. On Ash Wednesday, a cross will be placed on our foreheads as a reminder that we follow Christ and must forsake this world to be better prepared for the next. Let this be a day of preparation to work together on our journey of the cross.

Prayers
others may be added

To our saving God, we pray:

◆ Lord, hear our prayer.

May we possess hearts that are humble, we pray: ◆ May our world be more caring, we pray: ◆ May our lives be more sincere, we pray: ◆ May our work give you honor and glory, we pray: ◆ May the sick be healed, we pray: ◆ May those who have died share in eternal life, we pray: ◆

Our Father . . .

Loving God,
may our faith be professed on our lips
and in our lives.
Guide us on the journey of life
to serve the vulnerable and hurting
and bring prayer and joy to all we meet.
Through Christ our Lord.
Amen.

✝ To the upright I will show the saving power of God.

Wednesday, March 6, 2019
Ash Wednesday

✝ Be merciful, O Lord, for we have sinned.

Psalm 51
page 402

Reading
2 Corinthians 5:20—6:2

Brothers and sisters: We are ambassadors for Christ, as if God were appealing through us. We implore you on behalf of Christ, be reconciled to God. For our sake he made him to be sin who did not know sin, so that we might become the righteousness of God in him.

Working together, then, we appeal to you not to receive the grace of God in vain. For he says: / *In an acceptable time I heard you, / and on the day of salvation I helped you.* / Behold, now is a very acceptable time; behold, now is the day of salvation.

Reflection

As ambassadors for Christ, we are mindful during Lent of how we can reconcile not only with God but one another. Christ reconciled us with God through his death and modeled forgiveness while on the cross. There, he prayed for those crucifying him: "Father, forgive them, they know not what they do." As our Lenten journey begins again today, we have an opportunity to show that we belong to Christ during this acceptable time. During Lent, forgive someone you feel has wronged you. What better way could you follow Christ during these forty days than by making forgiveness integral to your daily life?

Prayers
others may be added

To our merciful God, we pray:

◆ Lord, have mercy.

Renew the Church in holiness, we pray: ◆ Inspire our leaders to model peaceful ways, we pray: ◆ Offer comfort to those who feel oppressed, we pray: ◆ Bring consolation to the homebound, we pray: ◆ Spare those who are sick from further suffering, we pray: ◆ Bring those who have died to the joys of everlasting life, we pray: ◆

Our Father . . .

O Lord,
throughout these forty days,
you call us to renewal of heart and mind.
Assist us as we seek to be true disciples
who show others Christ,
the true witness of love and life.
Through our Lord Jesus Christ, your Son,
who lives and reigns with the Holy Spirit,
one God, for ever and ever.
Amen.

✝ Be merciful, O Lord, for we have sinned.

Thursday, March 7, 2019
Thursday after Ash Wednesday

☩ Blessed are they who hope in the Lord.

Psalm 51 *page 402*

Reading *Luke 9:22–25*

Jesus said to his disciples, "The Son of Man must suffer greatly and be rejected by the elders, the chief priests, and the scribes, and be killed and on the third day be raised."

Then he said to all, "If anyone wishes to come after me, he must deny himself and take up his cross daily and follow me. For whoever wishes to save his life will lose it, but whoever loses his life for my sake will save it. What profit is there for one to gain the whole world yet lose or forfeit himself?"

Reflection

"What profit is there for one to gain the whole world yet lose or forfeit himself?" The Gospel portrays greatness differently than does secular culture. Jesus' followers deny themselves and take up their cross. Such a disciple leads with humility and openness to God's will. This way of living is countercultural to a society that considers wealth and worldly power as signs of greatness. A Christian's life, however, is modeled on that of Christ, who was rejected and then put to death.

Prayers *others may be added*

To our faithful God, we pray:

◆ Lord, hear our prayer.

May Church leaders seek wisdom through prayer, we pray: ◆ May elected officials guide their constituents with compassion, we pray: ◆ May married couples be strengthened in holiness, we pray: ◆ May those persecuted and in prison find hope, we pray: ◆ May the suffering find comfort and healing, we pray: ◆ May those who have died rejoice in heaven, we pray: ◆

Our Father . . .

O God,
you sent us Christ to show us
the way to you.
Trusting in your love,
we call out to you
to assist us in our ministry.
Help us spread your Word
to all we meet
and lift others with the Good News.
Through Christ our Lord.
Amen.

☩ Blessed are they who hope in the Lord.

Friday, March 8, 2019
Friday after Ash Wednesday

† A humble contrite heart, O God,
you will not spurn.

Psalm 51 *page 402*

Reading *Matthew 9:14–15*

The disciples of John approached Jesus and said, "Why do we and the Pharisees fast much, but your disciples do not fast?" Jesus answered them, "Can the guests mourn as long as the bridegroom is with them? The days will come when the bridegroom is taken away from them, and then they will fast."

Reflection

During the time of Jesus, fasting indicated mourning. Jesus notes, then, that it would not be fitting for the disciples to fast while he is with them. On Ash Wednesday and Good Friday, the Church asks us to eat small, simple meals as part of a penitential fast. Other types of fasting can be added to this discipline. At the beginning of this season, consider the following: How often does your tongue fast? How often do you fast from technology and other efforts that keep you from relating to friends, family, and God? What other types of fasting could help you grow closer to God?

Prayers *others may be added*

Placing our concerns with God,
we pray:

◆ Lord, hear our prayer.

May the Church seek more ways to serve the poor, we pray: ◆ May world leaders combine resources to care for those in the most need, we pray: ◆ May parishes renew efforts for their outreach, we pray: ◆ May vocations to serve in prison ministry grow, we pray: ◆ May the sick be made whole, we pray: ◆ May those who have died see the face of God, we pray: ◆

Our Father . . .

Gentle God,
you call our hearts to change
and be moved with compassion.
Grant that our sacrifices
be pleasing to you.
In humility, may we show
mercy and love to all we meet.
Through Christ our Lord.
Amen.

† A humble contrite heart, O God,
you will not spurn.

Saturday, March 9, 2019
Saturday after Ash Wednesday

✝ Teach me your way, O Lord.

Psalm 51 *page 402*

Reading *Luke 5:27–32*

Jesus saw a tax collector named Levi sitting at the customs post. He said to him, "Follow me." And leaving everything behind, he got up and followed him. Then Levi gave a great banquet for him in his house, and a large crowd of tax collectors and others were at table with them. The Pharisees and their scribes complained to his disciples, saying, "Why do you eat and drink with tax collectors and sinners?" Jesus said to them in reply, "Those who are healthy do not need a physician, but the sick do. I have not come to call the righteous but sinners."

Reflection

As we read the account of the call of Levi, we might recall how we have heard God's voice in our lives. God calls us just as he did the repentant Levi. The Pharisees thought that Jesus should only dine with those whose lives could stand up to scrutiny. Jesus, however, notes that he is with people where they are in life. We need to remember that God loves us even in our imperfections and sinfulness. He is present to reconcile us to him.

Prayers *others may be added*

To our God, who has called us, we pray:

◆ Lord, hear our prayer.

May the Church help the laity find ways to use their talents in service, we pray: ◆ May governments and businesses partner to train workers for the future, we pray: ◆ May young men and women hear God's call of service to a vocation in the Church, we pray: ◆ May the ailing find strength and healing, we pray: ◆ May those with chronic pain find comfort, we pray: ◆ May those who have died rest in peace, we pray: ◆

Our Father . . .

O God,
who pursues everyone with delight,
help us to renew our commitment
to follow and serve you
with a humble, contrite spirit.
Through our Lord Jesus Christ, your Son,
who lives and reigns with you in the unity
of the Holy Spirit,
one God, for ever and ever.
Amen.

✝ Teach me your way, O Lord.

Sunday, March 10, 2019

First Sunday of Lent

☩ Be with me, Lord, when I am in trouble.

Psalm 51

page 402

Reading

Luke 4:1–2

Filled with the Holy Spirit, Jesus returned from the Jordan and was led by the Spirit into the desert for forty days, to be tempted by the devil. He ate nothing during those days, and when they were over he was hungry.

Reflection

These two verses from the Gospel according to Luke show Jesus as "filled with the Holy Spirit" and then forty days later, "hungry." In our ministry and work, we may find ourselves filled with enthusiasm and then, perhaps sooner than forty days, exhausted. The Church gives us the opportunity during this holy season to renew ourselves and seek the Holy Spirit to remember the call of our baptismal covenant. The temptations we face each day can leave us weary. Let us be attentive to the Holy Spirit and ignore the idols that strive for our attention.

Prayers

others may be added

Turning to our God who strengthens us, we pray:

◆ Lord, hear our prayer.

For our pope and bishops, that they may lead us in renewal, we pray: ◆ For world leaders, that they may guide us to seek peace, we pray: ◆ For our Church, that she act as a sign of compassion in the world, we pray: ◆ For those who suffer trauma, we pray: ◆ For the environment, that we find ways to care for it, we pray: ◆ For those who have died, that they rest in peace, we pray: ◆

Our Father . . .

Lord God,
you sent Jesus into the desert
before the start of his ministry.
May we be delivered from sin
and darkness
to live anew your reign of love,
bringing Christian witness to the world.
Through Christ our Lord.
Amen.

☩ Be with me, Lord, when I am in trouble.

Monday, March 11, 2019
Lenten Weekday

☩ Your ways, O Lord, are Spirit and life.

Psalm 51
page 402

Reading
Matthew 25:31–40

Jesus said to his disciples: "When the Son of Man comes in his glory, and all the angels with him, he will sit upon his glorious throne, and all the nations will be assembled before him. And he will separate them one from another, as a shepherd separates the sheep from the goats. He will place the sheep on his right and the goats on his left. Then the king will say to those on his right, 'Come, you who are blessed by my Father. Inherit the kingdom prepared for you from the foundation of the world. For I was hungry and you gave me food, I was thirsty and you gave me drink, a stranger and you welcomed me, naked and you clothed me, ill and you cared for me, in prison and you visited me.' Then the righteous will answer him and say, 'Lord, when did we see you hungry and feed you, or thirsty and give you drink? When did we see you a stranger and welcome you, or naked and clothed you? When did we see you ill or in prison, and visit you?' And the king will say to them in reply, 'Amen, I say to you, whatever you did for one of the least brothers of mine, you did for me.'"

Reflection
When you feed, clothe, or comfort another, how often do you think that you are doing so for Christ? Jesus reminds us with such imagery that he is among us as we provide for the needs of our brothers and sisters. When we ignore someone, we are ignoring Christ.

Prayers
others may be added

Calling on God, who sees the needs of all, we pray:

◆ Graciously hear us, Lord.

May the Church's social justice ministries grow to meet growing needs, we pray: ◆ May nations work together to provide safe water and food, we pray: ◆ May our parish community grow in awareness of its mission, we pray: ◆ May we challenge our hearts to serve in new ways, we pray: ◆ May the sick be healed, we pray: ◆ May those we miss and mourn be brought to God's glory, we pray: ◆

Our Father . . .

Gracious God,
you call us to serve our brothers
and sisters,
especially the least among us.
Help us to answer the needs of others
with attitudes and actions
that build your reign.
Through Christ our Lord.
Amen.

☩ Your ways, O Lord, are Spirit and life.

Tuesday, March 12, 2019
Lenten Weekday

✝ From all their distress God rescues the just.

Psalm 51

page 402

Reading

Matthew 6:7–15

Jesus said to his disciples: "In praying, do not babble like the pagans, who think that they will be heard because of their many words. Do not be like them. Your Father knows what you need before you ask him.

"This is how you are to pray: / Our Father who art in heaven, / hallowed be thy name, / thy Kingdom come, / thy will be done, / on earth as it is in heaven. / Give us this day our daily bread; / and forgive us our trespasses, / as we forgive those who trespass against us; / and lead us not into temptation, / but deliver us from evil.

"If you forgive men their transgressions, your heavenly Father will forgive you. But if you do not forgive men, neither will your Father forgive your transgressions."

Reflection

Jesus provides a model for prayer and then instructs the disciples on the importance of forgiveness. Our prayer leads us to a circle of forgiveness. As we are challenged this Lent to remember that we are called to forgive, may we offer to God the person we are trying to forgive, requesting that God touch the individual's heart. God forgives; now it is our turn to live out his gift of love.

Prayers

others may be added

Trusting that God hears us, we turn in prayer:

◆ Lord, hear our prayer.

May the Church model forgiveness, we pray: ◆ May leaders forgive the debts of nations that struggle, we pray: ◆ May those who have been deeply hurt, trust again, we pray: ◆ May our example of prayer inspire others to a deeper prayer life, we pray: ◆ May the sick be comforted, we pray: ◆ May those who have died rest in peace, we pray: ◆

Our Father . . .

O God,
gaze toward your family,
and strengthen us
to radiate your love.
Help relationships to grow
in mutual respect and goodness
so that we may reflect
the peace and tranquility
of your kingdom.
Through Christ our Lord.
Amen.

✝ From all their distress God rescues the just.

Wednesday, March 13, 2019

Lenten Weekday

✝ A humble contrite heart, O God,
you will not spurn.

Psalm 51

page 402

Reading

Luke 11:29–32

While still more people gathered in the crowd Jesus said to them, "This generation is an evil generation; it seeks a sign, but no sign will be given it, except the sign of Jonah. Just as Jonah became a sign to the Ninevites, so will the Son of Man be to this generation. At the judgment the queen of the south will rise with the men of this generation and she will condemn them, because she came from the ends of the earth to hear the wisdom of Solomon, and there is something greater than Solomon here. At the judgment the men of Nineveh will arise with this generation and condemn it, because at the preaching of Jonah they repented, and there is something greater than Jonah here."

Reflection

Through signs, we know God and his ways. Jonah was a sign to the Ninevites, who heeded his words and repented. The Son of Man went unrecognized by many so they did not repent. The cross is a sign of our faith. As we begin prayer, we make the Sign of the Cross, invoking the Trinity and recalling the wood on which Christ died. That wood secured redemption and is a sign that God has forgiven and reconciled with us. For that reason, we adore the wood of the cross on Good Friday.

Prayers

others may be added

Trusting in the reconciling power of God, we pray:

◆ Lord, hear our prayer.

May Church leaders act as signs of forgiveness, we pray: ◆ May our parishioners participate in the Sacrament of Reconciliation, we pray: ◆ May those preparing for the sacraments grow in love of God, we pray: ◆ May civic leaders be witnesses to peace, we pray: ◆ May the sick be healed, we pray: ◆ May those who have died be led into eternal glory, we pray: ◆

Our Father . . .

O God,
regard the devotion of your people,
and help us to bear much fruit
through our acts of self-denial.
May we make the signs
of your love and forgiveness
integral to our lives.
Through Christ our Lord.
Amen.

✝ A humble contrite heart, O God,
you will not spurn.

Thursday, March 14, 2019
Lenten Weekday

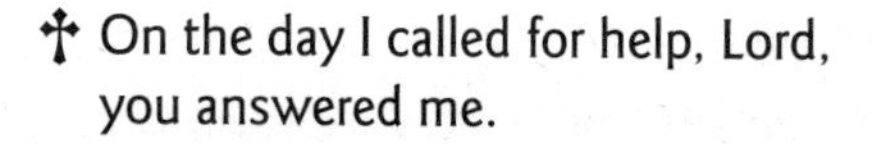

✝ On the day I called for help, Lord, you answered me.

Psalm 138 *page 420*

Reading *Matthew 7:7–12*

Jesus said to his disciples: "Ask and it will be given to you; seek and you will find; knock and the door will be opened to you. For everyone who asks, receives; and the one who seeks, finds; and to the one who knocks, the door will be opened. Which one of you would hand his son a stone when he asked for a loaf of bread, or a snake when he asks for a fish? If you, who are wicked, know how to give good things to your children, how much more will your heavenly Father give good things to those who ask him.

"Do to others whatever you would have them do to you. This is the law and the prophets."

Reflection

Have you met a person who wanted to know how to pray and talk to God, and at the same time said, "But, I don't want to bother God with my problems"? Such communication would not be dismissed in any other close relationship and should not be with God either. Faith grows through prayer, and that prayer includes asking, knocking, and trusting that God is listening. God may understand what we want to say before we do so, but for a relationship to grow, communication needs to include all parts of our lives.

Prayers *others may be added*

To the One who listens to our requests, we pray:

◆ Lord, hear our prayer.

May the Church help us discern through prayer, we pray: ◆ May government officials trust in God's plans, we pray: ◆ May doctors and nurses nurture their spiritual care, we pray: ◆ May youth open their hearts to God's ways, we pray: ◆ May cures be found for debilitating diseases, we pray: ◆ May those who have died be forgiven their sins, we pray: ◆

Our Father . . .

Discerning God,
you guide us in your ways,
and call us to trust anew.
Bestow a patient heart in us
so that we may live according to your will
and to what is good for all.
Through Christ our Lord.
Amen.

✝ On the day I called for help, Lord, you answered me.

Friday, March 15, 2019
Lenten Weekday

✝ Out of the depths I cry to you,
O Lord.

Psalm 130 *page 418*

Reading *Matthew 5:20–26*

Jesus said to his disciples: "I tell you, unless your righteousness surpasses that of the scribes and Pharisees, you will not enter into the Kingdom of heaven.

"You have heard that it was said to your ancestors, *You shall not kill; and whoever kills will be liable to judgment.* But I say to you, whoever is angry with his brother will be liable to judgment, and whoever says to his brother, *Raqa*, will be answerable to the Sanhedrin, and whoever says, 'You fool,' will be liable to fiery Gehenna. Therefore, if you bring your gift to the altar, and there recall that your brother has anything against you, leave your gift there at the altar, go first and be reconciled with your brother, and then come and offer your gift."

Reflection

Jesus asks us to talk with one another and seek reconciliation before offering gifts to God. During Lent, we especially focus on reconciling with one another and growing in relationships. Just as God does not keep grudges, neither should we. How can we work harder on forgiveness? Would it help to truly acknowledge how God has forgiven us? Consider how doing so will help you serve as a better ambassador for Christ.

Prayers *others may be added*

To the One who reconciles us with his love, we pray:

◆ Lord, hear our prayer.

May we show comfort to those in need of our love, we pray: ◆ May all learn the necessity of repentance, we pray: ◆ May wounds among estranged family members heal, we pray: ◆ May those who struggle financially find relief, we pray: ◆ May the cross be a fruit of new life for the sick, we pray: ◆ May those who have died enter eternal glory, we pray: ◆

Our Father . . .

O God,
grant your faithful,
a share in your new life.
Help us during our Lenten journey
to be renewed in spirit
and to be open to the grace
within the relationships
that bless our lives.
Through Christ our Lord.
Amen.

✝ Out of the depths I cry to you,
O Lord.

Saturday, March 16, 2019
Lenten Weekday

✝ Blessed are they who follow the law of the Lord.

Psalm 119 *page 414*

Reading *Matthew 5:43–48*

Jesus said to his disciples: "You have heard that it was said, *You shall love your neighbor and hate your enemy.* But I say to you, love your enemies and pray for those who persecute you, that you may be children of your heavenly Father, for he makes his sun rise on the bad and the good, and causes rain to fall on the just and the unjust. For if you love those who love you, what recompense will you have? Do not the tax collectors do the same? And if you greet your brothers only, what is unusual about that? Do not the pagans do the same? So be perfect, just as your heavenly Father is perfect."

Reflection

Today's Gospel presents a way of living that is difficult. After all, it is easy to love those who love us and often hard to imagine loving those who hate us. As Christians, we are to be different than the pagans. We have been called to holiness, to be perfect "just as your heavenly Father is perfect." Lent is a time to examine our lives to see how we can change our hearts to love our enemies. Perhaps during this season we can find small ways to lighten the load or say a prayer for an individual from whom we are estranged. If God "makes the sun shine on the bad and the good," shouldn't we do the same?

Prayers *others may be added*

To our heavenly Father, who models perfection, we pray:

◆ Lord, hear our prayer.

May love unite leaders in the Church, we pray: ◆ May leaders seek peaceful solutions, we pray: ◆ May youth share their gifts and talents for the world's betterment, we pray: ◆ May refugees find dignified shelter, we pray: ◆ May the sick be renewed in health and spirit, we pray: ◆ May those who have died be united with Mary and the saints in heaven, we pray: ◆

Our Father . . .

O God,
turn our hearts,
to the truth of your love.
May we seek out those
from whom we are estranged,
realizing they also are your children.
Accompany us with your compassion
as we seek to love one another.
Through Christ our Lord.
Amen.

✝ Blessed are they who follow the law of the Lord.

Sunday, March 17, 2019

Second Sunday of Lent

✝ The Lord is my light and my salvation.

Psalm 51 *page 402*

Reading *Luke 9:28b–35*

Jesus took Peter, John, and James and went up the mountain to pray. While he was praying, his face changed in appearance and his clothing became dazzling white. And behold, two men were conversing with him, Moses and Elijah, who appeared in glory and spoke of his exodus that he was going to accomplish in Jerusalem. Peter and his companions had been overcome by sleep, but becoming fully awake, they saw his glory and the two men standing with him. As they were about to part from him, Peter said to Jesus, "Master, it is good that we are here; let us make three tents, one for you, one for Moses, and one for Elijah." But he did not know what he was saying. While he was still speaking, a cloud came and cast a shadow over them, and they became frightened when they entered the cloud. Then from the cloud came a voice that said, "This is my chosen Son; listen to him."

Reflection

At the Transfiguration, we hear the Lord tell us to listen to his Son. The words from the Father in today's Gospel resemble those of the Gospel on the Feast of the Baptism of the Lord. Both times, the Father calls Jesus his Son. Today, we hear a mandate: "listen to him."

Prayers *others may be added*

To the Lord God, who sent his Son, we pray:

◆ Lord, hear our prayer.

For our hearts to be opened to respond to you through service in the Church, we pray: ◆ For civic leaders to listen to the cries of those most in need, we pray: ◆ For care of the planet, we pray: ◆ For the young to share their vocation openly, we pray: ◆ For the sick to be healed, we pray: ◆ For those who have died to be received into heaven, we pray: ◆

Our Father . . .

O God,
how good it is for us to be with you,
and know of your presence in our lives.
Help us to build tents of justice, love,
and light
that shower others with the goodness
of compassion that you have given us.
Through Christ our Lord.
Amen.

✝ The Lord is my light and my salvation.

Monday, March 18, 2019
Lenten Weekday

✝ Lord, do not deal with us according to our sins.

Psalm 130

page 418

Reading

Luke 6:36–38

Jesus said to his disciples: "Be merciful, just as your Father is merciful.

"Stop judging and you will not be condemned. Forgive and you will be forgiven. Give and gifts will be given to you; a good measure, packed together, shaken down, and overflowing, will be poured into your lap. For the measure with which you measure will in return be measured out to you."

Reflection

What do you "pack together"? Is it judgments? Condemnations? Forgiveness? What do you measure? Who does what? Jesus gives us many questions to ponder today as he challenges us to be merciful and loving. We do not need to measure the amount we love or forgive but seek to be totally committed and filled, "packed together" with an overflowing stream of forgiveness and acceptance of others, as God forgives and loves. One day at a time, let us act in this way. Aren't we blessed that God has a covenant of mercy and forgiveness? Let us witness this to others.

Prayers

others may be added

Turning to our merciful God, we pray:

◆ Lord, hear our prayer.

For tribunals in the Church, that they be open to review and renewal, we pray: ◆ For legislators, that their hearts be softened, we pray: ◆ For prison systems, that they show mercy to those in their care, we pray: ◆ For those imprisoned, that they turn to God's ways and love, we pray: ◆ For the sick who are held bondage to disease, we pray: ◆ For those who have died, that they rest in peace, we pray: ◆

Our Father . . .

Merciful God,
may your ways be our ways!
Help us not to remember
the iniquities of our past
but to bring pardon and peace to a world
thirsting for true justice and joy.
Through Christ our Lord.
Amen.

✝ Lord, do not deal with us according to our sins.

Tuesday, March 19, 2019

Solemnity of St. Joseph, Spouse of the Blessed Virgin Mary

✝ The son of David will live for ever.

Psalm 89

page 407

Reading

Matthew 1:18–21

This is how the birth of Jesus Christ came about. When his mother Mary was betrothed to Joseph, but before they lived together, she was found with child through the Holy Spirit. Joseph her husband, since he was a righteous man, yet unwilling to expose her to shame, decided to divorce her quietly. Such was his intention when, behold, the angel of the Lord appeared to him in a dream and said, "Joseph, son of David, do not be afraid to take Mary your wife into your home. For it is through the Holy Spirit that this child has been conceived in her. She will bear a son and you are to name him Jesus, because he will save his people from their sins."

Reflection

Sometimes God makes his plan known in dreams as we see in today's reading. The Gospel accounts never quote Joseph, but his actions speak volumes. He does not allow fear to guide his life but recognizes that God saves. Rather than questioning, he commits and follows God's commands. Oh, that we might become as trusting as Joseph and open ourselves more fully to doing the work of God in the world.

Prayers

others may be added

With trust in our God who saves,
we pray:

◆ Lord, hear our prayer.

For the continued renewal and protection of the Church, we pray: ◆ For expanded vision for civic leaders, we pray: ◆ For the unborn, that they be nurtured to birth, we pray: ◆ For medical research, that it improve the quality of life, we pray: ◆ For immigrants in search of stability, we pray: ◆ For those we miss and mourn, we pray: ◆

Our Father . . .

God of our ancestors,
you make your promises of old
come to birth through the actions
of your people.
Guide us in your ways
that we be zealous
in our work for justice
that your kingdom
may reign on this earth.
Through Christ our Lord.
Amen.

✝ The son of David will live for ever.

Wednesday, March 20, 2019
Lenten Weekday

✝ Save me, Lord, in your kindness.

Psalm 130 *page 418*

Reading *Matthew 20:20–23*

The mother of the sons of Zebedee approached Jesus with her sons and did him homage, wishing to ask him for something. He said to her, "What do you wish?" She answered him, "Command that these two sons of mine sit, one at your right and the other at your left, in your kingdom." Jesus said in reply, "You do not know what you are asking. Can you drink the chalice that I am going to drink?" They said to him, "We can." He replied, "My chalice you will indeed drink, but to sit at my right and at my left, this is not mine to give but is for those for whom it has been prepared by my Father."

Reflection

Our jealousies get in the way of our mission in the world. Worries over whether another's reward will be higher than ours distracts us from the service that is part of our discipleship. Today we are reminded that we are called to drink from the same cup or chalice as Christ in our service in the world. May we be able to connect our desires with the Lord's and go about our work without complaint.

Prayers *others may be added*

With confidence in our Lord, we pray:

◆ Lord, hear our prayer.

For missionaries in challenging circumstances, we pray: ◆ For the respect of all life, especially the unborn, we pray: ◆ For continued dialogue and respect among religions, we pray: ◆ For new members to volunteer in our parish, we pray: ◆ For healing of those who are sick, we pray: ◆ For those who have died, that they join the martyrs and saints, we pray: ◆

Our Father . . .

O God,
with our whole heart,
we wish to serve and witness to you.
Help us to serve zealously
and overcome obstacles with humility.
Through Christ our Lord.
Amen.

✝ Save me, Lord, in your kindness.

Thursday, March 21, 2019
Lenten Weekday

✝ Blessed are they who hope in the Lord.

Psalm 130 *page 418*

Reading *Jeremiah 17:5–10*

Thus says the LORD: / Cursed is the man who trusts in human beings, / who seeks his strength in flesh, / whose heart turns away from the LORD. / He is like a barren bush in the desert / that enjoys no change of season, / But stands in a lava waste, / a salt and empty earth. / Blessed is the man who trusts in the LORD, / whose hope is the LORD. / He is like a tree planted beside the waters / that stretches out its roots to the stream: / It fears not the heat when it comes, / its leaves stay green; / In the year of drought it shows no distress, / but still bears fruit. / More torturous than all else is the human heart, / beyond remedy; who can understand it? / I, the LORD, alone probe the mind and test the heart, / To reward everyone according to his ways, / according to the merit of his deeds.

Reflection

We hear in this reading from the prophet Jeremiah that the Lord alone knows the human heart. It is from that knowledge that the Lord will reward us for our good deeds. When we place our trust in ourselves and other human beings, we are like a barren bush in the desert. We are challenged to look forward to the fruit of our works. As we begin another season in nature, we recognize the circle of life. May we come from drought and winter, to fullness and spring, sharing in the bounty of creation that God shares with us.

Prayers *others may be added*

To our God who renews us, we pray:

◆ Lord, hear our prayer.

For charitable efforts of the Church to increase, we pray: ◆ For secular projects, that they benefit the common good, we pray: ◆ For favorable weather for crops, we pray: ◆ For those in prison to be visited and comforted, we pray: ◆ For the ill to be provided proper health care, we pray: ◆ For the deceased to be welcomed to the bosom of Abraham, we pray: ◆

Our Father . . .

Gracious God of our ancestors,
you invite us to participate
in your mission of compassion.
Guide our efforts of justice and love
so that others may feel
your welcome and wholeness
and be renewed in compassion.
Through Christ our Lord.
Amen.

✝ Blessed are they who hope in the Lord.

Friday, March 22, 2019
Lenten Weekday

✝ Remember the marvels the Lord has done.

Psalm 130

page 418

Reading

Matthew 21:42–43

[Jesus said to the chief priests and the elders of the people:] "Did you never read in the Scriptures:

The stone that the builders rejected
has become the cornerstone;
by the Lord has this been done,
and it is wonderful in our eyes?"

Reflection

Today's reading helps us recall that Jesus was rejected and crucified after showing more concern for the people than rules and laws. He would not hold back on the grace that God offers. We might want to review what we store up. Do we allow the fruits of the Kingdom to be lived freely to show the marvels of God? We must be sure not to let fear displace the love we are to share. Let us be careful to minister in the vineyard of the Lord.

Prayers

others may be added

To our Lord, our cornerstone, we pray:

◆ Lord, hear our prayer.

For the environment, that all nations make efforts to care for it, we pray: ◆ For recycling efforts, especially in our parishes, we pray: ◆ For freedom of religion, we pray: ◆ For the homeless and those disenfranchised, we pray: ◆ For nurses and other caregivers, we pray: ◆ For those we mourn and miss, we pray: ◆

Our Father . . .

Loving God,
you increase our trust
and challenge us not to be fearful.
Grant us health in mind and body
that we may attain the redemption
that you promise.
Through Christ our Lord.
Amen.

✝ Remember the marvels the Lord has done.

Saturday, March 23, 2019

Lenten Weekday

✝ The Lord is kind and merciful.

Psalm 130 *page 418*

Reading *Micah 7:14–15, 18–20*

Shepherd your people with your staff, / the flock of your inheritance, / That dwells apart in a woodland, / in the midst of Carmel. / Let them feed in Bashan and Gilead; / as in the days of old; / As in the days when you came from the land of Egypt, / show us wonderful signs.

Who is there like you, the God who removes guilt / and pardons sin for the remnant of his inheritance; / Who does not persist in anger forever, but delights rather in clemency, / And will again have compassion on us, treading underfoot our guilt? / You will cast into the depths of the sea all our sins; / You will show faithfulness to Jacob, / and grace to Abraham, / As you have sworn to our fathers / from the days of old.

Reflection

Nearing the Third Sunday of Lent, we reflect on how God consistently loves, cares, and demonstrates mercy to us. Though we have done nothing to merit God's gift of mercy, God continues to pardon us, delighting in clemency. During Lent, we work harder on imaging the face of God more clearly. Who is in need of your mercy? Let that person know that you have already forgiven him or her and want to renew the friendship.

Prayers *others may be added*

To our compassionate God, we pray:

◆ Hear us, gracious Lord.

For the Church, that she always act as a welcoming presence, we pray: ◆ For immigrants and refugees, that nations assist them, we pray: ◆ For renewal as we celebrate the sacraments, we pray: ◆ For cures to be found for diseases, we pray: ◆ For those who mourn the loss of a child, we pray: ◆ For those who have died, that they be granted eternal glory, we pray: ◆

Our Father . . .

O Guiding Light,
you walk with us on our journey of faith.
Teach us to stay true to our call.
May we share your gifts of grace
and reconciliation
until we at last obtain your promise.
Through Christ our Lord.
Amen.

✝ The Lord is kind and merciful.

Sunday, March 24, 2019
Third Sunday of Lent

✝ The Lord is kind and merciful.

Psalm 103

page 411

Reading

Luke 13:6–9

[Jesus] told them this parable: "There once was a person who had a fig tree planted in his orchard, and when he came in search of fruit on it but found none, he said to the gardener, 'For three years now I have come in search of fruit on this fig tree but have found none. So cut it down. Why should it exhaust the soil?' He said to him in reply, 'Sir, leave it for this year also, and I shall cultivate the ground around it and fertilize it; it may bear fruit in the future. If not you can cut it down.'"

Reflection

Just as the gardener is patient with the fig tree, willing to nurture it, so God is patient with us. God awaits our growth and willingness to live in him. To do that, we need to be open to the graces God provides. Do you take advantage of the ways the Church offers to nourish your spiritual life? We need to be mindful also to show patience with others, allowing them to bloom where they are planted.

Prayers

others may be added

Turning to the author of all life,
we pray:

◆ Lord, hear our prayer.

May the hungry be filled, we pray: ◆ May those who need care receive it, we pray: ◆ May world leaders bear good fruit in their work, we pray: ◆ May we work for peace and goodness, we pray: ◆ May doubters be awakened to trust and faith, we pray: ◆ May we always seek the city of heaven, we pray: ◆

Our Father . . .

God of every good grace,
direct our hearts and minds
to your service.
Help us fulfill your commands
and bring others to know of your mercy
until we are united in the halls of heaven.
Through Christ our Lord.
Amen.

✝ The Lord is kind and merciful.

Monday, March 25, 2019

Solemnity of the Annunciation of the Lord

✝ Here I am, Lord: I come to do your will.

Canticle of Mary

page 423

Reading

Hebrews 10:4–10

Brothers and sisters: It is impossible that the blood of bulls and goats take away sins. For this reason, when Christ came into the world, he said:

"Sacrifice and offering you did not desire, / but a body you prepared for me; / in holocausts and sin offerings you took no delight. / Then I said, 'As is written of me in the scroll / behold, I come to do your will, O God.'"

First he says, "Sacrifices and offerings, / holocausts and sin offerings, / you neither desired nor delighted in." These are offered according to the law. Then he says, "Behold, I come to do your will". He takes away the first to establish the second. By this "will," we have been consecrated through the offering of the Body of Jesus Christ once for all.

Reflection

"Behold, I come to do your will." God created Mary as a woman of faith, continuously open to doing God's will. Let us pray that we are willing to listen to God and follow through on what is asked of us. May we be open to grace and hope, as Mary was. Let us also see that that our obedience is our offering back to God. Our sacrifices will help bring about the birthing of Jesus Christ in the hearts of others, helping God's flesh to dwell among us.

Prayers

others may be added

Let us turn to God in confidence and hope, and pray:

◆ Hear us, gracious Lord.

May the hearts of Church leaders be open to new challenges, we pray: ◆ May community organizers look to the common good, we pray: ◆ May those in need find employment, we pray: ◆ May doubts be dampened with faith, we pray: ◆ May the downcast find comfort and strength, we pray: ◆ May the dead come to the fullness of eternal life, we pray: ◆

Our Father . . .

O Lord,
pour forth your grace into our hearts
that we who have known
the message of the angels and saints,
may, like Mary, trust in your Word.
Renew us to be
partakers of God's divine nature
and care for the mysteries
that have been entrusted to us.
Through Christ our Lord.
Amen.

✝ Here I am, Lord: I come to do your will.

Tuesday, March 26, 2019
Lenten Weekday

✝ Remember your mercies, O Lord.

Psalm 103

page 411

Reading

Matthew 18:21–22

Peter approached Jesus and said to him, "Lord, if my brother sins against me, how often must I forgive him? As many as seven times?" Jesus answered, "I say to you, not seven times but seventy-seven times."

Reflection

Besides the disciplines of prayer, fasting, and almsgiving, forgiveness can be considered a key practice during Lent. As we see in today's Gospel, forgiveness must be practiced continually. It is helpful to pray for the ability to forgive another and also for others to forgive you. Allow the Holy Spirit to move your heart to be in sync with God's heart, where mercy and compassion are found.

Prayers

others may be added

To our God of compassion, we pray:

◆ Lord, hear our prayer.

May Church leaders be models of forgiveness, we pray: ◆ May civic authorities trust in the gift of reconciliation, we pray: ◆ May justice systems emulate God's justice, we pray: ◆ May all, especially the unborn, be given inalienable rights, we pray: ◆ May those who suffer find relief, we pray: ◆ May those who have died be led to paradise, we pray: ◆

Our Father . . .

God of mercy and kindness,
you shower your people
with gifts of forgiveness.
May we continuously live
out reconciliation,
embracing the need to remove barriers
and foster unity and peace.
Through Christ our Lord.
Amen.

✝ Remember your mercies, O Lord.

Wednesday, March 27, 2019
Lenten Weekday

☩ Praise the Lord, Jerusalem!

Psalm 103 *page 411*

Reading *Matthew 5:17–19*
Jesus said to his disciples: "Do not think that I have come to abolish the law or the prophets. I have come not to abolish but to fulfill. Amen, I say to you, until heaven and earth pass away, not the smallest letter or the smallest part of a letter will pass from the law, until all things have taken place. Therefore, whoever breaks one of the least of these commandments and teaches others to do so will be called least in the Kingdom of heaven. But whoever obeys and teaches these commandments will be called greatest in the Kingdom of heaven."

Reflection
We know that Jesus came to fulfill the law. From Moses until Jesus' time, prophets were exhorting that the law was meant to be fulfilled through the people's lives. God's Law embodies the hopes of people. But these hopes need to be fulfilled in love. The greatest commandment is love. Over and over we hear that this is how Christ is fulfilled in our midst—when we love. When we choose to obey this law, the Kingdom of Heaven is at hand.

Prayers *others may be added*
To our God of love, we pray:

◆ Hear us, gracious Lord.

May the Church exude love as she enacts her mission, we pray: ◆ May community leaders serve with compassion, we pray: ◆ May all who protect us stay safe, we pray: ◆ May we be renewed in our spiritual lives during this Lent, we pray: ◆ May those who are sick be healed, we pray: ◆ May the dead come to the glory of heaven, we pray: ◆

Our Father . . .

God of our ancestors,
you bring us freedom
through your laws of love.
May we fulfill your dreams
in our actions of kindness and service
as we continue to strive
for goodness and mercy.
Through Christ our Lord.
Amen.

☩ Praise the Lord, Jerusalem!

Thursday, March 28, 2019
Lenten Weekday

✝ If today you hear God's voice,
harden not your hearts.

Psalm 95
page 408

Reading
Jeremiah 7:23–24

Thus says the LORD: This is what I commanded my people: Listen to my voice; then I will be your God and you shall be my people. Walk in all the ways that I command you, so that you may prosper.

But they obeyed not, nor did they pay heed. They walked in the hardness of their evil hearts and turned their backs, not their faces, to me. From the day that your fathers left the land of Egypt even to this day, I have sent you untiringly all my servants the prophets. Yet they have not obeyed me nor paid heed; they have stiffened their necks and done worse than their fathers. When you speak all these words to them, they will not listen to you either; when you call to them, they will not answer you. Say to them: This is the nation that does not listen to the voice of the LORD, its God, or take correction. Faithfulness has disappeared; the word itself is banished from their speech.

Reflection
Today's reading points out how generation after generation continues to act the same. Stubborn behaviors and attitudes become rock solid, making it difficult for the next generation to establish new patterns. We can become open-hearted people who do not hold on to the hate or evil that keeps us stubborn. Let us seek and examine our blind spots and open our hearts to God's will.

Prayers
others may be added

Seeking the Lord, who looks into our hearts, we pray:

◆ Lord, hear our prayer.

May the Church erode attitudes
that harbor stubbornness, we pray: ◆
May nations open their hearts to
refugees and migrants, we pray: ◆
May the lonely feel wanted, we pray: ◆
May those awaiting a transplant keep up hope, we pray: ◆ May the sick be renewed in health, we pray: ◆ May those who have died be received into heaven, we pray: ◆

Our Father . . .

O God,
create fresh hearts
that learn to grow
to be open to your will.
Teach us to be generous
in gratitude, care, and love,
so that we may witness to your Word.
Through our Lord Jesus Christ, your Son,
who lives and reigns with you in the unity
of the Holy Spirit,
one God, for ever and ever.
Amen.

✝ If today you hear God's voice,
harden not your hearts.

Friday, March 29, 2019
Lenten Weekday

✝ I am the Lord your God: hear my voice.

Psalm 103
page 411

Reading
Hosea 14:2–10

Thus says the LORD: / Return, O Israel, to the LORD, your God; / you have collapsed through your guilt. / Take with you words, / and return to the LORD; / Say to him, "Forgive all iniquity, / and receive what is good, that we may render / as offerings the bullocks from our stalls. / Assyria will not save us, / nor shall we have horses to mount; / We shall say no more, 'Our god,' / to the work of our hands; / for in you the orphan finds compassion." /

I will heal their defection, says the LORD, / I will love them freely; / for my wrath is turned away from them.

Reflection
A certain tenderness comes through our reading today. This blessed assurance that the Lord "will heal our defection" and freely love us helps us understand something about God's mercy and compassion. We are to savor this special gift as we share it with others as we extend forgiveness. In pardoning others, we are witnessing the goodness of our Lord in our lives.

Prayers
others may be added

Confident that God hears us, we pray:

◆ Lord, hear our prayer.

May the Church's ministries exude God's love, we pray: ◆ May efforts at peace blossom, we pray: ◆ May orphans of war find new families, we pray: ◆ May vocations to the consecrated life grow, we pray: ◆ May the sick recover, we pray: ◆ May the deceased receive God's mercy, we pray: ◆

Our Father . . .

Lord God,
you teach us to know your ways of love.
May we be prudent in the use of our gifts
and recognize their blessings
and importance
in continuing to share your compassion.
Through Christ our Lord.
Amen.

✝ I am the Lord your God: hear my voice.

Saturday, March 30, 2019

Lenten Weekday

† It is mercy I desire, and not sacrifice.

Psalm 103 *page 411*

Reading *Hosea 6:1–6*

"Come, let us return to the LORD, / it is he who has rent, but he will heal us; / he has struck us, but he will bind our wounds. / He will revive us after two days; / on the third day he will raise us up, / to live in his presence. / Let us know, let us strive to know the Lord; / as certain as the dawn is his coming, / and his judgment shines forth like the light of day! / He will come to us like the rain, / like spring rain that waters the earth."

What can I do with you, Ephraim? / What can I do with you, Judah? / Your piety is like a morning cloud, / like the dew that early passes away. For this reason I smote them through the prophets, / I slew them by the words of my mouth; / For it is love that I desire, not sacrifice, / and knowledge of God rather than burnt offerings.

Reflection

It must have been difficult for the audience of Hosea to hear that their works of sacrifice were not what God wanted. As we make sacrifices during Lent, we should examine our motivations. Do these sacrifices offer a way to bring us closer to God? Do they provide mercy and justice for those in need? Or are the sacrifices another way for us to be proud of ourselves? At the end of Lent, will we love God and neighbor more?

Prayers *others may be added*

Offering to God our hearts of concern, we pray:

◆ Merciful God, hear us.

May reforms from the Vatican bring healing, we pray: ◆ May world leaders work for the common good, we pray: ◆ May cures be found for infectious diseases, we pray: ◆ May benefactors know of our concern, we pray: ◆ May the ill find strength, we pray: ◆ May those who have died be welcomed in the new Jerusalem, we pray: ◆

Our Father . . .

Lord God,
it is not in sacrifices
that you take pleasure,
but in hearts open to loving and forgiving.
Give us strength
to renew our souls with your grace
and witness to your unbounded love and
mercy.
Through Christ our Lord.
Amen.

† It is mercy I desire, and not sacrifice.

Sunday, March 31, 2019

Fourth Sunday of Lent

✝ Taste and see the goodness of the Lord.

Psalm 34 *page 401*

Reading *Luke 15:11a, 13b, 14a, 14c, 20a, 20f–22a, 23b–24, 25, 28, 29, 31–32, 34*

[Jesus said:] "A man had two sons . . . the younger son collected all his belongings and set off to a distant country where he squandered his inheritance on a life of dissipation. When he had freely spent everything . . . he found himself in dire need. . . . Coming to his senses . . . he got up and went back to his father. While he was still a long way off, his father . . . ran to his son, embraced him, and kissed him. His son said to him, 'Father, I have sinned against heaven and against you; I no longer deserve to be called your son.' But his father ordered his servants . . . 'let us celebrate with a feast, because this son of mine was dead, and has come to life again; he was lost, and has been found.' . . . Now the older son had been out in the field and, on his way back, as he neared the house, he heard the sound of music and dancing. . . . He became angry. . . . He said to his father in reply, 'Look, all these years I served you and not once did I disobey your orders; yet you never gave me even a young goat to feast on with my friends. . . .' [His father] said to him, 'My son, you are here with me always; everything I have is yours. But now we must celebrate and rejoice, because your brother was dead and has come to life again; he was lost and has been found.' "

Reflection

This Gospel is often called the return of the prodigal son. Many people assume the word "prodigal" means lost. But the original meaning of the word is "yielding lavishly" or "abundant." Knowing the word's meaning gives us another take on this parable. How are we "prodigal"? Are we yielding with mercy like the Father? Or are we abundant with revenge like the son who stayed put and grew stonehearted? These three characters show ways of being prodigal. How do you choose to live?

Prayers *others may be added*

To our compassionate God, we pray:

◆ Lord, have mercy.

May the Church show mercy abundantly, we pray: ◆ May our daily living include sharing mercy, we pray: ◆ May nations seek peace, we pray: ◆ May the elect find strength in community, we pray: ◆ May the sick be healed, we pray: ◆ May the departed know eternal life, we pray: ◆

Our Father . . .

God of mercy and love,
you call on sinners
to renew their lives in you.
Grant to us, your servants,
hearts alive with forgiveness
following the example of Christ,
who lives and reigns with you in the unity
of the Holy Spirit,
one God, for ever and ever.
Amen.

✝ Taste and see the goodness of the Lord.

Monday, April 1, 2019
Lenten Weekday

✝ I will praise you, Lord, for you have rescued me.

Psalm 34 *page 401*

Reading *John 4:46–53*

[Jesus] returned to Cana in Galilee, where he had made the water wine. Now there was a royal official whose son was ill in Capernaum. When he heard that Jesus had arrived in Galilee from Judea, he went to him and asked him to come down and heal his son, who was near death. Jesus said to him, "Unless you people see signs and wonders, you will not believe." The royal official said to him, "Sir, come down before my child dies." Jesus said to him, "You may go; your son will live." The man believed what Jesus said to him and left. While the man was on his way back, his slaves met him and told him that his boy would live. He asked them when he began to recover. They told him, "The fever left him yesterday, about one in the afternoon." The father realized that just at that time Jesus had said to him, "Your son will live," and he and his whole household came to believe.

Reflection

The signs and wonders of Jesus are important for the Johannine community. With the first miracle occurring in Cana, the geographic location is a sign that a miracle will occur when the royal official asks for Jesus' help. This account shows that God heals even when the person who seeks him is outside the boundaries of culture and religion. Jesus knew the man had faith, even though he was not of the Jewish faith.

Prayers *others may be added*

Seeking all good, we pray:

◆ Graciously hear us, O Lord.

May farmers have favorable weather for planting, we pray: ◆ May the work of artists and musicians point to the glory of God, we pray: ◆ May nations help migrants find acceptance, we pray: ◆ May the Church welcome the diversity in her midst, we pray: ◆ May the ill be lifted up with Christ's healing, we pray: ◆ May God lead all who have died to the glory of heaven, we pray: ◆

Our Father . . .

God of all peoples,
you care for us and all our needs.
Guide our efforts
to renew your people
and make all know themselves
to be included in society and life
so that the common good may be accomplished.
Through Christ our Lord.
Amen.

✝ I will praise you, Lord, for you have rescued me.

Tuesday, April 2, 2019
Lenten Weekday

✝ The mighty Lord is with us; the God of Jacob is our refuge.

Psalm 34
page 401

Reading
John 5:2–9

Now there is in Jerusalem at the Sheep Gate a pool called in Hebrew Bethesda, with five porticoes. In these lay a large number of ill, blind, lame, and crippled. One man was there who had been ill for thirty-eight years. When Jesus saw him lying there and knew that he had been ill for a long time, he said to him, "Do you want to be well?" The sick man answered him, "Sir, I have no one to put me into the pool when the water is stirred up; while I am on my way, someone else gets down there before me." Jesus said to him, "Rise, take up your mat, and walk." Immediately the man became well, took up his mat, and walked.

Reflection
We are invited to "wade in the water." "Wade in the Water," the African American spiritual in which this line is sung, takes into account our baptismal call and the healing we are to offer others through our lives. Jesus performed his miracles, regardless of the day, time, or culture of the person. Through our ministry, we assist people to "wade in the water" to come to a rebirth in the waters of the Church. The waters are stirred. Are we ready to assist others to grow into the healing and wholeness that is Christian living?

Prayers
others may be added

With hope for rebirth this Easter, we pray:

◆ Lord, hear our prayer.

May all Christians be faithful to their baptismal call, we pray: ◆ May government officials assist, support, and seek to improve the lives of the disabled, we pray: ◆ May hermits be strengthened in their vocation, we pray: ◆ May good weather assist the growth of crops, we pray: ◆ May the sick be healed, we pray: ◆ May the deceased reach the glory of heaven, we pray: ◆

Our Father . . .

God of all goodness,
you wash us clean and make us whole
even when we do not expect your grace.
Stir the quenching powers of your Spirit
to aid our weakness
and make us faithful to your service.
Through Christ our Lord.
Amen.

✝ The mighty Lord is with us; the God of Jacob is our refuge.

Wednesday, April 3, 2019
Lenten Weekday

✝ The Lord is gracious and merciful.

Psalm 145
page 421

Reading
Isaiah 49:8–9, 12

Thus says the LORD: / In a time of favor I answer you, / on the day of salvation I help you; / and I have kept you and given you as a covenant to the people, / To restore the land / and allot the desolate heritages, / Saying to the prisoners: Come out! / To those in darkness: Show yourselves! / Along the ways they shall find pasture, / on every bare height shall their pastures be.

But Zion said, "The LORD has forsaken me; / my Lord has forgotten me." / Can a mother forget her infant, / be without tenderness for the child of her womb? / Even should she forget, / I will never forget you.

Reflection
Isaiah calls us to experience the comfort and care of our God. During our most difficult times, God will guide us if we look to him. As a woman never forgets her child, God never forgets us. We can extend God's love by reaching out to another. Sometimes encouraging words are enough for people to understand that God remembers them. Who might need your loving kindness?

Prayers
others may be added

Confident in God's gentle love,
we pray:

◆ Hear us, gracious Lord.

May the Church show the gentle care of a mother to those in need, we pray: ◆ May nations show concern for the environment and care for the planet, we pray: ◆ May those celebrating birthdays grow in holiness, we pray: ◆ May the lonely experience comfort, we pray: ◆ May the sick be healed, we pray: ◆ May those who have died be raised up, we pray: ◆

Our Father . . .

Abba, gracious God,
you care for us
as parents care for their children.
Hear the prayers of your people,
who long for your comfort and protection.
Through Christ our Lord.
Amen.

✝ The Lord is gracious and merciful.

Thursday, April 4, 2019
Lenten Weekday

✝ Remember us, O Lord, as you favor your people.

Psalm 34
page 401

Reading
Exodus 32:7–10, 11, 13–14

The LORD said to Moses, "Go down at once to your people whom you brought out of the land of Egypt, for they have become depraved. They have soon turned aside from the way I pointed out to them, making for themselves a molten calf and worshiping it, sacrificing to it and crying out, 'This is your God, O Israel, who brought you out of the land of Egypt!'" The LORD said to Moses, "I see how stiff-necked this people is. Let me alone, then, that my wrath may blaze up against them to consume them. Then I will make of you a great nation."

But Moses implored the LORD, his God, saying, "Why, O LORD, should your wrath blaze up against your own people, whom you brought out of the land of Egypt with such great power and with so strong a hand? . . . Remember your servants Abraham, Isaac and Israel, and how you swore to them by your own self, saying, 'I will make your descendants as numerous as the stars in the sky; and all this land that I promised, I will give your descendants as their perpetual heritage.'" So the Lord relented in the punishment he had threatened to inflict on his people.

Reflection
Often, the dialogues in Scripture are fascinating reminders of our prayer lives. God invites us to do many great works; sometimes, however, we are unsure of God's ways. We need to let go of this desire to fathom the Divine, and instead trust in God's goodness. We can be too "stiff-necked," or stubborn, to recognize the importance of God's purpose. Today, we ask God to open our minds and hearts to the divine will for us, a will that certainly brings wholeness and holiness to our world.

Prayers
others may be added

Lifting our hearts to the Lord,
we pray:

◆ Lord, hear our prayer.

May the Church's teachings help us to know Christ, we pray: ◆ May bishops unify their dioceses, we pray: ◆ May cures be found for agonizing diseases, we pray: ◆ May students preparing for new ventures trust in God's plan, we pray: ◆ May the ill return to health, we pray: ◆ May those who have died attain eternal life, we pray: ◆

Our Father . . .

O Lord,
confirm in us
your plan and care of our faith.
Let us trust in your goodness
and always know of your saving works
as you unfold your concern
for your people.
Through Christ our Lord.
Amen.

✝ Remember us, O Lord, as you favor your people.

Friday, April 5, 2019

Optional Memorial of St. Vincent Ferrer, Priest

✝ The Lord is near to broken hearts.

Psalm 34 *page 401*

Reading *John 7:25–30*

Some of the inhabitants of Jerusalem said, "Is [Jesus] not the one they are trying to kill? And look, he is speaking openly and they say nothing to him. Could the authorities have realized that he is the Christ? But we know where he is from. When the Christ comes, no one will know where he is from." So Jesus cried out in the temple area as he was teaching and said, "You know me and also know where I am from. Yet I did not come on my own, but the one who sent me, whom you do not know, is true. I know him, because I am from him, and he sent me." So they tried to arrest him, but no one laid a hand upon him, because his hour had not yet come.

Reflection

Early in John's account of the Gospel, Jesus' friends are concerned that his enemies are trying to kill him. Jesus was safe from their hands because "his hour had not yet come." We may have worries and concerns, but most likely have no reason to feel that our faith places us in peril. Serious dangers challenge people in other parts of the world. Ministers suffer for Christ as they witness the Gospel and try to teach and live the faith and practice acts of Christian charity. May we never be dissuaded from our faith but remain steadfast as followers of Jesus Christ.

Prayers *others may be added*

To our faithful God, we pray:

◆ Lord, hear our prayer.

May the Church seek to reconcile peoples, we pray: ◆ May nations desire to take steps toward peace, we pray: ◆ May the Dominican order be renewed in their preaching efforts, especially as they recall St. Vincent Ferrer, we pray: ◆ May efforts increase to make water safe in third-world countries, we pray: ◆ May burdens be lightened, we pray: ◆ May those who have died share in God's glory, we pray: ◆

Our Father . . .

Good and gracious God,
you help us travel the road to heaven.
Guide our Lenten ways
to help us fulfill our change of heart
and grow in holiness, charity, and prayer.
Through Christ our Lord.
Amen.

✝ The Lord is near to broken hearts.

Saturday, April 6, 2019

Lenten Weekday

✝ O Lord, my God, in you I take refuge.

Psalm 34

page 401

Reading

John 7:40–51

Some in the crowd who heard these words of Jesus said, "This is truly the Prophet." Others said, "This is the Christ." But others said, "The Christ will not come from Galilee, will he? Does not Scripture say that the Christ will be of David's family and come from Bethlehem, the village where David lived?" So a division occurred in the crowd because of him. Some of them even wanted to arrest him, but no one laid hands on him.

So the guards went to the chief priests and Pharisees, who asked them, "Why did you not bring him?" The guards answered, "Never before has anyone spoken like this man." So the Pharisees answered them, "Have you also been deceived? Have any of the authorities or the Pharisees believed in him? But this crowd, which does not know the law, is accursed." Nicodemus, one of their members who had come to him earlier, said to them, "Does our law condemn a man before it first hears him and finds out what he is doing?"

Reflection

Nicodemus suggested that the protocol of the law be followed before Jesus is condemned. No matter a person's background or the circumstances that bring them before authorities, they should be respected. What efforts do you make to communicate with those whose actions and attitude you cannot understand?

Prayers

others may be added

Seeking God alone as our refuge,
we pray:

◆ Lord, hear our prayer.

May renewed efforts of communication assist the Church's leadership, we pray: ◆ May leaders be open to dialogue with those with differing politics, we pray: ◆ May concern be given to collaboration in parish life, we pray: ◆ May vocations to married life be strengthened, we pray: ◆ May the sick be brought to health quickly, we pray: ◆ May the deceased share in eternal life, we pray: ◆

Our Father . . .

God of our ancestors and present age,
you seek out your people
and call us to renewed grace.
Guide our efforts
of dialogue and respect
to build a better world.
Through our Lord Jesus Christ, your Son,
who lives and reigns with you in the unity
of the Holy Spirit,
one God, for ever and ever.
Amen.

✝ O Lord, my God, in you I take refuge.

Sunday, April 7, 2019
Fifth Sunday of Lent

✝ The Lord has done great things for us; we are filled with joy.

Psalm 126 *page 417*

Reading *John 8:3–11*

The scribes and the Pharisees brought [to Jesus] a woman who had been caught in adultery and made her stand in the middle. They said to him, "Teacher, this woman was caught in the very act of committing adultery. Now in the law, Moses commanded us to stone such women. So what do you say?" They said this to test him, so that they could have some charge to bring against him. Jesus bent down and began to write on the ground with his finger. But when they continued asking him, he straightened up and said to them, "Let the one among you who is without sin be the first to throw a stone at her." Again he bent down and wrote on the ground. And in response, they went away one by one, beginning with the elders. So he was left alone with the woman before him. Then Jesus straightened up and said to her, "Woman, where are they? Has no one condemned you?" She replied, "No one, sir." Jesus said, "Neither do I condemn you. Go, and from now on do not sin any more."

Reflection

The mercy of God is apparent in our Scripture today as Jesus ministers to the woman caught in the act of adultery. The Gospel is a stark reminder of the contrast between God and humanity, for still in our time we are ready to seek out vengeance or condemnation rather than lift up others in mercy. We have opportunities to help others experience God's grace by loving the sinner while condemning the sin. It is our choice to assist in bringing about new things and eradicating old ways that call for punishments that equate to seeking "an eye for an eye." We are called to be agents of mercy.

Prayers *others may be added*

To our God of compassion, we pray:

◆ Lord, hear our prayer.

For renewed efforts at celebrating God's mercy, we pray: ◆ For debts between nations to be eradicated, we pray: ◆ For educators and formators of youth, we pray: ◆ For favorable weather for crops, we pray: ◆ For healing and wholeness for the sick, we pray: ◆ For the glory of God to be revealed to the deceased, we pray: ◆

Our Father . . .

God of gentleness and mercy,
you shower your servants
with your compassion and goodness.
Prompt us to be generous
with the gifts of love and kindness
as we witness your joy and care
in the midst of conflict and division.
Through Christ our Lord.
Amen.

✝ The Lord has done great things for us; we are filled with joy.

Monday, April 8, 2019
Lenten Weekday

✝ Though I walk in the valley of darkness, I fear no evil, for you are with me.

Psalm 130 *page 418*

Reading *John 8:12–19*

Jesus spoke to them again, saying, "I am the light of the world. Whoever follows me will not walk in darkness, but will have the light of life." So the Pharisees said to him, "You testify on your own behalf, so your testimony cannot be verified." Jesus answered and said to them, "Even if I do testify on my own behalf, my testimony can be verified, because I know where I came from and where I am going. But you do not know where I come from or where I am going. You judge by appearances, but I do not judge anyone. And even if I should judge, my judgment is valid, because I am not alone, but it is I and the Father who sent me. Even in your law it is written that the testimony of two men can be verified. I testify on my behalf and so does the Father who sent me." So they said to him, "Where is your father?" Jesus answered, "You know neither me nor my Father. If you knew me, you would know my Father also."

Reflection

Especially at penance services during Lent, we reflect on the darkness of sin and the brightness of light and goodness. We hear again how Christ is the Light of the World and how his followers will have "the light of life." As followers of Christ, we are to reflect his light in the way we care for others.

Prayers *others may be added*

Turning to the One who brings light to the world, we pray:

◆ Lord, graciously hear us.

For those who suffer mental illness, we pray: ◆ For children who need to be adopted, we pray: ◆ For peacekeepers, we pray: ◆ For scientists working on cures for diseases, we pray: ◆ For affordable health care, especially for those with long-term illness, we pray: ◆ For those who grieve the loss of a loved one, we pray: ◆

Our Father . . .

God of day and light,
you dwell in goodness and justice.
Help us testify to your Son,
who leads us in right judgment
to witness to your love.
Through Christ our Lord.
Amen.

✝ Though I walk in the valley of darkness, I fear no evil, for you are with me.

Tuesday, April 9, 2019
Lenten Weekday

✝ O Lord, hear my prayer, and let my cry come to you.

Psalm 130 *page 418*

Reading *Numbers 21:4–9*

From Mount Hor the children of Israel set out on the Red Sea road, to bypass the land of Edom. But with their patience worn out by the journey, the people complained against God and Moses, "Why have you brought us up from Egypt to die in this desert, where there is no food or water? We are disgusted with this wretched food!"

In punishment the LORD sent among the people saraph serpents, which bit the people so that many of them died. Then the people came to Moses and said, "We have sinned in complaining against the LORD, and you. Pray the LORD to take the serpents away from us." So Moses prayed for the people, and the LORD said to Moses, "Make a saraph and mount it on a pole, and whoever looks at it after being bitten will live." Moses accordingly made a bronze serpent and mounted it on a pole, and whenever anyone who had been bitten by a serpent looked at the bronze serpent, he lived.

Reflection

When the Hebrews railed against God in complaint, they were punished with poisonous snakes. Our complaints may poison us. Once we begin venting our wrath, venom can flow. It's important that we listen to ourselves and be aware of the gratitude (or lack thereof) within our speech. Try to hear yourself as God might. God raises us up and helps us mature, if only we request such aid and are patient with our struggle.

Prayers *others may be added*

Fearing the Lord and open to his love, we pray:

◆ Lord, hear our prayer.

For all nations to seek ways of peace, we pray: ◆ For the pope, that he be strengthened in holiness, we pray: ◆ For volunteers in soup kitchens and shelters, we pray: ◆ For those seeking food and water, we pray: ◆ For those awaiting an organ transplant, we pray: ◆ For those who have died, that they may see the glory of God, we pray: ◆

Our Father . . .

God of all hopefulness,
we begin this day
mindful of our sinfulness
and hoping for your blessings.
Teach us to be grateful
and learn the ways
of your goodness and generosity
so that we may aid
in the work of nourishing your people.
Through Christ our Lord.
Amen.

✝ O Lord, hear my prayer, and let my cry come to you.

Wednesday, April 10, 2019

Lenten Weekday

✝ Glory and praise for ever!

Psalm 130

page 418

Reading

John 8:31–38

Jesus then said to those Jews who believed in him, "If you remain in my word, you will truly be my disciples, and you will know the truth, and the truth will set you free." They answered him, "We are descendants of Abraham and have never been enslaved to anyone. How can you say, 'You will become free'?" Jesus answered them, "Amen, amen, I say to you, everyone who commits sin is a slave of sin. A slave does not remain in a household forever, but a son always remains. So if a son frees you, then you will truly be free. I know that you are descendants of Abraham. But you are trying to kill me, because my word has no room among you. I tell you what I have seen in the Father's presence; then do what you have heard from the Father."

Reflection

"The truth will set you free." Most of our lives, we seek to live and breathe the truth. We do so, knowing that we follow the way, the truth, and the life. It is good for us to reflect on our sinfulness and the ways we may get ourselves into trouble when we are not honest before God and others. Most of the time we may be too proud to observe our need for veracity. These last days of Lenten renewal are another chance for us to say with Pilate, "What is truth?" (John 18:38).

Prayers

others may be added

Lord, hear our prayer.

◆ To our Lord, who leads us to the truth, we pray:

For bishops, may they be supported in living out Christ's message, we pray: ◆ For civic leaders, that they seek honest ways to care for all, we pray: ◆ For those who struggle to forgive, we pray: ◆ For volunteers, that they experience renewal in their work, we pray: ◆ For healing of the sick, we pray: ◆ For all who have died, that they be brought to the way, the truth, and the life, we pray: ◆

Our Father . . .

God of faithfulness and love,
you call us to persevere
in truth and justice.
Make us your servants of compassion
who desire to forsake sin
and adhere to our call
to freedom in you.
Through Christ our Lord.
Amen.

✝ Glory and praise for ever!

Thursday, April 11, 2019
Lenten Weekday

✝ The Lord remembers his covenant for ever.

Psalm 130 *page 418*

Reading *Genesis 17:3–8*

When Abram prostrated himself, God spoke to him: "My covenant with you is this: you are to become the father of a host of nations. No longer shall you be called Abram; your name shall be Abraham, for I am making you the father of a host of nations. I will render you exceedingly fertile; I will make nations of you; kings shall stem from you. I will maintain my covenant with you and your descendants after you throughout the ages as an everlasting pact, to be your God and the God of your descendants after you. I will give to you and to your descendants after you the land in which you are now staying, the whole land of Canaan, as a permanent possession; and I will be their God."

Reflection

We are blessed to be part of a covenantal relationship with God. Lent helps us remember the covenant made at Baptism and the bond we have with the Holy Trinity. Our bond with the Trinity is the core of Christian life. Eucharistic Prayer for Reconciliation I states, "It is a bond so tight that it can never be broken." We may strain the bond with our sin, but we are assured that God will never turn away from us. For this bond and sacred relationship, we give thanks and praise.

Prayers *others may be added*

To our faithful God, we pray:

◆ Lord, hear our prayer.

For new ministers to serve the Church, we pray: ◆ For government leaders to work toward the common good, we pray: ◆ For more participation in the sacraments of healing, we pray: ◆ For the imprisoned, we pray: ◆ For the sick, we pray: ◆ For those who have died, we pray: ◆

Our Father . . .

God of our ancestors,
you have made us
the people of the new covenant.
Renew within us
compassion for all
so that we may serve others
knowing that we are one in the
Holy Spirit.
Through Christ our Lord.
Amen.

✝ The Lord remembers his covenant for ever.

Friday, April 12, 2019
Lenten Weekday

✝ In my distress, the Lord heard my voice.

Psalm 130
page 418

Reading
Jeremiah 20:10–13

I hear the whisperings of many: / "Terror on every side! / Denounce! let us denounce him!" / All those who were my friends / are on the watch for any misstep of mine. / "Perhaps he will be trapped; then we can prevail, / and take our vengeance on him." / But the LORD is with me, like a mighty champion: / my persecutors will stumble, they will not triumph. / In their failure they will be put to utter shame, / to lasting, unforgettable confusion. / O LORD of hosts, you who test the just, / who probe mind and heart, / Let me witness the vengeance you take on them, / for to you I have entrusted my cause. / Sing to the LORD, / praise the LORD, / For he has rescued the life of the poor / from the power of the wicked!

Reflection
How encouraged we are to know God is always willing to rescue us. As Jeremiah states, the Lord is with us. At times, we may feel that people are working against us. Though we may feel trapped, God will help us during rough periods. Putting our trust in God, we will make it through trials and testing. As the day brightens, we will feel God on our side.

Prayers
others may be added

Trusting in God who cares for us,
we pray:

◆ Hear us, gracious Lord.

For Catholic charitable agencies, that they lift up the poor, we pray: ◆ For government services to provide for the neglected, we pray: ◆ For safety of all troops and peacekeepers, we pray: ◆ For the renewal of environmental causes, we pray: ◆ For those in distress due to illness, we pray: ◆ For those who have died, that they feel God protecting them, we pray: ◆

Our Father . . .

O God,
you hear the cries of the poor,
and listen to those most in need.
Be our stronghold against evil
and temptation
and grant that we may always
long for your presence and care.
Through Christ our Lord.
Amen.

✝ In my distress, the Lord heard my voice.

Saturday, April 13, 2019

Lenten Weekday

✝ The Lord will guard us, as a shepherd guards the flock.

Psalm 130

page 418

Reading

John 11:45–53

Some of [the Jews] went to the Pharisees and told them what Jesus had done. So the chief priests and the Pharisees convened the Sanhedrin and said, "What are we going to do? This man is performing many signs. If we leave him alone, all will believe in him, and the Romans will come and take away both our land and our nation." But one of them, Caiaphas, who was high priest that year, said to them, "You know nothing, nor do you consider that it is better for you that one man should die instead of the people, so that the whole nation may not perish." He did not say this on his own, but since he was high priest for that year, he prophesied that Jesus was going to die for the nation, and not only for the nation, but also to gather into one the dispersed children of God. So from that day on they planned to kill him.

Reflection

The plot thickens in the last days of Jesus' life. Today, we hear some describe and justify the death of the Lord. They could not abide with the new way of life Jesus offered. Would we be any different? How often do we struggle with new ideas and trends that show us another way of being or thinking? May we be on guard against becoming the modern-day Pharisees and continue as disciples in mission for Christ.

Prayers

others may be added

To our faithful God, we pray:

◆ Lord, hear our prayer.

For those wishing to adopt a child, we pray: ◆ For victims of war and violence, we pray: ◆ For scientists researching cures for diseases, we pray: ◆ For the dying, that they receive God's mercy, we pray: ◆ For the ill, that their spirits be lifted, we pray: ◆ For those seeking meaningful employment, we pray: ◆

Our Father . . .

O God,
you strengthen your people
who seek you in times of trial.
May we disciples
assist in building up your reign
and resist the temptations of power
and vainglory.
Through Christ our Lord.
Amen.

✝ The Lord will guard us, as a shepherd guards the flock.

Sunday, April 14, 2019

Palm Sunday of the Passion of the Lord

✝ My God, my God, why have you abandoned me?

Psalm 27

page 399

Reading

Luke 19:36–40

As [Jesus] rode along, the people were spreading their cloaks on the road; and now as he was approaching the slope of the Mount of Olives, the whole multitude of his disciples began to praise God aloud with joy for all the mighty deeds they had seen. They proclaimed: / "Blessed is the king who comes / in the name of the Lord. / Peace in heaven / and glory in the highest." / Some of the Pharisees in the crowd said to him, "Teacher, rebuke your disciples." He said in reply, "I tell you, if they keep silent, the stones will cry out!"

Reflection

"As [Jesus] rode along" today's Gospel reading begins. All of us go on a journey with Christ, burdened with our cross. Though our travel is joyful, it also contains frustrations, disappointment, betrayals, and challenges. On each step of the way toward Jerusalem, Jesus is close at hand, united in our passion and sacrifice. Through this Holy Week, we have the opportunity to be transformed. Will you be open to being led to something new?

Prayers

others may be added

To the Father, who sent the Son to us, we pray:

◆ Lord, hear our prayer.

May the Church be renewed through the celebration of the Paschal Mystery, we pray: ◆ May lawmakers seek to serve the common good, we pray: ◆ May vocations to the consecrated life and the ordained priesthood increase, we pray: ◆ May conflicts and wars cease, we pray: ◆ May those who seek medical attention find compassion, we pray: ◆ May the light of God draw all to heaven, we pray: ◆

Our Father . . .

O God,
we call upon you and exalt you,
for you renew the face of the earth
with your Spirit.
Grant that our celebration
of your Son's passion and death
draw us ever closer
to obedient and humble service.
May your name be glorified,
for ever and ever.
Amen.

✝ My God, my God, why have you abandoned me?

Monday, April 15, 2019
Monday of Holy Week

✝ The Lord is my light and my salvation.

Psalm 27 *page 399*

Reading *John 12:1–5*

Six days before Passover Jesus came to Bethany, where Lazarus was, whom Jesus had raised from the dead. They gave a dinner for him there, and Martha served, while Lazarus was one of those reclining at table with him. Mary took a liter of costly perfumed oil made from genuine aromatic nard and anointed the feet of Jesus and dried them with her hair; the house was filled with the fragrance of the oil. Then Judas the Iscariot, one of his disciples, and the one who would betray him, said, "Why was this oil not sold for three hundred days' wages and given to the poor?"

Reflection

During Holy Week, we reflect on the days before Jesus' passion and death. knowing that Jesus will go to the cross soon after the dinner in Bethany gives us a perspective on the anointing that occurs there. Mary anoints Jesus for what is to come. We might consider the significant moments when faith is nurtured that occur at our family dinners. As Christians, we recognize the grace in the servant moments: when we prepare, enrich, and strengthen others. These are the moments that will transform lives and prepare people for eternal life.

Prayers *others may be added*

Seeking the grace of Holy Week,
we pray:

◆ Lord, hear our prayer.

May the celebration of the Paschal Mystery enrich the Church, we pray: ◆ May travelers reach their destination safely, we pray: ◆ May taxation codes be formed to be just and serve the common good, we pray: ◆ May young people hear the call to consecrated life, we pray: ◆ May the sick find strength and wholeness, we pray: ◆ May the dying be rewarded with eternal life, we pray: ◆

Our Father . . .

God of gentleness and compassion,
you enrich our lives
in moments of grace and care.
Help us to prepare for the
sacred mysteries
and be open to a renewal of our faith.
Through our Lord Jesus Christ, your Son,
who lives and reigns with you in the unity
of the Holy Spirit,
one God, for ever and ever.
Amen.

✝ The Lord is my light and my salvation.

Tuesday, April 16, 2019
Tuesday of Holy Week

✝ I will sing of your salvation.

Psalm 71
page 405

Reading
John 13:21b–27, 30

Jesus was deeply troubled and testified, "Amen, amen, I say to you, one of you will betray me." The disciples looked at one another, at a loss as to whom he meant. One of his disciples, the one whom Jesus loved, was reclining at Jesus' side. So Simon Peter nodded to him to find out whom he meant. He leaned back against Jesus' chest and said to him, "Master, who is it?" Jesus answered, "It is the one to whom I hand the morsel after I have dipped it." So he dipped the morsel and took it and handed it to Judas, son of Simon the Iscariot. After he took the morsel, Satan entered him. So Jesus said to him, "What you are going to do, do quickly." . . . So Judas took the morsel and left at once. And it was night.

Reflection
Betrayal is an experience unlikely to be forgotten. As we take in the betrayal of Christ, we recall any we have experienced. From the betrayal of Christ, from an evil act, eventually came our redemption. Sometimes a betrayal may lead to a transformation and eventually to growth and reconciliation. And sometimes none of that occurs. However we are after a betrayal, we can know that Christ has been in that place and that God is with us.

Prayers
others may be added

To our Lord, who is always with us,
we pray:

◆ Lord, hear our prayer.

May the Church help those who have betrayed another seek pardon and reconciliation, we pray: ◆ May leaders seek to restore liberties and freedom to those who have been betrayed, we pray: ◆ May those awaiting transplants receive them, we pray: ◆ May estranged families renew their efforts to communicate, we pray: ◆ May the sick find comfort, we pray: ◆ May the dying obtain everlasting life, we pray: ◆

Our Father . . .

O God,
you are the refuge of the poor,
hear our cries for help,
especially in times of trouble.
Strengthen our resolve
to focus on your mighty deeds of love
and reconciliation,
as Christ taught us
through his life and passion.
Through Christ our Lord.
Amen.

✝ I will sing of your salvation.

Wednesday, April 17, 2019
Wednesday of Holy Week

✝ Lord, in your great love, answer me.

Psalm 27 *page 399*

Reading *Matthew 26:14–19*

One of the Twelve, who was called Judas Iscariot, went to the chief priests and said, "What are you willing to give me if I hand him over to you?" They paid him thirty pieces of silver, and from that time on he looked for an opportunity to hand him over.

On the first day of the Feast of Unleavened Bread, the disciples approached Jesus and said, "Where do you want us to prepare for you to eat the Passover?" He said, "Go into the city to a certain man and tell him, 'The teacher says, "My appointed time draws near; in your house I shall celebrate the Passover with my disciples."'" The disciples then did as Jesus had ordered, and prepared the Passover.

Reflection

There is a contrast in this Gospel between Judas who has planned ahead in seeking an opportunity to destroy Jesus and the seemingly last-minute preparation for the Passover. You would think Passover preparations would have called for more careful planning. Yet this contrast of opportunity, betrayal, and celebration of what God has done for the Jewish people reminds us that we are given opportunities for good or ill will. What will we choose? How far in advance will we seek to prepare for the opportunities for good?

Prayers *others may be added*

Turning to the Lord who protects us, we pray:

◆ Lord, hear our prayer.

May a culture of life pervade our world, we pray: ◆ May the Church seek opportunities to promote justice, we pray: ◆ May we confront wrongdoing, we pray: ◆ May travelers reach their destinations safely, we pray: ◆ May those who are ill grow in wholeness, we pray: ◆ May the angels lead the dying to paradise, we pray: ◆

Our Father . . .

God of sympathy and joy,
you travel with us
along the path of insecurity.
Help us to seek you in all things,
and take opportunities to pause
to acknowledge your goodness and
mighty works.
Through Christ our Lord.
Amen.

✝ Lord, in your great love, answer me.

Thursday, April 18, 2019

Thursday of Holy Week (Holy Thursday)

☩ Our blessing cup is a communion with the blood of Christ.

Psalm 116 *page 413*

Reading *John 13:1–5, 12–15*

Before the feast of Passover, Jesus knew that his hour had come to pass from this world to the Father. He loved his own in the world and he loved them to the end. The devil had already induced Judas, son of Simon the Iscariot, to hand him over. So, during supper, fully aware that the Father had put everything into his power and that he had come from God and was returning to God, he rose from supper and took off his outer garments. He took a towel and tied it around his waist. Then he poured water into a basin and began to wash the disciples' feet and dry them with the towel around his waist.

So when he had washed their feet and put his garments back on and reclined at table again, he said to them, "Do you realize what I have done for you? You call me 'teacher' and 'master,' and rightly so, for indeed I am. If I, therefore, the master and teacher, have washed your feet, you ought to wash one another's feet. I have given you a model to follow, so that as I have done for you, you should also do."

Reflection

Jesus' act of service in washing the Apostles' feet is striking in its humility. Just as our Lord told the Apostles, "you ought to wash one another's feet," so should we act as servants. Jesus has given us "a model to follow." May we take it to heart and act likewise as we encounter others.

Prayers *others may be added*

To the One who seeks us, we pray:

◆ Hear us, gracious Lord.

Assist us as we take up the corporal works of mercy, we pray: ◆ Challenge those who would deny the deserving of opportunities, we pray: ◆ Strengthen people to work for religious liberty and freedom, we pray: ◆ Call all to respect human dignity and life, we pray: ◆ Heal those broken by sickness, we pray: ◆ Lift the dying to eternal glory, we pray: ◆

Our Father . . .

Dear Lord,
as we begin the Sacred Paschal Triduum,
may we faithfully recall your
Son's service,
and in remembering his table fellowship,
may we be hospitable to stranger, foe,
and friend,
seeking to unite all in a bond of
communion and love.
Through our Lord Jesus Christ, your Son,
who lives and reigns with you in the unity
of the Holy Spirit,
one God, for ever and ever.
Amen.

☩ Our blessing cup is a communion with the blood of Christ.

Friday, April 19, 2019
Friday of the Passion of the Lord (Good Friday)

☩ Abba, I put my life in your hands.

Psalm 31
page 400

Reading
Hebrews 4:14–16

Brothers and sisters: Since we have a great high priest who has passed through the heavens, Jesus, the Son of God, let us hold fast to our confession. For we do not have a high power who is unable to sympathize with our weaknesses, but one who has been similarly tested in every way, yet without sin. So let us confidently approach the throne of grace to receive mercy and to find grace for timely help.

Reflection
We approach this day with grace remembering God lifted up his Son for the salvation of the world. Through this salvation, we are helped in our time of need. May our faithful remembrance remind us that we, too, must die to ourselves and share the gift of our lives with others. May our prayers today be an opportunity to leave our sin, hurts, and challenges at the foot of Calvary, to grow through pain into new life. Christ died so that we might have new life. That new life started through his death on the cross to bring us glory.

Prayers
others may be added

In the glory of the cross, we pray:

◆ Lord, have mercy.

Guide the Church in your ways, we pray: ◆ Lead us to protect the stranger and guest, we pray: ◆ Give safe travel to visitors, we pray: ◆ Shield the unborn and elderly, we pray: ◆ Heal the sick, we pray: ◆ Lift up those we mourn to eternal life, we pray: ◆

Our Father . . .

O God,
you sent your Son to us
to deliver us from sin.
Trusting in your goodness and love,
we ask that you lead us
along the way of the cross
to the glory that awaits us in
your Kingdom,
where you live and reign in unity with the
Son and Holy Spirit,
one God, for ever and ever.
Amen.

☩ Abba, I put my life in your hands.

Saturday, April 20, 2019
Holy Saturday

✝ Lord, send out your Spirit and renew the face of the earth.

Psalm 104
page 411

Reading
Romans 6:3–11

Brothers and sisters: Are you unaware that we who are baptized into Christ Jesus were baptized into his death? We were indeed buried with him through baptism into death, so that, just as Christ was raised from the dead by the glory of the Father, we too might live in newness of life.

For if we have grown into union with him through a death like his, we shall also be united with him in the resurrection. We know that our old self was crucified with him, so that our sinful body might be done away with, that we might no longer be in slavery to sin. For a dead person has been absolved from sin. If, then, we have died with Christ, we believe that we shall also live with him. We know that Christ, raised from the dead, dies no more; death no longer has power over him. As to his death, he died to sin once and for all; as to his life, he lives for God. Consequently, you too must think of yourselves as being dead to sin and living for God in Christ Jesus.

Reflection
Today is one of preparation as homes are readied for Easter dinner and churches are decorated for the celebration of the Resurrection of the Lord. It is also a day when we pause to contemplate what it means to us to reflect both on Christ's death and Resurrection. In the quiet, we consider what it means to be baptized into Christ Jesus and his death. We have died to ourselves during Lent to more fully take on Christ. Take time to pray for those who will profess their faith for the first time at tonight's Vigil.

Prayers
others may be added

To the Father, who brings us newness of life, we pray:

◆ Lord, hear us.

May our worship enliven our spirits, we pray: ◆ May those who have no faith be guided to hear your voice, we pray: ◆ May the elect be encouraged by support from the parish, we pray: ◆ May travelers be safe, we pray: ◆ May those with serious diseases be healed, we pray: ◆ May those who are dying share in the glory of the resurrection, we pray: ◆

Our Father . . .

All-powerful God of heaven and earth,
unite your people
through these sacred events
and mysteries.
Help us to serve in mission
and to seek out those most in need,
following the example of your Son
who calls us forth
to live out our baptismal calling.
Through Christ our Lord.
Amen.

✝ Lord, send out your Spirit and renew the face of the earth.

Sunday, April 21, 2019

Easter Sunday of the Resurrection of the Lord

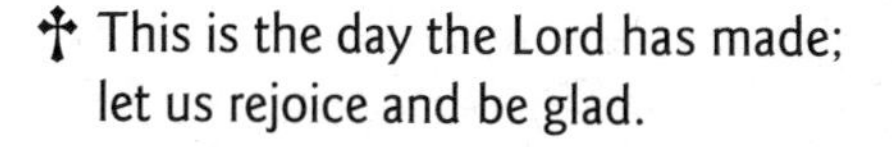

✝ This is the day the Lord has made;
let us rejoice and be glad.

Victimae Paschali Laudes *page 424*

Reading *Luke 24:1–8*

At daybreak on the first day of the week the women who had come from Galilee with Jesus took the spices they had prepared and went to the tomb. They found the stone rolled away from the tomb; but when they entered, they did not find the body of the Lord Jesus. While they were puzzling over this, behold, two men in dazzling garments appeared to them. They were terrified and bowed their faces to the ground. They said to them, "Why do you seek the living one among the dead? He is not here, but he has been raised. Remember what he said to you while he was still in Galilee, that the Son of Man must be handed over to sinners and be crucified, and rise on the third day." And they remembered his words.

Reflection

In spite of the danger, the women arrived at the tomb to carry out the Jewish prescriptions for burial. They could have abandoned Jesus, but remained faithful as he had been to them. Finding the stone rolled away, they faced two men in dazzling garments who queried, "Why do you seek the living one among the dead?" God rolls away stones in our lives to make all things new. How have your practices during Lent opened you to this new life?

Prayers *others may be added*

Turning to the Lord of life, we pray:

◆ Gracious Lord, hear us.

May Christians lift their voices to praise God throughout Easter time, we pray: ◆ May regions experiencing conflict find paths to reconciliation, we pray: ◆ May families discover ways to work together peacefully, we pray: ◆ May the faith of the neophytes renew parishes, we pray: ◆ May those in need of a transplant receive one, we pray: ◆ May the dying be received into heaven, we pray: ◆

Our Father . . .

God of the living,
you raised up your Son
to renew the world in holiness.
Grant us the fortitude
to continue to strive to follow
the ways of holiness
that Jesus modeled.
Through our Lord Jesus Christ, your Son,
who lives and reigns with you in the unity
of the Holy Spirit,
one God, for ever and ever.
Amen.

✝ This is the day the Lord has made;
let us rejoice and be glad.

Monday, April 22, 2019

Monday within the Octave of Easter

✝ Keep me safe, O God; you are my hope.

Victimae Paschali Laudes *page 424*

Reading *Matthew 28:8–14*

Mary Magdalene and the other Mary went away quickly from the tomb, fearful yet overjoyed, and ran to announce the news to his disciples. And behold, Jesus met them on their way and greeted them. They approached, embraced his feet, and did him homage. Then Jesus said to them, "Do not be afraid. Go tell my brothers to go to Galilee, and there they will see me."

While they were going, some of the guard went into the city and told the chief priests all that had happened. The chief priests assembled with the elders and took counsel; then they gave a large sum of money to the soldiers, telling them, "You are to say to him, 'His disciples came by night and stole him while we were asleep.' And if this gets to the ears of the governor, we will satisfy him and keep you out of trouble."

Reflection

The fear and joy that overtake Mary Magdalene and the other Mary capture our Christian life. We are sometimes anxious over what will happen, but also filled with joy that we share the blessing of the life of a follower of Christ. Today's Gospel reminds us not to be afraid as it encourages us to share our joy, our blessings, and our news of our faith day after day. We are to continuously go to "Galilee," or our communities, to see Christ at work in our lives.

Prayers *others may be added*

Let us praise God with our prayers:

◆ Lord, hear our prayer.

Renew the Church with a spirit of joy, we pray: ◆ Rid our community of corruption, we pray: ◆ Affirm vocations to the consecrated life, we pray: ◆ Encourage seekers in the way of Catholic Christians, we pray: ◆ Grant health to all who are suffering, we pray: ◆ Bring to eternal life those awaiting the promise, we pray: ◆

Our Father . . .

Loving God,
you offer hope to the faithful.
Strengthen the neophytes
to share their faith with others.
Help all to put into action
the faith of the Risen Lord,
who lives and reigns with you in the unity
of the Holy Spirit,
one God, for ever and ever.
Amen.

✝ Keep me safe, O God; you are my hope.

Tuesday, April 23, 2019
Tuesday within the Octave of Easter

✝ The earth is full of the goodness of the Lord.

Victimae Paschali Laudes *page 424*

Reading *John 20:11–18*

Mary Magdalene stayed outside the tomb weeping. And as she wept, she bent over into the tomb and saw two angels in white sitting there, one at the head and one at the feet where the Body of Jesus had been. And they said to her, "Woman, why are you weeping?" She said to them, "They have taken my Lord, and I don't know where they laid him." When she had said this, she turned around and saw Jesus there, but did not know it was Jesus. Jesus said to her, "Woman, why are you weeping? Whom are you looking for?" She thought it was the gardener and said to him, "Sir, if you carried him away, tell me where you laid him, and I will take him." Jesus said to her, "Mary!" She turned and said to him in Hebrew, "Rabbouni," which means Teacher. Jesus said to her, "Stop holding on to me, for I have not yet ascended to the Father. But go to my brothers and tell them, 'I am going to my Father and your Father, to my God and your God.'" Mary went and announced to the disciples, "I have seen the Lord," and then reported what he had told her.

Reflection

In the encounters after the Resurrection, it is fascinating that Jesus remained a mystery to those who had been close to him. They were holding on to what they knew. To take part in the new life that Christ offers, we need to be willing to open ourselves to be transformed in him.

Prayers *others may be added*

With joy in our hearts, we pray:

◆ Gracious Lord, hear us.

Grant success to new projects in our parish, we pray: ◆ Help the neophytes to keep their zeal, we pray: ◆ Reconcile nations in turmoil, we pray: ◆ Protect the unborn, we pray: ◆ Show mercy to the sick, we pray: ◆ Mercifully grant those who have died a place in the kingdom, we pray: ◆

Our Father . . .

Lord God,
you have brought us to faith.
Grant that, through the Easter mysteries
that we celebrate,
we be compelled to share the joy
of the life you bring to us.
May we rejoice with the neophytes
that we have been called
to bear your name.
Through Christ our Lord.
Amen.

✝ The earth is full of the goodness of the Lord.

Wednesday, April 24, 2019
Wednesday within the Octave of Easter

✝ Rejoice, O hearts that seek the Lord.

Victimae Paschali Laudes *page 424*

Reading *Luke 24:13–16*

That very day, the first day of the week, two of Jesus' disciples were going to a village seven miles from Jerusalem called Emmaus, and they were conversing about all the things that had occurred. And it happened that while they were conversing and debating, Jesus himself drew near and walked with them, but their eyes were prevented from recognizing him.

Reflection

On this fourth day of Easter, we continue to reflect on "all the things that had occurred." Just as the disciples walked to Emmaus pondering what had happened from the Last Supper through finding the tomb empty, we reflect on what the passion, death, and Resurrection mean in our lives. The readings during this Octave of Easter help us go deeper in examining our life in Christ. The disciples in the Gospel considered the events of the previous day while on a seven-mile walk. We know that Christ is risen and always with us. We only need to allow him to remove what keeps us from seeing him in our midst.

Prayers *others may be added*

To our Lord, who is with us always, we pray:

◆ Gracious Lord, hear us.

Stir our hearts to share the gifts of the Holy Spirit, we pray: ◆ Grant in us a love of Scripture, we pray: ◆ Renew our leaders to work for the common good, we pray: ◆ Assist the Body of Christ as it seeks unity, we pray: ◆ Heal those whose hearts are broken, we pray: ◆ Lead the dying to eternal life, we pray: ◆

Our Father . . .

Loving God,
you walk with us
on the journey of faith.
Teach us to trust in your ways,
and echo songs of joy in our hearts,
renewing our lives in Easter joy.
Through Christ our Lord.
Amen.

✝ Rejoice, O hearts that seek the Lord.

Thursday, April 25, 2019

Thursday within the Octave of Easter

† O Lord our God, how wonderful
your name in all the earth!

Victimae Paschali Laudes *page 424*

Reading *Luke 24:35–39*

The disciples of Jesus recounted what had taken place along the way, and how they had come to recognize him in the breaking of bread.

While they were still speaking about this, he stood in their midst and said to them, "Peace be with you." But they were startled and terrified and thought that they were seeing a ghost. Then he said to them, "Why are you troubled? And why do questions arise in your hearts? Look at my hands and my feet, that it is I myself. Touch me and see, because a ghost does not have flesh and bones as you can see I have." And as he said this, he showed them his hands and his feet. While they were still incredulous for joy and were amazed, he asked them, "Have you anything here to eat?" They gave him a piece of baked fish; he took it and ate it in front of them.

Reflection

As we hear Jesus' words "Peace be with you" to the Apostles, we can be assured of Christ's forgiveness no matter what we have done. When we celebrate Mass, we are extended peace, nurtured with the Eucharist, and sent to live that peace in the world. No matter what occurs in our day, Christ assures us we have no reason to be troubled. Rest in the knowledge that he is with you on your journey.

Prayers *others may be added*

To our Lord, who walks with us,
we pray:

◆ Lord, hear our prayer.

Renew the Church in hope and joy, we pray: ◆ Heal a world wounded by division, we pray: ◆ Strengthen the faith of the sick, we pray: ◆ Assist those who work on behalf of orphans, refugees, and the displaced, we pray: ◆ Inspire leaders to work for peace, we pray: ◆ Grant the deceased the joys of the kingdom of God, we pray: ◆

Our Father . . .

Blessed God of all peace and joy,
you gather those who are troubled
in spirit.
May all who have been reborn in Baptism
experience your healing power
over sin and anxiety.
May your name be praised through
all ages.
Through our Lord Jesus Christ, your Son,
who lives and reigns with you in the unity
of the Holy Spirit,
one God, for ever and ever.
Amen.

† O Lord our God, how wonderful
your name in all the earth!

Friday, April 26, 2019

Friday within the Octave of Easter

✝ The stone rejected by the builders
has become the cornerstone.

Victimae Paschali Laudes *page 424*

Reading *John 21:1–7a*

Jesus revealed himself again to his disciples at the Sea of Tiberias. He revealed himself in this way. Together were Simon Peter, Thomas called Didymus, Nathanael from Cana in Galilee, Zebedee's sons, and two others of his disciples. Simon Peter said to them, "I am going fishing." They said to him, "We also will come with you." So they went out and got into the boat, but that night they caught nothing. When it was already dawn, Jesus was standing on the shore; but the disciples did not realize that it was Jesus. Jesus said to them, "Children, have you caught anything to eat?" They answered him, "No." So he said to them, "Cast the net over the right side of the boat and you will find something." So they cast it, and were not able to pull it in because of the number of fish. So the disciple whom Jesus loved said to Peter, "It is the Lord."

Reflection

Today, many people think of fishing as a leisurely pursuit. In the time of Jesus, though, people needed to fish so that they could eat. Fishing provided their meals and their livelihood. This time the disciples caught nothing until Jesus appeared. It is like that in our lives, too. When we depend on God, what we desire is accomplished. When we rely only on ourselves, little goes right.

Prayers *others may be added*

To the One who renew us, we pray:

◆ Gracious Lord, hear our prayer.

May the neophytes be strengthened in their new life, we pray: ◆ May legislators be stirred to enact laws to protect all life, we pray: ◆ May young people see the need to heed the call to ministry, we pray: ◆ May peace come to families in need of healing, we pray: ◆ May the infirm be safeguarded, we pray: ◆ May the dying be granted life everlasting, we pray: ◆

Our Father . . .

Eternal God,
you enlighten and draw us to you
through the sacraments.
May these mysteries permeate our lives
so that we know and serve you gladly.
Through our Lord Jesus Christ, your Son,
who lives and reigns with you in the unity
of the Holy Spirit,
one God, for ever and ever.
Amen.

✝ The stone rejected by the builders
has become the cornerstone.

Saturday, April 27, 2019

Saturday within the Octave of Easter

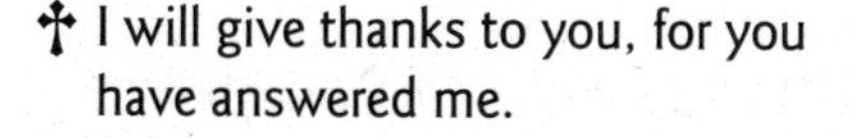

✝ I will give thanks to you, for you have answered me.

Victimae Paschali Laudes *page 424*

Reading *Mark 16:9–15*

When Jesus had risen, early on the first day of the week, he appeared first to Mary Magdalene, out of whom he had driven seven demons. She went and told his companions who were mourning and weeping. When they heard that he was alive and had been seen by her, they did not believe.

After this he appeared in another form to two of them along on their way to the country. They returned and told the others; but they did not believe them either.

But later, as the Eleven were at table, he appeared to them and rebuked them for their unbelief and hardness of heart because they had not believed those who saw him after he had been raised. He said to them, "Go into the whole world and proclaim the Gospel to every creature."

Reflection

Should we be surprised when people do not believe us when we tell of our life in Christ? No matter whether another takes us seriously, we should be steadfast in our belief and continue to share the life we are called to live. Evangelization is challenging, hard work. May we take seriously our call to "Go into the whole world and proclaim the Gospel to every creature."

Prayers *others may be added*

To the source of our hope and joy,
let us pray:

◆ Lord, hear our prayer.

May the evangelization efforts of the Church be strengthened, we pray: ◆ May civic leaders work in harmony, we pray: ◆ May children on school break be protected, we pray: ◆ May many be drawn to mission work to share the Gospel, we pray: ◆ May those who suffer disease be healed, we pray: ◆ May the dying be commended to the Communion of Saints, we pray: ◆

Our Father . . .

God of all grace and goodness,
your love transforms all believers.
Guide your ministers
to serve your Word
and trust in the Spirit of truth
so that all may come to know
and deepen their life in you.
Through Christ our Lord.
Amen.

✝ I will give thanks to you, for you have answered me.

Sunday, April 28, 2019

Second Sunday of Easter

✝ Give thanks, for the Lord is good,
God's love is everlasting.

Psalm 118 *page 414*

Reading *John 20:24–29*

Thomas, called Didymus, one of the Twelve, was not with them when Jesus came. So the other disciples said to him, "We have seen the Lord." But Thomas said to them, "Unless I see the mark of the nails in his hands and put my finger into the nailmarks and put my hand into his side, I will not believe."

Now a week later his disciples were again inside and Thomas was with them. Jesus came, although the doors were locked, and stood in their midst and said, "Peace be with you." Then he said to Thomas, "Put your finger here and see my hands, and bring your hand and put it into my side, and do not be unbelieving, but believe." Thomas answered and said to him, "My Lord and my God!" Jesus said to him, "Have you come to believe because you have seen me? Blessed are those who have not seen and have believed."

Reflection

Each year on this Second Sunday of Easter we are faced with confronting our sense of doubt and faith. Like Thomas, we are called to examine the mysteries of life, especially the mystery of what it means to have life in Christ. We reach out again from the uncertainties and fears of our present age to recall that Christ is always wishing us peace, always breathing this gift upon us. This Spirit renews us to strengthen our faith and helps us go forward to profess "My Lord and my God!"

Prayers *others may be added*

To our Lord, who brings us peace,
we pray:

◆ Lord, hear our prayer.

For the Church's mission of mercy, may it reach those who need to feel forgiven, we pray: ◆ For the poor, that medical care be provided to them, we pray: ◆ For teachers, that they be renewed in their service, we pray: ◆ For missionaries in adverse conditions, we pray: ◆ For the sick, that they recover, we pray: ◆ For those we miss and mourn, we pray: ◆

Our Father . . .

God of tenderness and mercy,
you call us to share our belief in you
and minister to those in need of
your care.
Guide our efforts of evangelization
so that we may bring others
to know of your love for them.
Through Christ our Lord.
Amen.

✝ Give thanks, for the Lord is good,
God's love is everlasting.

Monday, April 29, 2019

Memorial of St. Catherine of Siena, Virgin and Doctor of the Church

✝ Blessed are all who take refuge in the Lord.

Psalm 66

page 403

Reading

John 3:1–8

There was a Pharisee named Nicodemus, a ruler of the Jews. He came to Jesus at night and said to him, "Rabbi, we know that you are a teacher who has come from God, for no one can do these things that you are doing unless God is with him." Jesus answered and said to him, "Amen, amen, I say to you, unless one is born from above, he cannot see the Kingdom of God." Nicodemus said to him, "How can a man once grown old be born again? Surely he cannot reenter his mother's womb and be born again, can he?" Jesus answered, "Amen, amen, I say to you, unless one is born of water and Spirit he cannot enter the Kingdom of God. What is born of flesh is flesh and what is born of spirit is spirit. Do not be amazed that I told you, 'You must be born from above.' The wind blows where it wills, and you can hear the sound it makes, but you do not know where it comes from or where it goes; so it is with everyone who is born of the Spirit."

Reflection

"You must be born from above." Today's Gospel helps us remember that our Baptism gives us new life. It is a life that we are to live boldly in the knowledge that the Spirit empowers us to share our faith.

Prayers

others may be added

With St. Catherine and all theologians, we pray:

◆ Lord, have mercy.

That Catholics seek a deeper understanding of God's presence in our lives, we pray: ◆ For the neophytes, we pray: ◆ For others to join in our faith and be born again in Christ, we pray: ◆ For those preparing for First Communion and Confirmation, we pray: ◆ For the sick, that they be cured, we pray: ◆ For the dying, that they be received into paradise, we pray: ◆

Our Father . . .

God of day,
you shed your light
on all who are drawn to you.
Grant that we be steadfast
in courageously sharing our gift of faith.
May we support others
as they seek to grow closer to your Son,
who lives and reigns with you in the unity
of the Holy Spirit,
one God, for ever and ever.
Amen.

✝ Blessed are all who take refuge in the Lord.

Tuesday, April 30, 2019
Easter Weekday

✝ The Lord is king and robed in majesty.

Psalm 66
page 403

Reading
Acts 4:32–37

The community of believers was of one heart and mind, and no one claimed that any of his possessions was his own, but they had everything in common. With great power the Apostles bore witness to the resurrection of the Lord Jesus, and great favor was accorded them all. There was no needy person among them, for those who owned property or houses would sell them, bring the proceeds of the sale, and put them at the feet of the Apostles, and they were distributed to each according to need.

Thus Joseph, also named by the Apostles Barnabas (which is translated "son of encouragement"), a Levite, a Cypriot by birth, sold a piece of property that he owned, then brought the money and put it at the feet of the Apostles.

Reflection

It is inspiring that the first Christians were able to detach themselves from possessions and live communally. Barnabas' selling his property and giving the proceeds to the Apostle is a concrete example of how early believers used their property. Though most Christians do not forsake their property today, we are to have more regard for the welfare of others than our possessions. It is good to always review how attached we are to what we own.

Prayers
others may be added

Looking to our Lord, who provides for us, we pray:

◆ Lord, graciously hear us.

For the nurturing of servant leadership, we pray: ◆ For civic leaders, that they seek to work in harmony, we pray: ◆ For the elderly, that their needs be met, we pray: ◆ For an end to the death penalty, we pray: ◆ For the ill to be healed, we pray: ◆ For those who have died, that they see God's glory, we pray: ◆

Our Father . . .

Almighty God,
you inspire us
to ways of living together in harmony.
Help us serve others,
and in serving them,
build up the Body of Christ.
Through our Lord Jesus Christ, your Son,
who lives and reigns with you in the unity
of the Holy Spirit,
one God, for ever and ever.
Amen.

✝ The Lord is king and robed in majesty.

Wednesday, May 1, 2019
Optional Memorial of St. Joseph the Worker

✝ Lord, give success to the work of our hands.

Psalm 66
page 403

Reading
Matthew 13:54–58

Jesus came to his native place and taught the people in their synagogue. They were astonished and said, "Where did this man get such wisdom and mighty deeds? Is he not the carpenter's son? Is not his mother named Mary and his brothers James, Joseph, Simon, and Judas? Are not his sisters all with us? Where did this man get all this?" And they took offense at him. But Jesus said to them, "A prophet is not without honor except in his native place and in his own house." And he did not work many mighty deeds there because of their lack of faith.

Reflection
On the day in which many nations honor their workers, Catholics look to St. Joseph the Worker, who provided for his family through a trade. Many people are known by their work and even draw their strongest identity through how they make a living. Skills practiced at work often nurture self-worth and bring happiness. When those skills are attributed to God, our faith can be deepened. No matter the type of work we do, we pray that it give glory to God and that we never fail to see our value in the divine plan.

Prayers
others may be added

Turning to the Lord, who provides for our every need, we pray:

◆ Lord, hear our prayer.

For laborers to toil in the Church's mission, we pray: ◆ For those who provide for our manufacturing needs, we pray: ◆ For the safety of those who work with their hands, we pray: ◆ For the care of the earth, we pray: ◆ For those searching for cures, we pray: ◆ For those who have died, that they reach the glory of heaven, we pray: ◆

Our Father . . .

Gracious God,
you gave us St. Joseph
as a model of work and service.
May we serve you and one another
to build up the Body of Christ
and give glory to your name.
Through Christ our Lord.
Amen.

✝ Lord, give success to the work of our hands.

Thursday, May 2, 2019

Memorial of St. Athanasius, Bishop and Doctor of the Church

✝ The Lord hears the cry of the poor.

Psalm 66

page 403

Reading

John 3:31–36

The one who comes from above is above all. The one who is of the earth is earthly and speaks of earthly things. But the one who comes from heaven is above all. He testifies to what he has seen and heard, but no one accepts his testimony. Whoever does accept his testimony certifies that God is trustworthy. For the one whom God sent speaks the words of God. He does not ration his gift of the Spirit. The Father loves the Son and has given everything over to him. Whoever believes in the Son has eternal life, but whoever disobeys the Son will not see life, but the wrath of God remains upon him.

Reflection

Like today's saint, we are to seek the things of heaven. Amid the details of our daily life, we need to remove our focus from what John describes as "earthly things" and be attentive to the words of Christ. The Church has given us these fifty days of Easter to reflect joyfully on the love God has for us. As we ponder how the Father's love sent the Son to redeem us, we rejoice that our acceptance of this gift merits eternal life for us.

Prayers

others may be added

Putting our trust in God, we pray:

◆ Lord, hear our prayer.

For theologians to connect us to God's message, we pray: ◆ For this National Day of Prayer to transform our nation, we pray: ◆ For parish ministries to reach past the church doors, we pray: ◆ For economic policies that take in the needs of the marginalized, we pray: ◆ For the ill to be eased of suffering, we pray: ◆ For the dying, that they see the face of God, we pray: ◆

Our Father . . .

God of all ages,
you sent your Son
that we might have eternal life.
Assist us as we seek
to put our trust in you
and deepen our faith.
May we be worthy
to share eternal life with you.
Through Christ our Lord.
Amen.

✝ The Lord hears the cry of the poor.

Friday, May 3, 2019

Feast of Sts. Philip and James, Apostles

† Their message goes out through all the earth.

Psalm 19 *page 397*

Reading *John 14:7–14*

Jesus said to Thomas: "If you know me, then you will also know my Father. From now on you do know him and have seen him." Philip said to him, "Master, show us the Father, and that will be enough for us." Jesus said to him, "Have I been with you for so long a time and you still do not know me, Philip? Whoever has seen me has seen the Father. How can you say, 'Show us the Father'? Do you not believe that I am the Father and the Father is in me? The words that I speak to you I do not speak on my own. The Father who dwells in me is doing his works. Believe me that I am in the Father and the Father is in me, or else, believe because of the works themselves. Amen, amen, I say to you, whoever believes in me will do the works that I do, and will be greater ones than these, because I am going to the Father. And whatever you ask in my name, I will do, so that the Father may be glorified in the Son. If you ask anything of me in my name, I will do it."

Reflection

As Christians, we seek to grow in knowing the Master each day. Sometimes, like Philip, we do not recognize the Father in our midst. It is important to spend a portion of each day considering God's action in our lives. Spending time in such reflection will help us grow in awareness of God's presence.

Prayers *others may be added*

To our Lord, whose glory is among us, we pray:

◆ Hear us, gracious Lord.

For missionaries sharing the Gospel of Jesus Christ, we pray: ◆ For renewed efforts to help migrants, we pray: ◆ For those preparing for First Communion, we pray: ◆ For caretakers, we pray: ◆ For the sick, we pray: ◆ For those we miss and mourn, we pray: ◆

Our Father . . .

Loving God,
you choose Apostles and disciples
to prepare a place
for your message to renew our world.
Help us to advance the message
of your Son,
so that with the Holy Spirit
our world be re-created
to help us attain the glories of eternal life.
Through Christ our Lord.
Amen.

† Their message goes out through all the earth.

Saturday, May 4, 2019

Easter Weekday

✝ Lord, let your mercy be on us, as we place our trust in you.

Psalm 66

page 403

Reading

John 6:16–20

When it was evening, the disciples of Jesus went down to the sea, embarked in a boat, and went across the sea to Capernaum. It had already grown dark, and Jesus had not yet come to them. The sea was stirred up because a strong wind was blowing. When they had rowed about three or four miles, they saw Jesus walking on the sea and coming near the boat, and they began to be afraid. But he said to them, "It is I. Do not be afraid."

Reflection

The story of the Apostles in a boat on a stormy sea is our story. Storms often confront us in the form of issues and challenges that leave us feeling as though rocked among the waves. Yet, we have nothing to be afraid of in these storms—Christ always walks with us, easing the strong winds. In the psalm response today, we tell of our trust in the Lord. May we take those words to heart, recalling God's mercy.

Prayers

others may be added

In complete trust, we pray:

◆ Graciously hear us, Lord.

For leaders in the Church, that they trust the Spirit, we pray: ◆ For civic officials, that they not allow fear to keep them from acting with integrity, we pray: ◆ For the safety of those who work on the seas, we pray: ◆ For renewed efforts to help those in debt, we pray: ◆ For cures for the sick, we pray: ◆ For the dying, that the angels guide them to paradise, we pray: ◆

Our Father . . .

O God who calms all storms,
we give you praise and acclamation!
Grant us courage
to renew our efforts of living our faith
until we are one with you
in the glories of the kingdom.
Through our Lord Jesus Christ, your Son,
who lives and reigns with you in the unity
of the Holy Spirit,
one God, for ever and ever.
Amen.

✝ Lord, let your mercy be on us, as we place our trust in you.

Sunday, May 5, 2019

Third Sunday of Easter

✝ I will praise you, Lord, you have rescued me.

Psalm 30 *page 400*

Reading *John 21:15–19*

When they had finished breakfast, Jesus said to Simon Peter, "Simon, son of John, do you love me more than these?" Simon Peter answered him, "Yes, Lord, you know that I love you." Jesus said to him, "Feed my lambs. He then said to Simon Peter a second time, "Simon, son of John, do you love me?" Simon Peter answered him, "Yes, Lord, you know that I love you." Jesus said to him, "Tend my sheep." Jesus said to him the third time, "Simon, son of John, do you love me?" Peter was distressed that Jesus had said to him a third time, "Do you love me?" and he said to him, "Lord, you know everything; you know that I love you." Jesus said to him, "Feed my sheep. Amen, amen, I say to you, when you were younger, you used to dress yourself and go where you wanted; but when you grow old, you will stretch out your hands, and someone else will dress you and lead you where you do not want to go." He said this signifying by what kind of death he would glorify God. And when he had said this, he said to him, "Follow me."

Reflection

We receive the same call as Simon Peter to feed the Lord's sheep. Three times Christ questions Peter's love and then directs him to care for the flock. How many times do we need to be told? How is our love for God evident by the way we live? Consider who needs to be fed in your life and who needs your loving attention.

Prayers *others may be added*

In a spirit of serving God, we pray:

◆ Lord, hear our prayer.

Inspire the Church as she seeks to follow your command to feed your sheep, we pray: ◆ Teach leaders to share their vision and gifts, we pray: ◆ Open hearts to vocations in the consecrated life, we pray: ◆ Bring people to consider a calling to the diaconate, we pray: ◆ Heal the sick and needy, we pray: ◆ Lead the dying to eternal glory, we pray: ◆

Our Father . . .

Gentle shepherd and guide,
inspire us to true service
with loving hearts and minds
focusing on the ever increasing needs
of your kingdom.
May we be open to your Son
and his vision and witness of
faithful discipleship.
Through Christ our Lord.
Amen.

✝ I will praise you, Lord, you have rescued me.

Monday, May 6, 2019
Easter Weekday

✝ Blessed are they who follow the law of the Lord!

Psalm 30 *page 400*

Reading *John 6:22–29*

[After Jesus had fed the five thousand men, his disciples saw him walking on the sea.] The next day, the crowd that remained across the sea saw that there had been only one boat there, and that Jesus had not gone along with his disciples in the boat, but only his disciples had left. Other boats came from Tiberias near the place where they had eaten the bread when the Lord gave thanks. When the crowd saw that neither Jesus nor his disciples were there, they themselves got into the boats and came to Capernaum looking for Jesus. And when they found him across the sea they said to him, "Rabbi, when did you get here?" Jesus answered them and said, "Amen, amen, I say to you, you are looking for me not because you saw signs but because you ate the loaves and were filled. Do not work for food that perishes but for the food that endures for eternal life, which the Son of Man will give you. For on him the Father, God, has set his seal." So they said to him, "What can we do to accomplish the works of God?" Jesus answered and said to them, "This is the work of God, that you believe in the one he sent."

Reflection

When the disciples ask what they should do, Jesus tells them to believe. We may feel that we have an overwhelming number of things to accomplish. As today's reading points out, Christ will accomplish it. Let us not be plagued with worry; let us put our faith first and know that all else will fall in line. That way, we will do the essential work of God.

Prayers *others may be added*

Trusting in God's compassion, we pray:

◆ **Lord, hear our prayer.**

Renew the Church in her ministries, we pray: ◆ Inspire members of many denominations to participate in ecumenical dialogue, we pray: ◆ Assist those seeking to develop ministries for the imprisoned, we pray: ◆ Bring legislators to a respect for life from conception to natural death, we pray: ◆ Aid those who seek relief from pain, we pray: ◆ Accompany the dying as they journey with the angels to paradise, we pray: ◆

Our Father . . .

God of all the ages,
continue to feed us
with the bread of eternal life.
Help us always to put our prayer life first
so that we may accomplish your works
by treating all in need
with dignity and respect
and give glory to your name.
Through Christ our Lord.
Amen.

✝ Blessed are they who follow the law of the Lord!

Tuesday, May 7, 2019

Easter Weekday

✝ Into your hands, O Lord, I commend my spirit.

Psalm 30

page 400

Reading

Acts 7:55–60

Stephen, filled with the Holy Spirit, looked up intently to heaven and saw the glory of God and Jesus standing at the right hand of God, and Stephen said, "Behold, I see the heavens opened and the Son of Man standing at the right hand of God." But they cried out in a loud voice, covered their ears, and rushed upon him together. They threw him out of the city, and began to stone him. The witnesses laid down their cloaks at the feet of a young man named Saul. As they were stoning Stephen, he called out, "Lord Jesus, receive my spirit." Then he fell to his knees and cried out in a loud voice, "Lord, do not hold this sin against them"; and when he said this, he fell asleep.

Reflection

As he was stoned, Stephen echoed the words of Jesus on the cross (Luke 23:34 and 46). Following Jesus' example, the first martyr asked the Lord to receive his spirit and then asked forgiveness for those who were killing him. Stephen is a model not only of faith for us, but of forgiveness as well. When have you asked the Lord to forgive someone who has wronged you? We may not need to die for our faith, but we need to pray for those who have harmed us.

Prayers

others may be added

With open hearts and hands, we pray:

◆ Lord, hear our prayer.

Care for those who devote themselves to the Church's charitable ministries, we pray: ◆ Inspire our community leaders to work for the common good, we pray: ◆ Assist parents as they seek to nurture their families, we pray: ◆ Aid farmers as they work in the field, we pray: ◆ Heal those afflicted by illness, we pray: ◆ Welcome the departed to eternal life, we pray: ◆

Our Father . . .

Gracious God,
we commit our lives to doing your will.
Lead us through our trials and suffering
into the goodness of the promise to come.
Through Christ our Lord.
Amen.

✝ Into your hands, O Lord, I commend my spirit.

Wednesday, May 8, 2019
Easter Weekday

✝ Let all the earth cry out to God with joy.

Psalm 30
page 400

Reading
John 6:35–40

Jesus said to the crowds, "I am the bread of life; whoever comes to me will never hunger, and whoever believes in me will never thirst. But I told you that although you have seen me, you do not believe. Everything that the Father gives me will come to me, and I will not reject anyone who comes to me, because I came down from heaven not to do my own will but the will of the one who sent me. And this is the will of the one who sent me, that I should not lose anything of what he gave me, but that I should raise it on the last day. For this is the will of my Father, that everyone who sees the Son and believes in him may have eternal life, and I shall raise him on the last day."

Reflection

"I am the bread of life; whoever comes to me will never hunger." We sing phrases close to these words during the Communion hymn "I am the Bread of Life," by Suzanne Toolan. The words of the hymn reinforce our understanding that Christ nourishes us in the Eucharist. If we believe in God, we will have all that we need. We will attain life everlasting.

Prayers
others may be added

Aware of the goodness God provides, we pray:

◆ Lord, hear our prayer.

Sustain the Church in holiness, we pray: ◆ Assist leaders who seek to bring peace where there is discord, we pray: ◆ Encourage Christians who work for unity, we pray: ◆ Come to the aid of those in need of water and food, we pray: ◆ Help scientists researching cures for diseases, we pray: ◆ Lead the dying to the glory of the kingdom, we pray: ◆

Our Father . . .

Bread of Life and Chalice of Blessing,
guide your people with that
which sustains
to a future full of hope and promise.
Sustain us now and always,
in your love and kindness
so that we may always serve you
in gladness
and guide others to your truth.
Through Christ our Lord.
Amen.

✝ Let all the earth cry out to God with joy.

Thursday, May 9, 2019
Easter Weekday

✝ Let all the earth cry out to God with joy.

Psalm 30

page 400

Reading

John 6:44–51

Jesus said to the crowds: "No one can come to me unless the Father who sent me draw him, and I will raise him on the last day. It is written in the prophets: / *They shall all be taught by God.* / Everyone who listens to my Father and learns from him comes to me. Not that anyone has seen the Father except the one who is from God; he has seen the Father. Amen, amen, I say to you, whoever believes has eternal life. I am the bread of life. Your ancestors ate the manna in the desert but they died; this is the bread that comes from heaven so that one may eat it and not die. I am the living bread that came down from heaven; whoever eats this bread will live forever; and the bread that I will give is my flesh for the life of the world."

Reflection

As Jesus continues the discourse on the Bread of Life, we hear how God brings eternal life to those who eat of the living bread. God calls us to live and feast forever. What a great gift and promise. Our task is to help others see this faith, this gift, and desire to be fed through the Eucharist. Through consecrated bread, we know God is with us. May we open ourselves to the graces that accompany the Body and Blood of Christ.

Prayers

others may be added

To our God who nourishes us,
we pray:

◆ Hear our prayer.

Bless the Church with an increase in numbers of those who seek to serve others, we pray: ◆ Guide leaders of the third-world countries to discover ways to provide clean water, we pray: ◆ Amend divisions among Christians, we pray: ◆ Return to the fold those who do not worship, we pray: ◆ Aid those in prison, we pray: ◆ Unite the sinners and saints among us, we pray: ◆

Our Father . . .

God everlasting,
you provide heavenly food for us.
Grant that we may always desire
to be fed from your table.
May we be renewed in holiness
and appreciate the mysteries
and reach out to sustain those in need.
Through Christ our Lord.
Amen.

✝ Let all the earth cry out to God with joy.

Friday, May 10, 2019

Memorial of St. Damien de Veuster, Priest

✝ Go out to all the world and tell the Good News.

Psalm 30

page 400

Reading

John 6:52–58

The Jews quarreled among themselves, saying, "How can this man give us his flesh to eat?" Jesus said to them, "Amen, amen, I say to you, unless you eat the flesh of the Son of Man and drink his blood, you do not have life within you. Whoever eats my flesh and drinks my blood has eternal life, and I will raise him on the last day. For my flesh is true food, and my blood is true drink. Whoever eats my flesh and drinks my blood remains in me and I in him. Just as the living Father sent me and I have life because of the Father, so also the one who feeds on me will have life because of me. This is the bread that came down from heaven. Unlike your ancestors who ate and still died, whoever eats this bread will live forever."

Reflection

Today we honor St. Damien, a priest of the Fathers of the Sacred Hearts of Jesus and Mary. Damien left Belgium for mission work in Hawaii. Once he learned that those with Hansen's disease (leprosy) were segregated with no spiritual or medical aid, he requested to work with them. As he ministered to them, he also became a victim of Hansen's disease. He died at age forty-nine during Holy Week. Taking the Gospel message to heart, he gave his life for others. This is giving true flesh to another.

Prayers

others may be added

To our God of compassion, we pray:

◆ Hear us, gracious Lord.

Open hearts to heed the call to serve in the vineyard, we pray: ◆ Guide leaders to make wise choices for the well-being of others, we pray: ◆ Help doctors and nurses care for the suffering, we pray: ◆ Encourage scientists as they seek to find cures for contagious diseases, we pray: ◆ Renew those who are tired and weary, we pray: ◆ Enlighten those seeking eternal glory, we pray: ◆

Our Father . . .

God of the poor and ill,
you sent St. Damien help
to minister to the suffering.
Encourage us to be the face of Christ
to those who are most in need.
Grant peace and tranquility to all
who provide witness
as your servant Damian did
to those cast from society.
Through Christ our Lord.
Amen.

✝ Go out to all the world and tell the Good News.

Saturday, May 11, 2019
Easter Weekday

☩ How shall I make a return to the Lord for all the good he has done for me?

Psalm 30 *page 400*

Reading *John 6:60–69*

Many of the disciples of Jesus who were listening said, "This saying is hard; who can accept it?" Since Jesus knew that his disciples were murmuring about this, he said to them, "Does this shock you? What if you were to see the Son of Man ascending to where he was before? It is the Spirit that gives life, while the flesh is of no avail. The words I have spoken to you are Spirit and life. But there are some of you who do not believe." Jesus knew from the beginning the ones who would not believe and the one who would betray him. And he said, "For this reason I have told you that no one can come to me unless it is granted him by my Father."

As a result of this, many of his disciples returned to their former way of life and no longer walked with him. Jesus then said to the Twelve, "Do you also want to leave?" Simon Peter answered him, "Master, to whom shall we go? You have the words of eternal life. We have come to believe and are convinced that you are the Holy One of God."

Reflection

The choice to follow Christ can be a difficult one. At times, we may be tempted to leave our commitment to our baptismal call and go another way as did some of the disciples. Yet, as Peter says, and we echo with our lives, we are "convinced" that the "Holy One of God" will sustain us. How can we do anything else but follow?

Prayers *others may be added*

In trust and confidence, we pray:

◆ **Lord, hear our prayer.**

Shape hearts and minds to continue
to desire life in Christ, we pray: ◆
Assist those seeking renewable energies
to sustain our planet, we pray: ◆
Aid workers in conflict-ridden regions,
we pray: ◆ Support peacekeeping efforts,
we pray: ◆ Heal the downtrodden,
we pray: ◆ Lead the dying to the heavenly
banquet, we pray: ◆

Our Father . . .

O Holy God,
you feed and sustain us
with your life-giving food.
Help us to live in your Spirit
and renew the face of the earth
through your gifts
so that all may know
the glories of your Reign.
Through our Lord Jesus Christ, your Son,
who lives and reigns with you in the unity
of the Holy Spirit,
one God, for ever and ever.
Amen.

☩ How shall I make a return to the Lord for all the good he has done for me?

Sunday, May 12, 2019
Fourth Sunday of Easter

✝ We are God's people, the sheep of his flock.

Psalm 100 *page 410*

Reading *John 10:27–30*

Jesus said, "My sheep hear my voice; I know them, and they follow me. I give them eternal life, and they shall never perish. No one can take them out of my hand. My Father, who has given them to me, is greater than all, and no one can take them out of the Father's hand. The Father and I are one."

Reflection

The verbs in this short Gospel highlights key aspects of our faith life. Jesus reminds us to "hear" and to "follow" and tells us that we will not be taken from the Father. The Shepherd is always giving to those who listen. Our lives are to reflect Christ's and we are to be open to shepherding others. In our discipleship, we can let those we encounter know of the gift of eternal life that we are offered. At the same time, we have a role as sheep who always listen and pay attention to the Good Shepherd.

Prayers *others may be added*

To the Lord who shepherds us,
we pray:

◆ Lord, hear our prayer.

For our pope, bishops, and pastors, that they never waver from closely following Christ, we pray: ◆ For mothers, living and deceased, we pray: ◆ For those who farm and raise cattle, we pray: ◆ For openness to hear, listen, and communicate well, we pray: ◆ For the suffering, we pray: ◆ For the dying, that the Good Shepherd leads them to glory, we pray: ◆

Our Father . . .

Gentle Shepherd and guide,
help us to be open to your Word
and renew our efforts
to lead all to your pasture.
Bless our mothers,
who were created in your pastoral image.
May all know your ways
and guide others to the promise
that is won
in the unity of the Son and Spirit,
one God, for ever and ever.
Amen.

✝ We are God's people, the sheep of his flock.

Monday, May 13, 2019

Easter Weekday

☩ Athirst is my soul for the living God.

Psalm 100

page 410

Reading

John 10:1–6

Jesus said "Amen, amen, I say to you, whoever does not enter a sheepfold through the gate but climbs over elsewhere is a thief and a robber. But whoever enters through the gate is the shepherd of the sheep. The gatekeeper opens it for him, and the sheep hear his voice, as he calls his own sheep by name and leads them out. When he has driven out all his own, he walks ahead of them, and the sheep follow him, because they recognize his voice. But they will not follow a stranger; they will run away from him, because they do not recognize the voice of strangers." Although Jesus used this figure of speech, they did not realize what he was trying to tell them.

Reflection

Christ gives us a direction; however, sometimes we act rebelliously, confident that our way is better. When I was a child, I climbed over our property fence rather than go through the gate. I preferred a challenge to easy access and was rewarded with torn jeans and cuts that needed stitches. Ignoring the gatekeeper makes life harder. Will we listen and follow or proceed on a path that brings difficulties?

Prayers

others may be added

Hearing the voice of the Shepherd,
we pray:

◆ Lord, hear our prayer.

For leaders in the Church, that they seek the Holy Spirit, we pray: ◆ For civic officials, that they hear the cries of their people, we pray: ◆ For protection of all human life, we pray: ◆ For vocations to the consecrated life, we pray: ◆ For healing of the ill, we pray: ◆ For the dead, we pray: ◆

Our Father . . .

Gentle Shepherd,
you lead all your flock
to a path of righteousness and goodness.
Protect our path
and help us
to listen and serve you faithfully.
Through Christ our Lord.
Amen.

☩ Athirst is my soul for the living God.

Tuesday, May 14, 2019
Feast of St. Matthias, Apostle

† The Lord will give him a seat with the leaders of his people.

Psalm 113 *page 412*

Reading *Acts 1:15–17, 21, 23–26*

[Peter] said, "My brothers and sisters . . . Judas was numbered among us and was allotted a share in this ministry. Therefore, it is necessary that one of the men who accompanied us the whole time the Lord Jesus came and went among us . . . become with us a witness to his resurrection." So they proposed two, Joseph called Barsabbas, who was also known as Justus, and Matthias. Then they prayed, "You, Lord, who know the hearts of all, show which one of these two you have chosen to take the place in this apostolic ministry from which Judas turned away to go to his own place." Then they gave lots to them, and the lot fell upon Matthias, and he was counted with the Eleven Apostles.

Reflection

Today, as we honor St. Matthias, we reflect on his call to be of service to the Church. When lots were distributed, the disciples depended on the Lord to show them who should join the Eleven. What trust they had in God! Today, too, we seek women and men to come forward to serve in the Church's life. Some parishes have difficulty engaging leaders. Perhaps we need to suggest that parishioners spend time discerning their call. They may just hear the Spirit calling them to leadership.

Prayers *others may be added*

To our God, who calls out to us,
we pray:

◆ **Lord, hear our prayer.**

For parishioners, that they will discern their call to serve in parish ministries, we pray: ◆ For community agencies, that they will be renewed, we pray: ◆ For protection for those in public safety, we pray: ◆ For peace in troubled regions, we pray: ◆ For healing for those who suffer, we pray: ◆ For the beloved dead to enter their heavenly reward, we pray: ◆

Our Father . . .

Discerning God,
you call us to serve you
and faithfully share our gifts and talents.
May we never allow fears or worry
to keep ourselves and others
from the mission of your Church.
Grant that we be steadfast
in bringing the Good News to all
and building the Body of Christ.
Through Christ our Lord.
Amen.

† The Lord will give him a seat with the leaders of his people.

Wednesday, May 15, 2019

Optional Memorial of St. Isidore

✝ O God, let all the nations praise you!

Psalm 100

page 410

Reading

Acts 12:24—13:5a

The word of God continued to spread and grow.

After Barnabas and Saul completed their relief mission, they returned to Jerusalem, taking with them John, who is called Mark.

Now there were in the Church at Antioch prophets and teachers: Barnabas, Symeon who was called Niger, Lucius of Cyrene, Manaen who was a close friend of Herod the tetrarch, and Saul. While they were worshiping the Lord and fasting, the holy Spirit said, "Set apart for me Barnabas and Saul for the work to which I have called them." Then, completing their fasting and prayer, they laid hands on them and sent them off.

So they, sent forth by the Holy Spirit, went down to Seleucia and from there sailed to Cyprus. When they arrived in Salamis, they proclaimed the word of God in the Jewish synagogues.

Reflection

As the Acts of the Apostles tells of the mission of the early Church, much attention is paid to the names of those serving the Church. Centuries later, unfamiliar with these individuals, we may think of the listing of names as details. But those details are important in the Acts of the Apostles, for they show how the faith was spread. Perhaps we need to pay attention to our details through fasting and prayer. Take a day of rest in the middle of the week and discern how God is using your hands to preach the Word. We have a powerful mission, built on the faithful Apostles and disciples.

Prayers

others may be added

With St. Isidore the farmer, we offer our prayers:

◆ Lord, graciously hear us.

For missionary efforts to spread Christianity, we pray: ◆ For the well-being of farmers, we pray: ◆ For the protection of global resources, we pray: ◆ For efforts to respect all human life, we pray: ◆ For the neglected, we pray: ◆ For the dying, that the angels accompany them, we pray: ◆

Our Father . . .

Loving God,
you guide us on the pilgrimage of life
to share your faith and truth.
Help us to be faithful
to your message of love
and serve those most in need of your care.
Through Christ our Lord.
Amen.

✝ O God, let all the nations praise you!

Thursday, May 16, 2019
Easter Weekday

✝ Forever I will sing the goodness of the Lord.

Psalm 89

page 407

Reading

John 13:16–20

When Jesus had washed the disciples' feet, he said to them: "Amen, amen, I say to you, no slave is greater than his master nor any messenger greater than the one who sent him. If you understand this, blessed are you if you do it. I am not speaking of all of you. I know those whom I have chosen. But so that the Scripture might be fulfilled, / *The one who ate my food has raised his heel against me.* / From now on I am telling you before it happens, so that when it happens you may believe that I AM. Amen, amen, I say to you, whoever receives the one I send receives me, and whoever receives me receives the one who sent me."

Reflection

After the foot washing, Jesus begins his final discourse. He explains that those who wash feet will be blessed and that those who receive him receive the Father. As we accept the mission of Christ, we need to remember the humility that accompanies it. No matter the work we do, washing feet falls into our ministry.

Prayers

others may be added

To the Father who sent the Son,
we pray:

◆ Lord, hear our prayer.

For growth in Church ministries, we pray: ◆ For civic plans for expansion and development, that they be made in concert with the needs of the whole community, we pray: ◆ For an increased interest in the study of the New Testament, we pray: ◆ For the protection of those who seek to keep us safe, we pray: ◆ For the elderly, we pray: ◆ For the deceased, we pray: ◆

Our Father . . .

O God,
you call us
to share the Good News.
Help us to be receptive to your Word
and live it throughout our day,
bringing others to know the joy
of life in the kingdom.
Through our Lord Jesus Christ, your Son,
who lives and reigns with you in the unity
of the Holy Spirit,
one God, for ever and ever.
Amen.

✝ Forever I will sing the goodness of the Lord.

Friday, May 17, 2019
Easter Weekday

✝ You are mine; this day I have begotten you.

Psalm 100 *page 400*

Reading *John 14:1–6*

Jesus said to his disciples, "Do not let your hearts be troubled. You have faith in God; have faith also in me. In my Father's house there are many dwelling places. If there were not, would I have told you that I am going to prepare a place for you? And if I go and prepare a place for you, I will come back again and take you to myself, so that where I am you also may be. Where I am going you know the way." Thomas said to him, "Master, we do not know where you are going; how can we know the way?" Jesus said to him, "I am the way and the truth and the life. No one comes to the Father except through me."

Reflection

No fear, no troubles. Those are promises of Jesus to us. We are being called out of our cynicism and worries to trust in the truth and our place in salvation. As Christ tells the disciples that he will prepare a dwelling place for them, he also tells us. We know the way to where Jesus is going because we have come to know him. When we open our minds and hearts, and still our need to control, we allow faith to grow.

Prayers *others may be added*

With open hearts and minds, we pray:

◆ Lord, hear us.

For leaders in the Church, that they seek guidance from the Holy Spirit, we pray: ◆ For civic leaders, that they care for the least of our society, we pray: ◆ For chefs and cooks who remember St. Paschal Baylon, their patron, we pray: ◆ For those in need of clean water, we pray: ◆ For caregivers, we pray: ◆ For those we mourn, we pray: ◆

Our Father . . .

God of promise and life,
you lead us through the journeys of life
and prepare a place for us.
Guide us to relinquish our fears
so that we might trust and know
your will.
Through Christ our Lord.
Amen.

✝ You are mine; this day I have begotten you.

Saturday, May 18, 2019
Easter Weekday

✝ All the ends of the earth have seen the saving power of God.

Psalm 98 *page 410*

Reading *John 14:7–14*

Jesus said to his disciples: "If you know me, then you will also know my Father. From now on you do know him and have seen him." Philip said to him, "Master, show us the Father, and that will be enough for us." Jesus said to him, "Have I been with you for so long a time and you still do not know me, Philip? Whoever has seen me has seen the Father. How can you say, 'Show us the Father'? Do you not believe that I am the Father and the Father is in me? The words that I speak to you I do not speak on my own. The Father who dwells in me is doing his works. Believe me that I am in the Father and the Father is in me, or else, believe because of the works themselves. Amen, amen, I say to you, whoever believes in me will do the works that I do, and will be greater ones than these, because I am going to the Father. And whatever you ask in my name, I will do, so that the Father may be glorified in the Son. If you ask anything of me in my name, I will do it."

Reflection

We may sometimes feel the same exacerbation that Christ demonstrates after hearing the demand "show us the Father." After our good deeds and service, some may criticize. Ours is a culture that would like signs and wonders. When beset with such situations, we know that God will support us.

Prayers *others may be added*

To our God, who is there for our seeking, we pray:

◆ **Lord, hear our prayer.**

For Church leaders, that they feel supported in their efforts, we pray: ◆ For civic leaders, that they be strengthened through reliance on God, we pray: ◆ For parents, that they see the fruits of their sacrifices, we pray: ◆ For students preparing for graduation, we pray: ◆ For the sick, may they be healed, we pray: ◆ For the dying, that they experience the glory of heaven, we pray: ◆

Our Father . . .

Faithful God,
you hear the prayers of your people.
May we always seek you with humility.
Bless us this day and throughout the
weekend as we seek renewal.
Through Christ our Lord.
Amen.

✝ All the ends of the earth have seen the saving power of God.

Sunday, May 19, 2019
Fifth Sunday of Easter

✝ I will praise your name for ever, my king and my God.

Psalm 145

page 421

Reading

John 13:31–33a, 34–35

Jesus said, "Now is the Son of Man glorified, and God is glorified in him. If God is glorified in him, God will also glorify him in himself, and God will glorify him at once. My children, I will be with you only a little while longer. I give you a new commandment: love one another. As I have loved you, so you also should love one another. This is how all will know that you are my disciples, if you have love for one another."

Reflection

After Judas leaves the Last Supper, Jesus gives the disciples the new commandment: love one another. No matter what happens in our lives, we are called to love as Jesus did. We are known as Christ's disciples by how we love, even when we need to love through the pain and rejection within our lives. Under some circumstances, to love in such a way requires extraordinary faith. Jesus loved even the one who betrayed him. He forgave those who hanged him on the cross. We are to forgive, too.

Prayers

others may be added

Trusting our all-loving God, we pray:

◆ Lord, hear our prayer.

That leaders in the Church always seek to reflect God's love, we pray: ◆ That civic authorities bridge health-care gaps, we pray: ◆ That young people be open to a vocation in the Church, we pray: ◆ That the children receiving their First Communion during Easter Time grow in holiness, we pray: ◆ That caregivers be gifted with patience, we pray: ◆ That the dying see the face of God, we pray: ◆

Our Father . . .

Almighty God,
you love us abundantly.
and teach us that we should love
in the same way.
May we follow the example set by our
Lord Jesus Christ,
so that all may see
that we are your Son's disciples.
Through Christ our Lord.
Amen.

✝ I will praise your name for ever, my king and my God.

Monday, May 20, 2019
Easter Weekday

✝ Not to us, O Lord, but to your name give the glory.

Psalm 145
page 421

Reading
John 14:21–26

Jesus said to his disciples: "Whoever has my commandments and observes them is the one who loves me. Whoever loves me will be loved by my Father, and I will love him and reveal myself to him." Judas, not the Iscariot, said to him, "Master, then what happened that you will reveal yourself to us and not to the world?" Jesus answered and said to him, "Whoever loves me will keep my word, and my Father will love him, and we will come to him and make our dwelling with him. Whoever does not love me does not keep my words; yet the word you hear is not mine but that of the Father who sent me.

"I have told you this while I am with you. The Advocate, the Holy Spirit whom the Father will send in my name—he will teach you everything and remind you of all that I told you."

Reflection

In a number of ways, people advocate for us throughout our lives. We are blessed that Jesus sent the Holy Spirit as Advocate to lead and guide us in loving. As long as we seek the Spirit, we will be spurred on in the ways of love that the Lord taught the disciples. Follow through with loving another by inviting someone to Mass, an event at the parish, or even a movie. Through our actions, this commandment becomes real for others.

Prayers
others may be added

To the Father, who sent the Holy Spirit to us, we pray:

◆ Graciously hear us, O Lord.

That our pope and bishops never waver from reflecting God's love, we pray: ◆ That the common good may be achieved in our country, we pray: ◆ That all life may be respected and abortions end, we pray: ◆ That students find summer employment, we pray: ◆ That all in need be assisted by the many forms of healing, we pray: ◆ That the dying may shine in God's everlasting love, we pray: ◆

Our Father . . .

All-loving God,
you guide us in ways of loving
and sharing our faith.
Give us zeal for serving your people.
May our trust in you grow
and may the Advocate help us
to grow more fully into the image of your Son, our Lord Jesus Christ,
who lives and reigns with you in the unity of the Holy Spirit,
one God, for ever and ever.
Amen.

✝ Not to us, O Lord, but to your name give the glory.

Tuesday, May 21, 2019
Easter Weekday

✝ Your friends make known the glorious splendor of your kingdom.

Psalm 145 *page 421*

Reading *John 14:27–31a*

Jesus said to his disciples: "Peace I leave with you; my peace I give to you. Not as the world gives do I give it to you. Do not let your hearts be troubled or afraid. You heard me tell you, 'I am going away and I will come back to you.' If you loved me, you would rejoice that I am going to the Father; for the Father is greater than I. And now I have told you this before it happens, so that when it happens you may believe. I will no longer speak much with you, for the ruler of the world is coming. He has no power over me, but the world must know that I love the Father and that I do just as the Father has commanded me."

Reflection

It is amazing how many times Jesus shares the gift of peace with his disciples. Early on, the Church placed the Sign of Peace within the Mass. Every day is an opportunity for us to share peace with others. Doing so can be challenging, for the gift of peace must be freely offered and accepted. May our reflection on Jesus' sharing of peace make extending peace to others integral to our lives.

Prayers *others may be added*

In peace and trust, we pray:

◆ Lord, hear our prayer.

That peacemakers around the globe be supported in their efforts, we pray: ◆ That troops and those who protect be kept safe, we pray: ◆ That wars end quickly, we pray: ◆ That random acts of kindness spread and renew faith in the goodness of humankind, we pray: ◆ That the sick be given hope, we pray: ◆ That the dying shine in glory within the heavenly realm, we pray: ◆

Our Father . . .

Gracious God,
you offer us the generous spirit of peace
to share with others and reflect you.
Help us to maintain and do your will
and continue the gift of love
so that our world be truly transformed
in the spirit of peace and trust.
Through Christ our Lord.
Amen.

✝ Your friends make known the glorious splendor of your kingdom.

Wednesday, May 22, 2019

Optional Memorial of St. Rita of Cascia, Religious

✝ Let us go rejoicing to the house of the Lord.

Psalm 122 *page 416*

Reading *John 15:1–8*

Jesus said to his disciples: "I am the true vine, and my Father is the vine grower. He takes away every branch in me that does not bear fruit, and everyone that does he prunes so that it bears more fruit. You are already pruned because of the word that I spoke to you. Remain in me, as I remain in you. Just as a branch cannot bear fruit on its own unless it remains on the vine, so neither can you unless you remain in me. I am the vine, you are the branches. Whoever remains in me and I in him will bear much fruit, because without me you can do nothing. Anyone who does not remain in me will be thrown out like a branch and wither; people will gather them and throw them into a fire and they will be burned. If you remain in me and my words remain in you, ask for whatever you want and it will be done for you. By this is my Father glorified, that you bear much fruit and become my disciples."

Reflection

Pruning is a necessity for new growth. For us, pruning may mean the trimming of our egos for growth in humility. Today, perhaps we can begin recognizing the necessity of seeking God's help to prune areas within us. Regular pruning is necessary. As we grow in some areas, we need to allow the removal of weeds in other spots. When that is done, the Spirit of God will blossom.

Prayers *others may be added*

Trusting in God's care for us, we pray:

◆ **Lord, hear our prayer.**

For leaders in the Church, that they focus on the true necessities for growth, we pray: ◆ For civic authorities, that they be mindful of the care of nature, we pray: ◆ For efforts to enhance our forests, we pray: ◆ For Augustinians, who enjoy the devotions of St. Rita of Cascia, we pray: ◆ For those needing transplants, we pray: ◆ For the deceased on their journey to heaven, we pray: ◆

Our Father . . .

Lord God,
you are the vine, we are the branches
and you call us
into a special communion with you.
Teach us your ways of humility
so that we may not fear change
and renewal
in our lives and the world in which
we live.
Through Christ our Lord.
Amen.

✝ Let us go rejoicing to the house of the Lord.

Thursday, May 23, 2019
Easter Weekday

✝ Proclaim God's marvelous deeds to all the nations.

Psalm 122

page 416

Reading

John 15:9–11

Jesus said to his disciples: "As the Father loves me, so I also love you. Remain in my love. If you keep my commandments, you will remain in my love, just as I have kept my Father's commandments and remain in his love.

"I have told you this so that my joy might be in you and your joy might be complete."

Reflection

How do we remain in God's love? How do we keep the commandments? Loving is the key element to Christianity and our life in Christ. I cannot help but think of this G. K. Chesterton quote: "The Christian ideal has not been tried and found wanting; it has been found difficult and left untried." This could be a harsh judgment on many of us today, especially those who work in ministry. By witnessing to loving works, we live and keep the commandments. What loving deed do we need to share? What will show others our joy?

Prayers

others may be added

Turning to our loving God, we pray:

◆ Lord, hear our prayer.

For the Church's charitable organizations, that they be strengthened, we pray: ◆ For those recovering from natural disasters, we pray: ◆ For the homebound, we pray: ◆ For students, that they secure summer employment, we pray: ◆ For the sick, that they recover, we pray: ◆ For those we miss and mourn, we pray: ◆

Our Father . . .

Loving God,
you call us to stay close to your love
and commandments of joy.
Heed the calls of your people
who ask for your guidance and support
in living your Gospel of service.
Through Christ our Lord.
Amen.

✝ Proclaim God's marvelous deeds to all the nations.

Friday, May 24, 2019
Easter Weekday

✝ I will give you thanks among the peoples, O Lord.

Psalm 122 *page 416*

Reading *John 15:12–16*

Jesus said to his disciples: "This is my commandment: love one another as I love you. No one has greater love than this, to lay down one's life for one's friends. You are my friends if you do what I command you. I no longer call you slaves, because a slave does not know what his master is doing. I have called you friends, because I have told you everything I have heard from my Father. It was not you who chose me, but I who chose you and appointed you to go and bear fruit that will remain, so that whatever you ask the Father in my name he may give you."

Reflection

"Love one another as I love you." We are to love to the degree that Jesus loved, which means we are to love as if another's life means more than ours. Most of us will not be called to give our life for another, but we will be called to die to our egos and selfishness for another. Fulfilling this commandment means living with humility as Jesus did. When we do that, we are acting as a friend of Jesus.

Prayers *others may be added*

Trusting in God's care for us, we pray:

◆ Lord, hear our prayer.

For clergy and church workers in troubled parts of the world, we pray: ◆ For married couples to be strengthened, we pray: ◆ For leaders, that they truly serve their constituents, we pray: ◆ For efforts toward peace, we pray: ◆ For those awaiting a cure for a disease, we pray: ◆ For the dying, that the angels lead them to paradise, we pray: ◆

Our Father . . .

Heavenly Father,
you gave us your Son
as a witness of love.
Help us remain faithful
to your commands
that all may know us
as your servants of the Gospel.
Through Christ our Lord.
Amen.

✝ I will give you thanks among the peoples, O Lord.

Saturday, May 25, 2019
Easter Weekday

✝ Let all the earth cry out to God with joy.

Psalm 122

page 416

Reading

John 15:18–21

Jesus said to his disciples: "If the world hates you, realize that it hated me first. If you belonged to the world, the world would love its own; but because you do not belong to the world, and I have chosen you out of the world, the world hates you. Remember the word I spoke to you, 'No slave is greater than his master.' If they persecuted me, they will also persecute you. If they kept my word, they will also keep yours. And they will do all these things to you on account of my name, because they do not know the One who sent me."

Reflection

Today's Gospel leaves no doubt that following Christ is difficult. Disciples will be subject to hate and persecution, just as Jesus was. Persecution will come because others do not know God. Christians can rest assured that they are united with Christ, who knows the Father intimately. The love of the Father and the Son will guide you to the right paths.

Prayers

others may be added

To the Father, who is united with us in love, we pray:

◆ Lord, hear our prayer.

For the suffering Church in parts of the world, we pray: ◆ For governments, that they ensure religious freedom, we pray: ◆ For vocations to serve in vowed or ordained life, we pray: ◆ For justice and freedom, we pray: ◆ For compassionate caregivers in nursing facilities, may they receive support, we pray: ◆ For bereavement ministers, we pray: ◆

Our Father . . .

Everlasting God,
you chose us as your faithful disciples
to serve you and our sisters and brothers.
Guide our efforts to share your love
and make our service ever faithful
to your will
until you come again in glory.
Through Christ our Lord.
Amen.

✝ Let all the earth cry out to God with joy.

Sunday, May 26, 2019

Sixth Sunday of Easter

✝ O God, let all the nations praise you!

Psalm 67 *page 404*

Reading *John 14:23–28*

[Jesus said,] "Whoever loves me will keep my word, and my Father will love him, and we will come to him and make our dwelling with him. Whoever does not love me does not keep my words; yet the word you hear is not mine but that of the Father who sent me.

"I have told you this while I am with you. The Advocate, the Holy Spirit whom the Father will send in my name, will teach you everything and remind you of all that I told you. Peace I leave with you; my peace I give to you. Not as the world gives do I give it to you. Do not let your hearts be troubled or afraid. You heard me tell you, 'I am going away and I will come back to you.' If you loved me, you would rejoice that I am going to the Father; for the Father is greater than I."

Reflection

This Gospel reminds us that God will make a place within those who love Jesus. Not only will God dwell within them but so will the peace that Christ leaves with them. How often do we hear words of peace? Enough to believe, live, and feel them? What would it be like for people to hear daily: the peace of the Lord be with you. What reaction might that draw when said to others? We are called to continue to breathe peace so that people will not be afraid, but will trust and believe.

Prayers *others may be added*

One in the Spirit, we pray:

◆ Hear us, gracious Lord.

May parishes work for unity and peace, we pray: ◆ May world leaders stress the need for reconciliation, we pray: ◆ May prisoners find ways to deepen their faith, we pray: ◆ May we be grateful for those who died in service to our country, we pray: ◆ May travelers reach their destination safely, we pray: ◆ May the sick regain their health, we pray: ◆

Our Father . . .

God of peace and promise,
you lead your people
in unity with the Spirit
who comforts us.
Strengthen our efforts
to bravely work for peace
in a world of despair and fear
so that all may come to realize
the greatest gift of love.
Through Christ our Lord.
Amen.

✝ O God, let all the nations praise you!

Monday, May 27, 2019
Easter Weekday

✝ The Lord takes delight in his people.

Psalm 67
page 404

Reading
Acts 16:11–15

We set sail from Troas, making a straight run for Samothrace, and on the next day to Neapolis, and from there to Philippi, a leading city in that district of Macedonia and a Roman colony. We spent some time in that city. On the sabbath we went outside the city gate along the river where we thought there would be a place of prayer. We sat and spoke with the women who had gathered there. One of them, a woman named Lydia, a dealer in purple cloth, from the city of Thyatira, a worshiper of God, listened, and the Lord opened her heart to pay attention to what Paul was saying. After she and her household had been baptized, she offered us an invitation, "If you consider me a believer in the Lord, come and stay at my home," and she prevailed on us.

Reflection
Even today, at the site of the Baptism of Lydia, there is a flowing stream, with a carved cross in a shrine beside it. A chapel erected at the site is named Lydia's Baptistery and is used only for Baptisms. This site of the historic conversion of Lydia is a reminder that our Baptism is a significant moment that calls us to hospitality and service. In what way does our service deepen our relationship with Christ?

Prayers
others may be added

To the Lord, who strengthens us,
we pray:

◆ Graciously hear us, O Lord.

May evangelization efforts grow, we pray: ◆ May world leaders allow religious freedom, we pray: ◆ May children seeking adoption find homes, we pray: ◆ May favorable weather help crops grow, we pray: ◆ May the ill find comfort, we pray: ◆ May the dying be led into glory, we pray: ◆

Our Father . . .

Good and gracious God,
you called us into a relationship
at our Baptism that we may share
in a communion of love and friendship.
Guide our steps
with words and actions
to shape the world in your vision.
Through Christ our Lord.
Amen.

✝ The Lord takes delight in his people.

Tuesday, May 28, 2019
Easter Weekday

† Your hand saves me, O Lord.

Psalm 67 *page 404*

Reading *John 16:5–11*

Jesus said to his disciples: "Now I am going to the one who sent me, and not one of you asks me, 'Where are you going?' But because I told you this, grief has filled your hearts. But I tell you the truth, it is better for you that I go. For if I do not go, the Advocate will not come to you. And when he comes he will convict the world in regard to sin and righteousness and condemnation: sin, because they do not believe in me; righteousness, because I am going to the Father and you will no longer see me; condemnation, because the ruler of this world has been condemned."

Reflection

Each day we wake up with the blessing of an Advocate who accompanies us on our journey. In truth, sometimes we only seek counsel when we are in trouble. Christ sent us this guide to be there for all our needs. It is valuable to remember that we share with God all the parts of our life and that the Spirit is always with us.

Prayers *others may be added*

Trusting in the Spirit, we pray:

◆ Lord, hear our prayer.

May Church leaders always seek the Spirit's counsel, we pray: ◆ May special interests not cloud the judgment of elected officials, we pray: ◆ May young people be kept free from harm, we pray: ◆ May those recovering from disasters find relief, we pray: ◆ May the sick be healed, we pray: ◆ May the grieving find comfort, we pray: ◆

Our Father . . .

O God,
you give us your Spirit,
that we may have life to the fullest.
Through your guidance,
may we always call
upon your wisdom
to lead us safely
into the journey before us,
where you live and reign with our Lord
Jesus Christ, your Son,
in the unity of the Holy Spirit,
one God, for ever and ever.
Amen.

† Your hand saves me, O Lord.

Wednesday, May 29, 2019
Easter Weekday

✝ Heaven and earth are full of your glory.

Psalm 148 *page 422*

Reading *John 16:12–15*

Jesus said to his disciples: "I have much more to tell you, but you cannot bear it now. But when he comes, the Spirit of truth, he will guide you to all truth. He will not speak on his own, but he will speak what he hears, and will declare to you the things that are coming. He will glorify me, because he will take from what is mine and declare it to you. Everything that the Father has is mine; for this reason I told you that he will take from what is mine and declare it to you."

Reflection

Little by little, our life unfolds, just as our knowledge of God does. If we were to know everything that would happen to us at once, could we bear it? The unfolding of knowledge about God allows us time to ponder and accept the truth. We then can trust in God's wisdom and grace for us today.

Prayers *others may be added*

Placing our faith in God's plan,
we pray:

◆ Lord, hear our prayer.

May Church leaders continue to trust in the Holy Spirit, we pray: ◆ May civic leaders work for the common good, we pray: ◆ May those bound for prison be kept safe, we pray: ◆ May vocations to the single life be strengthened, we pray: ◆ May the sick regain their health, we pray: ◆ May the dead reach God's glory, we pray: ◆

Our Father . . .

God of all time and seasons,
we trust in your providential care for us.
Give us courage and patience anew
that your Spirit guide us
and provide the fortitude and wisdom
we need.
Through Christ our Lord.
Amen.

✝ Heaven and earth are full of your glory.

Thursday, May 30, 2019
Easter Weekday

✝ The Lord has revealed to the nations his saving power.

Psalm 148
page 422

Reading
John 16:16–20

Jesus said to his disciples: "A little while and you will no longer see me, and again a little while later and you will see me." So some of his disciples said to one another, "What does this mean that he is saying to us, 'A little while and you will not see me, and again a little while and you will see me,' and 'Because I am going to the Father'?" So they said, "What is this 'little while' of which he speaks? We do not know what he means." Jesus knew that they wanted to ask him, so he said to them, "Are you discussing with one another what I said, 'A little while and you will not see me, and again a little while and you will see me'? Amen, amen, I say to you, you will weep and mourn, while the world rejoices; you will grieve, but your grief will become joy."

Reflection
The disciples were perplexed. They could not understand how Jesus could be seen and then not seen. Neither could they grasp why they would mourn and then rejoice. In our lives, we know what it is to grieve a loved one but then to be comforted with the knowledge that the person is with God. Our faith tells us that heaven is the ultimate goal and so we can experience joy as well as grief with a death. Meanwhile, we ask God to help us with this "little while."

Prayers
others may be added

Uniting our prayers with heaven,
we pray:

◆ Lord, hear our prayer.

May we be inspired through the witness of leaders in the Church, we pray: ◆ May civic officials seek peace, we pray: ◆ May teachers and students have patience, we pray: ◆ May restaurant workers be treated with dignity, we pray: ◆ May those needing transplants receive them, we pray: ◆ May we find consolation when we miss and mourn our loved ones, we pray: ◆

Our Father . . .

O God, our shelter and strength,
you guide us along paths of holiness
until we are reunited with you in glory.
Make us open to you in times of sadness.
Help all who mourn to find comfort,
faith, and consolation in your
loving care.
Through Christ our Lord.
Amen.

✝ The Lord has revealed to the nations his saving power.

Friday, May 31, 2019
Feast of the Visitation of the Blessed Virgin Mary

✝ Among you is the great and Holy One of Israel.

Canticle of Mary *page 423*

Reading *Romans 12:9–16*

Brothers and sisters: Let love be sincere; hate what is evil, hold on to what is good; love one another with mutual affection; anticipate one another in showing honor. Do not grow slack in zeal, be fervent in spirit, serve the Lord. Rejoice in hope, endure in affliction, persevere in prayer. Contribute to the needs of the holy ones, exercise hospitality. Bless those who persecute you, bless and do not curse them. Rejoice with those who rejoice, weep with those who weep. Have the same regard for one another; do not be haughty but associate with the lowly; do not be wise in your own estimation.

Reflection

Such fervent spirit Mary had as she approached Elizabeth with words of praise for God on her lips. She rejoiced that God had blessed her and zealously proclaimed the mightly deeds of the Lord. Never was she wise in her own estimation but attributed all honor to God, who gave a promise of mercy.

Prayers *others may be added*

With Mary, we praise and seek God's favor as we pray:

◆ Lord, hear our prayer.

May Mary's zeal inspire leaders in the Church, we pray: ◆ May Mary's peace inspire reconciliation among peoples, we pray: ◆ May all children be welcomed, we pray: ◆ May parents who have lost a child find comfort and strength, we pray: ◆ May Mary's visit inspire ecumenical dialogue, we pray: ◆ May all who have died rejoice with Mary and the saints, we pray: ◆

Our Father . . .

God of hospitality and wholeness,
you inspired Mary to listen and serve.
Help us to be open to these same gifts
and the working of the Word and Spirit
within our own lives,
so that we may be your faithful servants,
for ever and ever.
Amen.

✝ Among you is the great and Holy One of Israel.

Saturday, June 1, 2019
Memorial of St. Justin, Martyr

✝ The Lord delivered me from all my fears.

Psalm 34 *page 401*

Reading *1 Corinthians 1:18–25*

Brothers and sisters: The message of the cross is foolishness to those who are perishing, but to us who are being saved it is the power of God. For it is written: *I will destroy the wisdom of the wise, / and the learning of the learned I will set aside.*

Where is the wise one? Where is the scribe? Where is the debater of this age? Has not God made the wisdom of the world foolish? For since in the wisdom of God the world did not come to know God through wisdom, it was the will of God through the foolishness of the proclamation to save those who have faith. For Jews demand signs and Greeks look for wisdom, but we proclaim Christ crucified, a stumbling block to Jews and foolishness to Gentiles, but to those who are called, Jews and Greeks alike, Christ the power of God and the wisdom of God. For the foolishness of God is wiser than human wisdom, and the weakness of God is stronger than human strength.

Reflection

Justin, a second-century martyr "lived the folly of the cross," preaching Christ and the power of the Gospel. Saints help us gain better perspective on our vocation and the demands of Christian living. Our job may not be to write a defense of the faith but we still need to share our faith. Pray for strength and wisdom to fulfill your discipleship.

Prayers *others may be added*

To our all-powerful God, we pray:

◆ Hear us, gracious Lord.

May catechists be strong in sharing the Gospel, we pray: ◆ May peacekeepers never lose heart, we pray: ◆ May missionaries continue their zeal for the faith, we pray: ◆ May parents resolve to bring their children to Mass, we pray: ◆ May tears be wiped away from those who mourn, we pray: ◆ May those in need of healing find comfort, we pray: ◆

Our Father . . .

O God,
you give us martyrs such as Justin
to teach us the importance of the faith.
Continue to guide your Church
to be a living witness to your truth
and become steadfast in your love
and service.
Through Christ our Lord.
Amen.

✝ The Lord delivered me from all my fears.

Sunday, June 2, 2019

Solemnity of the Ascension of the Lord / Seventh Sunday of Easter

✝ God mounts the throne to shouts of joy: a blare of trumpets for the Lord.

Psalm 118 *page 414*

Reading *Luke 24:46–53*

Jesus said to his disciples: "Thus it is written that the Christ would suffer and rise from the dead on the third day and that repentance, for the forgiveness of sins, would be preached in his name to all the nations, beginning from Jerusalem. You are witnesses of these things. And behold I am sending the promise of my Father upon you; but stay in the city until you are clothed with power from on high."

Then he led them out as far as Bethany, raised his hands, and blessed them. As he blessed them he parted from them and was taken up to heaven. They did him homage and then returned to Jerusalem with great joy, and they were continually in the temple praising God.

Reflection

Both Luke's versions of the Ascension today from Acts and the Gospel are proclaimed today. The Gospel states that Christ blessed the disciples as he was raised to heaven. At the end of Mass, we are blessed as we go forth to live out the mission of the Church to announce the Good News in word and deed. In our worship and service, we hand on the faith. The angel in the reading from Acts asks the disciples why they are standing around. We also need to be about the work of the Lord.

Prayers *others may be added*

In a spirit of joy, we pray:

◆ Lord, hear our prayer.

Help the Church grow in service to others, we pray: ◆ Remove the blindness of leaders who do not see the common good, we pray: ◆ Allow hearts to be moved to consider the consecrated and ordained life, we pray: ◆ Confirm the faith of those who doubt, we pray: ◆ Bring comfort to the sick, we pray: ◆ Welcome the dying to the glory of your kingdom, we pray: ◆

Our Father . . .

Reconciling God,
you grant us wisdom and mercy.
Mold us into Christ's likeness
so that we may be imitators of your love.
Through our Lord Jesus Christ, your Son,
who lives and reigns with you in the unity
of the Holy Spirit,
one God, for ever and ever.
Amen.

✝ God mounts the throne to shouts of joy: a blare of trumpets for the Lord.

Monday, June 3, 2019

Memorial of St. Charles Lwanga and Companions, Martyrs

✝ Sing to God, O kingdoms of the earth.

Psalm 124

page 417

Reading

Acts 19:1–7

While Apollos was in Corinth, Paul traveled through the interior of the country and down to Ephesus where he found some disciples. He said to them, "Did you receive the Holy Spirit when you became believers?" They answered him, "We have never even heard that there is a Holy Spirit." He said, "How were you baptized?" They replied, "With the baptism of John." Paul then said, "John baptized with a baptism of repentance, telling the people to believe in the one who was to come after him, that is, in Jesus." When they heard this, they were baptized in the name of the Lord Jesus. And when Paul laid his hands on them, the Holy Spirit came upon them, and they spoke in tongues and prophesied. Altogether there were about twelve men.

Reflection

As Paul traveled, he found that some who had been baptized by John the Baptist were not later baptized in the name of the Father, Son, and Holy Spirit. John's baptism was one of repentance, preparing people for the coming of Christ. These followers from Ephesus believed in Christ but had not known of the Spirit. When baptized, they received the gifts of the Spirit. Charles Lwanga's strong faith did not waver when he was burned at the stake.

Prayers

others may be added

In union with all the faithful and saints, we pray:

◆ Lord, hear our prayer.

Send forth missionaries to evangelize, we pray: ◆ Help the poor receive what they need, we pray: ◆ Open the hearts of your followers so that they do not judge others, we pray: ◆ Assist those who are sick to patiently await their recovery, we pray: ◆ Purify the souls of the dead so that they may rejoice with the martyrs and saints, we pray: ◆

Our Father . . .

O God,
send the power of your Spirit upon us,
so that like your saints and martyrs,
we may faithfully live and share
the Good News of salvation.
Help us remain faithful to your service
and sow the seeds of justice and peace.
Through Christ our Lord.
Amen.

✝ Sing to God, O kingdoms of the earth.

Tuesday, June 4, 2019
Easter Weekday

☩ Sing to God, O kingdoms of the earth.

Psalm 68 *page 404*

Reading *Acts 20:19–24*

[Paul said:] "I served the Lord with all humility and with the tears and trials that came to me because of the plots of the Jews, and I did not at all shrink from telling you what was for your benefit, or from teaching you in public or in your homes. I earnestly bore witness for both Jews and Greeks to repentance before God and to faith in our Lord Jesus. But now, compelled by the Spirit, I am going to Jerusalem. What will happen to me there I do not know, except that in one city after another the Holy Spirit has been warning me that imprisonment and hardships await me. Yet I consider life of no importance to me, if only that I may finish my course and the ministry that I received from the Lord Jesus, to bear witness to the Gospel of God's grace.

Reflection

Paul's explanation of his departure to the leaders of the church of Ephesus is a reminder that the Spirit can guide us to leave one place for another. Paul has taught and been persecuted in Ephesus and knows that further trials await him in Jerusalem. Hardship does not matter to him; his ministry is his priority. As did St. Paul, we need to trust the Holy Spirit to lead us through any ordeal.

Prayers *others may be added*

Trusting the wisdom of God, we pray:

◆ Lord, hear our prayer.

Encourage parishes in their efforts to work for peace, we pray: ◆ Aid community leaders seeking to provide clothing for the homeless, we pray: ◆ Bless the work of laborers, we pray: ◆ Encourage pastoral leaders who carry heavy burdens, we pray: ◆ Heal the brokenhearted, we pray: ◆ Raise the dead to glory, we pray: ◆

Our Father . . .

Spirit of the Living God,
awaken in us the sense of your call.
Renew our efforts to be your laborers,
and as living witnesses of your Son,
spread the message of the Good News.
Through our Lord Jesus Christ, your Son,
who lives and reigns with you in the unity
of the Holy Spirit,
one God, for ever and ever.
Amen.

☩ Sing to God, O kingdoms of the earth.

Wednesday, June 5, 2019

Memorial of St. Boniface, Bishop and Martyr

✝ Sing to God, O kingdoms of the earth.

Psalm 68 *page 404*

Reading *John 17:11b–19*

Jesus prayed, saying: "I gave them your word, and the world hated them, because they do not belong to the world any more than I belong to the world. I do not ask that you take them out of the world but that you keep them from the Evil One. They do not belong to the world any more than I belong to the world. Consecrate them in the truth. Your word is truth. As you sent me into the world, so I sent them into the world. And I consecrate myself for them so that they also may be consecrated in truth."

Reflection

As we near the end of the Farewell Discourse, Jesus prays for the disciples and asks that they be consecrated in the truth. Secular culture can challenge our beliefs. How comforting it is to know that Jesus prays for us and that the Advocate is here to guard, protect, and guide, keeping us in a spirit of joy and love. We are united to Christ, who will pray us through our worldly adventures.

Prayers *others may be added*

Turning to our Lord, who protects us, we pray:

◆ Lord, hear our prayer.

Guide efforts of renewal in the Church, we pray: ◆ Encourage leaders of nations who are working to mend fences, we pray: ◆ Assist students who are seeking summer employment, we pray: ◆ Renew efforts at improving health care, we pray: ◆ Heal those awaiting transplants, we pray: ◆ Lead the recently deceased to eternal glory, we pray: ◆

Our Father . . .

Lord God,
you send the Advocate
to assist us in living as your holy people.
Encourage us to be open
to what the Spirit brings.
May we use our talents and gifts
to partner with you in the recreating
of the face of the earth.
Through Christ our Lord.
Amen.

✝ Sing to God, O kingdoms of the earth.

Place Stamp
Here

DAILY PRAYER RENEWAL
LITURGY TRAINING PUBLICATIONS
3949 SOUTH RACINE AVENUE
CHICAGO, IL 60609-2523

Thursday, June 6, 2019
Optional Memorial of St. Norbert, Bishop

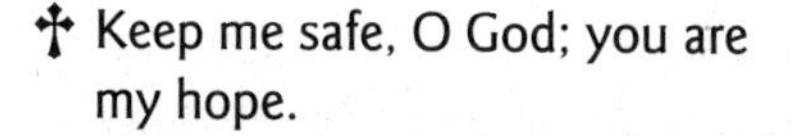

✝ Keep me safe, O God; you are my hope.

Psalm 68 *page 404*

Reading *John 17:20–24*

Jesus prayed, saying: "I pray not only for them, but also for those who will believe in me through their word, so that they may all be one, as you, Father, are in me and I in you, that they also may be in us, that the world may believe that you sent me. And I have given them the glory you gave me, so that they may be one, as we are one, I in them and you in me, that they may be brought to perfection as one, that the world may know that you sent me, and that you loved them even as you loved me. Father, they are your gift to me. I wish that where I am they also may be with me, that they may see my glory that you gave me, because you loved me before the foundation of the world."

Reflection

On this last day of the Farewell Discourse, we marvel that Jesus prays not only for the disciples but for us. We, of course, believe through the word of those first followers. Jesus prays that our love resemble the love that he and the Father have for each other. Such love will bring perfection and unity just as the Father and Son are in communion in their perfect love.

Prayers *others may be added*

To our God whose love is perfect,
we pray:

◆ Lord, hear our prayer.

Enlighten our bishops as they continue to seek your will, we pray: ◆ Render justice through our nation's leaders, we pray: ◆ Sustain the vision of St. Norbert in Eucharistic activity, we pray: ◆ Assist parishes as they seek to feed the hungry, we pray: ◆ Comfort the poor in spirit, we pray: ◆ Prepare the terminally ill for eternal salvation, we pray: ◆

Our Father . . .

Lord God,
during this Easter Time,
you have called us to rejoice
in the power of the Resurrection.
Receive the prayers of your people
and assist us in leading lives of Easter joy.
Through our Lord Jesus Christ, your Son,
who lives and reigns with you in the unity
of the Holy Spirit,
one God, for ever and ever.
Amen.

✝ Keep me safe, O God; you are my hope.

Friday, June 7, 2019
Easter Weekday

✝ The Lord has established his throne in heaven.

Psalm 118 *page 414*

Reading *John 21:15–19*

[Jesus] said to Simon Peter, "Simon, son of John, do you love me more than these?" He said to him, "Yes, Lord, you know that I love you." He said to him, "Feed my lambs." He then said to him a second time, "Simon, son of John, do you love me?" He said to him, "Yes, Lord, you know that I love you." He said to him, "Tend my sheep." He said to him the third time, "Simon, son of John, do you love me?" Peter was distressed that he had said to him a third time, "Do you love me?" and he said to him, "Lord, you know everything; you know that I love you." Jesus said to him, "Feed my sheep."

Reflection

The Apostles have just finished the breakfast Jesus cooked when he questions and then instructs Peter. In these directives, we hear how we are to live in the Risen Lord. First, we are to feed others through God's Word and love. Second, we are to more deeply follow the Lord. As Jesus queries Peter three times about his love, we understand that our commitment to our faith is not a halfhearted one. During each Easter Time as we read this Gospel, we become more aware that as we share in the Eucharist, we are to love, no matter the difficulty in doing so.

Prayers *others may be added*

To the Lord, who raises up the lowly, we pray:

◆ Graciously hear us, O Lord.

Strengthen Church leaders to govern wisely, we pray: ◆ Provide government officials wisdom to seek peace, we pray: ◆ Assist parishioners to discern a calling to liturgical ministry, we pray: ◆ Guide those seeking meaningful employment and better wages, we pray: ◆ Heal the sick, we pray: ◆ Awaken those who have died to everlasting life, we pray: ◆

Our Father . . .

Gracious God,
hear the desires and needs
of those who cry out to you.
During these last days of Easter Time,
ask the Holy Spirit
to renew efforts of love and service
within all of your people,
so that we may faithfully serve the needs of all.
Through Christ our Lord.
Amen.

✝ The Lord has established his throne in heaven.

Saturday, June 8, 2019
Easter Weekday

✝ The just will gaze on your face, O Lord.

Psalm 118 *page 414*

Reading *John 21:20–25*

Peter turned and saw the disciple following whom Jesus loved, the one who had also reclined upon his chest during the supper and had said, "Master, who is the one who will betray you?" When Peter saw him, he said to Jesus, "Lord, what about him?" Jesus said to him, "What if I want him to remain until I come? What concern is it of yours? You follow me." So the word spread among the brothers that that disciple would not die. But Jesus had not told him that he would not die, just "What if I want him to remain until I come? What concern is it of yours?"

It is this disciple who testifies to these things and has written them, and we know that his testimony is true. There are also many other things that Jesus did, but if these were to be described individually, I do not think the whole world would contain the books that would be written.

Reflection

This last moment in John's Gospel helps us consider our attentiveness to following Christ. So often, we worry about others and their business. Jesus says, "What concern is it of yours?" Rather, we are to be concerned about following, living, and testifying to the Gospel. This account reminds us that we are writing a narrative of Good News as we live and work as the beloved disciple today.

Prayers *others may be added*

Mindful of the needs of others, and ourselves we pray:

◆ Graciously hear us, O Lord.

Encourage those discerning the religious life, we pray: ◆ Renew efforts of peace and reconciliation among nations, we pray: ◆ Help the unemployed find work, we pray: ◆ Safeguard those who travel this summer, we pray: ◆ Sustain those awaiting surgery, we pray: ◆ Provide comfort to the dying, we pray: ◆

Our Father . . .

Spirit of truth and life,
you guide us along the path of service.
Make your people strong
in holiness and goodness
to witness to your ways
and bear confidence to the Gospel.
Through Christ our Lord.
Amen.

✝ The just will gaze on your face, O Lord.

Sunday, June 9, 2019
Pentecost Sunday

✝ Lord send out your Spirit, and renew the face of the earth.

Psalm 104 *page 411*

Reading *John 14:15–16, 23b–26*

[Jesus said,] "If you love me, you will keep my commandments. And I will ask the Father, and he will give you another Advocate to be with you always.

"Whoever loves me will keep my word, and my Father will love him, and we will come to him and make our dwelling with him. Whoever does not love me does not keep my words; yet the word you hear is not mine but that of the Father who sent me.

"I have told you this while I am with you. The Advocate, the Holy Spirit that the Father will send in my name, will teach you everything and remind you of all that I told you."

Reflection

God is continuing to teach us many lessons. The Advocate is here to remind us and teach us "everything." Are we willing to listen and learn? No matter our age or education, the Spirit can lead us to deepen our life in the Lord. This Pentecost, we take to heart the message that love and the Commandments are intertwined. The Advocate is here to help us understand that.

Prayers *others may be added*

Confident in the Spirit's power,
we pray:

◆ Graciously hear us, O Lord.

Refresh the Church and its leadership, we pray: ◆ Affirm the efforts of those who work for peace, we pray: ◆ Draw unbelievers to the catechumenate, we pray: ◆ Protect the unborn and elderly, we pray: ◆ Heal the ill, we pray: ◆ Bring the dying to eternal life, we pray: ◆

Our Father . . .

Spirit of the Living God,
fall afresh on us
and remold us into your image.
Guide us along the ways of love
and help us to serve you earnestly
as we learn new ways of living
that strengthen our faith.
Through Christ our Lord.
Amen.

✝ Lord send out your Spirit, and renew the face of the earth.

Monday, June 10, 2019
Memorial of the Blessed Virgin Mary, Mother of the Church

† Glorious things are told of you,
O city of God.

Canticle of Mary *page 423*

Reading *John 19:25–27*

Standing by the cross of Jesus were his mother and his mother's sister, Mary the wife of Clopas, and Mary of Magdala. When Jesus saw his mother and the disciple there whom he loved, he said to his mother, "Woman, behold, your son." Then he said to the disciple, "Behold, your mother." And from that hour the disciple took her into his home.

Reflection

As Mary stood at the foot of the Cross, Jesus gave his followers over to her as he told the beloved disciple, "Behold your mother." The disciple represented all who would follow the Son of God, all whom Mary would welcome as her own. In the Acts of the Apostles, we see that Mary prays with the Apostles in the upper room. Through the centuries, Mary has been called the Mother of the Church, and at the close of the third session of the Second Vatican Council, Pope Paul VI declared her "the Mother of the Church, that is to say of all Christian people."

Prayers *others may be added*

To our Lord, who treasured us enough to entrust us to his mother, we pray:

◆ Lord, hear our prayer.

For the Church, that she seek out Mary during struggles, we pray: ◆ For world leaders, that they seek peaceful solutions to conflict, we pray: ◆ For those who are motherless, that they receive the support they need, we pray: ◆ For all who grieve the loss of a child to violence, we pray: ◆

Our Father . . .

Lord Jesus,
in your wisdom,
you gave us your mother
to watch over us.
May we always look to her
as a woman of strength
and model of faith,
for without fear,
she answered your call.
You live and reign with the Father
in the unity of the Holy Spirit,
one God, for ever and ever.

† Glorious things are told of you,
O city of God.

Tuesday, June 11, 2019

Memorial of St. Barnabas, Apostle

✝ The Lord has revealed to the nations his saving power.

Psalm 98

page 410

Reading

Acts 11:21b–26

In those days a great number who believed turned to the Lord. The news about them reached the ears of the Church in Jerusalem, and they sent Barnabas to go to Antioch. When he arrived and saw the grace of God, he rejoiced and encouraged them all to remain faithful to the Lord in firmness of heart, for he was a good man, filled with the Holy Spirit and faith. And a large number of people was added to the Lord. Then he went to Taurus to look for Saul, and when he had found him he brought him to Antioch. For a whole year they met with the Church and taught a large number of people. And it was in Antioch that the disciples were first called Christians.

Reflection

God set apart Barnabas and Saul just as God has called and set us apart to continue the work of spreading the Good News. Whether we catechize through the hospitality we offer or preach through kind acts, we too rejoice when others come to know the Lord. Apostles such as Barnabas are noted briefly in Scripture. Their faithful lives highlight that they followed Christ's mandate "to make disciples of all nations" (Matthew 28:19). We do this through our words and actions.

Prayers

others may be added

To our Lord, who blesses us with faith, we pray:

◆ Lord, hear our prayer.

For missionaries, that they not lose heart, we pray: ◆ For peacemakers working for justice, we pray: ◆ For safety for those traveling on vacation, we pray: ◆ For those seeking meaningful employment we pray: ◆ For the sick and those who care for them, we pray: ◆ For the deceased, we pray: ◆

Our Father . . .

Loving God,
you call us to serve the Gospel
and bring your Word
to all we encounter.
Help us to work for your reign
and share the joys of the Good News
by our preaching, teaching, and actions.
Through Christ our Lord.
Amen.

✝ The Lord has revealed to the nations his saving power.

Wednesday, June 12, 2019
Weekday

✝ Holy is the Lord our God.

Psalm 34

page 401

Reading

2 Corinthians 3:4–11

Brothers and sisters: Such confidence we have through Christ toward God. Not that of ourselves we are qualified to take credit for anything as coming from us; rather, our qualification comes from God, who has indeed qualified us as ministers of a new covenant, not of letter but of spirit; for the letter brings death, but the Spirit gives life.

Now if the ministry of death, carved in letters on stone, was so glorious that the children of Israel could not look intently at the face of Moses because of its glory that was going to fade, how much more will the ministry of the Spirit be glorious? For if the ministry of condemnation was glorious, the ministry of righteousness will abound much more in glory. Indeed, what was endowed with glory has come to have no glory in this respect because of the glory that surpasses it. For if what was going to fade was glorious, how much more will what endures be glorious.

Reflection

Paul reminds us that our faith is from God. Through the Spirit, we are able to be ministers of the new covenant. The goodness of this ministry is reflected in the glory that we give to God. Our deeds, words, and actions come from the Source that created us. As we praise God, we return all to him.

Prayers

others may be added

To our Lord, who is worthy of our praise and honor, we pray:

◆ Lord, hear our prayer.

For the Church, that she reflect God's glory, we pray: ◆ For civic authorities, that they care for the earth's resources we pray: ◆ For the imprisoned, that they be shown hope, we pray: ◆ For the homeless, that they receive shelter, we pray: ◆ For those who are depressed, that their spirits be renewed, we pray: ◆ For those who have died, that they be welcomed to the glory of the Kingdom, we pray: ◆

Our Father . . .

God of power and might,
we praise you
for your goodness and care for us.
Help us in our ministry
to serve you and honor your name
by the way we reflect your deeds
and place our trust in you.
Through Christ our Lord.
Amen.

✝ Holy is the Lord our God.

Thursday, June 13, 2019
Memorial of St. Anthony of Padua, Priest and Doctor of the Church

✝ The glory of the Lord will dwell in our land.

Psalm 34

page 401

Reading

2 Corinthians 4:3–6

Brothers and sisters: Even though our Gospel is veiled, it is veiled for those who are perishing, in whose case the god of this age has blinded the minds of the unbelievers, so that they may not see the light of the Gospel of the glory of Christ, who is the image of God. For we do not preach ourselves but Jesus Christ as Lord, and ourselves as your slaves for the sake of Jesus. For God who said, *Let light shine out of darkness*, has shone in our hearts to bring to light the knowledge of the glory of God on the face of Jesus Christ.

Reflection

Although the candle we received at our Baptism may be hidden away in an attic, the light of our faith should always beam brightly, illuminating God's works. We do not hide behind a veil but boast Christ and live his identity for all the world to see. We need light to see through the darkness and sin that pervade our world. God's brightness begins with our living that spark of faith that shines in our hearts.

Prayers

others may be added

Confident that God hears our needs, we pray:

◆ Lord, hear our prayer.

For the protection of the elderly, we pray: ◆ For people who are lost to the faith, that through the intercession of St. Anthony of Padua, they may be found, we pray: ◆ For vocations to the priesthood, diaconate, or consecrated life, we pray: ◆ For the safety of those who protect us we pray: ◆ For the sick, we pray: ◆ For all who have died, we pray: ◆

Our Father . . .

Gentle God,
you call us to your marvelous light
to shine your glory on our world.
Teach us to know
the places where we must shower
your love and care with Gospel faith
and help others to see your presence.
Through our Lord Jesus Christ, your Son,
who lives and reigns with you in the unity
of the Holy Spirit,
one God, for ever and ever.
Amen.

✝ The glory of the Lord will dwell in our land.

Friday, June 14, 2019
Weekday

✝ To you, Lord, I will offer a sacrifice of praise.

Psalm 116 *page 413*

Reading *2 Corinthians 4:7–11*

Brothers and sisters: We hold this treasure in earthen vessels, that the surpassing power may be of God and not from us. We are afflicted in every way, but not constrained; perplexed, but not driven to despair; persecuted, but not abandoned; struck down but not destroyed; always carrying about in the Body the dying of Jesus, so that the life of Jesus may also be manifested in our body. For we who live are constantly being given up to death for the sake of Jesus, so that the life of Jesus may be manifested in our mortal flesh.

Reflection

It is remarkable to think that God repeatedly works through us to bring Christ's glory. We are placed in particular circumstances to "manifest" Christ. Though we may not feel worthy to do so, the reading shows that there is no reason to give into any fear, for even in our weakness, we show forth the life of Christ. Through our lives, we live out the Paschal Mystery, the dying and rising of Christ. As we do so, we present Christ to the world.

Prayers *others may be added*

To our Lord, who would never abandon us, we pray:

◆ Graciously hear us, O Lord.

For concern for all in our communities, we pray: ◆ For our leadership skills to grow so that we increasingly image Christ, we pray: ◆ For renewed efforts at protecting life we pray: ◆ For the earth, that our care for it praise God, we pray: ◆ For the sick, that they be healed in mind and spirit, we pray: ◆ For those who have died, that God's glory be revealed to them, we pray: ◆

Our Father . . .

Lord God,
each day, you lift us up in glory
so that we may be your instruments
of grace and mercy.
Teach us the ways we may share our gifts
and bring about your reign
in a fragile world that awaits your justice.
Through Christ our Lord.
Amen.

✝ To you, Lord, I will offer a sacrifice of praise.

Saturday, June 15, 2019
Weekday

✝ The Lord is kind and merciful.

Psalm 103

page 411

Reading

2 Corinthians 5:14, 20–21

Brothers and sisters: The love of Christ impels us, once we have come to the conviction that one died for all; therefore, all have died. He indeed died for all, so that those who live might no longer live for themselves but for him who for their sake died and was raised.

So we are ambassadors for Christ, as if God were appealing through us. We implore you on behalf of Christ, be reconciled to God. For our sake he made him to be sin who did not know sin, so that we might become the righteousness of God in him.

Reflection

As each generation learns what it means to die to themselves, they take the Christian message to others. Paul emphasizes that we learn to die to ourselves after realizing that Christ died so that we may live for him. As ambassadors of Christ, we extend the love of God as we reconcile with others and ask them to reconcile with God. With Christ's death and Resurrection, God works through us to bring others to reconciliation. How will you represent God in the world today?

Prayers

others may be added

With Christ, we lift our prayer to God, as we pray:

◆ Lord, hear our prayer.

For leaders in the Church, that they light the way to reconciliation, we pray: ◆ For world leaders, that they be intent on fostering peace, we pray: ◆ For students in summer school, that they apply themselves to their studies, we pray: ◆ For those in law enforcement and the citizens they protect, that they seek good relations with each other, we pray: ◆ For those on life support, that they be strengthened, we pray: ◆ For God's mercy on those seeking to enter heaven, we pray: ◆

Our Father . . .

Righteous and loving God,
you implore us to be your witnesses
and be true to the message
of reconciliation.
Guide our efforts of peace and forgiveness
so that others may see Christ alive in us
and trust that they will be renewed
through his grace.
Through Christ our Lord.
Amen.

✝ The Lord is kind and merciful.

Sunday, June 16, 2019
Solemnity of the Most Holy Trinity

✝ O Lord, our God, how wonderful
your name in all the earth.

Psalm 8
page 396

Reading
John 16:12–14

Jesus said to his disciples: "I have much more to tell you, but you cannot bear it now. But when he comes, the Spirit of truth, he will guide you to all truth. He will not speak on his own, but he will speak what he hears, and will declare to you the things that are coming. He will glorify me, because he will take from what is mine and declare it to you."

Reflection
We live in an age in which we often do not need to wait to know something. Advancements in science allow parents to know the gender of a child months prior to birth and for genes to be mapped to determine possible future ailments. Jesus tells the disciples something that is contrary to our time. He tells them to wait. They are to await guidance from the Spirit of truth. When do you pray to the Spirit for guidance? How hard is it to await the reply? As we await the Spirit, we are putting our trust in God.

Prayers
others may be added

Giving all honor and glory to God,
we pray:

◆ Lord, hear our prayer.

Help couples to make their marriages a reflection of Trinitarian love, we pray: ◆ Guide world leaders to be servants of goodness, joy, and peace, we pray: ◆ Heal the broken-hearted, we pray: ◆ Strengthen missioners in faith, we pray: ◆ Affirm those called to study theology and be of service to God's Word, we pray: ◆ Awaken the dead to eternal life, we pray: ◆

Our Father . . .

Almighty God,
you mirror communion and love
and draw us deeper into your care.
Renew us in your life and ways
so that we may better serve your image
in our actions, words, and deeds.
We ask this through the true Godhead,
living for ever and ever.
Amen.

✝ O Lord, our God, how wonderful
your name in all the earth.

Monday, June 17, 2019
Weekday

✝ The Lord has made known salvation.

Psalm 98

page 410

Reading

Matthew 5:38–42

Jesus said to his disciples: "You have heard that it was said, / *An eye for an eye and a tooth for a tooth.* / But I say to you, offer no resistance to one who is evil. When someone strikes you on your right cheek, turn the other one to him as well. If anyone wants to go to law with you over your tunic, hand him your cloak as well. Should anyone press you into service for one mile, go with him for two miles. Give to the one who asks of you, and do not turn your back on one who wants to borrow."

Reflection

In the world in which we live, seeking revenge is sometimes lauded. Television dramas often glorify evil and destruction of good. Moviegoers applaud when the enemy gets what they see as coming to him or her. Jesus' teaching in today's Gospel is completely contrary to such views. Continuing the Sermon on the Mount, Jesus tells his followers to offer the other cheek when one cheek is struck, to go the extra mile, and to give to the one who asks. God's justice and ways of seeing the world are different than ours. Our task is to seek to conform our heart to God's ways.

Prayers

others may be added

To our merciful Lord, we pray:

◆ Lord, hear our prayer.

May people work together to end the death penalty in our country, we pray: ◆ May nations seek the ways of peace, we pray: ◆ May atrocities against humanity cease, we pray: ◆ May travelers be safe, we pray: ◆ May the ill recover, we pray: ◆ May our beloved dead know the glory of heaven, we pray: ◆

Our Father . . .

Gracious God,
help us understand your ways and justice.
Keep our minds and hearts
open to learning the ways of love
and compassion.
May we offer mercy and care
to all those we find difficult.
Through Christ our Lord.
Amen.

✝ The Lord has made known salvation.

Tuesday, June 18, 2019
Weekday

☩ Praise the Lord, my soul!

Psalm 98

page 410

Reading

Matthew 5:43–48

Jesus said to his disciples: "You have heard that it was said, / *You shall love your neighbor and hate your enemy.* / But I say to you, love your enemies and pray for those who persecute you, that you may be children of your heavenly Father, for he makes his sun rise on the bad and the good, and causes rain to fall on the just and the unjust. For if you love those who love you, what recompense will you have? Do not the tax collectors do the same? And if you greet your brothers only, what is unusual about that? Do not the pagans do the same? So be perfect, just as your heavenly Father is perfect."

Reflection

Jesus calls us to love the individuals in our lives who are the hardest for us to love. Those who have persecuted us or treated us badly are to be loved and prayed for; otherwise, we are acting the same as a pagan. If our aim is to be as perfect as the heavenly Father, we need to love even the most difficult, even an enemy. Let us give special attention and prayer to the one or two difficult persons in our lives and ask for God's guidance and assistance as we do so.

Prayers

others may be added

Confident in God's love, we pray:

◆ Lord, hear our prayer.

May justice and mercy play a large role in the Church's tribunals, we pray: ◆ May nations take steps to end torture, we pray: ◆ May prisoners experience peace and love, we pray: ◆ May there be an increase in participation and attendance at Mass, we pray: ◆ May those awaiting transplants receive assurance, we pray: ◆ May those who have died reach eternal glory, we pray: ◆

Our Father . . .

All loving God,
you shower your care
on all your people and nations.
Guide our efforts of peace and mercy
that we may grant love and compassion
to witness to your Son,
who lives and reigns with you in the unity
of the Holy Spirit,
one God, for ever and ever.
Amen.

☩ Praise the Lord, my soul!

Wednesday, June 19, 2019
Weekday

✝ Blessed the one who fears the Lord.

Psalm 98 *page 410*

Reading *2 Corinthians 9:6–8*

Brothers and sisters, consider this: Whoever sows sparingly will also reap sparingly, and whoever sows bountifully will also reap bountifully. Each must do as already determined, without sadness or compulsion, for God loves a cheerful giver. Moreover, God is able to make every grace abundant for you, so that in all things, always having all you need, you may have an abundance for every good work.

Reflection

Paul reminds us of the richness God give us and how we are generously blessed. The encouragement we seek from others is always there with God, who abundantly cares for us. We are charged with seeing and hearing this encouragement. More importantly, we are called to give and share from our harvest. Sometimes people do not see their blessings or understand that they have talents and strengths to offer another. It is important to acknowledge what we have and recognize that we are called to be generous stewards and give thanks always.

Prayers *others may be added*

To the Lord, who blesses us, we pray:

◆ Graciously hear us, O Lord.

May the Church always be open to sharing her blessings, we pray: ◆ May our government welcome those most in need, we pray: ◆ May interfaith collaboration to support charitable organizations continue, we pray: ◆ May work to renew peace in troubled regions be sustained, we pray: ◆ May the sick recover, we pray: ◆ May the angels lead those who have died to paradise, we pray: ◆

Our Father . . .

Generous and caring God,
you shelter your people with
many blessings
as you provide for all their needs.
Assist us in our efforts
to be cheerful givers,
to lend our support to others,
and to help them recognize the richness
of their blessings.
Through Christ our Lord.
Amen.

✝ Blessed the one who fears the Lord.

Thursday, June 20, 2019
Weekday

☩ Your works, O Lord, are justice and truth.

Psalm 116

page 413

Reading

Matthew 6:7–15

Jesus said to his disciples: "In praying, do not babble like the pagans, who think that they will be heard because of their many words. Do not be like them. Your Father knows what you need before you ask him.

"This is how you are to pray: / Our Father who art in heaven, / hallowed be thy name, / thy Kingdom come, / thy will be done, / on earth as it is in heaven. / Give us this day our daily bread; / and forgive us our trespasses, / as we forgive those who trespass against us; / and lead us not into temptation, / but deliver us from evil.'

"If you forgive men their transgressions, your heavenly Father will forgive you. But if you do not forgive men, neither will your Father forgive your transgressions."

Reflection

As Jesus continues to teach from the Mount, he shows us how to pray. In the Lord's Prayer, we praise God, state our openness to his will, and make a request for our needs and forgiveness. Praying in this way leads us closer to God and the path of the Christian. Be attentive today to the words of the Our Father, noticing that you are praying that the Lord's name be respected as holy. Your careful prayer can bring you more in communion with God and closer to his will.

Prayers

others may be added

To the Father, who gives us our daily bread, we pray:

◆ Lord, hear our prayer.

May the pope bring hope to the Church he leads, we pray: ◆ May the president, governor, and local leaders dedicate time to prayer and openness to God's will, we pray: ◆ May all have the freedom to pray and worship, we pray: ◆ May those studying this summer find courage and strength in their education, we pray: ◆ May healing come quickly to those recovering from surgery, we pray: ◆ May the grieving find comfort, we pray: ◆

Our Father . . .

O God,
you give us our daily bread and so much more.
May we live in praise to you,
always seeking your will.
Teach us to be patient
and allow our hearts to be moved
so that our longings be in harmony with your ways.
Through Christ our Lord.
Amen.

☩ Your works, O Lord, are justice and truth.

Friday, June 21, 2019

Memorial of St. Aloysius Gonzaga, Religious

✝ From all their distress God rescues the just.

Psalm 98

page 410

Reading

Matthew 6:19–23

Jesus said to his disciples: "Do not store up for yourselves treasures on earth, where moth and decay destroy, and thieves break in and steal. But store up treasures in heaven, where neither moth nor decay destroys, nor thieves break in and steal. For where your treasure is, there also will your heart be.

"The lamp of the body is the eye. If your eye is sound, your whole body will be filled with light; but if your eye is bad, your whole body will be in darkness. And if the light in you is darkness, how great will the darkness be."

Reflection

Sometimes it is good to review what we value and store up. It is easy to collect many things that do not belong in our lives. How much anger do you hold in a closet in your heart? Do you hold in kindness or is it always available to share? How are you doing on storing up forgiveness or are you happy to distribute it? Where does light need to be shed? What do you need to cast out? Christ provides light for our reflection so that we can choose what to keep and allow to grow and what to cast aside.

Prayers

others may be added

Confident in God's assistance,
we pray:

◆ Lord, hear our prayer.

May the Church continue to care for those who are neglected, we pray: ◆ May our nation see the treasures and resources of the earth and use them for the common good, we pray: ◆ May vacationers be refreshed, we pray: ◆ May young men join the Jesuits through the inspiration of St. Aloysius Gonzaga, we pray: ◆ May those who suffer the agony of addiction be healed, we pray: ◆ May wholeness come to the grieving, we pray: ◆

Our Father . . .

God of all gifts and treasures,
you call your people to wholeness
and renew our lives with your goodness.
Draw all to know the values
that your life and teachings espoused.
May we seek for our treasures
to be those we store in heaven.
Through Christ our Lord.
Amen.

✝ From all their distress God rescues the just.

Saturday, June 22, 2019
Weekday

☩ Taste and see the goodness of the Lord.

Psalm 34 *page 410*

Reading *Matthew 6:24–27*

Jesus said to his disciples: "No one can serve two masters. He will either hate one and love the other, or be devoted to one and despise the other. You cannot serve God and mammon.

"Therefore I tell you, do not worry about your life, what you will eat or drink, or about your body, what you will wear. Is not life more than food and the body more than clothing? Look at the birds in the sky; they do not sow or reap, they gather nothing into barns, yet your heavenly Father feeds them. Are not you more important than they? Can any of you by worrying add a single moment to your life-span?"

Reflection

Why do we waste so much time worrying? In today's reading, Jesus reminds us that there is no reason for distress, for God cares for our needs. Anxiety, stress, and worry come from our fear and desire for control. Through prayer, we can give our concerns to God. When we are anxious, our cares may overrun our life and our desire to be God's light and servant to others. During times of anxiety, we focus on ourselves and not on God's Kingdom and rule. This is another day to "let God" and "let go." This may be easily said but difficult to implement.

Prayers *others may be added*

Open to trusting God's ways and will, we pray:

◆ Lord, hear our prayer.

May the Church help her members grow in trusting God, we pray: ◆ May leaders in our community seek wisdom through collaboration, we pray: ◆ May those preparing for the Sacrament of Matrimony put their focus on the gifts the sacrament offers, we pray: ◆ May migrants find a welcoming home, we pray: ◆ May health-care workers find ways to relieve the stress of the sick, we pray: ◆ May the angels lead the dying to paradise, we pray: ◆

Our Father . . .

God of the heavens and earth,
you seek to lead us to the joys of heaven.
Guide your friends
along the path to righteousness
so that we may partner with you
to build a world of justice and freedom
where all are united in your love.
Through Christ our Lord.
Amen.

☩ Taste and see the goodness of the Lord.

Sunday, June 23, 2019

Solemnity of the Most Holy Body and Blood of Christ (Corpus Christi)

✝ You are a priest for ever, in the line of Melchizedek.

Psalm 116

page 413

Reading

Luke 9:12–17

The Twelve approached him and said, "Dismiss the crowd so that they can go to the surrounding villages and farms and find lodging and provisions; for we are in a deserted place here." He said to them, "Give them some food yourselves." They replied, "Five loaves and two fish are all we have, unless we ourselves go and buy food for all these people." Now the men there numbered about five thousand. Then he said to his disciples, "Have them sit down in groups of about fifty." They did so and made them all sit down. Then taking the five loaves and the two fish, and looking up to heaven, he said the blessing over them, broke them, and gave them to the disciples to set before the crowd. They all ate and were satisfied.

Reflection

Jesus looked lovingly on the crowd and provided for them. Through the Eucharist, God continues to offer food for the journey. At Mass, we offer our lives up and Christ nourishes us at the table of the Lord. We then are dismissed to "go and announce the Gospel," making our lives nourishment for others. At times we may feel we are living in a deserted place and barren. But we can always come to the Eucharist to eat and be satisfied. We trust that God's love is bountiful, and we give that love to others.

Prayers

others may be added

To our Lord, who feeds us, we pray:

◆ Lord, hear our prayer.

That members of the priesthood of the baptized be open to sharing their gifts, we pray: ◆ That the ordained may never stifle their spirit of giving, we pray: ◆ That rulers of nations generously preserve the resources of their peoples, we pray: ◆ That those who go hungry be fed, we pray: ◆ That the sick recover, we pray: ◆ That those who have died share in the resurrection, we pray: ◆

Our Father . . .

Lord God,
you gave us your Son
so that we may feed
on the Eucharist,
the everlasting memorial of love
and thanksgiving.
May we always share your gifts
as we seek to renew the face of the earth
to bring about your reign.
Through our Lord Jesus Christ, your Son,
who lives and reigns with you in the unity
of the Holy Spirit,
one God, for ever and ever.
Amen.

✝ You are a priest for ever, in the line of Melchizedek.

Monday, June 24, 2019

Solemnity of the Nativity of St. John the Baptist

† I praise you, for I am wonderfully made.

Psalm 71

page 405

Reading

Luke 1:57–66

When the time arrived for Elizabeth to have her child she gave birth to a son. Her neighbors and relatives heard that the Lord had shown his great mercy toward her, and they rejoiced with her. When they came on the eighth day to circumcise the child, they were going to call him Zechariah after his father, but his mother said in reply, "No. He will be called John." But they answered her, "There is no one among your relatives who has this name." So they made signs, asking his father what he wished him to be called. He asked for a tablet and wrote, "John is his name," and all were amazed.

Reflection

Some families spend months poring over names as they determine what a baby will be called. Other families know that the child will be given a family name. The parents of John the Baptist left the choosing of the name to God. When the angel told the couple that Elizabeth would give birth, she gave them the name John, which means "the Lord has shown favor." The Church celebrates John's birth because he pointed the way to Jesus. All who bear the name Christian are to show others Christ by how they live.

Prayers

others may be added

To our Lord, who has blessed us,
we pray:

◆ Lord, hear our prayer.

That the Church may always be a beacon showing the world Christ, we pray: ◆ That our parish community may be an inspiration of faith and service, we pray: ◆ That efforts to rebuild neighborhoods may thrive, we pray: ◆ That those awaiting a child may experience a safe delivery, we pray: ◆ That mothers who are hospitalized recover quickly, we pray: ◆ That those who have lost a child may be comforted, we pray: ◆

Our Father . . .

O God,
you gave Elizabeth and Zechariah a child
who would point the way to your Son.
May we be as open to your plan
of salvation
as were the parents of John the Baptist.
Teach us to be strong in spirit,
and trusting in your providence
so that we might point others to
your glory.
Through Christ our Lord.
Amen.

† I praise you, for I am wonderfully made.

Tuesday, June 25, 2019
Weekday

✝ The just will live in the presence of the Lord.

Psalm 116 *page 413*

Reading *Genesis 13:2, 5–12*

Abram was very rich in livestock, silver, and gold.

Lot, who went with Abram, also had flocks and herds and tents, so that the land could not support them if they stayed together; their possessions were so great that they could not dwell together. There were quarrels between the herdsmen of Abram's livestock and those of Lot's. . . .

So Abram said to Lot: "Let there be no strife between you and me, or between your herdsmen and mine, for we are kinsmen. Is not the whole land at your disposal? Please separate from me. If you prefer the left, I will go to the right; if you prefer the right, I will go to the left." Lot looked about and saw how well watered the whole Jordan Plain was as far as Zoar, like the LORD's own garden, or like Egypt. (This was before the LORD had destroyed Sodom and Gomorrah.) Lot, therefore, chose for himself the whole Jordan Plain and set out eastward. Thus they separated from each other; Abram stayed in the land of Canaan, while Lot settled among the cities of the Plain, pitching his tents near Sodom.

Reflection

When Abraham heeded the Lord's call to leave the land of his kin, his nephew Lot accompanied him. Now that they were settled, each had considerable animals and herdsmen, so living close together was no longer suitable. Understanding this, Abraham recognized that change was needed. This story reminds us of the value of letting our egos go and giving others an opportunity. Change can be difficult but it is often necessary to allow God's plan to flourish.

Prayers *others may be added*

Confident in God's plan for us,
we pray:

◆ **Lord, hear our prayer.**

That leaders in the Church model discernment as they make decisions, we pray: ◆ That civic leaders serve the common good, we pray: ◆ That children in summer learning programs seek to advance in knowledge, we pray: ◆ That those in treatment may find assistance, we pray: ◆ That the sick recover quickly, we pray: ◆ That those who have died enter eternal glory, we pray: ◆

Our Father . . .

Loving God,
you guide your people
across desert paths and bountiful gardens
to discover your presence among us.
Help us to work toward your good
and lead others to the paths
of righteousness.
Through Christ our Lord.
Amen.

✝ The just will live in the presence of the Lord.

Wednesday, June 26, 2019
Weekday

☩ The Lord remembers his covenant for ever.

Psalm 116
page 413

Reading
Matthew 7:15–20

Jesus said to his disciples: "Beware of false prophets, who come to you in sheep's clothing, but underneath are ravenous wolves. By their fruits you will know them. Do people pick grapes from thornbushes, or figs from thistles? Just so, every good tree bears good fruit, and a rotten tree bears bad fruit. A good tree cannot bear bad fruit, nor can a rotten tree bear good fruit. Every tree that does not bear good fruit will be cut down and thrown into the fire. So by their fruits you will know them."

Reflection

As we consider the people in our lives, sometimes we find it necessary to take stock of the good or the ill that they bear. Periodically, we need to enter into discernment about our lives, considering what has borne good fruit and where our choices are taking us. We may see that pruning is needed in our lives to enrich our relationship with God and family members. Such times of reflection allow us to take a hard look at our lives and reflect on the fruit that we bear. Are people able to see that we are Christians by how we live? Would those we encounter say that we are bearing good fruit or bad? Jesus invites us to listen, look, and review the fruit our relationship with God and others bears.

Prayers
others may be added

Turning to God, we pray:

◆ Lord, hear our prayer.

That leaders in the Church stay mindful of their role to call people to service, we pray: ◆ That the president and Congress discern the ways to help our nation bear good fruit, we pray: ◆ That farmers experience renewal as they care for crops, we pray: ◆ That we each take sufficient time to discern, we pray: ◆ That those making serious healthcare decisions trust in God's ways, we pray: ◆ That angels lead those who have died to paradise, we pray: ◆

Our Father . . .

Ever-faithful God,
you call us into a deeper spirit
to learn your ways of truth.
Guide our vocation
and help us remain true to your ways.
Through Christ our Lord.
Amen.

☩ The Lord remembers his covenant for ever.

Thursday, June 27, 2019
Weekday

☩ Give thanks to the Lord for he is good.

Psalm 116 *page 413*

Reading *Matthew 7:21, 24–27*

Jesus said to his disciples: "Not everyone who says to me, 'Lord, Lord,' will enter the Kingdom of heaven, but only the one who does the will of my Father in heaven.

"Everyone who listens to these words of mine and acts on them will be like a wise man who built his house on rock. The rain fell, the floods came, and the winds blew and buffeted the house. But it did not collapse; it had been set solidly on rock. And everyone who listens to these words of mine but does not act on them will be like a fool who built his house on sand. The rain fell, the floods came, and the winds blew and buffeted the house. And it collapsed and was completely ruined."

Reflection

From recent disasters, we know too well the devastation of flooding. Such damage is similar to what occurs in our lives when we do not listen and act appropriately. When we are deaf to God's voice, we might as well be standing in a poorly built home during turbulent weather. However, when we remain faithful to God's Word and follow his ways, we find that we are on a firm foundation. As long as we rely on God, our lives can withstand the many storms that come our way.

Prayers *others may be added*

Confident in God's power and guidance, we pray:

◆ Merciful Lord, hear our prayer.

That the pope and bishops remain faithful to their calling, we pray: ◆ That civic authorities seek the common good, we pray: ◆ That teachers enjoy their vacations and return in the fall renewed, we pray: ◆ That those on vacation remain safe, we pray: ◆ That the sick be assured of God's healing presence, we pray: ◆ That those who have died be welcomed to the heavenly banquet, we pray: ◆

Our Father . . .

O God of wind and flame,
you guide us with your mighty hand
through the challenges of our daily lives.
Lead us forward to know your ways
and assist us in building your reign
so that all may grow in faith.
Through our Lord Jesus Christ, your Son,
who lives and reigns with you in the unity
of the Holy Spirit,
one God, for ever and ever.
Amen.

☩ Give thanks to the Lord for he is good.

Friday, June 28, 2019

Solemnity of the Most Sacred Heart of Jesus

✝ The Lord is my shepherd;
there is nothing I shall want.

Psalm 23

page 398

Reading

Luke 15:3–7

[Jesus said:]
"What man among you having a hundred sheep and losing one of them would not leave the ninety-nine in the desert and go after the lost one until he finds it? And when he does find it, he sets it on his shoulders with great joy and, upon his arrival home, he calls together his friends and neighbors and says to them, 'Rejoice with me because I have found my lost sheep.' I tell you, in just the same way there will be more joy in heaven over one sinner who repents than over ninety-nine righteous people who have no need of repentance."

Reflection

This reading portrays a compassionate shepherd who is so aware of a lost sheep that he knows when one among a hundred is missing. Not only does the shepherd set aside everything to look for the sheep but rejoices when it is found. God, too, is aware when we are lost and seeks us. Though ninety-nine in our company may be steadfast in the faith, God is attentive to the one who has strayed. We, too, need to be open to and caring of those who lose their way.

Prayers

others may be added

Turning to our compassionate God,
we pray:

◆ Merciful Lord, hear our prayer.

For the Church, that she always seek to act with mercy and compassion, we pray: ◆ For world leaders, that they work for peace, we pray: ◆ For those who work the land, we pray: ◆ For dialogue among Christians, Muslims, and Jews, we pray: ◆ For the sick to recover, we pray: ◆ For those who have died, that they find rest in God's mercy, we pray: ◆

Our Father . . .

Gentle Shepherd, loving God,
you call us to seek you
with a sincere heart.
Help us to show your face
to those who are searching
for love and forgiveness.
Through Christ our Lord.
Amen.

✝ The Lord is my shepherd; there is nothing I shall want.

Saturday, June 29, 2019

Solemnity of Sts. Peter and Paul, Apostles

✝ The angel of the Lord will rescue those who fear the Lord.

Psalm 118

page 414

Reading

Matthew 16:13–19

When Jesus went into the region of Caesarea Philippi he asked his disciples, "Who do people say that the Son of Man is?" They replied, "Some say John the Baptist, others Elijah, still others Jeremiah or one of the prophets." He said to them, "But who do you say that I am?" Simon Peter said in reply, "You are the Christ, the Son of the living God." Jesus said to him in reply, "Blessed are you, Simon son of Jonah. For flesh and blood has not revealed this to you, but my heavenly Father. And so I say to you, you are Peter, and upon this rock I will build my Church, and the gates of the netherworld shall not prevail against it. I will give you the keys to the Kingdom of heaven. Whatever you bind on earth shall be bound in heaven; and whatever you loose on earth shall be loosed in heaven."

Reflection

Caesarea Philippi was known for its monuments to many gods. This was a likely place, then, for Jesus to ask the disciples who they believed him to be, for some people thought Jesus to be a certain god. We are invited also to contemplate the question. Imagine that Jesus asks, "Who do you say that I am?" Christ counted on Peter and Paul to lead the Church. We continue their work of spreading the Good News. To do so, we should know who Christ is in our lives.

Prayers

others may be added

Trusting in the God who saves,
we pray:

◆ **Lord, hear our prayer.**

That our bishops help us emulate their strong leadership, we pray: ◆ That all who serve in government roles may seek to serve the least, we pray: ◆ That our parish may grow in service to build God's reign, we pray: ◆ That those who desire to become Catholic may be strengthened in their resolve, we pray: ◆ That the sick may be made whole, we pray: ◆ That Sts. Peter and Paul may welcome those who have died to the heavenly banquet, we pray: ◆

Our Father . . .

Almighty God,
you gave Sts. Peter and Paul
a strong faith to witness to you.
Grant us the courage
to follow their example
and carry on their witness.
Guide our efforts in acclaiming
Jesus Christ
as the Son of the living God.
Through Christ our Lord.
Amen.

✝ The angel of the Lord will rescue those who fear the Lord.

Sunday, June 30, 2019

Thirteenth Sunday in Ordinary Time

✝ *You are my inheritance, O Lord.*

Psalm 16

page 396

Reading

Luke 9:51–62

When the days for Jesus' being taken up were fulfilled, he resolutely determined to journey to Jerusalem, and he sent messengers ahead of him. On the way they entered a Samaritan village to prepare for his reception there, but they would not welcome him because the destination of his journey was Jerusalem. When the disciples James and John saw this they asked, "Lord, do you want us to call down fire from heaven to consume them?" Jesus turned and rebuked them, and they journeyed to another village.

As they were proceeding on their journey someone said to him, "I will follow you wherever you go." Jesus answered him, "Foxes have dens and birds of the sky have nests, but the Son of Man has nowhere to rest his head."

And to another he said, "Follow me." But he replied, "Lord, let me go first and bury my father." But he answered him, "Let the dead bury their dead. But you, go and proclaim the kingdom of God." And another said, "I will follow you, Lord, but first let me say farewell to my family at home." To him Jesus said, "No one who sets a hand to the plow and looks to what was left behind is fit for the kingdom of God."

Reflection

As Jesus calls people, we hear legitimate reasons for putting off the call to follow. Jesus replies that another can bury the dead or bid farewell. What keeps you from following Christ? Are there things that you need to release or allow to die so that you may freely follow Christ? If anger or past hurts are holding you back, it may be time to say goodbye to them and move on. Today Jesus may be urging you not to look back.

Prayers

others may be added

Confident that God is leading us,
we pray:

◆ Lord, hear our prayer.

For Church leaders, that they may possess courage and strength to move forward, we pray: ◆ For legislators, that they act boldly for the good of the nation, we pray: ◆ For the health of doctors and nurses, we pray: ◆ For those preparing to travel, that their journeys be safe, we pray: ◆ For the sick, we pray: ◆ For the grieving, that they be comforted, we pray: ◆

Our Father . . .

Ever-faithful God,
you lead us along our journey.
Renew our minds and hearts
so that we may follow you more closely.
Grant us the courage to release past hurts
and take on our call as disciples
to bring your Good News to all we meet.
Through Christ our Lord.
Amen.

✝ *You are my inheritance, O Lord.*

Monday, July 1, 2019
Memorial of St. Junípero Serra, Priest

✝ The Lord is kind and merciful.

Psalm 16
page 396

Reading
Matthew 8:18–22

When Jesus saw a crowd around him, he gave orders to cross to the other shore. A scribe approached and said to him, "Teacher, I will follow you wherever you go." Jesus answered him, "Foxes have dens and birds of the sky have nests, but the Son of Man has nowhere to rest his head." Another of his disciples said to him, "Lord, let me go first and bury my father." But Jesus answered him, "Follow me, and let the dead bury their dead."

Reflection
Imagine Jesus giving you the order "to cross to the other shore." Following this command could get you to a new place in your life. Sometimes we feel unable to move forward, but Christ's words can help us see that we can redirect our lives on another path. Is Christ calling you to step forth in courage to follow him? Our ego and sometimes our plans need to be buried as we seek to go where Christ leads.

Prayers
others may be added

Trusting in God's path for us, we pray:

◆ Lord, hear our prayer.

For those who lead ministries in the Church, that they may be open to new directions, we pray: ◆ For the citizens of Canada, as they celebrate their national holiday, we pray: ◆ For missionaries who assist in the efforts of the Gospel, we pray: ◆ For vocations to Franciscan orders, we pray: ◆ For healing among races, especially Native American peoples, we pray: ◆ For those who have died, we pray: ◆

Our Father . . .

Good and gracious God,
you call us to follow you more intently.
Grant us courage
to do your will
and be open to new efforts
of walking in the steps of the Gospel.
Through Christ our Lord.
Amen.

✝ The Lord is kind and merciful.

Tuesday, July 2, 2019
Weekday

✝ O Lord, your mercy is before my eyes.

Psalm 89
page 407

Reading
Matthew 8:23–27

As Jesus got into a boat, his disciples followed him. Suddenly a violent storm came up on the sea, so that the boat was being swamped by waves; but he was asleep. They came and woke him, saying, "Lord, save us! We are perishing!" He said to them, "Why are you terrified, O you of little faith?" Then he got up, rebuked the winds and the sea, and there was great calm. The men were amazed and said, "What sort of man is this, whom even the winds and the sea obey?"

Reflection
"Why are you terrified, O you of little faith?" How often could Jesus say these words to us? When storms beset our lives, we might call out to be saved as though we are about to perish. God is ready to calm the rough spots in our lives if we trust him enough to seek his help. What a comfort this is to know that he can rebuke not only the wind and sea but whatever troubles us.

Prayers
others may be added

To the Lord who calms the seas, we pray:

◆ Lord, hear our prayer.

For those who suffer from natural disasters, especially flooding and tornadoes, we pray: ◆ For our community, that it be open to the work of God in our midst, we pray: ◆ For our bishops, that they assure and gently lead their faithful, we pray: ◆ For those who suffer from mental illness, we pray: ◆ For those awaiting transplants, we pray: ◆ For the grieving, that they be comforted, we pray: ◆

Our Father . . .

God of the storms and calm,
you offer us assurance
when we are most troubled.
Renew our inner most being
so that we may bring your concern
to all in need.
Through Christ our Lord.
Amen.

✝ O Lord, your mercy is before my eyes.

Wednesday, July 3, 2019

Feast of St. Thomas, Apostle

✝ Go out to all the world and tell the Good News.

Psalm 117 *page 413*

Reading *John 20:24–29*

Thomas, called Didymus, one of the Twelve, was not with them when Jesus came. So the other disciples said to him, "We have seen the Lord." But Thomas said to them, "Unless I see the mark of the nails in his hands and put my finger into the nailmarks and put my hand into his side, I will not believe." Now a week later his disciples were again inside and Thomas was with them. Jesus came, although the doors were locked, and stood in their midst and said, "Peace be with you." Then he said to Thomas, "Put your finger here and see my hands, and bring your hand and put it into my side, and do not be unbelieving, but believe." Thomas answered and said to him, "My Lord and my God!" Jesus said to him, "Have you come to believe because you have seen me? Blessed are those who have not seen and have believed."

Reflection

I have often wondered what it would have been like to be in Thomas' shoes during the passion, death, and Resurrection of Christ. It is hard to imagine what he was thinking, feeling, and fearing, as Jesus carried the cross and then was hanged. Yet, we know that Thomas became a true believer and fully committed himself to going to the ends of the earth to share the Gospel. This disciple helps us feel the peace Christ offers and go forward to live the faith. He came to believe because of what he saw. Many came to believe through Thomas' faith.

Prayers *others may be added*

Trusting in the Lord's plan, we pray:

◆ **Lord, hear our prayer.**

For missionaries, that their teaching and preaching be respectful of other cultures, we pray: ◆ For civic leaders, that they seek the common good, we pray: ◆ For engineers, that they be inspired to design creatively, we pray: ◆ For vocations to serve the Church, we pray: ◆ For those awaiting a transplant, that they be provided with patience, we pray: ◆ For those who have died, we pray: ◆

Our Father . . .

Loving God,
you offer us peace
even when we struggle with faith.
May we acknowledge and worship you
as the true Lord.
Grant us the will to serve you
and proclaim your mighty deeds
to all we meet.
Through Christ our Lord.
Amen.

✝ Go out to all the world and tell the Good News.

Thursday, July 4, 2019
Weekday

☩ I will walk in the presence of the Lord, in the land of the living.

Psalm 16 *page 396*

Reading *Matthew 9:1–8*

After entering a boat, Jesus made the crossing, and came into his own town. And there people brought to him a paralytic lying on a stretcher. When Jesus saw their faith, he said to the paralytic, "Courage, child, your sins are forgiven." At that, some of the scribes said to themselves, "This man is blaspheming." Jesus knew what they were thinking, and said, "Why do you harbor evil thoughts? Which is easier, to say, 'Your sins are forgiven,' or to say, 'Rise and walk'? But that you may know that the Son of Man has authority on earth to forgive sins"—he then said to the paralytic, "Rise, pick up your stretcher, and go home." He rose and went home. When the crowds saw this they were struck with awe and glorified God who had given such authority to men.

Reflection

Some of the scribes in this Gospel were so distracted by the law that they were unable to witness the miracles taking place before them. If we, too, allow rules to take the place of healing acts, we would be putting up roadblocks to the Good News. Take the opportunity today to see how you can glorify God rather than criticize. You may be opening up ways for God to work through you.

Prayers *others may be added*

To our Lord who heals, we pray:

◆ Lord, hear our prayer.

For leaders in the Church, that they let the joy of the Gospel shine through them, we pray: ◆ For civic authorities to glorify God in their deeds, we pray: ◆ For citizens of our nation, that they grow in kindness and interest in liberties for all, we pray: ◆ For healing among factions in our country, we pray: ◆ For those seeking miracles to cure the sick, we pray: ◆ For those who died in service to our country, we pray: ◆

Our Father . . .

God of all peoples and nations,
you recognize the needs of our world.
Teach us to be open to your ways
so that your good may be the authority
we seek.
Through Christ our Lord.
Amen.

☩ I will walk in the presence of the Lord, in the land of the living.

Friday, July 5, 2019

Optional Memorial of St. Anthony Zaccaria, Priest

☩ Give thanks to the Lord, for he is good.

Psalm 89

page 407

Reading

Matthew 9:9–13

As Jesus passed by, he saw a man named Matthew sitting at the customs post. He said to him, "Follow me." And he got up and followed him. While he was at table in his house, many tax collectors and sinners came and sat with Jesus and his disciples. The Pharisees saw this and said to his disciples, "Why does your teacher eat with tax collectors and sinners?" He heard this and said, "Those who are well do not need a physician, but the sick do. Go and learn the meaning of the words, / *I desire mercy, not sacrifice.* / I did not come to call the righteous but sinners."

Reflection

Matthew, as well as Jesus' other disciples, must have been taken aback when Jesus told them to beware of men who would hand them over to the courts. Still, Jesus told his followers that the Spirit would speak through them and that those who endured would be saved. Do you ever wonder what you have gotten into by being a Christian? We have a choice to follow Christ by showing mercy and goodness. Sometimes we will be castigated for following the Lord. Always, we are assured that God will be with us when we follow his ways. How will you show Christ to others today?

Prayers

others may be added

Following the Lord more intently,
we pray:

◆ Lord, hear us.

For physicians under the patronage of St. Anthony Zaccaria, we pray: ◆ For vocations to the Barnabites, founded by St. Anthony, we pray: ◆ For safety for all who are traveling on vacation, we pray: ◆ For farmers, that they may reap a good harvest, we pray: ◆ For the healing of the sick, we pray: ◆ For those who have died, that they be welcomed to enter eternal life, we pray: ◆

Our Father . . .

Loving God,
you call us to serve without honor.
Grant that we may remain faithful
to you and endure through trials
and persecution
so that we rejoice at the heavenly banquet
one day.
Through our Lord Jesus Christ, your Son,
who lives and reigns with you in the unity
of the Holy Spirit,
one God, for ever and ever.
Amen.

☩ Give thanks to the Lord, for he is good.

Saturday, July 6, 2019

Optional Memorial of St. Maria Goretti, Virgin and Martyr

☩ Praise the Lord for the Lord is good!

Psalm 16

page 396

Reading

Matthew 9:14–17

The disciples of John approached Jesus and said, "Why do we and the Pharisees fast much, but your disciples do not fast?" Jesus answered them, "Can the wedding guests mourn as long as the bridegroom is with them? The days will come when the bridegroom is taken away from them, and then they will fast. No one patches an old cloak with a piece of unshrunken cloth, for its fullness pulls away from the cloak and the tear gets worse. People do not put new wine into old wineskins. Otherwise the skins burst, the wine spills out, and the skins are ruined. Rather, they pour new wine into fresh wineskins, and both are preserved."

Reflection

Jesus does not seem to give a direct answer to John's disciples. Those disciples may have fasted, as was the custom as signs of mourning and in repentance. Jesus' disciples, though, had reason to rejoice while in his presence. His death and their mourning would come soon enough. Jesus offered new life to believers. His disciples, then, had no need to practice old ways. May we know when to fast and when to rejoice.

Prayers

others may be added

In faith and trust, we pray:

◆ Lord, hear us.

For efforts of renewal in the Church, we pray: ◆ For those who, like St. Maria Goretti, suffer for their faith, we pray: ◆ For legislators, that they seek aid for the marginalized, we pray: ◆ For those who have not been born, that they be protected, we pray: ◆ For all awaiting surgery, we pray: ◆ For the souls in purgatory, we pray: ◆

Our Father . . .

Life-giving God,
you show us new ways
and call us to feast
on the richness of life in you.
Grant that we, your disciples,
may be strengthened in our faith
so that we might show your truth
to all your people.
Through Christ our Lord.
Amen.

☩ Praise the Lord for the Lord is good!

Sunday, July 7, 2019

Fourteenth Sunday in Ordinary Time

✝ Let all the earth cry out to God with joy.

Psalm 66

page 403

Reading

Luke 10:1–9

The Lord appointed seventy-two others whom he sent ahead of him in pairs to every town and place he intended to visit. He said to them, "The harvest is abundant but the laborers are few; so ask the master of the harvest to send out laborers for his harvest. Go on your way; behold, I am sending you like lambs among wolves. Carry no money bag, no sack, no sandals; and greet no one along the way. Into whatever house you enter, first say, 'Peace to this household.' If a peaceful person lives there, your peace will rest on him; but if not, it will return to you. Stay in the same house and eat and drink what is offered to you, for the laborer deserves his pay. Do not move about from one house to another. Whatever town you enter and they welcome you, eat what is set before you, cure the sick in it and say to them, 'The Kingdom of God is at hand for you.'"

Reflection

Going with one other person to another city to preach the Gospel may not be our vocation. However, we are doing God's work when we wish peace to those we meet. No matter the circumstance or place, a Christian is to act as an instrument of peace. The Eucharist empowers us to bring Christ's peace to others. As we witness Christ in our lives, may we emanate the peace that we have received.

Prayers

others may be added

Give glory to God, we pray:

◆ Lord, hear us.

That people of all nations may know religious freedom, we pray: ◆ That bishops may act with zeal as they spread the Good News in their dioceses, we pray: ◆ That those persecuted for the faith may stand courageous, we pray: ◆ That travelers may arrive safely at their destination, we pray: ◆ That the sick may recover, we pray: ◆ That those who have lived their faith may enter into paradise, we pray: ◆

Our Father . . .

O God,
you give us all we need
to serve the Gospel.
Grant us peace and strength,
that we may live and witness to your Son,
whose Cross is our glory and salvation.
May we embrace our cross
and proclaim to the ends of the earth
your saving power.
Through our Lord Jesus Christ, your Son,
who lives and reigns with you in the unity
of the Holy Spirit,
one God, for ever and ever.
Amen.

✝ Let all the earth cry out to God with joy.

Monday, July 8, 2019
Weekday

✝ In you, my God, I place my trust.

Psalm 66
page 403

Reading
Matthew 9:18–22

While Jesus was speaking, an official came forward, knelt down before him, and said, "My daughter has just died. But come, lay your hand on her, and she will live." Jesus rose and followed him, and so did his disciples. A woman suffering hemorrhages for twelve years came up behind him and touched the tassel on his cloak. She said to herself, "If only I can touch his cloak, I shall be cured." Jesus turned around and saw her, and said, "Courage, daughter! Your faith has saved you." And from that hour the woman was cured.

Reflection

Both the official and the woman needed courage to cross social barriers to approach Jesus for healing. It must not have been easy for a Roman soldier to ask Jesus to heal his child. The woman who hemorrhaged should not have been around Jesus; yet she was touching his garment. The soldier's and the woman's need and faith were great enough that they presented themselves to Jesus. May we never fear requesting the Lord's help and always give gratitude to God.

Prayers
others may be added

With great courage, we pray:

◆ Lord, hear our prayer.

That those with incurable diseases find healing, we pray: ◆ That those awaiting transplants receive them, we pray: ◆ That nurses and doctors trust that their touch will heal, we pray: ◆ That an increasing number of people seek to serve others through the vocation of health care, we pray: ◆ That those who care for the sick find strength, we pray: ◆ That those who have died find eternal rest, we pray: ◆

Our Father . . .

O Lord,
you heed our calls for healing.
Grant that in times of doubt,
we have strength and courage.
Renew the life-giving presence
of wholeness and healing
so that we may all witness faith
and strengthen the Body of Christ.
Through Christ our Lord.
Amen.

✝ In you, my God, I place my trust.

Tuesday, July 9, 2019

Optional Memorial of St. Augustine Zhao Rong, Priest, and Companions, Martyrs

✝ In justice, I shall behold your face, O God.

Psalm 66

page 403

Reading

Matthew 9:35–38

Jesus went around to all the towns and villages, teaching in their synagogues, proclaiming the Gospel of the Kingdom, and curing every disease and illness. At the sight of the crowds, his heart was moved with pity for them because they were troubled and abandoned, like sheep without a shepherd. Then he said to his disciples, "The harvest is abundant but the laborers are few; so ask the master of the harvest to send out laborers for his harvest."

Reflection

St. Augustine Zhao Rong and the 119 other martyrs that Pope John Paul II canonized on October 1, 2000, labored in the vineyard knowing that death could be a consequence of their ministry. St. Augustine had been a soldier in China, but having witnessed the patience of a bishop who was martyred, he became a Catholic, entered the seminary and was ordained a priest. He died in 1815. The eighty-six companions from China and thirty-three from other countries were both lay people and religious. They were martyred between 1648 and 1930. Each heeded the call to be a laborer to bring Christ's healing presence.

Prayers

others may be added

In communion with the saints,
we pray:

◆ Lord, hear our prayer.

That the Church continue her efforts of evangelization, we pray: ◆ That world leaders work that all may worship freely, we pray: ◆ That all may have access to clean water, we pray: ◆ That the Church in China be strengthened, we pray: ◆ That the ill find healing, we pray: ◆ That those who have died be welcomed into the kingdom, we pray: ◆

Our Father . . .

O God,
you provided the saints and martyrs
with the fortitude to spread your Word
in dangerous circumstances.
Grant that we may enthusiastically labor
in your vineyard,
serving you and others.
Through Christ our Lord.
Amen.

✝ In justice, I shall behold your face, O God.

Wednesday, July 10, 2019
Weekday

☩ Let your mercy be on us, O God,
as we place our trust in you.

Psalm 145 *page 421*

Reading *Matthew 10:1, 5–7*

Jesus summoned his Twelve disciples and gave them authority over unclean spirits to drive them out and to cure every disease and every illness. . . .

Jesus sent out these Twelve after instructing them thus, "Do not go into pagan territory or enter a Samaritan town. Go rather to the lost sheep of the house of Israel. As you go, make this proclamation: 'The Kingdom of heaven is at hand.'"

Reflection

Just as Jesus summoned the Twelve, God calls each Christian. With our Baptism, we became part of the Body of Christ and took on the responsibility of priest, prophet, and king. Our vocation as a Christian brings us to tell others of how God has worked in our lives. Just as these disciples did not go to pagan territories or Samaritan towns, our evangelization is with those we encounter each day.

Prayers *others may be added*

To our Lord, who summons us,
we pray:

◆ Lord, hear our prayer.

That men and women serve the Church in the consecrated life, we pray: ◆ That religious women and men be strengthened in their vocation, we pray: ◆ That Bible camps this summer help God's Word come alive in youngsters, we pray: ◆ That renewable energy be developed quickly, we pray: ◆ That the sick recover, we pray: ◆ That those we mourn enter God's glory, we pray: ◆

Our Father . . .

Lord God,
you have called us to follow you
and to share our gifts and talents.
Guide our efforts to bring a healing touch
to family, friends, and coworkers.
Through our Lord Jesus Christ, your Son,
who lives and reigns with you in the unity
of the Holy Spirit,
one God, for ever and ever.
Amen.

☩ Let your mercy be on us, O God,
as we place our trust in you.

Thursday, July 11, 2019
Memorial of St. Benedict, Abbot

✝ Remember the marvels the Lord has done.

Psalm 66

page 403

Reading

Matthew 10:7–13

Jesus said to his Apostles: "As you go, make this proclamation: 'The Kingdom of heaven is at hand.' Cure the sick, raise the dead, cleanse the lepers, drive out demons. Without cost you have received; without cost you are to give. Do not take gold or silver or copper for your belts; no sack for the journey, or a second tunic, or sandals, or walking stick. The laborer deserves his keep. Whatever town or village you enter, look for a worthy person in it, and stay there until you leave. As you enter a house, wish it peace. If the house is worthy, let your peace come upon it; if not, let your peace return to you."

Reflection

Anyone who has stayed at a Benedictine guest house would have experienced the hospitality for which the order is known. Benedictines are especially attentive to welcoming people as they would Christ. The saint we honor today provided guidance for monastics in the Rule of St. Benedict. In directing how to live the monastic life, Benedict connected work and prayer, noting that work should be done alongside contemplation. We, too, can draw from the Rule, bringing peace to those we meet.

Prayers

others may be added

To our Lord, who calls us to comfort one another, we pray:

◆ Lord, hear our prayer.

That the Church continue to reach out in hospitality, we pray: ◆ That world leaders engage in peace talks where needed, we pray: ◆ That more men and women answer the call to serve as Benedictines, we pray: ◆ That workers in the food industry stay safe as they care for others, we pray: ◆ That the sick be made whole, we pray: ◆ That those who have died feast at the banquet table of heaven, we pray: ◆

Our Father . . .

Loving God,
you gave us St. Benedict
as a witness of your love.
Teach us to be generous
to all in need of hospitality.
Through the inspiration of St. Benedict,
may we guide others to know
the healing power of your compassion.
Through Christ our Lord.
Amen.

✝ Remember the marvels the Lord has done.

Friday, July 12, 2019
Weekday

✝ The salvation of the just comes from God.

Psalm 66

page 403

Reading

Matthew 10:17–22

[Jesus said to his disciples,] "Beware of men, for they will hand you over to the courts and scourge you in their synagogues, and you will be led before governors and kings for my sake as a witness before them and the pagans. When they hand you over, do not worry about how you are to speak or what you are to say. You will be given at that moment what you are to say. For it will not be you who speak but the Spirit of your Father speaking through you. Brother will hand over brother to death, and the father his child; children will rise up against parents and have them put to death. You will be hated by all because of my name, but whoever endures to the end will be saved."

Reflection

Jesus is clear on the risks of living the faith. However, he also provides reassurance that those challenged because of their beliefs will be protected. When called upon to speak, the Spirit will speak for them. This passage points out the need to put trust in God alone. A brother, father, or child may fail an individual. God, however, will be there to accompany followers during trials and will save those who cling to the faith.

Prayers

others may be added

Confident in the Lord's ways, we pray:

◆ Lord, hear our prayer.

That the Church provide hope to all who look to her, we pray: ◆ That witnesses to the faith move civic authorities to work for justice for all, we pray: ◆ That those who suffer for the faith may be strengthened, we pray: ◆ That we grow in our trust of God, we pray: ◆ That the sick feel the support of our prayers, we pray: ◆ That those who have died be welcomed into the company of the martyrs, we pray: ◆

Our Father . . .

O God,
you protect all who call out to you.
May we continue to place our trust
in you.
Grant that in times of distress,
we look to you to calm our fears.
Through our Lord Jesus Christ, your Son,
who lives and reigns with you in the unity
of the Holy Spirit,
one God, for ever and ever.
Amen.

✝ The salvation of the just comes from God.

Saturday, July 13, 2019
Optional Memorial of St. Henry

✝ Be glad you lowly ones; may your hearts be glad.

Psalm 145 *page 421*

Reading *Matthew 10:24–29*

Jesus said to his Apostles: "No disciple is above his teacher, no slave above his master. It is enough for the disciple that he become like his teacher, for the slave that he become like his master. If they have called the master of the house Beelzebul, how much more those of his household!

"Therefore do not be afraid of them. Nothing is concealed that will not be revealed, nor secret that will not be known. What I say to you in the darkness, speak in the light; what you hear whispered, proclaim on the housetops. And do not be afraid of those who kill the body but cannot kill the soul; rather, be afraid of the one who can destroy both soul and body in Gehenna. Are not two sparrows sold for a small coin? Yet not one of them falls to the ground without your Father's knowledge."

Reflection

Jesus continues to teach his followers not to allow fear to deter them from speaking their faith. He directs them to "speak in the light" and "proclaim on the housetops" what he tells them. They are not to worry that they will be in danger because no one can harm their soul. How do you live out your trust in the Lord?

Prayers *others may be added*

To our compassionate Lord, we pray:

◆ Lord, hear our prayer.

That leaders in the Church grow in a humble spirit, we pray: ◆ That, through the intercession of St. Henry, couples who long for a child may conceive, we pray: ◆ That the faithful will take to heart their duty to be good stewards, we pray: ◆ That those who protect us may remain free from harm, we pray: ◆ That the suffering may be given relief, we pray: ◆ That those who have died rest forever in hope and glory, we pray: ◆

Our Father . . .

Almighty God,
you call us to be of true service.
Guide our actions
to boldly proclaim your glory
not only from housetops,
but through the joy of our lives.
Through Christ our Lord.
Amen.

✝ Be glad you lowly ones; may your hearts be glad.

Sunday, July 14, 2019
Fifteenth Sunday in Ordinary Time

☩ The precepts of the Lord give joy to the heart.

Psalm 19 *page 397*

Reading *Luke 10:30–35*

[Jesus said:] "A man fell victim to robbers as he went down from Jerusalem to Jericho. They stripped and beat him and went off leaving him half-dead. A priest happened to be going down that road, but when he saw him, he passed by on the opposite side. Likewise a Levite came to the place, and when he saw him, he passed by on the opposite side. But a Samaritan traveler who came upon him was moved with compassion at the sight. He approached the victim, poured oil and wine over his wounds and bandaged them. Then he lifted him up on his own animal, took him to an inn, and cared for him. The next day he took out two silver coins and gave them to the innkeeper with the instruction, 'Take care of him. If you spend more than what I have given you, I shall repay you on my way back.' "

Reflection

For centuries, societies have tried to answer the question "Who is my neighbor?" Today's reading depicts a person who offers mercy to a stranger in answer to this question. As a Christian, our response to another should be to provide mercy. That is especially true when the person cannot reciprocate. Today's Gospel account portrays mercy well since it personifies not only a good deed but how another is acknowledged and accorded dignity. Whom do you encounter who would be grateful for your recognition?

Prayers *others may be added*

To our merciful Father, we pray:

◆ Hear us, O Lord.

May the Church be a place of mercy and welcome, we pray: ◆ May rulers govern with justice, we pray: ◆ May the intercession of St. Kateri Tekakwitha bring reconciliation among tribes and nations, we pray: ◆ May we forgive those who wrong us, we pray: ◆ May the sick recover, we pray: ◆ May the doors of eternity be open to all who have died, we pray: ◆

Our Father . . .

Merciful God,
you teach us compassion and care
for all your people.
Help us to be open to console
those burdened and in strife
so that all may come to know your love.
Through Christ our Lord.
Amen.

☩ The precepts of the Lord give joy to the heart.

Monday, July 15, 2019

Memorial of St. Bonaventure,
Bishop and Doctor of the Church

✝ Our help is in the name of the Lord.

Psalm 119

page 414

Reading

Matthew 10:34–36

Jesus said to his Apostles: "Do not think that I have come to bring peace upon the earth. I have come to bring not peace but the sword. For I have come to set a man against his father, a daughter against her mother, and a daughter-in-law against her mother-in-law; and one's enemies will be those of his household."

Reflection

Jesus explains that one's faith can endanger relationships. Our peace is found in Christ, when he is foremost in our lives. However, that does not mean that family and friends will support our faith. Sometimes issues of faith will draw us away from our loved ones. We need to be aware that our comfort and refuge is in God.

Prayers

others may be added

To God, our refuge, we pray:

◆ **Lord, hear our prayer.**

May the Church lead with courage, we pray: ◆ May missionaries rely on God for strength, we pray: ◆ May global initiatives for safe water be encouraged, we pray: ◆ May St. Bonaventure continue to inspire theologians, we pray: ◆ May those awaiting transplants be provided patience, we pray: ◆ May eternal happiness come to the deceased, we pray: ◆

Our Father . . .

Lord God,
you are always with us on our journey.
Grant that your earthly family
be united in a bond of love.
May we strive to emulate your love
during our most difficult moments
when those close to us challenge
our faith.
Through our Lord Jesus Christ, your Son,
who lives and reigns with you in the unity
of the Holy Spirit,
one God, for ever and ever.
Amen.

✝ Our help is in the name of the Lord.

Tuesday, July 16, 2019

Optional Memorial of Our Lady of Mount Carmel

✝ Turn to the Lord in your need, and you will live.

Canticle of Mary *page 423*

Reading *Matthew 12:46–50*

While Jesus was speaking to the crowds, his mother and his brothers appeared outside, wishing to speak with him. Someone told him, "Your mother and your brothers are standing outside, asking to speak with you." But he said in reply to the one who told him, "Who is my mother? Who are my brothers?" And stretching out his hand toward his disciples, he said, "Here are my mother and my brothers. For whoever does the will of my heavenly Father is my brother, and sister, and mother."

Reflection

At Mount Carmel, the prophet Elijah listened for God in the wind, an earthquake, and fire. Finally, he heard him in the silence. Centuries later, a group of hermits on Mount Carmel built and dedicated a chapel to the Blessed Virgin Mary. They prayed for her protection and her help in contemplative prayer. Today, people across the world wear the scapular of Our Lady of Mount Carmel as a sign of a special relationship with her and their interest in imitating her. Mary, who is regarded as the first disciple, is a model of a person who does the will of God.

Prayers *others may be added*

With Mary, we bring our intentions to God:

◆ Lord, hear our prayer.

May peace reign in the Holy Land, we pray: ◆ May vocations to the Carmelite orders increase, we pray: ◆ May those seeking meaningful employment find it quickly, we pray: ◆ May the faithful be drawn to Bible studies in parishes, we pray: ◆ May cures be found for cancer and other diseases, we pray: ◆ May those who have died be granted eternal life, we pray: ◆

Our Father . . .

O God,
through Our Lady of Mount Carmel,
you inspire us to seek to do your will
and to contemplate your Word.
May we continue to witness to you
through humble acts of love.
Through Christ our Lord.
Amen.

✝ Turn to the Lord in your need, and you will live.

Wednesday, July 17, 2019
Weekday

✝ The Lord is kind and merciful.

Psalm 103
page 411

Reading
Matthew 11:25–27

At that time Jesus exclaimed: "I give praise to you, Father, Lord of heaven and earth, for although you have hidden these things from the wise and the learned you have revealed them to the childlike. Yes, Father, such has been your gracious will. All things have been handed over to me by my Father. No one knows the Son except the Father, and no one knows the Father except the Son and anyone to whom the Son wishes to reveal him."

Reflection
Today we hear Jesus lift his voice in praise of the Father. He gives thanks that the Lord has revealed his ways to the childlike and then acknowledges that only the Father knows him. Consider your prayer life. How often do you spend time praising God for what you have been given? Do you ever think that God knows you better than anyone, even those closest to you? We can model our prayer after Jesus'.

Prayers
others may be added

To our Lord, who is always open to us, we pray:

◆ Lord, hear our prayer.

May those who suffer the effects of natural disaster know of our support, we pray: ◆ May the desperate and hurting find comfort and strength, we pray: ◆ May those who suffer from depression find solace, we pray: ◆ May those hoping to conceive a child experience good news, we pray: ◆ May the sick be healed, we pray: ◆ May those who have died be received into heaven, we pray: ◆

Our Father . . .

Loving God,
you call us into an intimate relationship
of prayer and communication.
Teach us to be patient, open,
and courageous.
Through our lives of service and prayer,
may we come to know you intimately.
Through Christ our Lord.
Amen.

✝ The Lord is kind and merciful.

Thursday, July 18, 2019
Optional Memorial of St. Camillus de Lellis, Priest

✝ The Lord remembers his covenant for ever.

Psalm 103

page 411

Reading

Matthew 11:28–30

Jesus said to the crowds: "Come to me, all you who labor and are burdened, and I will give you rest. Take my yoke upon you and learn from me, for I am meek and humble of heart; and you will find rest for yourselves. For my yoke is easy, and my burden light."

Reflection

Some of us are weary from physical labor and others from the stress of a demanding work schedule or trying to meet the needs of both children and grandparents. Taking refuge in the Lord is welcome. St. Camillus followed the Lord's example by founding an order to care for the sick and bring Christ's healing presence to others. As we approach others with a humble spirit, may we be mindful of reaching out with a caring touch.

Prayers

others may be added

To Christ who heals us, we pray:

◆ Lord, hear our prayer.

May the Church offer hope to those in need of healing, we pray: ◆ May workers in health care be strengthened in their vocation, we pray: ◆ May scientists receive support in their efforts to find cures for diseases, we pray: ◆ May training support those studying to be healthcare professionals, we pray: ◆ May those awaiting transplants see reason to be patient, we pray: ◆ May all souls find heavenly comfort, we pray: ◆

Our Father . . .

Gracious God and healer,
you offer us a light burden
if only we trust in you.
Grant that we may lift the burdens
from those who are sick and suffering
so that they may feel your presence.
Through Christ our Lord.
Amen.

✝ The Lord remembers his covenant for ever.

Friday, July 19, 2019
Weekday

☩ I will take the cup of salvation and call on the name of the Lord.

Psalm 116

page 413

Reading

Matthew 12:1–8

Jesus was going through a field of grain on the sabbath. His disciples were hungry and began to pick the heads of grain and eat them. When the Pharisees saw this, they said to him, "See, your disciples are doing what is unlawful to do on the sabbath." He said to them, "Have you not read what David did when he and his companions were hungry, how he went into the house of God and ate the bread of offering, which neither he nor his companions but only the priests could lawfully eat? Or have you not read in the law that on the sabbath the priests serving in the temple violate the sabbath and are innocent? I say to you, something greater than the temple is here. If you knew what this meant, *I desire mercy, not sacrifice*, you would not have condemned these innocent men. For the Son of Man is Lord of the sabbath."

Reflection

Jesus taught the necessity of going beyond regulations to see the meaning behind them. There was no reason for the disciples to go hungry simply to uphold a law. With an allowance of mercy, they ate the heads of grain. When have you had difficulty distinguishing when a rule should be kept or mercy offered?

Prayers

others may be added

To the God of our longing, we pray:

◆ Lord, hear us.

May the Church offer the light of hope, we pray: ◆ May government officials find ways to feed the hungry, we pray: ◆ May those seeking meaningful employment, especially recent graduates, find work, we pray: ◆ May men and women serve God in a vocation to the religious life, we pray: ◆ May healing come quickly to the sick, we pray: ◆ May those who have recently died be welcomed to eternal life, we pray: ◆

Our Father . . .

Life-giving God,
you sustain us with many blessings.
Assist us in the mission
of witness to your Gospel of mercy
so that all may know
of your compassion
and desire to work to build your reign.
Through Christ our Lord.
Amen.

☩ I will take the cup of salvation and call on the name of the Lord.

Saturday, July 20, 2019
Weekday

✝ Give thanks to the Lord for God's mercy is for ever.

Psalm 136 *page 420*

Reading *Matthew 12:14–21*

The Pharisees went out and took counsel against Jesus to put him to death.

When Jesus realized this, he withdrew from that place. Many people followed him, and he cured them all, but he warned them not to make him known. This was to fulfill what had been spoken through Isaiah the prophet:

Behold, my servant whom I have chosen, / my beloved in whom I delight; / I shall place my Spirit upon him, / and he will proclaim justice to the Gentiles. / He will not contend or cry out, / nor will anyone hear his voice in the streets. / A bruised reed he will not break, / a smoldering wick he will not quench, / until he brings justice to victory. / And in his name the Gentiles will hope.

Reflection

In times of trouble, Jesus gives us a model of what to do when we feel threatened and worried: pray in a special place. In this private space, we will feel the Holy Spirit's guidance and care. More importantly, as God's servants, may we too be a place or haven for hope for others. Just as our Lord was a hope to the Gentiles so should we offer hope to those we encounter throughout the day.

Prayers *others may be added*

To the God of peace, we pray:

◆ Lord, hear our prayer.

May the Church always be a sanctuary for those in need, we pray: ◆ May migrants find a welcoming nation in which to live, we pray: ◆ May marriages be strengthened through prayer, we pray: ◆ May children be adopted quickly and live in hope, we pray: ◆ May the sick experience renewal, we pray: ◆ May the angels lead the dead to paradise, we pray: ◆

Our Father . . .

Ever-loving God,
you guide us
to paths of prayer and contemplation
where we grow in knowledge of you.
May we always seek you
as our shelter and strength.
Grant that we may increase our desire to offer mercy
to those who are entrusted to us.
Through Christ our Lord.
Amen.

✝ Give thanks to the Lord for God's mercy is for ever.

Sunday, July 21, 2019
Sixteenth Sunday in Ordinary Time

☩ The just will live in the presence of the Lord.

Psalm 116 *page 413*

Reading *Luke 10:38–42*

Jesus entered a village where a woman whose name was Martha welcomed him. She had a sister named Mary who sat beside the Lord at his feet listening to him speak. Martha, burdened with much serving, came to him and said, "Lord, do you not care that my sister has left me by myself to do the serving? Tell her to help me." The Lord said to her in reply, "Martha, Martha, you are anxious and worried about many things. There is need of only one thing. Mary has chosen the better part and it will not be taken from her."

Reflection

"Martha, Martha, you are anxious and worried about many things." We can replace our name with Martha's and imagine how easily Jesus could comment on how we concern ourselves with things that do not matter. Take a moment to close your eyes and be with the Lord to discern what is important. Today we have a chance to choose "the better part," and to be led to this better place, be it at the Lord's feet or another place.

Prayers *others may be added*

Placing our trust in the Lord, we pray:

◆ Lord, hear our prayer.

That parishes find ways to open their doors throughout the day for all to pray, we pray: ◆ That civic leaders grow in wisdom, we pray: ◆ That retreat centers have resources to stay afloat and expand their mission, we pray: ◆ That quality care be provided at the end of life, we pray: ◆ That all may be made whole, especially the sick, we pray: ◆ That those who have died be welcomed to paradise, we pray: ◆

Our Father . . .

Loving God,
you offer hospitality
to those who seek you.
Grant always
that we, your children,
may choose to be in your presence
and listen to your Word and guidance.
Through Christ our Lord.
Amen.

☩ The just will live in the presence of the Lord.

Monday, July 22, 2019

Feast of St. Mary Magdalene

✝ My soul is thirsting for you, O Lord my God.

Psalm 63

page 403

Reading

John 20:11–18

Mary Magdalene stayed outside the tomb weeping. And as she wept, she bent over into the tomb and saw two angels in white sitting there, one at the head and one at the feet where the Body of Jesus had been. And they said to her, "Woman, why are you weeping?" She said to them, "They have taken my Lord, and I don't know where they laid him." When she had said this, she turned around and saw Jesus there, but did not know it was Jesus. Jesus said to her, "Woman, why are you weeping? Whom are you looking for?" She thought it was the gardener and said to him, "Sir, if you carried him away, tell me where you laid him, and I will take him." Jesus said to her, "Mary!" She turned and said to him in Hebrew, "Rabbouni," which means Teacher. Jesus said to her, "Stop holding on to me, for I have not yet ascended to the Father. But go to my brothers and tell them, 'I am going to my Father and your Father, to my God and your God.'" Mary went and announced to the disciples, "I have seen the Lord," and then reported what he had told her.

Reflection

Mary Magdalene, who is known as the "Apostle to the Apostles," did not waver when the Lord told her to witness to his Resurrection. She reminds us that we cannot keep the experience of our Lord to ourselves. Through how we live, we proclaim that the Lord is with us through our joys and sorrows.

Prayers

others may be added

With confidence in the Resurrection, we pray:

◆ Lord, hear our prayer.

Strengthen the leaders of the Church, we pray: ◆ Encourage women and men to consider the life of the vowed religious, we pray: ◆ Aid those who minister to the needs of the poor, we pray: ◆ Assist those in ministries of hospitality to receive people joyfully, we pray: ◆ Forgive the leaders who do not strive for harmony and peace, we pray: ◆ Lift those who have died to eternal glory, we pray: ◆

Our Father . . .

Loving God,
you gave Mary Magdalene
a share in your Good News.
Encourage us in joining her joyful
proclamation that Jesus Christ lives.
Guide our efforts to praise and proclaim
that the Risen Lord transforms our lives.
Through Christ our Lord.
Amen.

✝ My soul is thirsting for you, O Lord my God.

Tuesday, July 23, 2019

Optional Memorial of St. Bridget, Religious

✝ Let us sing to the Lord who has covered himself in glory.

Psalm 63

page 403

Reading

Matthew 12:46–50

While Jesus was speaking to the crowds, his mother and his brothers appeared outside, wishing to speak with him. Someone told him, "Your mother and your brothers are standing outside, asking to speak with you." But he said in reply to the one who told him, "Who is my mother? Who are my brothers?" And stretching out his hand toward his disciples, he said, "Here are my mother and my brothers. For whoever does the will of my heavenly Father is my brother, and sister, and mother."

Reflection

Jesus continuously invites his followers to look at the bigger picture. Our family consists of our blood relatives but also of the members of the Church, wherever they are located. The Nicene Creed uses the word "catholic" to describe the Church, meaning the Church is universal. We are linked to those who do God's will, whether they are in our home, community, or across the sea. The people on both heaven and earth make up the Mystical Body of Christ.

Prayers

others may be added

With knowledge of God's care for all, we pray:

◆ Lord, hear our prayer.

Support the Church as she reaches out to other ecclesial communities, we pray: ◆ Challenge government leaders to broaden their vision, we pray: ◆ Strengthen those who work for family support networks, we pray: ◆ Heal divisions among family members, we pray: ◆ Through the example of St. Bridget, may couples be renewed in their vocation of love and service, we pray: ◆ Assist the dying to enjoy a vision of God, we pray: ◆

Our Father . . .

Lord,
you have provided us a family
within the Church.
May we join with them in building
a world
faithful to your vision of an
inclusive community,
where all may grow together as sister,
brother, mother, and father
caring for all and living the Good News
of salvation.
Through Christ our Lord.
Amen.

✝ Let us sing to the Lord who has covered himself in glory.

Wednesday, July 24, 2019

Optional Memorial of St. Sharbel Makhlūf, Priest

☩ The Lord gave them bread
from heaven.

Psalm 63

page 403

Reading

Matthew 13:1–9

On that day, Jesus went out of the house and sat down by the sea. Such large crowds gathered around him that he got into a boat and sat down, and the whole crowd stood along the shore. And he spoke to them at length in parables, saying: "A sower went out to sow. And as he sowed, some seed fell on the path, and birds came and ate it up. Some fell on rocky ground, where it had little soil. It sprang up at once because the soil was not deep, and when the sun rose it was scorched, and it withered for lack of roots. Some seed fell among thorns, and the thorns grew up and choked it. But some seed fell on rich soil and produced fruit, a hundred or sixty or thirtyfold. Whoever has ears ought to hear."

Reflection

During the summer, we are asked to be alert, listen, and reflect on how the Word is sprouting and others are growing in faith. Jesus wants us to recognize that we have been charged with discipleship and should continue scattering good seed. No matter how we judge the worthiness of the soil, and no matter what we think the measurable outcome will be, God's Word should be invested. God regularly throws seeds, modeling his hope for us.

Prayers

others may be added

To our God, who nourishes us,
we pray:

◆ Lord, hear our prayer.

Inspire Church leaders to continuously seek to renew their spirits, we pray: ◆ Through the intercession of St. Sharbel, guide the church of Lebanon and other places of strife, we pray: ◆ Encourage leaders to reform prisons, we pray: ◆ Keep safe all who are vacationing, we pray: ◆ Heal the wounded, we pray: ◆ Guide the dying to the path to heaven, we pray: ◆

Our Father . . .

Gracious God,
you nurture and care for your people
and assist us in our journey to eternal life.
May we always look to the eternal Light,
Jesus Christ,
and be guided
to blossom and bear
much fruit for your world.
Through Christ our Lord.
Amen.

☩ The Lord gave them bread
from heaven.

Thursday, July 25, 2019

Feast of St. James, Apostle

✝ Those who sow in tears shall reap rejoicing.

Psalm 126

page 417

Reading

2 Corinthians 4:7–15

Brothers and sisters: We hold this treasure in earthen vessels, that the surpassing power may be of God and not from us. We are afflicted in every way, but not constrained; perplexed, but not driven to despair; persecuted, but not abandoned; struck down, but not destroyed; always carrying about in the body the dying of Jesus, so that the life of Jesus may also be manifested in our body. For we who live are constantly being given up to death for the sake of Jesus, so that the life of Jesus may be manifested in our mortal flesh.

So death is at work in us, but life in you. Since, then, we have the same spirit of faith, according to what is written, *I believed, therefore I spoke*, we too believe and therefore speak, knowing that the one who raised the Lord Jesus will raise us also with Jesus and place us with you in his presence. Everything indeed is for you, so that the grace bestowed in abundance on more and more people may cause the thanksgiving to overflow for the glory of God.

Reflection

This feast day reading reminds us that no matter what comes our way, God's grace will indeed strengthen and guide us. It is, after all, from God that all power comes. We may be afflicted and persecuted at times, but we carry within us what we have received. Throughout our difficulties, are we able to remain a thankful people? Our gratitude comes from "knowing that the one who raised the Lord Jesus will raise us also and place us in his presence." May we always allow praise and thanksgiving to permeate our lives.

Prayers

others may be added

Proclaiming God's Word to the world, we pray:

◆ Lord, hear us.

Bestow grace on all Church leaders
to boldly proclaim the Good News,
we pray: ◆ Encourage world leaders
as they work to be instruments of peace,
we pray: ◆ Help communities establish
systems to procure safe water, we pray: ◆
Expand employment opportunities,
especially for recent graduates,
we pray: ◆ Heal those awaiting cancer
treatments, we pray: ◆ Give light and
comfort to those who are dying,
we pray: ◆

Our Father . . .

Almighty God,
you led St. James, as you do us,
to share the treasures of the faith
to the ends of the world.
Renew our efforts
to sow seeds of love and compassion
to build your reign of justice and good.
Through Christ our Lord.
Amen.

✝ Those who sow in tears shall reap rejoicing.

Friday, July 26, 2019
Memorial of Sts. Joachim and Anne,
Parents of the Blessed Virgin Mary

✝ God will give the throne of David.

Psalm 132 *page 419*

Reading *Sirach 44:1, 10–15*

Now will I praise those godly men,
our ancestors, each in his
own time:
These were godly men
whose virtues have not
been forgotten;
Their wealth remains in
their families,
their heritage with
their descendants;
Through God's covenant with them
their family endures,
their posterity for their sake.

And for all time their progeny
will endure,
their glory will never be
blotted out;
Their bodies are peacefully
laid away,
but their name lives on and on.
At gatherings their wisdom is retold,
and the assembly proclaims
their praise.

Reflection

We honor the parents of Mary, who reared her in her faith. Just as Joachim and Anne entrusted Mary with virtue and prepared her for her vocation as "God bearer," our parents, grandparents, godparents, and other "wisdom" women and men taught us to pray and strengthened us for our vocation as a Christian disciple. The wisdom we share, generation to generation, holds us together as the family of God and ensures the prosperity of God's holy people.

Prayers *others may be added*

From one generation to the next, we entrust our prayers to God:

◆ Lord, hear our prayer.

Strengthen the family of the Church, we pray: ◆ Assist governments in providing just service to support families, we pray: ◆ Provide new vocations to the ordained and vowed religious, we pray: ◆ Help us to foster a profound respect for all human life, we pray: ◆ Aid caregivers who support the elderly who are sick, we pray: ◆ Bring all the dying to the Communion of Saints, we pray: ◆

Our Father . . .

Provident God,
you grant many blessings
to all who cry out to you in need.
Sustain our families
so that protected by the Holy Spirit
we may continue the traditions
of faithfulness and service.
Through Christ our Lord.
Amen.

✝ God will give the throne of David.

Saturday, July 27, 2019
Weekday

✝ Offer to God a sacrifice of praise.

Psalm 63 *page 403*

Reading *Matthew 13:24–29*

Jesus proposed a parable to the crowds, saying: "The kingdom of heaven may be likened to a man who sowed good seed in his field. While everyone was asleep his enemy came and sowed weeds all through the wheat, and then went off. When the crop grew and bore fruit, the weeds appeared as well. The slaves of the householder came to him and said, 'Master, did you not sow good seed in your field? Where have the weeds come from?' He answered, 'An enemy has done this.' His slaves said to him, 'Do you want us to go and pull them up?' He replied, 'No, if you pull up the weeds you might uproot the wheat along with them. Let them grow together until harvest.'"

Reflection

How patient God is with us as we grow together. God waits for us to bear fruit, to come to "the harvest" of heaven when ready. All of us grow so that we may influence one another. The perfectionists among us may want especially to recognize that God not only tolerates imperfections but welcomes them. What must we welcome in our lives to shape us, mold us, and beyond that, help us see that we are to grow together in the same field?

Prayers *others may be added*

Trusting in God's plans for us,
we pray:

◆ Lord, hear our prayer.

Assist the Church in being open to learning from people of various cultures, we pray: ◆ Help civic authorities to be mindful of the common good, we pray: ◆ Encourage us to rely on the Holy Spirit as we seek to bear good fruit, we pray: ◆ Provide farmers with fortitude to reap a bountiful harvest, we pray: ◆ Give patience to scientists looking for cures for diseases, we pray: ◆ Guide the dying to your eternal glory, we pray: ◆

Our Father . . .

O God of the harvest,
you call your servants
to bear good works and service
to your name.
Help us to be patient
and learn from your ways,
that we may share in your goodness
and come to your eternal field in heaven,
where you are Lord for ever and ever.
Amen.

✝ Offer to God a sacrifice of praise.

Sunday, July 28, 2019

Seventeenth Sunday in Ordinary Time

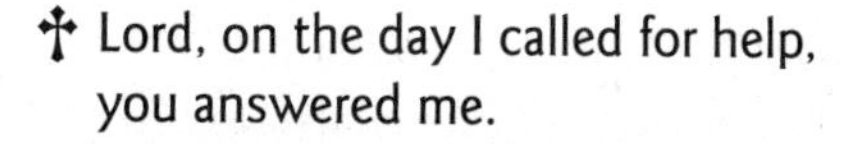

✝ Lord, on the day I called for help,
you answered me.

Psalm 138 *page 420*

Reading *Luke 11:9–13*

[Jesus said:] "And I tell you, ask and you will receive; seek and you will find; knock and the door will be opened to you. For everyone who asks, receives; and the one who seeks, finds; and to the one who knocks, the door will be opened. What father among you would hand his son a snake when he asks for a fish? Or hand him a scorpion when he asks for an egg? If you then, who are wicked, know how to give good gifts to your children, how much more will the Father in heaven give the Holy Spirit to those who ask him?"

Reflection

After giving the disciples the Lord's Prayer, Jesus continues to teach them to pray. He tells them the heart of communication with God is to ask, knock, search, and trust. Again, we are reminded that God does what is best for us. Even in our sinfulness, we know to gift our children with what is good. How much more does God do for us by providing the Holy Spirit? Take time today to examine your prayer life. Do you value time in prayer? Is anything missing from your prayer life?

Prayers *others may be added*

Turning to God with confidence,
we pray:

◆ Lord, hear our prayer.

That we, as a Church, will grow in the varied ways of prayer, we pray: ◆ That world leaders pray and work together for peace, we pray: ◆ That scientists be inspired to search for new ways to care for the earth, we pray: ◆ That vacationers have a safe holiday, we pray: ◆ That the sick find comfort and healing, we pray: ◆ That the dying be led to eternal life, we pray: ◆

Our Father . . .

Praised be to you, O God,
who knows our needs
and calls us to open the door
to share in a deeper life and relationship
with you.
Continually renew our efforts
to grow together in love
and recognize the gift of your care.
Through Christ our Lord.
Amen.

✝ Lord, on the day I called for help,
you answered me.

Monday, July 29, 2019

Memorial of St. Martha

✝ I will bless the Lord at all times.

Psalm 34 *page 401*

Reading *John 11:19–24*

Many of the Jews had come to Martha and Mary to comfort them about their brother [Lazarus, who had died]. When Martha heard that Jesus was coming, she went to meet him; but Mary sat at home. Martha said to Jesus, "Lord, if you had been here, my brother would not have died. But even now I know that whatever you ask of God, God will give you." Jesus said to her, "Your brother will rise." Martha said to him, "I know he will rise, in the resurrection on the last day."

Reflection

Why did Martha come to believe in Christ? Christ was patient as she came to believe and supported her throughout the process. Martha experienced the healing, wholeness, and life that Christ brought to her. She trusted and came to believe that Christ is "the resurrection and the life." Christ took her busy spirit and allowed it to deepen so that she could grow to be a person of profound faith. Christ awaits also our responses of faith.

Prayers *others may be added*

Turning to God with confidence,
we pray:

◆ Lord, hear us.

That Church leaders boldly share that Christ brings his life to us, we pray: ◆ That government officials respect all human life, we pray: ◆ That those suffering from the weather and natural disasters find comfort, we pray: ◆ That sacristans and other church volunteers know of our profound gratitude for their service to us, we pray: ◆ That the terminally ill be comforted, we pray: ◆ That those in purgatory be led to their eternal reward, we pray: ◆

Our Father . . .

God of hospitality,
you call all your servants, like Martha,
to grow in holiness and faithfulness
and to acknowledge you
as God of the living and the dead.
Bring your people to trust ever more
deeply in your Son,
who leads all the faithful to the halls
of heaven.
Through Christ our Lord.
Amen.

✝ I will bless the Lord at all times.

Tuesday, July 30, 2019
Weekday

✝ The Lord is kind and merciful.

Psalm 103

page 411

Reading

Matthew 13:36–41

Jesus dismissed the crowds and went into the house. His disciples approached him and said, "Explain to us the parable of the weeds in the field." He said in reply, "He who sows good seed is the Son of Man, the field is the world, the good seed the children of the Kingdom. The weeds are the children of the Evil One, and the enemy who sows them is the Devil. The harvest is the end of the age, and the harvesters are angels. Just as weeds are collected and burned up with fire, so will it be at the end of the age. The Son of Man will send his angels, and they will collect out of his Kingdom all who cause others to sin and all evildoers. They will throw them into the fiery furnace, where there will be wailing and grinding of teeth. Then the righteous will shine like the sun in the Kingdom of their Father. Whoever has ears ought to hear."

Reflection

Sometimes we are like the disciples and want everything explained to us as clearly as possible. It is possible to agonize over the details and keep asking God questions only to realize we are holding back from living out our call. We continuously renew our covenant at the Eucharist and our challenge is to grow as the good seed, building the Kingdom of God.

Prayers

others may be added

Confident that God will nurture us,
we pray:

◆ Lord, hear our prayer.

That our parish leaders never tire from encouraging our faith to grow, we pray: ◆ That civic authorities build earthly cities that reflect God's justice, we pray: ◆ That the poor benefit from our generosity, we pray: ◆ That good weather bring farmers an abundant harvest, we pray: ◆ That the sick recover quickly, we pray: ◆ That the dying enter eternal life, we pray: ◆

Our Father . . .

Gentle God,
you lead us to a righteous life.
Guide us to ignore the allure
of those who would lead us to sin
so that we may rest in your grace.
Through our Lord Jesus Christ, your Son,
who lives and reigns with you in the unity
of the Holy Spirit,
one God, for ever and ever.
Amen.

✝ The Lord is kind and merciful.

Wednesday, July 31, 2019

Memorial of St. Ignatius Loyola, Priest

✝ Holy is the Lord our God.

Psalm 103

page 411

Reading

Matthew 13:44–46

Jesus said to his disciples: "The Kingdom of heaven is like a treasure buried in a field, which a person finds and hides again, and out of joy goes and sells all that he has and buys that field. Again, the Kingdom of heaven is like a merchant searching for fine pearls. When he finds a pearl of great price, he goes and sells all that he has and buys it."

Reflection

Today's reading helps us consider how we regard our faith. Would we be like the person who sells all he has so that he can be in possession of such a gift as the Kingdom of God? Do we consider our faith as important as the man who purchases the pearl of great price? How do you nurture your gift of faith? Do you see it as a treasure? Earlier in Matthew's account of the Gospel (5:16), Jesus states, "your light must shine before others, that they may see your good deeds and glorify your heavenly Father." Never bury or sell this gift.

Prayers

others may be added

To God, who gifts us with faith, we pray:

◆ Lord, hear our prayer.

That our religious leaders encourage members to share their talents, we pray: ◆ That the Jesuit order continue to flourish in its mission, we pray: ◆ That students and teachers treasure the wealth of their knowledge, we pray: ◆ That those who regularly drive for a living be kept safe, we pray: ◆ That the sick be healed quickly, we pray: ◆ That the faithful departed be welcomed to the heavenly banquet, we pray: ◆

Our Father . . .

God of hidden majesty,
you call us forth to build your Kingdom
and share our treasure for your glory.
Keep us under your watchful care
and strengthen our resolve to be faithful
to our baptismal call.
Through Christ our Lord.
Amen.

✝ Holy is the Lord our God.

Thursday, August 1, 2019

Memorial of St. Alphonsus Liguori, Bishop and Doctor of the Church

✝ How lovely is your dwelling place, O Lord, mighty God.

Psalm 84 *page 406*

Reading *Matthew 13:47–50*

Jesus said to the disciples: "The Kingdom of heaven is like a net thrown into the sea, which collects fish of every kind. When it is full they haul it ashore and sit down to put what is good into buckets. What is bad they throw away. Thus it will be at the end of the age. The angels will go out and separate the wicked from the righteous and throw them into the fiery furnace, where there will be wailing and grinding of teeth."

"Do you understand all these things?" They answered, "Yes." And he replied, "Then every scribe who has been instructed in the Kingdom of heaven is like the head of a household who brings from his storeroom both the new and the old." When Jesus finished these parables, he went away from there.

Reflection

The seriousness by which we are called to be "good" is laid out in the reading today. The image of the wicked being tossed in the furnace is striking. Near the end of this Gospel reading, Jesus asks the disciples if they understand. Do we understand well enough to conform our lives to live righteously? Do we hold back on building up the Kingdom of God or being open to doing good?

Prayers *others may be added*

Turning to our faithful Lord, we pray:

◆ Lord, hear our prayer.

That our bishops continue to seek to be transparent in leading the Church, we pray: ◆ That civic authorities work for the common good, we pray: ◆ That refugees find a welcome home, we pray: ◆ That more men seek to follow in the footsteps of St. Alphonsus and serve the church as Redemptorists, we pray: ◆ That the sick be healed, we pray: ◆ That those who have died be nourished at the heavenly banquet, we pray: ◆

Our Father . . .

O God,
you raise us up, like St. Alphonsus,
to be people who live our faith with zeal
and witness for the common good.
Strengthen us that we may care
for the needs of our community
and bring the beauty of your reign.
Through Christ our Lord.
Amen.

✝ How lovely is your dwelling place, O Lord, mighty God.

Friday, August 2, 2019
Optional Memorial of St. Peter Julian Eymard, Priest

✝ Sing with joy to God our help.

Psalm 103 *page 411*

Reading *Matthew 13:54–58*

Jesus came to his native place and taught the people in their synagogue. They were astonished and said, "Where did this man get such wisdom and mighty deeds? Is he not the carpenter's son? Is not his mother named Mary and his brothers James, Joseph, Simon, and Judas? Are not his sisters all with us? Where did this man get all this?" And they took offense at him. But Jesus said to them, "A prophet is not without honor except in his native place and in his own house." And he did not work many mighty deeds there because of their lack of faith.

Reflection

It is hard to go back to our childhood roots or places. St. Peter Julian Eymard was able, through his constant zeal and ardent love of the Eucharist, to help people focus on Christ in this sacrament of thanksgiving. Our challenge is to point others to Christ and do so prophetically, do so, so that we may honor the gifts of God. Living the Eucharist fully, in all its facets, will help others see Christ's presence, and not the idiosyncrasies we left behind in that childhood place.

Prayers *others may be added*

To the Lord, who sent his Son to us, we pray:

◆ Lord, hear our prayer.

That the Church grow in unity around the Eucharist, we pray: ◆ That community leaders seek to serve the needs of all, we pray: ◆ That reconciliation may occur in countries at war, we pray: ◆ That through the inspiration of St. Peter Julian Eymard, more men and woman serve in a eucharistic vocation and ministry in the Church, especially in the Congregation of the Blessed Sacrament, we pray: ◆ That cures be found for challenging diseases, we pray: ◆ That those who have died be welcome to the heavenly banquet, we pray: ◆

Our Father . . .

Gracious God of our ancestors,
you guide your Church
in leadership and wisdom.
Help us to serve you prophetically
with wisdom and grace.
Through Christ our Lord.
Amen.

✝ Sing with joy to God our help.

Saturday, August 3, 2019
Weekday

✝ O God, let all the nations praise you!

Psalm 119 *page 414*

Reading *Matthew 14:6–12*

But at a birthday celebration for Herod, the daughter of Herodias performed a dance before the guests and delighted Herod so much that he swore to give her whatever she might ask for. Prompted by her mother, she said, "Give me here on a platter the head of John the Baptist." The king was distressed, but because of his oaths and the guests who were present, he ordered that it be given, and he had John beheaded in the prison. His head was brought in on a platter and given to the girl, who took it to her mother. His disciples came and took away the corpse and buried him; and they went and told Jesus.

Reflection

With this reading, we see John the Baptist's life taken out of revenge. Daily through the news, we hear of lives that are expunged senselessly. We cannot turn away but must work to sensitize people to violence. John the Baptist was killed for speaking the truth. As we prepare for the Lord's Day, we recognize that many have given their life for Christ. May we speak up for those who are unafraid and live courageously.

Prayers *others may be added*

Confident that the Lord guides and strengthens us, we pray:

◆ Lord, hear our prayer.

That the faithful allow themselves to be strengthened by the witness of martyrs, we pray: ◆ That politicians work for peace in cities, we pray: ◆ That strife and friction between enemies may end, we pray: ◆ That faiths across the world unite in charity to care for all, we pray: ◆ That surgeon's hands be steady, we pray: ◆ That the angels accompany to heaven those who have died, we pray: ◆

Our Father . . .

O God of justice and peace,
renew efforts to unite your people.
Sow seeds of love and care in us
so that we may always witness these gifts
and bring compassion to those who hurt
because of hatred and division.
Through Christ our Lord.
Amen.

✝ O God, let all the nations praise you!

Sunday, August 4, 2019

Eighteenth Sunday in Ordinary Time

✝ In every age, O Lord, you have been our refuge.

Psalm 90

page 408

Reading

Luke 12:16–20

Then [Jesus] told [the crowd] a parable. "There was a rich man whose land produced a bountiful harvest. He asked himself, 'What shall I do, for I do not have space to store my harvest?' And he said, 'This is what I shall do: I shall tear down my barns and build larger ones. There I shall store all my grain and other goods and I shall say to myself, "Now as for you, you have so many good things stored up for many years, rest, eat, drink, be merry!"' But God said to him, 'You fool, this night your life will be demanded of you; and the things you have prepared, to whom will they belong?' Thus will it be for the one who stores up treasure for himself but is not rich in what matters to God."

Reflection

Our consumer culture thrives on possessions and accumulating more and more things. It is no wonder we become obsessed with stuff. We are invited to form a different sort of relationship with possessions. This relationship would have regard for what matters in life. As many have found, giving away things not only lightens the burden on the earth but also helps us achieve our ultimate happiness found in God alone. Examine whether your treasure is in your possessions.

Prayers

others may be added

In giving of our prayers, we receive God's grace to live:

◆ Lord, hear our prayer.

For the Church, that she be steadfast in evangelization efforts, we pray: ◆ For countries in need, that other nations share their wealth, we pray: ◆ For affordable housing in cities, we pray: ◆ For safe travels for vacationers, we pray: ◆ For the well-being of the sick, we pray: ◆ For those we miss and mourn, we pray: ◆

Our Father . . .

Loving God,
you have taught us that
our heart will be where our treasure is.
Help us to aim for what the
Kingdom offers.
May we share our riches
with our brothers and sisters,
always seeking their welfare.
Through Christ our Lord.
Amen.

✝ In every age, O Lord, you have been our refuge.

Monday, August 5, 2019
Weekday

✝ Sing with joy to God our help.

Psalm 90 *page 408*

Reading *Matthew 14:15–20*

When it was evening, the disciples approached [Jesus] and said, "This is a deserted place and it is already late; dismiss the crowds so that they can go to the villages and buy food for themselves." Jesus said to them, "There is no need for them to go away; give them some food yourselves." But they said to him, "Five loaves and two fish are all we have here." Then he said, "Bring them here to me," and he ordered the crowds to sit down on the grass. Taking the five loaves and the two fish, and looking up to heaven, he said the blessing, broke the loaves, and gave them to the disciples, who in turn gave them to the crowds. They all ate and were satisfied.

Reflection

The feeding of the five thousand takes place shortly after John the Baptist's death. After being told about the beheading of John, Jesus went in a boat to a deserted place to be alone. Soon, people found Jesus, and he cured their sick. Despite his grief, Jesus ministered, even to the concern for the physical nourishment of the people. He took the bread, blessed, broke, and gave it to feed the multitudes. An abundance was left. God always gives us more than we ever need.

Prayers *others may be added*

With confidence in our care, we pray to God:

◆ Lord, hear our prayer.

For renewal in the Church's charitable ministries, we pray: ◆ For world leaders, that they inspire their citizens to share their wealth, we pray: ◆ For the rebuilding of places suffering from natural disasters, we pray: ◆ For efforts to make our world safer, we pray: ◆ For those who work to prevent diseases, we pray: ◆ For mourners who have lost a loved one, we pray: ◆

Our Father . . .

Bountiful God,
you satisfy the hungry heart
and teach us to be generous with
our gifts.
Fill the longings of our world
by encouraging our generosity
so that others may come to experience
the satisfaction of our compassion
that comes through you.
Through Christ our Lord.
Amen.

✝ Sing with joy to God our help.

Tuesday, August 6, 2019

Feast of the Transfiguration of the Lord

✝ The Lord is king, the most high over all the earth.

Psalm 145 *page 421*

Reading *Luke 9:28b–31*

Jesus took Peter, John, and James and went up the mountain to pray. While he was praying his face changed in appearance and his clothing became dazzling white. And behold, two men were conversing with him, Moses and Elijah, who appeared in glory and spoke of his exodus that he was going to accomplish in Jerusalem.

Reflection

We are grateful that Peter, John, and James did not keep the experience of the Transfiguration to themselves; after the Resurrection they proclaimed it. They recognized that this gift of knowing Christ is not meant to be kept in some sacred location but is to boldly shine for all to see. Christ allowed the Apostles to see him transfigured so that they and we would be transformed. This transformation propels us to seek a meaningful relationship with Christ and to be heralds of the Gospel.

Prayers *others may be added*

To our Lord of glory, we pray:

◆ Lord, hear our prayer.

For Church leaders on pilgrimage in the Holy Land, we pray: ◆ For legislators, that they abolish the death penalty, we pray: ◆ For an end to nuclear weapons, we pray: ◆ For the development of renewable energies, we pray: ◆ For the sick to recover, we pray: ◆ For the dead to see the glory of God, we pray: ◆

Our Father . . .

O God,
who guides us through the peaks and valleys of life,
let us be renewed in our faith journey
as we follow the steps of your Son
to the glory of your Kingdom,
where you live and reign in the unity of the Holy Spirit,
one God, for ever and ever.
Amen.

✝ The Lord is king, the most high over all the earth.

Wednesday, August 7, 2019
Weekday

☩ Remember us, O Lord, as you favor your people.

Psalm 90

page 408

Reading

Matthew 15:21–28

At that time Jesus withdrew to the region of Tyre and Sidon. And behold, a Canaanite woman of that district came and called out, "Have pity on me, Lord, Son of David! My daughter is tormented by a demon." But he did not say a word in answer to her. His disciples came and asked him, "Send her away, for she keeps calling out after us." He said in reply, "I was sent only to the lost sheep of the house of Israel." But the woman came and did him homage, saying, "Lord, help me." He said in reply, "It is not right to take the food of the children and throw it to the dogs." She said, "Please, Lord, for even the dogs eat the scraps that fall from the table of their masters." Then Jesus said to her in reply, "O woman, great is your faith! Let it be done for you as you wish." And her daughter was healed from that hour.

Reflection

This woman's faith was so great that she did not fear Jesus' response. She knew that he taught the Jews. Surely, she knew of their status as the Chosen People. None of this deterred her, for she was a mother in need of a cure for her daughter, and she had faith that Jesus could cast out demons. She would confront him until he cured her child. In this passage, we see that faith extended to the Gentiles.

Prayers

others may be added

Opening our hearts and minds,
we pray:

◆ Lord, hear our prayer.

For leaders in the Church to trust the movement of the Holy Spirit, we pray: ◆ For civic authorities to listen to the needs of the poor, we pray: ◆ For those in prison, we pray: ◆ For the humane care of animals, we pray: ◆ For the sick awaiting transplants, we pray: ◆ For those who grieve the loss of a loved one, we pray: ◆

Our Father . . .

Gentle and loving God,
you hear the cries
of those who call to you in mercy.
Accept our desires for healing
and help us to endure the trials and
worries of our day
so that we may be assured
of your compassion and care.
Through Christ our Lord.
Amen.

☩ Remember us, O Lord, as you favor your people.

Thursday, August 8, 2019

Memorial of St. Dominic, Priest

✝ If today you hear God's voice,
harden not your hearts.

Psalm 95 *page 408*

Reading *Matthew 16:13–20*

Jesus went into the region of Caesarea Philippi and he asked his disciples, "Who do people say that the Son of Man is?" They replied, "Some say John the Baptist, others Elijah, still others Jeremiah or one of the prophets." He said to them, "But who do you say that I am?" Simon Peter said in reply, "You are the Christ, the Son of the living God." Jesus said to him in reply, "Blessed are you, Simon son of Jonah. For flesh and blood has not revealed this to you, but my heavenly Father. And so I say to you, you are Peter, and upon this rock I will build my church, and the gates of the netherworld shall not prevail against it. I will give you the keys to the kingdom of heaven. Whatever you bind on earth shall be bound in heaven; and whatever you loose on earth shall be loosed in heaven." Then he strictly ordered his disciples to tell no one that he was the Christ.

Reflection

When Jesus queries the disciples, "Who do you say that I am?" Peter replies with a profession of faith. If you were asked who Jesus is in your life, how would you reply? Would you say that you are his follower and profess not only who he is but who you are as a Christian? May we reveal by how we live that Christ is the lord of our life.

Prayers *others may be added*

To our Lord, who gives us faith,
we pray:

◆ Lord, hear our prayer.

For our pope, may he be healthy, we pray: ◆ For peacekeeping efforts among nations, we pray: ◆ For the Dominican order, may its members continue their mission of preaching, we pray: ◆ For those preparing for marriage, we pray: ◆ For those suffering from depression, we pray: ◆ For those we miss and mourn, we pray: ◆

Our Father . . .

Lord God,
you called Peter, Dominic,
and all your disciples
to dare to confess their faith
and boldly live out service and justice.
Help us to bring your Word
to life in our community
and devote ourselves
to living your truth.
Through Christ our Lord.
Amen.

✝ If today you hear God's voice,
harden not your hearts.

Friday, August 9, 2019
Weekday

✝ I remember the deeds of the Lord.

Psalm 90
page 408

Reading
Matthew 16:24–27

Jesus said to his disciples, "Whoever wishes to come after me must deny himself, take up his cross, and follow me. For whoever wishes to save his life will lose it, but whoever loses his life for my sake will find it. What profit would there be for one to gain the whole world and forfeit his life? Or what can one give in exchange for his life? For the Son of Man will come with his angels in his Father's glory, and then he will repay everyone according to his conduct."

Reflection

After Peter professes that Jesus is the Christ, the Son of the living God, the Apostles are told the cost of discipleship. Christ explains that following him entails denying oneself and taking up a cross. Christians lose their life in order to find life in Christ. Each day we die to ourselves to rise in Christ. Through that dying to ourselves, we find ourselves, for our identity is in Christ. Should we seek our identity in the things of this world, we lose ourselves, for we are pulling ourselves away from God. As we pray daily, we draw closer to God and the life that he gives.

Prayers
others may be added

To our God, who leads us to life in him, we pray:

◆ Lord, hear our prayer.

For pastors faced with difficult decisions, we pray: ◆ For unity among Christian churches and communities, we pray: ◆ For government leaders, that they be open to the poor, we pray: ◆ For the safety of those who protect us, we pray: ◆ For the healing of mind and spirit of those who feel dejected, we pray: ◆ For all who have been marked with the sign of faith, we pray: ◆

Our Father . . .

God of our ancestors,
you lead us daily
to know the glory of the Risen Lord.
Help us to take up our crosses
each day, paying little heed
to their weight,
for they bring us closer
to our life of glory in you.
Through Christ our Lord.
Amen.

✝ I remember the deeds of the Lord.

Saturday, August 10, 2019
Feast of St. Lawrence, Deacon and Martyr

✝ Blessed the one who is gracious and lends to those in need.

Psalm 112 *page 412*

Reading *John 12:24–26*

Jesus said to his disciples: "Amen, amen, I say to you, unless a grain of wheat falls to the ground and dies, it remains just a grain of wheat; but if it dies, it produces much fruit. Whoever loves his life loses it, and whoever hates his life in this world will preserve it for eternal life. Whoever serves me must follow me, and where I am, there also will my servant be. The Father will honor whoever serves me."

Reflection

As the archdeacon of Rome, Lawrence looked after the Church's treasury and the giving of alms to the poor. He was executed in 258 after the emperor declared that bishops, priests, and deacons should be put to death. Since Lawrence was to turn over the Church's wealth before being killed, he requested three days to gather the funds and the goods. In that time, he distributed the Church's property to the poor. To his death, Lawrence bore much fruit, serving and following the Lord. We can look to his example as one who preserved his life and gained eternal life.

Prayers *others may be added*

To our compassionate God, we pray:

◆ Lord, hear our prayer.

For more men to serve the Church as deacons, we pray: ◆ For deacons, that they always seek to grow in their service of the Church, we pray: ◆ For legislators to sacrifice for the common good, we pray: ◆ For renewed efforts to find employment for all who seek work, we pray: ◆ For ministers who care for the sick, we pray: ◆ For bereavement ministers as they comfort the grieving, we pray: ◆

Our Father . . .

O God,
you gave St. Lawrence the wisdom
to care for both the Church's financial affairs and the poor.
May we always treasure the gifts of heaven
and love the people of earth,
who share their gifts and talents for your glory.
Through Christ our Lord.
Amen.

✝ Blessed the one who is gracious and lends to those in need.

Sunday, August 11, 2019

Nineteenth Sunday in Ordinary Time

✝ Happy the people the Lord has chosen to be his own.

Psalm 34

page 401

Reading

Luke 12:35–38

Jesus said to his disciples: "Gird your loins and light your lamps and be like servants who await their master's return from a wedding, ready to open immediately when he comes and knocks. Blessed are those servants whom the master finds vigilant on his arrival. Amen, I say to you, he will gird himself, have them recline at table, and proceed to wait on them. And should he come in the second or third watch and find them prepared in this way, blessed are those servants."

Reflection

In the United States, elementary, high school, and college students are spending hours daily practicing soccer or football. They aim to be ready for the season. Do we place as much energy into being ready for heaven? Does there seem to be an uneven contrast with our preparation for things of this earth and for the next life? Scripture regularly reminds us to be vigilant as we await the Master. How can you direct your life more toward readying yourself for Christ's coming?

Prayers

others may be added

Turning to our Lord who awaits us, we pray:

◆ Lord, hear us.

Cleanse and sanctify your Church and her leaders, we pray: ◆ Assist leaders of nations as they seek to reconcile their differences, we pray: ◆ Inspire young people to be open to a vocation in the cloistered life, we pray: ◆ Guide vacationers to safe travels, we pray: ◆ Heal the sick, we pray: ◆ Receive the souls of the dead, we pray: ◆

Our Father . . .

Inspired by your Word, O God,
we travel onward as pilgrims keeping our lamps lit.
Encourage us to live with hearts
that seek you
so that we will be ready for your coming.
Through our Lord Jesus Christ, your Son,
who lives and reigns with you in the unity of the Holy Spirit,
one God, for ever and ever.
Amen.

✝ Happy the people the Lord has chosen to be his own.

Monday, August 12, 2019

Optional Memorial of St. Jane Frances de Chantal, Religious

† Praise the Lord, Jerusalem.

Psalm 34

page 401

Reading

Matthew 17:24–27

When they [Jesus and his disciples] came to Capernaum, the collectors of the temple tax approached Peter and said, "Does not your teacher pay the temple tax?" "Yes," he said. When he came into the house, before he had time to speak, Jesus asked him, "What is your opinion, Simon? From whom do the kings of the earth take tolls or census tax? From their subjects or from foreigners?" When he said, "From foreigners," Jesus said to him, "Then the subjects are exempt. But that we may not offend them, go to the sea, drop in a hook, and take the first fish that comes up. Open its mouth and you will find a coin worth twice the temple tax. Give that to them for me and for you."

Reflection

Scripture scholars say that this text reflects material Matthew wished to include in the Gospel about Peter and the early Church. The passage directs that members of the Church act as part of the society in which they live. Today, we recognize that paying taxes provides for the well-being of our society. We are to offer our gifts and tithing to make our society better. As citizens of the world, we need to share our gifts to make life better for everyone.

Prayers

others may be added

To our compassionate God, we pray:

◆ Lord, hear our prayer.

Assist pastors in their ministry, we pray: ◆ Protect community leaders as they work toward the common good, we pray: ◆ Support the Congregation of the Visitation and those inspired by the vision of St. Jane Frances de Chantal, we pray: ◆ Aid those who long for meaningful employment, we pray: ◆ Comfort the sick, we pray: ◆ Commend to your care all who have died, we pray: ◆

Our Father . . .

Strengthen your people, Lord,
to be of service to your world.
May our efforts at preserving the faith
lead us to be companions to the needy
and examples of your shining light.
Through Christ our Lord.
Amen.

† Praise the Lord, Jerusalem.

Tuesday, August 13, 2019
Weekday

✝ Forever will I sing the goodness of the Lord.

Psalm 34 *page 401*

Reading *Matthew 18:1–5, 10*

The disciples approached Jesus and said, "Who is the greatest in the Kingdom of heaven?" He called a child over, placed it in their midst, and said, "Amen, I say to you, unless you turn and become like children, you will not enter the Kingdom of heaven. Whoever humbles himself like this child is the greatest in the Kingdom of heaven. And whoever receives one child such as this in my name receives me.

"See that you do not despise one of these little ones, for I say to you that their angels in heaven always look upon the face of my heavenly Father."

Reflection

In the time of Jesus, children had no rights, putting them among the humblest of humankind. Since our social values accord honor and greatness, the disciples queried Jesus about who would be greatest in heaven. His response of pointing to a child portrays the role of humility in the Christian life. Only through embracing a humble attitude will we enter God's Kingdom.

Prayers *others may be added*

Trusting in God, who helps us,
we pray:

◆ Lord, hear our prayer.

Encourage ministers in the Church
as they seek to take a humble posture
in welcoming others, we pray: ◆
Guide politicians to be honest and just,
we pray: ◆ Protect the children in our
religious-education programs, we pray: ◆
Support those working to care for the
earth, we pray: ◆ Heal those who have
cancer, we pray: ◆ Bring to eternal glory
all the dead, we pray: ◆

Our Father . . .

Gracious God,
you call us to humble service
and childlike trust and faith.
Guide your people
as they mature on their journey.
Grant that they seek to serve you
as they offer mercy and reconciliation
to those they encounter.
Through Christ our Lord.
Amen.

✝ Forever will I sing the goodness of the Lord.

Wednesday, August 14, 2019

Memorial of St. Maximilian Kolbe, Priest and Martyr

✝ Blessed be God who filled my soul with fire!

Psalm 85

page 407

Reading

Matthew 18:15–17

Jesus said to his disciples: "If your brother sins against you, go and tell him his fault between you and him alone. If he listens to you, you have won over your brother. If he does not listen, take one or two others along with you, so that 'every fact may be established on the testimony of two or three witnesses.' If he refuses to listen to them, tell the Church. If he refuses to listen even to the Church, then treat him as you would a Gentile or a tax collector."

Reflection

A wrong may be committed either with intention or unintentionally. In either case, the matter will not be settled until the individuals discuss it. In this passage, Christ sets out a path for reconciliation. Though it may be difficult, we need to allow the other person a chance to listen to us. Only if there is a refusal to listen should the person enlist another's help. Carefully read Christ's wisdom and the pattern he sets forth for right relating. Hard conversations require humility and a recognition that we are called to minister as Christ to one another.

Prayers

others may be added

To our God of mercy, we pray:

◆ Lord, hear our prayer.

Guide leaders in the Church to humbly listen to the concerns of their members, we pray: ◆ Help civic authorities draw from the good counsel of others, we pray: ◆ Nurture the talents of artists to bring hope and joy, we pray: ◆ Lead those who hunger to places that will feed them, we pray: ◆ Strengthen the weak, we pray: ◆ Encourage us to look to St. Maximilian for inspiration in living humbly for others, we pray: ◆

Our Father . . .

O God,
you gave St. Maximilian the fortitude
to give his life to save another.
May our interest in the welfare of others
be more than our concern for ourselves.
Grant that we may proceed humbly
in all our dealings with others.
Through Christ our Lord.
Amen.

✝ Blessed be God who filled my soul with fire!

Thursday, August 15, 2019

Solemnity of the Assumption of the Blessed Virgin Mary

☩ The queen stands at your hand, arrayed in gold.

Canticle of Mary

page 423

Reading

Luke 1:39–45

Mary set out in those days and traveled to the hill country in haste to a town of Judah, where she entered the house of Zechariah and greeted Elizabeth. When Elizabeth heard Mary's greeting, the infant leaped in her womb, and Elizabeth, filled with the Holy Spirit, cried out in a loud voice and said, "Blessed are you among women, and blessed is the fruit of your womb. And how does this happen to me, that the mother of my Lord should come to me? For at the moment the sound of your greeting reached my ears, the infant in my womb leaped for joy. Blessed are you who believed that what was spoken to you by the Lord would be fulfilled."

Reflection

In 1950, Pope Pius XII declared the doctrine of the Assumption. This doctrine teaches that Mary was taken to heaven body and soul. But that is not the only teaching contained within the doctrine. Mary, the model disciple, points the way for us in life and death. Not only are we to live as she did, but the doctrine of the Assumption assures us that one day we will be reunited with our bodies. At the resurrection of the dead, our bodies will join our souls in eternal glory. The banquet of the Lord is our ultimate destination, just as it was Mary's.

Prayers

others may be added

To the Lord, who blesses us, we pray:

◆ Lord, hear our prayer.

Help your Church be of one mind and heart, we pray: ◆ Direct the hearts of civic leaders to care for the least among us, we pray: ◆ Grant us grace as we act with hospitality to those who need help, we pray: ◆ Guide those who are pregnant to proper health care, we pray: ◆ Assist those who mourn the loss of a child, we pray: ◆ May those who have died rejoice with Mary and all the saints, we pray: ◆

Our Father . . .

O God,
let us, like Mary,
look forward to the promise of heaven.
Guide us in our life's journey
to trust in you
so that we be led to our eternal reward.
Through Christ our Lord.
Amen.

☩ The queen stands at your hand, arrayed in gold.

Friday, August 16, 2019
Weekday

✝ God's mercy endures forever.

Psalm 34 *page 401*

Reading *Matthew 19:3–6*

Some Pharisees approached Jesus, and tested him, saying, "Is it lawful for a man to divorce his wife for any cause whatever?" He said in reply, "Have you not read that from the beginning the Creator *made them male and female* and said, *For this reason a man shall leave his father and mother and be joined to his wife, and the two shall become one flesh?* So they are no longer two, but one flesh. Therefore, what God has joined together, man must not separate."

Reflection

In the apostolic exhortation *The Joy of Love*, Pope Francis upholds the sanctity of the Sacrament of Matrimony and urges pastoral effort to strengthen marriages. He also prescribes mercy and patience when accompanying those whose marriages have ended in divorce. He encourages people who are in complicated situations to speak to their pastors and he asks priests to "listen with sensitivity and serenity." As we accompany others, we are to pay attention to the mercy God has extended to us.

Prayers *others may be added*

To our merciful God, we pray:

◆ Lord, hear our prayer.

Strengthen our parish leaders so they act out of mercy, we pray: ◆ Free world leaders from all evil, we pray: ◆ Help couples focus on the spiritual as they prepare for the Sacrament of Matrimony, we pray: ◆ Support those who are called to the religious life, we pray: ◆ Heal the sick, we pray: ◆ Welcome those who have died to eternal life, we pray: ◆

Our Father . . .

God of love and mercy,
you call your servants to communion.
Help us encourage and affirm
the dignity of married life.
May all couples enjoy
the fruits of the sacrament
and witness to the joy that they share.
Through Christ our Lord.
Amen.

✝ God's mercy endures forever.

Saturday, August 17, 2019
Weekday

† You are my inheritance, O Lord.

Psalm 34

page 401

Reading

Matthew 19:13–15

Children were brought to Jesus that he might lay his hands on them and pray. The disciples rebuked them, but Jesus said, "Let the children come to me, and do not prevent them; for the Kingdom of heaven belongs to such as these." After he placed his hands on them, he went away.

Reflection

"Let the children come to me." By our Baptism, we became adopted children of God. That adoption brought us into a special relationship with God and others in the family of God. We are members of the Mystical Body of Christ. In this world, we act humbly as children as we do the work of Christ. When we arrive in the next world, we will share in God's love at the eternal banquet. As children of God, there is always a place for us.

Prayers

others may be added

To our loving Father, we pray:

◆ Lord, hear us.

Bless the leaders of the Church, we pray: ◆ Guide legislators to enact laws that protect children, we pray: ◆ Be attentive to the cries of children, we pray: ◆ Provide shelter and relief for all refugees and immigrants, we pray: ◆ Renew the health of all the sick, we pray: ◆ Welcome into eternal life all who have died, we pray: ◆

Our Father . . .

Good and gracious God,
you welcome all to come and experience
your loving embrace.
Teach us to be hospitable
and reveal Christ to others
as we extend kindness.
Through Christ our Lord.
Amen.

† You are my inheritance, O Lord.

Sunday, August 18, 2019
Twentieth Sunday in Ordinary Time

✝ Lord, come to my aid!

Psalm 40
page 402

Reading
Luke 12:49–53

Jesus said to his disciples: "I have come to set the earth on fire, and how I wish it were already blazing! There is a baptism with which I must be baptized, and how great is my anguish until it is accomplished! Do you think that I have come to establish peace on the earth? No, I tell you, but rather division. From now on a household of five will be divided, three against two and two against three; a father will be divided against his son and a son against his father, a mother against her daughter and a daughter against her mother, a mother-in-law against her daughter-in-law and a daughter-in-law against her mother-in-law."

Reflection
Jesus reminds us that responding as a Christian sometimes stirs up anger and resentment in family and friends. While peace will come with the Kingdom of God, doing the will of God may cause rifts among loved ones. Those that are closest to us will sometimes disagree on the necessity of following the path of righteousness. They may desire to take an easier way and want us to do so also. At such times, we need to be sure to find our peace in God, not in humankind. God will always be our refuge and aid.

Prayers
others may be added

Confident that God hears us, we pray:

◆ Lord, hear us.

That leaders in the Church never waver in presenting the Gospel, we pray: ◆ That government officials use their office for the zeal of Christian values, we pray: ◆ That teachers and students be blessed and safe in their new school year, we pray: ◆ That those on vacation return safely, we pray: ◆ That those on transplant lists receive a transplant, we pray: ◆ That all who have died rest in peace, we pray: ◆

Our Father . . .

All-powerful God,
you share your light of truth
and passionately call us
to transform our world.
Guide our efforts to live our
faith zealously.
Through Christ our Lord.
Amen.

✝ Lord, come to my aid!

Monday, August 19, 2019
Weekday

✝ Remember us, O Lord, as you favor your people.

Psalm 40

page 402

Reading

Matthew 19:16–22

A young man approached Jesus and said, "Teacher, what good must I do to gain eternal life?" . . . Jesus said to him, "If you wish to be perfect, go, sell what you have and give to the poor, and you will have treasure in heaven. Then come, follow me." When the young man heard this statement, he went away sad, for he had many possessions.

Reflection

"What must I do to gain eternal life?" Each time we read today's Scripture passage we are faced with Jesus looking into our hearts and providing a tough answer. Today we have another chance to assess our progress toward holiness, for only holiness brings about perfection. Are we making choices that bring us closer to our Lord? Are there things that we need to banish from our life so that we can become closer to God? What steps can you make to become holy?

Prayers

others may be added

To our holy Lord, we pray:

◆ Lord, hear our prayer.

That our parish ministers help us on our journey toward holiness, we pray: ◆ That elected officials work toward the common good, we pray: ◆ That life be respected from conception until natural death, we pray: ◆ That refugees be cared for, we pray: ◆ That Christ's healing renew the sick, we pray: ◆ That the martyrs and saints welcome those who have died into heaven, we pray: ◆

Our Father . . .

O God,
you give us what we need
to attain eternal life.
Teach us to be mindful of ways in which we may grow
and strengthen our relationship with you and one another.
Help us see how we might find ways
to come closer to you.
May we always find our perfection in you.
Through Christ our Lord.
Amen.

✝ Remember us, O Lord, as you favor your people.

Tuesday, August 20, 2019

Memorial of St. Bernard, Abbot and Doctor of the Church

☩ The Lord speaks of peace to his people.

Psalm 40

page 402

Reading

Matthew 19:27–30

[Peter said to Jesus,] "We have given up everything and followed you. What will there be for us?" Jesus said to them, "Amen, I say to you that you who have followed me, in the new age, when the Son of Man is seated on his throne of glory, will yourselves sit on twelve thrones, judging the twelve tribes of Israel. And everyone who has given up houses or brothers or sisters or father or mother or children or lands for the sake of my name will receive a hundred times more, and will inherit eternal life. But many who are first will be last, and the last will be first."

Reflection

Peter's query to Jesus is similar to one many would make in our day. Human beings often want to know what they will get out of something. If we follow Jesus, do we get something in return? If there is no reward, why would we bother to take the risk? Jesus tells Peter that those who have given up much will inherit eternal life. But he also cautions that "many who are first will be last." We cannot depend on our status on earth to correspond with our place in the heavenly realm. What is first in this world will not lead us to what is first for God. Putting God first makes all things possible.

Prayers

others may be added

To our Lord, who calls us to follow, we pray:

◆ Lord, hear our prayer.

That leaders in the Church always seek to place the things of God first, we pray: ◆ That our legislators strive for the greater good, we pray: ◆ That justice and peace may reign in our world, we pray: ◆ That St. Bernard continue to inspire people to heed the call to monastic vocations, we pray: ◆ That the sick be provided with patience, we pray: ◆ That those who mourn find hope, we pray: ◆

Our Father . . .

Gracious God,
you care for your people
through trial, tribulation, and turmoil.
Help us to follow you in all things.
Support us when we are tempted to doubt
so that we may feel your presence always.
Through Christ our Lord.
Amen.

☩ The Lord speaks of peace to his people.

Wednesday, August 21, 2019
Memorial of St. Pius X, Pope

✝ Lord, in your strength our hearts are glad!

Psalm 89 *page 407*

page 407

Reading *Matthew 20:8–15*

"When it was evening the owner of the vineyard said to his foreman, 'Summon the laborers and give them their pay, beginning with the last and ending with the first.' When those who had started about five o'clock came, each received the usual daily wage. So when the first came, they thought that they would receive more, but each of them also got the usual wage. And on receiving it they grumbled against the landowner, saying, 'These last ones worked only one hour, and you have made them equal to us, who bore the day's burden and the heat.' He said to one of them in reply, 'My friend, I am not cheating you. Did you not agree with me for the usual daily wage? Take what is yours and go. What if I wish to give this last one the same as you? Or am I not free to do as I wish with my own money? Are you envious because I am generous?' "

Reflection

Jesus uses a parable about how the owner of a vineyard distributes wages to illustrate the bountiful love of God. When workers received the same wage no matter the hours worked, some protested. The owner may not have acted logically, but generosity flows from mercy not logic. God, too, is generous beyond reason, showering his love without cost. St. Pius X desired that more people avail themselves of God's love in the Eucharist. He lowered the age of reception of Communion to age seven, and he recommended that the faithful receive Communion frequently.

Prayers *others may be added*

To our generous God, we pray:

◆ Lord, hear our prayer.

That bishops seek always to act from compassion, we pray: ◆ That rulers of nations be guided to work for peace through justice, we pray: ◆ That prisoners may find comfort and strength, we pray: ◆ That through the inspiration of St. Pius X, a devotion to the Eucharist grow, we pray: ◆ That all awaiting transplants be provided with patience, we pray: ◆ That those who have died be welcomed at the heavenly banquet, we pray: ◆

Our Father . . .

All-caring God,
you are generous beyond measure.
May we be mindful of your goodness
when a neighbor seeks our mercy.
As we rejoice in your compassion,
may we serve you and others with joy.
Through Christ our Lord.
Amen.

✝ Lord, in your strength our hearts are glad!

Thursday, August 22, 2019

Memorial of the Queenship of the Blessed Virgin Mary

✝ Here I am, Lord, I come to do your will.

Canticle of Mary *page 423*

Reading *Matthew 22:1–14*

Jesus again in reply spoke to the chief priests and the elders of the people in parables saying, "The Kingdom of heaven may be likened to a king who gave a wedding feast for his son. He dispatched his servants to summon the invited guests to the feast, but they refused to come. A second time he sent other servants, saying, 'Tell those invited: "Behold, I have prepared my banquet, my calves and fattened cattle are killed, and everything is ready; come to the feast."' Some ignored the invitation and went away, one to his farm, another to his business. The rest laid hold of his servants, mistreated them, and killed them. The king was enraged and sent his troops, destroyed those murderers, and burned their city. Then the king said to his servants, 'The feast is ready, but those who were invited were not worthy to come. Go out, therefore, into the main roads and invite to the feast whomever you find.' . . . But when the king came in to meet the guests he saw a man there not dressed in a wedding garment. He said to him, 'My friend, how is it that you came in here without a wedding garment?' But he was reduced to silence. Then the king said to his attendants, 'Bind his hands and feet, and cast him into the darkness outside, where there will be wailing and grinding of teeth.' Many are invited, but few are chosen."

Reflection

Why would some invited to a banquet refuse to attend while others kill the servants? Consider the response to the invitation to the heavenly banquet. Martyrs' blood attests that some have killed those who invited them. Others have ignored the invitation. Today we recognize Mary's willingness to answer yes to God. May we follow her example.

Prayers *others may be added*

Trusting in God, with Mary, we pray:

◆ Hear us, O Lord.

That the Church always welcome the invitation of the bridegroom, we pray: ◆ That nations be open to immigrants, we pray: ◆ That youth accept the invitation to expand their minds, we pray: ◆ That clothing be available to all in need, we pray: ◆ That all in hospice be strengthened spiritually for their journey home, we pray: ◆ That the grieving be comforted, we pray: ◆

Our Father . . .

Lord God,
you chose Mary to be a faithful disciple
and led her to the glory of heaven.
May we serve you
and share our resources
with those most in need,
welcoming all with mercy.
Through Christ our Lord.
Amen.

✝ Here I am, Lord, I come to do your will.

Friday, August 23, 2019

Optional Memorial of St. Rose of Lima, Virgin

✝ Praise the Lord, my soul!

Psalm 40 *page 402*

Reading *Matthew 22:34–40*

When the Pharisees heard that Jesus had silenced the Sadducees, they gathered together, and one of them a scholar of the law, tested him by asking, "Teacher, which commandment in the law is the greatest?" Jesus said to him, "You shall love the Lord, your God, with all your heart, with all your soul, and with all your mind. This is the greatest and the first commandment. The second is like it: You shall love your neighbor as yourself. The whole law and the prophets depend on these two commandments."

Reflection

Jesus tells us that the whole law and the prophets stand on two commands. These two Commandments, then, deserve our attention. Take time today to sit silently with this Gospel. What does it mean to love God with your entire being and to love your neighbor as yourself? Ponder what you leave out in your love of God. Is it your heart? Is it your mind? How can you love God more fully?

Prayers *others may be added*

With St. Rose, we turn to a loving God and pray:

◆ **Lord, hear our prayer.**

That the faithful be open to the grace of the sacraments, we pray: ◆ That civic leaders seek to create more employment opportunities, we pray: ◆ That college students receive the financial help they need, we pray: ◆ That through the inspiration of St. Rose, Third Order Dominicans prosper in their spiritual life, we pray: ◆ That the sick recover, we pray: ◆ That the dead rise to glory, we pray: ◆

Our Father . . .

O God,
you set St. Rose of Lima
on fire with your love and zeal
to inspire her generation
to understand your commands.
Grant that we may be open
to your love,
and spread that love to others.
Through Christ our Lord.
Amen.

✝ Praise the Lord, my soul!

Saturday, August 24, 2019

Feast of St. Bartholomew, Apostle

✝ Your friends make known, O Lord, the glorious splendor of your kingdom.

Psalm 145

page 421

Reading

John 1:45–49

Philip found Nathanael and told him, "We have found the one about whom Moses wrote in the law, and also the prophets, Jesus son of Joseph, from Nazareth." But Nathanael said to him, "Can anything good come from Nazareth?" Philip said to him, "Come and see." Jesus saw Nathanael coming toward him and said of him, "Here is a true child of Israel. There is no duplicity in him." Nathanael said to him, "How do you know me?" Jesus answered and said to him, "Before Philip called you, I saw you under the fig tree." Nathanael answered him, "Rabbi, you are the Son of God; you are the King of Israel."

Reflection

With the call of Nathanael, we have a chance to reflect on how we have responded to our vocation as a Christian. Are we as enthusiastic as Nathanael, or have we become complacent? No matter where we are from, good comes from us. Jesus sees us where we are and invites us to a journey that will lead to new places. Today we honor St. Bartholomew, who is said to have traveled as far as India, inviting people to "come and see."

Prayers

others may be added

With the Apostles, we turn to God and pray:

◆ Lord, hear our prayer.

That the Church maintain a missionary spirit, we pray: ◆ That community leaders promote the common good for all, we pray: ◆ That people may come forward to serve the apostolic faith, we pray: ◆ That farmers be given strength to gather the harvest, we pray: ◆ That the sick may preach the goodness of God with the example of their lives, we pray: ◆ That those who have died receive a joyful welcome to heaven, we pray: ◆

Our Father . . .

Heavenly God,
you called your Apostles,
especially Bartholomew,
to serve you to the ends of the earth,
fearlessly sharing the Good News.
Guide our efforts at evangelization
and help us to renew the face of the earth.
Through Christ our Lord.
Amen.

✝ Your friends make known, O Lord, the glorious splendor of your kingdom.

Sunday, August 25, 2019

Twenty-First Sunday in Ordinary Time

☩ Go out to all the world and tell the good news.

Psalm 117

page 413

Reading

Luke 13:23–25, 29

Someone asked him, "Lord, will only a few people be saved?" He answered them, "Strive to enter through the narrow gate, for many, I tell you, will attempt to enter but will not be strong enough. After the master of the house has arisen and locked the door, then will you stand outside knocking and saying, 'Lord, open the door for us.' He will say to you in reply, 'I do not know where you are from.' And people will come from the east and the west and from the north and the south and will recline at table in the kingdom of God."

Reflection

"I do not know where you are from." Jesus knows those who have lived as he has commanded. Calling ourselves Christians and abiding minimally to the faith does not merit a person the Kingdom of God. Jesus tells his followers to enter by the narrow gate. Have you conformed your life to Christ's? Have you done the hard work of getting to know him by bringing him into your heart?

Prayers

others may be added

To our Lord, who seeks our hearts, we pray:

◆ Lord, hear our prayer.

For our parishes, that they take to heart the call to evangelize, we pray: ◆ For our elected officials, that they be guided to care for the common good, we pray: ◆ For respect for all life from conception to natural death, we pray: ◆ For those who do not believe in God, that they be inspired by our faithful witness, we pray: ◆ For healthcare workers, that they know that their touch heals, we pray: ◆ For caregivers at funeral homes, we pray: ◆

Our Father . . .

Lord God,
you call us this Lord's Day
to renew our covenant with you
and continue to build the kingdom
of love and justice.
Guide our efforts at evangelization
so that we may bring others
to the banquet feast
you prepare for us.
Through Christ our Lord.
Amen.

☩ Go out to all the world and tell the good news.

Monday, August 26, 2019
Weekday

✝ The Lord takes delight in his people.

Psalm 117
page 413

Reading
Matthew 23:16–22

Jesus said to the crowds and to his disciples: "Woe to you, blind guides, who say, 'If one swears by the temple, it means nothing, but if one swears by the gold of the temple, one is obligated.' Blind fools, which is greater, the gold, or the temple that made the gold sacred? And you say, 'If one swears by the altar, it means nothing, but if one swears by the gift on the altar, one is obligated.' You blind ones, which is greater, the gift, or the altar that makes the gift sacred? One who swears by the altar swears by it and all that is upon it; one who swears by the temple swears by it and by him who dwells in it; one who swears by heaven swears by the throne of God and by him who is seated on it."

Reflection

As Jesus nears his passion and death, he reminds the Pharisees of their responsibility to be honest witnesses for God. We also need to examine ourselves to uncover hypocrisy. Our challenge is to see incongruities before they are so enmeshed in our lives that we do not notice them. We need to be aware of our blind spots. With such awareness, we can be more open to the work of God in our midst.

Prayers
others may be added

To the God who longs for us, we pray:

◆ Lord, hear our prayer.

For priests, that they seek always to be aware of their humble posture before others, we pray: ◆ For leaders of nations, that they be compassionate to the least among us, we pray: ◆ For awareness and sensitivity to all cultures, we pray: ◆ For those who seek meaningful employment, we pray: ◆ For the sick, that they recover, we pray: ◆ For the dying, that they enter into the light of God, we pray: ◆

Our Father . . .

Wondrous God,
you challenge us to be open to you
so that we grow in holiness.
Teach us your ways
so that we may renew our lives
and make a perfect sacrifice of praise.
Through Christ our Lord.
Amen.

✝ The Lord takes delight in his people.

Tuesday, August 27, 2019

Memorial of St. Monica

✝ You search me and you know me,
O Lord.

Psalm 117

page 413

Reading

Matthew 23:23–26

Jesus said: "Woe to you, scribes and Pharisees, you hypocrites. You pay tithes of mint and dill and cummin, and have neglected the weightier things of the law: judgment and mercy and fidelity. But these you should have done, without neglecting the others. Blind guides, who strain out the gnat and swallow the camel!

"Woe to you, scribes and Pharisees, you hypocrites. You cleanse the outside of cup and dish, but inside they are full of plunder and self-indulgence. Blind Pharisee, cleanse first the inside of the cup, so that the outside also may be clean."

Reflection

On the way to Jerusalem, Jesus continues to admonish the Pharisees. On the outside, they appear to adhere closely to the faith, but Jesus desires that their interior lives reflect their beliefs. Both tithing and mercy are important and one should not be valued more than the other. Jesus directs the Pharisees to work on their inner life and the exterior will follow. We are not entirely unlike the leaders at that time. We can find also that it is easier to sit in judgment over others than to lead humble lives filled with compassion. Like St. Monica, may we seek to possess a mother's love and patience in our lives today.

Prayers

others may be added

To our Lord, who desires a pure heart, we pray:

◆ Lord, hear our prayer.

For deacons, may they seek to serve the Church humbly, we pray: ◆ For those who work in social service agencies, we pray: ◆ For insurance workers to administer with gentleness, we pray: ◆ For respect and care for our planet, we pray: ◆ For those in a coma, may they be reawakened, we pray: ◆ For the souls in purgatory, we pray: ◆

Our Father . . .

Good and loving God,
you gave St. Monica a heart filled
with love for her children.
May we respond to your call
to deeper holiness and love.
Uncover in us
the gifts of mercy and humility
that we may always be open
to serving with gentleness and kindness.
Through Christ our Lord.
Amen.

✝ You search me and you know me,
O Lord.

Wednesday, August 28, 2019

Memorial of St. Augustine, Bishop and Doctor of the Church

✝ You have searched me and you know me, Lord.

Psalm 119

page 414

Reading

Matthew 23:27–32

Jesus said, "Woe to you, scribes and Pharisees, you hypocrites. You are like whitewashed tombs, which appear beautiful on the outside, but inside are full of dead men's bones and every kind of filth. Even so, on the outside you appear righteous, but inside you are filled with hypocrisy and evildoing.

"Woe to you, scribes and Pharisees, you hypocrites. You build the tombs of the prophets and adorn the memorials of the righteous, and you say, 'If we had lived in the days of our ancestors, we would not have joined them in shedding the prophets' blood.' Thus you bear witness against yourselves that you are the children of those who murdered the prophets; now fill up what your ancestors measured out!"

Reflection

Again, Jesus instructs the Pharisees that their outer appearances do not matter if they do not possess clean hearts. These messages help us consider whether we work harder to show that we are good people than we work at becoming good people. If our good deeds are empty, others will notice. In the same vein, when our actions come from an interior life that seeks to be conformed to Christ, our goodness will be obvious. Righteous acts will flow from a compassionate heart.

Prayers

others may be added

With hearts open to God, we pray:

◆ Lord, hear our prayer.

For theologians, that they continue to reveal God's beauty to us, we pray: ◆ For world leaders, that they act as instruments of peace, we pray: ◆ For vocations to the Augustinian orders, we pray: ◆ For catechumens, we pray: ◆ For the sick, we pray: ◆ For those who have died, that they be welcomed at the heavenly banquet, we pray: ◆

Our Father . . .

Gracious God,
you reveal your truths in uncommon ways
to those who seek you
with a sincere heart.
Guide our thoughts
so that our souls rest only in you.
Through Christ our Lord.
Amen.

✝ You have searched me and you know me, Lord.

Thursday, August 29, 2019
Memorial of the Passion of St. John the Baptist

✝ I will sing your salvation.

Psalm 71

page 405

Reading

Mark 6:17–22, 24

Herod was the one who had John the Baptist arrested and bound in prison on account of Herodias, the wife of his brother Philip, whom he had married. John had said to Herod, "It is not lawful for you to have your brother's wife." Herodias harbored a grudge against him and wanted to kill him but was unable to do so. Herod feared John, knowing him to be a righteous and holy man, and kept him in custody. When he heard him speak he was very much perplexed, yet he liked to listen to him. She had an opportunity one day when Herod, on his birthday, gave a banquet for his courtiers, his military officers, and the leading men of Galilee. Herodias' own daughter came in and performed a dance that delighted Herod and his guests. The king said to the girl, "Ask of me whatever you wish and I will grant it to you." She went out and said to her mother, "What shall I ask for?" She replied, "The head of John the Baptist." The girl hurried back to the king's presence and made her request, "I want you to give me at once on a platter the head of John the Baptist."

Reflection

John the Baptist's honest pronouncements incurred the wrath of a vengeful woman. Sometimes honesty hurts us also. Instead of stewing over a person or incident, it is wise to examine the truth in what another states. Another's critique could prompt positive change and goodness. Having reflected on a friend's or coworker's point, we can see how we might improve at pointing others toward Jesus Christ.

Prayers

others may be added

Confident in the Lord's saving power, we pray:

◆ Lord, hear our prayer.

For missionaries who face adversaries, we pray: ◆ For peacekeepers with the United Nations, we pray: ◆ For healing and concord for families in crisis, we pray: ◆ For respect for elders, we pray: ◆ For efforts to find cures for diseases, we pray: ◆ For the path of glory for all the deceased, we pray: ◆

Our Father . . .

God of goodness,
you sent John the Baptist
to prepare the way for your Son.
Give us strength in temptation
and help us to make your paths straight
to lead others to your glory.
Through Christ our Lord.
Amen.

✝ I will sing your salvation.

Friday, August 30, 2019
Weekday

✝ Rejoice in the Lord, you just!

Psalm 136 *page 420*

Reading *Matthew 25:1–13*

Jesus told his disciples this parable: "The kingdom of heaven will be like ten virgins who took their lamps and went out to meet the bridegroom. Five of them were foolish and five were wise. The foolish ones, when taking their lamps, brought no oil with them, but the wise brought flasks of oil with their lamps. Since the bridegroom was long delayed, they all became drowsy and fell asleep. At midnight, there was a cry, 'Behold, the bridegroom! Come out to meet him!' Then all those virgins got up and trimmed their lamps. The foolish ones said to the wise, 'Give us some of your oil, for our lamps are going out.' But the wise ones replied, 'No, for there may not be enough for us and you. Go instead to the merchants and buy some for yourselves.' While they went off to buy it, the bridegroom came and those who were ready went into the wedding feast with him. Then the door was locked. Afterwards the other virgins came and said, 'Lord, Lord, open the door for us!' But he said in reply, 'Amen, I say to you, I do not know you.' Therefore, stay awake, for you know neither the day nor the hour."

Reflection

In many areas of our lives, we are urged to be prepared. Christ's caution for readiness is particularly striking because it pertains to eternal life. Our preparations in this life will determine our happiness in the next. Jesus points out that we cannot be tending to details when he comes for us. Are you paying attention to the needs of your soul? How can you prepare better for the next life?

Prayers *others may be added*

To our God of surprises, we pray:

◆ Lord, hear us.

For the pope, that he help us stay alert to the signs of our times, we pray: ◆ For community leaders, that they persist in working for the common good, we pray: ◆ For teachers and students in this new school year, we pray: ◆ For those communities seeking new leadership to build their parish, we pray: ◆ For the sick and those who care for them, we pray: ◆ For all who have died, that they be led to eternal life, we pray: ◆

Our Father . . .

Almighty God of heaven and earth,
you guide your servants on their journey.
Teach us to long for the things of heaven
and not be anxious over earthly matters.
Through Christ our Lord.
Amen.

✝ Rejoice in the Lord, you just!

Saturday, August 31, 2019
Weekday

✝ The Lord comes to rule the earth with justice.

Psalm 117 *page 413*

Reading *1 Thessalonians 4:9–11*

Brothers and sisters: On the subject of fraternal charity you have no need for anyone to write you, for you yourselves have been taught by God to love one another. Indeed, you do this for all the brothers throughout Macedonia. Nevertheless we urge you, brothers and sisters, to progress even more, and to aspire to live a tranquil life, to mind your own affairs, and to work with your own hands, as we instructed you.

Reflection

St. Paul points out that he cannot teach the Thessalonians how to love, because they have learned this from God. He points out, though, that they can always improve on how they love one another. St. Paul encourages the people of Thessalonica to continue to seek to live without worry and to stay busy. Have you ever felt self-satisfied in your relationships with God and others? Just as St. Paul directed the Thessalonians, we are to continue to progress in our ways of loving one another and God.

Prayers *others may be added*

To the ever-present Lord, we pray:

◆ Lord, hear our prayer.

For tribunals, that they be compassionate to those seeking annulments, we pray: ◆ For judges, that they grow in wisdom, we pray: ◆ For progress in developing renewable energy, we pray: ◆ For the safety of those in prison, we pray: ◆ For the health and well-being of all, we pray: ◆ For the dying, that angels lead them to the gates of heaven, we pray: ◆

Our Father . . .

O God,
you have shown us how to love.
Grant that we may always seek to lift up
our joys, talents, and gifts for your glory.
Renew our efforts to love one another
in works of charity and justice
that transform our world into your reign.
Through Christ our Lord.
Amen.

✝ The Lord comes to rule the earth with justice.

Sunday, September 1, 2019

Twenty-Second Sunday in Ordinary Time

† God, in your goodness, you have made a home for the poor.

Psalm 68

page 404

Reading

Luke 14:8–11

[Jesus] told a parable to those who had been invited [to the sabbath], noticing how they were choosing the places of honor at the table. "When you are invited by someone to a wedding banquet, do not recline at table in the place of honor. A more distinguished guest than you may have been invited by him, and the host who invited both of you may approach you and say, 'Give your place to this man,' and then you would proceed with embarrassment to take the lowest place. Rather, when you are invited, go and take the lowest place so that when the host comes to you he may say, 'My friend, move up to a higher position.' Then you will enjoy the esteem of your companions at the table. For everyone who exalts himself will be humbled, but the one who humbles himself will be exalted."

Reflection

"Everyone who exalts himself will be humbled, but the one who humbles himself will be exalted." It is good for us to reflect on our humility. Those who are humble are aware of their relationship with God and others. They do not pretend to be greater than or less than another. Truly great leaders know that they are in relationship with those they serve. When Jesus washed the feet of the Apostles, he taught them that servant leaders humble themselves. Whom do you need to assist today? How will that help another see God in their midst?

Prayers

others may be added

To the Lord, who knows our heart, we pray:

◆ Lord, hear our prayer.

That leaders in the Church always seek to be servant leaders, we pray: ◆ That civic authorities lead with humility, we pray: ◆ That victims of abuse be shown kindness and compassion, we pray: ◆ That catechists prepare well for their lessons ahead, we pray: ◆ That the sick feel the healing presence of Christ, we pray: ◆ That the deceased be welcomed to heaven, we pray: ◆

Our Father . . .

Lord God,
you make a place and home for all.
May we serve you and your people,
making known the message
of your love and compassion.
Guide our efforts at building
your kingdom.
Through our Lord Jesus Christ, your Son,
who lives and reigns with you in the unity
of the Holy Spirit,
one God, for ever and ever.
Amen.

† God, in your goodness, you have made a home for the poor.

Monday, September 2, 2019
Weekday

✝ The Lord comes to judge the earth.

Psalm 68

page 404

Reading

Luke 4:16–21

Jesus came to Nazareth, where he had grown up, and went according to his custom into the synagogue on the sabbath day. He stood up to read and was handed a scroll of the prophet Isaiah. He unrolled the scroll and found the passage where it was written:

The Spirit of the Lord is upon me, / because he has anointed me / to bring glad tidings to the poor. / He has sent me to proclaim liberty to captives / and recovery of sight to the blind, / to let the oppressed go free, / and to proclaim a year acceptable to the Lord.

Rolling up the scroll, he handed it back to the attendant and sat down, and the eyes of all in the synagogue looked intently at him. He said to them, "Today this Scripture passage is fulfilled in your hearing."

Reflection

Returning to his hometown at the beginning of his ministry, Jesus picks up the scroll to read that the Lord has anointed him to proclaim liberty to the captive and sight to the blind. Christians were anointed at Baptism and made priest, prophet, and king in Jesus Christ. When we live as doers of the Word, we bring this Scripture to life in our community. Do you know someone who is oppressed? Who needs you to proclaim the Good News to them?

Prayers

others may be added

Confident in the Lord's guidance,
we pray:

◆ Lord, hear our prayer.

That the Church proclaim liberty to captives through care for refugees, we pray: ◆ That community leaders seek to care for the marginalized, we pray: ◆ That those who labor and are burdened find relief, we pray: ◆ That those who work in oppressive conditions be provided relief, we pray: ◆ That travelers reach their destination safely, we pray: ◆ That those who have died join our God in glory, we pray: ◆

Our Father . . .

God, ever ancient and new,
you teach us the ways of your reign
and guide us toward a communion
of love.
Strengthen our effort
to live out your vision as we seek
to proclaim your goodness to all.
Through Christ our Lord.
Amen.

✝ The Lord comes to judge the earth.

Tuesday, September 3, 2019

Memorial of St. Gregory the Great, Pope and Doctor of the Church

✝ I believe that I shall see the good things of the Lord in the land of the living.

Psalm 63

page 403

Reading

Luke 4:31–37

Jesus went down to Capernaum, a town of Galilee. He taught them on the sabbath, and they were astonished at his teaching because he spoke with authority. In the synagogue there was a man with the spirit of an unclean demon, and he cried out in a loud voice, "What have you to do with us, Jesus of Nazareth? Have you come to destroy us? I know who you are—the Holy One of God!" Jesus rebuked him and said, "Be quiet! Come out of him!" Then the demon threw the man down in front of them and came out of him without doing him any harm. They were all amazed and said to one another, "What is there about his word? For with authority and power he commands the unclean spirits, and they come out." And news of him spread everywhere in the surrounding region.

Reflection

When Jesus rebukes the demon, others are amazed at the impact of his word. Most of us will never come across someone who is possessed. However, we will come upon times when the Word of God will comfort, console, and instruct. As we become closer to the Lord through prayer and Scripture, we may find that we are drawn to rely on the Word to reach others. May we put our trust in God and ask him to speak through us.

Prayers

others may be added

To our healing God, we pray:

◆ Lord, hear our prayer.

That the people in ministry teach with love, we pray: ◆ That through the intercession of St. Gregory, we have a renewed affection for liturgical music, we pray: ◆ That nations work for relief of refugees and migrants, we pray: ◆ That students seek wisdom, we pray: ◆ That healing come to all who are ill, we pray: ◆ That those who have died be brought into the light of Christ, we pray: ◆

Our Father . . .

Loving God,
your Word has the power
to cast out demons
and bring healing and goodness to all.
As heralds of the Good News,
may we draw others to your Word
that they may feel your protection.
Through Christ our Lord.
Amen.

✝ I believe that I shall see the good things of the Lord in the land of the living.

Wednesday, September 4, 2019
Weekday

✝ I trust in the mercy of God for ever.

Psalm 63 *page 403*

Reading *Luke 4:38–44*

After Jesus left the synagogue, he entered the house of Simon. Simon's mother-in-law was afflicted with a severe fever, and they interceded with him about her. He stood over her, rebuked the fever, and it left her. She got up immediately and waited on them.

At sunset, all who had people sick with various diseases brought them to him. He laid his hands on each of them and cured them. And demons also came out from many, shouting, "You are the Son of God." But he rebuked them and did not allow them to speak because they knew that he was the Christ.

At daybreak, Jesus left and went to a deserted place. The crowds went looking for him, and when they came to him, they tried to prevent him from leaving them. But he said to them, "To the other towns also I must proclaim the good news of the Kingdom of God, because for this purpose I have been sent." And he was preaching in the synagogues of Judea.

Reflection

As we read of Jesus' life of prayer and spreading the Good News, we may reflect on how we live. It is apparent that Jesus did nothing without prayer. He prayed at the synagogue and then healed people. Before traveling to continue preaching, he prayed. His desire to proclaim God's Kingdom far and wide prevented him from staying in one place. How do you live out the Gospel? Do you rely on prayer before you act?

Prayers *others may be added*

Turning to our Lord, we pray:

◆ **Lord, hear our prayer.**

That the Gospel be brought to those in need, we pray: ◆ That civic authorities seek to work for the common good, we pray: ◆ That those who work in hospitality see the Good News in their efforts to make people comfortable, we pray: ◆ That our parish may always be a place of faithful stewardship, we pray: ◆ That the sick and those who care for them experience the strength of Christ, we pray: ◆ That those who have died may rest in the Lord, we pray: ◆

Our Father . . .

Gracious God,
you call us to serve you
and those who are most in need.
Heal the troubles in our world,
and guide our efforts
to bring your Good News
to the downtrodden and afflicted
so that they may be raised up in hope.
Through Christ our Lord.
Amen.

✝ I trust in the mercy of God for ever.

Thursday, September 5, 2019
Weekday

✝ The Lord has made known
his salvation.

Psalm 63
page 403

Reading
Luke 5:4–10

[Jesus] said to Simon, "Put out into deep water and lower your nets for a catch." Simon said in reply, "Master, we have worked hard all night and have caught nothing, but at your command I will lower the nets." When they had done this, they caught a great number of fish and their nets were tearing. They signaled to their partners in the other boat to come to help them. They came and filled both boats so that the boats were in danger of sinking. When Simon Peter saw this, he fell at the knees of Jesus and said, "Depart from me, Lord, for I am a sinful man." For astonishment at the catch of fish they had made seized him and all those with him, and likewise James and John, the sons of Zebedee, who were partners of Simon. Jesus said to Simon, "Do not be afraid; from now on you will be catching men."

Reflection

Peter must have been moved by the preaching and teaching of Jesus to follow his command instantly. Christ also interrupts our busy lives and invites us to "put out into deep water." At times, we need help to realize that disruptions and changes in plans, especially when least expected, are opportunities for ministry and sharing of gifts. May we never tire from being open to possibilities. As Jesus said, "Do not be afraid."

Prayers
others may be added

Confident in the Lord's care, we pray:

◆ Lord, hear our prayer.

That women and men seek to be of service through the vowed life, we pray: ◆ That world leaders assist people who are in need of water and other vital resources, we pray: ◆ That those recovering from natural disasters know of our support, we pray: ◆ That prisoners keep their strength and courage, we pray: ◆ That the sick find hope in Christ, we pray: ◆ That the faithful departed be guided to their eternal reward, we pray: ◆

Our Father . . .

Heavenly Father,
you come to our aid
when our work brings little result.
Teach us to be open
and have courage in following your Son
so that we may put aside our pride
and share everything for your glory.
Through Christ our Lord.
Amen.

✝ The Lord has made known
his salvation.

Friday, September 6, 2019
Weekday

✝ Come with joy into the presence of the Lord.

Psalm 100 *page 410*

Reading *Luke 5:33–39*

The scribes and Pharisees said to Jesus, "The disciples of John the Baptist fast often and offer prayers, and the disciples of the Pharisees do the same; but yours eat and drink." Jesus answered them, "Can you make the wedding guests fast while the bridegroom is with them? But the days will come, and when the bridegroom is taken away from them, then they will fast in those days." And he also told them a parable. "No one tears a piece from a new cloak to patch an old one. Otherwise, he will tear the new and the piece from it will not match the old cloak. Likewise, no one pours new wine into old wineskins. Otherwise, the new wine will burst the skins, and it will be spilled, and the skins will be ruined. Rather, new wine must be poured into fresh wineskins. And no one who has been drinking old wine desires new, for he says, 'The old is good.'"

Reflection

Pope Francis teaches people to be open to other attitudes. In this Gospel, one group of people sees the necessity of fasting while another forgoes the discipline. Jesus' disciples do not fast because they are with the one they have awaited. John's disciples cannot see this. Pope Francis strived to change the heart of the Church for the poor. We are called to be open to seeing another way. Through humility, we open ourselves to serve in new ways. May we pray that we never close ourselves off from inspiration from God.

Prayers *others may be added*

Looking to God, who makes all things new, we pray:

◆ Lord, hear us.

That the Church seek always to grow and change with God's help, we pray: ◆ That community leaders assist those in need, we pray: ◆ That farmers and fishers have an abundant harvest, we pray: ◆ That youth at football games and other sports events remain safe and free from harm, we pray: ◆ That the sick recover, we pray: ◆ That the dying reach the heavenly banquet, we pray: ◆

Our Father . . .

Good and gracious God,
you call us to change and grow
in every time, season, and place.
May we celebrate your goodness
and be mindful of your Spirit
who guides our future
and our efforts to be constant in love.
Through Christ our Lord.
Amen.

✝ Come with joy into the presence of the Lord.

Saturday, September 7, 2019
Weekday

✝ God is my help.

Psalm 66 *page 403*

Reading *Luke 6:1–5*

While Jesus was going through a field of grain on a sabbath, his disciples were picking the heads of grain, rubbing them in their hands, and eating them. Some Pharisees said, "Why are you doing what is unlawful on the sabbath?" Jesus said to them in reply, "Have you not read what David did when he and those who were with him were hungry? How he went into the house of God, took the bread of offering, which only the priests could lawfully eat, ate of it, and shared it with his companions?" Then he said to them, "The Son of Man is lord of the sabbath."

Reflection

Another journey and another rule that Jesus allows to be broken. We might consider if we let rules keep us from witnessing to the Lord. Do we ever see it necessary to go against social norms so that Christ may break into the world? At times, those norms are unspoken ones. Though our society claims to be open, racism, ageism, and sexism still take a role in decision making. Do we try to educate our associates to accord dignity to all, no matter race, age, or sex. Do our lives reflect compassion for others? We must be mindful not to value rules more than mercy.

Prayers *others may be added*

Confident in God's care for us,
we pray:

◆ Gracious Lord, hear our prayer.

That our parish leaders be open to ways of deepening our Christian life, we pray: ◆ That leaders of nations strive to model peace and unity, we pray: ◆ That our elected officials work for just wages for all, we pray: ◆ That those who protect us be kept free from harm, we pray: ◆ That those with incurable diseases experience miraculous healing, we pray: ◆ That the angels lead the dying to paradise, we pray: ◆

Our Father . . .

God of day and darkness,
you bring light to your people.
Keep us faithful to your path
of justice and righteousness
so that all may be provided hope
and live in your goodness.
Through Christ our Lord.
Amen.

✝ God is my help.

Sunday, September 8, 2019

Twenty-Third Sunday in Ordinary Time

☩ In every age, O Lord, you have been our refuge.

Psalm 51 *page 402*

Reading *Luke 14:25–27*

Great crowds were traveling with Jesus, and he turned and addressed them, "If anyone comes to me without hating his father and mother, wife and children, brothers and sisters, and even his own life, he cannot be my disciple. Whoever does not carry his own cross and come after me cannot be my disciple."

Reflection

Today's reading invites us to reflect on what possesses us and what we need to leave behind to love the Lord fully. What do you value in your life? Do you value any of those things or people more than you value the Lord? A scene from the 1986 movie *The Mission* vividly portrays the need to cut out what holds us back from climbing the mountain of the Lord. We do not go to heaven with what weighs us down. What is the Lord inviting you to let go during this day?

Prayers *others may be added*

Turning to our faithful Lord, we pray:

◆ Lord, hear our prayer.

Assist the Church in finding ways to care for the poor and needy, we pray: ◆ Encourage leaders of nations to seek justice, we pray: ◆ Grant heads of companies the wisdom to value workers more than profits, we pray: ◆ Unite families in crisis and conflict, we pray: ◆ Inspire researchers to develop drugs to cure disease, we pray: ◆ Show the dying your face, we pray: ◆

Our Father . . .

O Lord,
you teach us your ways and truth.
Grant that we may desire
to deepen our faith.
May we give honor to you
and not the things of this earth.
Through Christ our Lord.
Amen.

☩ In every age, O Lord, you have been our refuge.

Monday, September 9, 2019

Memorial of St. Peter Claver, Priest

☩ In God is my safety and my glory.

Psalm 51

page 402

Reading

Luke 6:6–11

On a certain sabbath Jesus went into the synagogue and taught, and there was a man there whose right hand was withered. The scribes and the Pharisees watched him closely to see if he would cure on the sabbath so that they might discover a reason to accuse him. But he realized their intentions and said to the man with the withered hand, "Come up and stand before us." Then Jesus said to them, "I ask you, is it lawful to do good on the sabbath rather than to do evil, to save life rather than to destroy it?" Looking around at them all, he then said to him, "Stretch out your hand." He did so and his hand was restored. But they became enraged and discussed what they might do to Jesus.

Reflection

Jesus did not protest rules. However, he would not allow a rule to prevent him from curing someone. The scribes and Pharisees are presented as obsessed with the Law. This obsession blinded them to the love that undergirded the Law. They had lost track of the reason God presented them with the Law. When are you unable to see as God might see? Is it possible for you to remove the blinders that narrow your vision?

Prayers

others may be added

To our healing Lord, we pray:

◆ Hear us, gracious Lord.

That the Church continue to work to inform the faithful of her teachings on justice, we pray: ◆ That those who are underemployed find ways to use their talents, we pray: ◆ That victims of trafficking be freed, we pray: ◆ That our community work for racial equality, we pray: ◆ That the sick be healed, we pray: ◆ That the dying be led to paradise, we pray: ◆

Our Father . . .

O God,
your love for us is bountiful.
May we strive
to abide by your Commandments
and through them show our love
for all you have given us.
Grant that our hearts be open
to your life-giving ways.
Through Christ our Lord.
Amen.

☩ In God is my safety and my glory.

Tuesday, September 10, 2019
Weekday

✝ The Lord is compassionate toward all his works.

Psalm 95

page 408

Reading

Luke 6:12–19

Jesus departed to the mountain to pray, and he spent the night in prayer to God. When day came, he called his disciples to himself, and from them he chose Twelve, whom he also named Apostles: Simon, whom he named Peter, and his brother Andrew, James, John, Philip, Bartholomew, Matthew, Thomas, James the son of Alphaeus, Simon who was called a Zealot, and Judas the son of James, and Judas Iscariot, who became a traitor.

And he came down with them and stood on a stretch of level ground. A great crowd of his disciples and a large number of the people from all Judea and Jerusalem and the coastal region of Tyre and Sidon came to hear him and to be healed of their diseases; and even those who were tormented by unclean spirits were cured. Everyone in the crowd sought to touch him because power came forth from him and healed them all.

Reflection

Only after a night of prayer does Jesus choose the Apostles. We, too, should be careful to pray and discern the will of God before making a decision. How will we know what God desires if we have not spent time alone with him? Solitude with God allows us to renew our relationship and sense of purpose in working for God's Kingdom.

Prayers

others may be added

To the Lord of our longing, we pray:

◆ Graciously hear us, O Lord.

Help catechists to model ways of praying for their students, we pray: ◆ Assist leaders to help the community respect the Lord's Day, we pray: ◆ Encourage coaches of school sports to honor the body and the spirit during practices, we pray: ◆ Assist the lonely and aged in their challenges, we pray: ◆ Grant patience to the anxious awaiting results from medical testing, we pray: ◆ Show the dying their path to eternal life, we pray: ◆

Our Father . . .

Loving God,
you call your people to serve you.
Grant that the faithful
take to heart opportunities
to discern their next steps
and your will.
Through Christ our Lord.
Amen.

✝ The Lord is compassionate toward all his works.

Wednesday, September 11, 2019
Weekday

✝ The Lord is compassionate toward all his works.

Psalm 95 *page 408*

Reading *Colossians 3:1–11*

Brothers and sisters: If you were raised with Christ, seek what is above, where Christ is seated at the right hand of God. Think of what is above, not of what is on earth. For you have died, and your life is hidden with Christ in God. When Christ your life appears, then you too will appear with him in glory.

Put to death, then, the parts of you that are earthly: immorality, impurity, passion, evil desire, and the greed that is idolatry. Because of these the wrath of God is coming upon the disobedient. By these you too once conducted yourselves, when you lived in that way. But now you must put them all away: anger, fury, malice, slander, and obscene language out of your mouths. Stop lying to one another, since you have taken off the old self with its practices and have put on the new self, which is being renewed, for knowledge, in the image of its creator. Here there is not Greek and Jew, circumcision and uncircumcision, barbarian, Scythian, slave, free; but Christ is all and in all.

Reflection

As Patriot Day is celebrated today, we should be especially mindful of the type of life this reading calls us to lead. As Christians, we have been raised with Christ and are subject to a higher calling. We are to seek life, work for the good of others, and not allow ourselves to be caught up in vengefulness or anger. People of every nation have been made in the image and likeness of God. The faithful give thanks that God shows us his face in so many.

Prayers *others may be added*

Trusting in God's protection, we pray:

◆ Lord, hear our prayer.

Aid the Church as it strives to show your love and mercy, we pray: ◆ Guide world leaders to be instruments of peace, we pray: ◆ Heal all who carry hate and vengeance in their hearts, we pray: ◆ Renew dialogue among world religions, we pray: ◆ Support first responders who suffer from diseases incurred during their rescue efforts on 9/11, we pray: ◆ Lead those who have died in service to our country to eternal glory, we pray: ◆

Our Father . . .

Lord God,
on this special day of remembrance,
guide our efforts at peacekeeping.
May we be your faithful witnesses
of love and mercy,
willing to share our gifts with all we meet
to build your reign of justice and good.
Through Christ our Lord.
Amen.

✝ The Lord is compassionate toward all his works.

Thursday, September 12, 2019
Optional Memorial of the Holy Name of Mary

✝ Let everything that breathes praise the Lord.

Psalm 90
page 408

Reading
Colossians 3:12–16

Brothers and sisters: Put on, as God's chosen ones, holy and beloved, heartfelt compassion, kindness, humility, gentleness, and patience, bearing with one another and forgiving one another, if one has a grievance against another; as the Lord has forgiven you, so must you also do. And over all these put on love, that is, the bond of perfection. And let the peace of Christ control your hearts, the peace into which you were also called in one Body. And be thankful. Let the word of Christ dwell in you richly, as in all wisdom you teach and admonish one another, singing psalms, hymns, and spiritual songs with gratitude in your hearts to God.

Reflection
The name of Mary, who lived as God desired, is honored because she is the Mother of God. She was chosen for a special role, but we are also chosen. As God's chosen ones, St. Paul directs that we are to act in a certain manner. We are to live with compassion, forgiving one another, allowing the peace of Christ to rule our hearts. Always we are to live in gratitude, praising God in song. Such a life may seem too difficult, but we have Mary to follow and to lead us in her way of discipleship.

Prayers
others may be added

With Mary, we turn to God to share our prayers and petitions:

◆ Lord, hear our prayer.

Assist leaders in the Church as they seek to witness forgiveness with compassion, we pray: ◆ Lead community leaders to bring citizens to care for the earth and the environment, we pray: ◆ Help couples strengthen their marriages through living in gratitude, we pray: ◆ Nurture musicians as they try to build parish music ministries, we pray: ◆ Aid scientists researching cures for diseases, we pray: ◆ Show the dying your glorious presence, we pray: ◆

Our Father . . .

O God,
you have shown us your ways.
Help us to keep your Word dwelling
in our hearts so that
we might be holy as you are holy.
May we join with creation in praise
to you,
always lifting our voices in gratitude.
Through Christ our Lord.
Amen.

✝ Let everything that breathes praise the Lord.

Friday, September 13, 2019

Memorial of St. John Chrysostom, Bishop and Doctor of the Church

✝ *You are my inheritance, O Lord.*

Psalm 90 *page 408*

Reading *I Timothy 1:1–2, 12–14*

Paul, an Apostle of Christ Jesus by command of God our savior and of Christ Jesus our hope, to Timothy, my true child in faith: grace, mercy, and peace from God the Father and Christ Jesus our Lord.

I am grateful to him who has strengthened me, Christ Jesus our Lord, because he considered me trustworthy in appointing me to the ministry. I was once a blasphemer and a persecutor and an arrogant man, but I have been mercifully treated because I acted out of ignorance in my unbelief. Indeed, the grace of our Lord has been abundant, along with the faith and love that are in Christ Jesus.

Reflection

Paul's greetings remind us of the joy and fellowship we should share with others. Too often we find ourselves too busy to properly acknowledge one another's presence. But by doing so, we strengthen and support those in need of grace and peace. The way we witness and preach helps us to become the golden-tongued leaders of today, just as was John Chrysostom, who was known for his gift of preaching. His authentic teaching helped others grow from ignorance to belief. May we recognize our active role in supporting others' faith.

Prayers *others may be added*

Directing our thoughts to our merciful Lord, we pray:

◆ Lord, hear our prayer.

Inspire the faithful to support the efforts of Catholic charitable organizations, we pray: ◆ Assist leaders of relief efforts in places suffering from natural disaster, we pray: ◆ Through the intercession of St. John, support deacons, priests, and bishops as they seek to be renewed in their preaching and teaching, we pray: ◆ Move hearts to develop a profound respect for all human life, we pray: ◆ Heal the sick and strengthen those who care for them, we pray: ◆ Show the light of your face to all who are dying, we pray: ◆

Our Father . . .

O God,
you gave John Chrysostom
a golden tongue
to teach and enlighten
the people of his time.
Help us as we craft our words
so that others may know
of your goodness.
Through Christ our Lord.
Amen.

✝ You are my inheritance, O Lord.

Saturday, September 14, 2019
Feast of the Exaltation of the Holy Cross

✝ Do not forget the works of the Lord!

Psalm 90 *page 408*

Reading *John 3:13–17*

Jesus said to Nicodemus: "No one has gone up to heaven except the one who has come down from heaven, the Son of Man. And just as Moses lifted up the serpent in the desert, so must the Son of Man be lifted up, so that everyone who believes in him may have eternal life."

For God so loved the world that he gave his only Son, so that everyone who believes in him might not perish but might have eternal life. For God did not send his Son into the world to condemn the world, but that the world might be saved through him.

Reflection

Throughout the year we hear in the Gospel: take up your cross and follow the Lord. When Christ was raised on the cross to his death, he transformed a symbol of hate to one of love. We die to ourselves as we take up our cross and live for others. With the cross raised in our lives, we speak and act as a member of Christ's Body. At our Baptism, we were signed with the cross and claimed for Christ. As part of the Body of Christ, we live out that sign in the world, working to be God's transformative agent of love.

Prayers *others may be added*

Glorying in the cross of Christ,
we pray:

◆ Lord, hear our prayer.

Protect all who seek to evangelize, we pray: ◆ Inspire our civic leaders as they face difficulties, we pray: ◆ Aid us as we face our crosses, we pray: ◆ Strengthen all who long for meaningful employment, we pray: ◆ Heal the broken-hearted, we pray: ◆ Grant eternal life to the dying, we pray: ◆

Our Father . . .

Dear Lord,
you so loved the world
that you sent us your Son
to be glorified on the Tree of Life.
Renew our resolve to take up our cross
and strengthen us in the mysteries
of faith.
Through Christ our Lord.
Amen.

✝ Do not forget the works of the Lord!

Sunday, September 15, 2019

Twenty-Fourth Sunday in Ordinary Time

✝ I will rise and go to my father.

Psalm 51

page 402

Reading

Luke 15:3–7

[Jesus said:]
"What man among you having a hundred sheep and losing one of them would not leave the ninety-nine in the desert and go after the lost one until he finds it? And when he does find it, he sets it on his shoulders with great joy and, upon his arrival home, he calls together his friends and neighbors and says to them, 'Rejoice with me because I have found my lost sheep.' I tell you, in just the same way there will be more joy in heaven over one sinner who repents than over ninety-nine righteous people who have no need of repentance."

Reflection

Christ tells many parables to support our faith, guide us when we sin, and gives us hope to return to God at any time. People who stay away from the Church because of a feeling that they are terrible sinners need us to provide hope. Christ's parables first give us hope that nothing can ever keep us away from God's mercy, love, and forgiveness. There is no reason to feel lost; our loving God will always find us. We might encourage others to think of the Church as the "lost and found" area for our time on earth.

Prayers

others may be added

Turning to our merciful God, we pray:

◆ Lord, hear our prayer.

For renewed efforts to welcome Catholics to return to the sacraments, we pray: ◆ For migrants seeking a place of rest and refreshment, we pray: ◆ For the incarcerated who feel lost in society, we pray: ◆ For the lonely and lost who need to find a place in others' lives, we pray: ◆ For cures to be found for cancer, we pray: ◆ For those we miss and mourn, we pray: ◆

Our Father . . .

Merciful God,
you always call us back to you
and readily extend forgiveness.
Shelter those in need of your care
and guide our efforts
to strengthen and support
those who are seeking renewal
of their faith
and a closer bond with the Church.
Through Christ our Lord.
Amen.

✝ I will rise and go to my father.

Monday, September 16, 2019

Memorial of St. Cornelius, Pope, and Cyprian, Bishop, Martyrs

✝ Blessed be the Lord, who has heard my prayer.

Psalm 51

page 402

Reading

1 Timothy 2:1–8

Beloved: First of all, I ask that supplications, prayers, petitions, and thanksgivings be offered for everyone, for kings and for all in authority, that we may lead a quiet and tranquil life in all devotion and dignity. This is good and pleasing to God our savior, who wills everyone to be saved and to come to knowledge of the truth. / For there is one God. / There is also one mediator between God and men, / the man Christ Jesus, / who gave himself as ransom for all.

This was the testimony at the proper time. For this I was appointed preacher and Apostle (I am speaking the truth, I am not lying), teacher of the Gentiles in faith and truth.

It is my wish, then, that in every place the men should pray, lifting up holy hands, without anger or argument.

Reflection

Cyprian and Cornelius struggled for unity in the Church, seeking to keep members together in spite of theological controversies and persecutions from emperors. In this pastoral letter, we hear of the need to do well and please God, to lead a "tranquil life in all devotion and dignity." Though difficulties face us, we seek wisdom so that our life becomes a prayer of thanksgiving that glorifies God.

Prayers

others may be added

Seeking God's help, we pray:

◆ Lord, hear our prayer.

For bishops, may they be strengthened in hope, we pray: ◆ For unity among Christian communities, we pray: ◆ For catechists, we pray: ◆ For Catholic charities, that they continue to share God's love, we pray: ◆ For caregivers, that they provide a healing touch, we pray: ◆ For the dying, that they join the martyrs and saints, we pray: ◆

Our Father . . .

O God,
you guide martyrs, saints and sinners.
Strengthen our resolve to serve you
and your people.
May we be provided with fortitude
when our days are full of toil
and adversity challenges us.
Through Christ our Lord.
Amen.

✝ Blessed be the Lord, who has heard my prayer.

Tuesday, September 17, 2019
Optional Memorial of St. Robert Bellarmine, Bishop and Doctor of the Church

✝ I will walk with blameless heart.

Psalm 51 *page 402*

Reading *Luke 7:11–17*

Jesus journeyed to a city called Nain, and his disciples and a large crowd accompanied him. As he drew near to the gate of the city, a man who had died was being carried out, the only son of his mother, and she was a widow. A large crowd from the city was with her. When the Lord saw her, he was moved with pity for her and said to her, "Do not weep." He stepped forward and touched the coffin; at this the bearers halted, and he said, "Young man, I tell you, arise!" The dead man sat up and began to speak, and Jesus gave him to his mother. Fear seized them all, and they glorified God, exclaiming, "A great prophet has arisen in our midst," and "God has visited his people." This report about him spread through the whole of Judea and in all the surrounding region.

Reflection

Jesus knew that the death of this widow's son meant that she would lose not only social status but would struggle to put bread on the table. Without her asking, Jesus restored the son to life. We, too, are to notice the pain of others and reach out in compassion. May we understand that our presence can help renew another's spirit. Our reaching out to a person who is in pain extends the presence and grace of God.

Prayers *others may be added*

Trusting in the Lord's goodness,
we pray:

◆ Hear us, gracious Lord.

For leaders in the Church, that they always seek to witness compassion in their ministry, we pray: ◆ For civic agencies, that they provide care for those most in need, we pray: ◆ For the Society of Jesus, that through the intercession of Robert Bellarmine, more men join the order, we pray: ◆ For teachers, may they receive the support they need, we pray: ◆ For people suffering from emotional difficulties, that they find healing, we pray: ◆ For those who have died, that they be welcomed to heaven, we pray: ◆

Our Father . . .

God of healing,
you brought a man back to life
and provided a mother joy.
You call us to arise
to serve the needs of others.
Renew in all the Church
a desire to be a sign of healing
and an instrument of your peace.
Through Christ our Lord.
Amen.

✝ I will walk with blameless heart.

Wednesday, September 18, 2019
Weekday

✝ How great are the works of the Lord!

Psalm 51 *page 402*

Reading *Luke 7:31–35*

Jesus said to the crowds: "To what shall I compare the people of this generation? What are they like? They are like children who sit in the marketplace and call to one another, / 'We played the flute for you, but you did not dance. / We sang a dirge, but you did not weep.' / For John the Baptist came neither eating food nor drinking wine, and you said, 'He is possessed by a demon.' The Son of Man came eating and drinking and you said, 'Look, he is a glutton and a drunkard, a friend of tax collectors and sinners.' But wisdom is vindicated by all her children."

Reflection

Sometimes the expectations of others can be frustrating. One day a person might say, "I wish you would do this," and on another, "Oh, you should have done it that way." The resulting frustration can divert us from our purpose and drain energy. The Scriptures show us that prophets and leaders have needed to work to stay focused on their call. Their mission was not to please people but to follow the plan that God had for them. Today we need to continue to concentrate on the vision that God provides and not lose our way to the changing expectations of others.

Prayers *others may be added*

To our Lord who guides us, we pray:

◆ Lord, hear our prayer.

For the pope, that he never waver as he seeks to follow the Lord, we pray: ◆ For community leaders, that they not fear speaking prophetically, we pray: ◆ For those looking for employment, we pray: ◆ For renewed efforts to support alternative energy renewal, we pray: ◆ For healing of mind and body for those who are depressed, we pray: ◆ For those who have died, that they be welcomed to the banquet of the Lord, we pray: ◆

Our Father . . .

O Lord,
you perform marvelous deeds
in our midst.
Help us always to be mindful
of our expectations of others
and assist them in bringing forth
your vision of holiness and love.
Through Christ our Lord.
Amen.

✝ How great are the works of the Lord!

Thursday, September 19, 2019
Weekday

✝ How great are the works of the Lord.

Psalm 103 *page 411*

page 411

Reading *Luke 7:36–39, 44–47*

A . . . Pharisee invited Jesus to dine with him, and he entered the Pharisee's house and reclined at table. Now there was a sinful woman in the city who learned that he was at table in the house of the Pharisee. Bringing an alabaster flask of ointment, she stood behind him at his feet weeping and began to bathe his feet with her tears. Then she wiped them with her hair, kissed them, and anointed them with the ointment. When the Pharisee who had invited him saw this he said to himself, "If this man were a prophet, he would know who and what sort of woman this is who is touching him, that she is a sinner." Then he [Jesus] turned to the woman and said to Simon, "Do you see this woman? When I entered your house you did not give me water for my feet, but she has bathed them with her tears and wiped them with her hair. You did not give me a kiss, but she has not ceased kissing my feet since the time I entered. You did not anoint my head with oil, but she anointed my feet with ointment. So I tell you, her many sins have been forgiven; hence, she has shown great love. But the one to whom little is forgiven, loves little."

Reflection

When the Pharisee sees the woman anointing Jesus, he thinks of her sin. Jesus, however, sees this woman's humility. The Pharisee obeys the Law, but Jesus points out that he has forsaken kindness, hospitality, and acts of humility. We are left wondering how to show love for God. Do we do so through obeying the Commandments or through virtues such as humility?

Prayers *others may be added*

Turning to our merciful Lord, we pray:

◆ **Lord, hear our prayer.**

For parishioners who show the face of God to those they meet, we pray: ◆ For hospital volunteers, that they feel support for their service, we pray: ◆ For the lonely and abandoned, that they find solace, we pray: ◆ For social workers, that their work be done with wisdom, we pray: ◆ For nurses and other health-care providers, we pray: ◆ For all who work in bereavement ministry, we pray: ◆

Our Father . . .

Loving God,
you point the way for us
to enter into relationship with you.
May we always seek to greet others
with humility and kindness
so that they may feel the warmth
of your compassion and mercy.
Through Christ our Lord.
Amen.

✝ How great are the works of the Lord.

Friday, September 20, 2019

Memorial of Sts. Andrew Kim Tae-gŏn, Priest, and Paul Chŏng Ha-sang, and Companions, Martyrs

✝ Blessed the poor in spirit, the Kingdom of heaven is theirs!

Psalm 103

page 411

Reading

Luke 8:1–3

Jesus journeyed from one town and village to another, preaching and proclaiming the good news of the Kingdom of God. Accompanying him were the Twelve and some women who had been cured of evil spirits and infirmities. Mary, called Magdalene, from whom seven demons had gone out, Joanna, the wife of Herod's steward Chuza, Suzanna, and many others who provided for them out of their resources.

Reflection

Today's Gospel highlights the companionship that Jesus had with men and women during his ministry. For Jesus, as for us, friendship is important and provides graces that draw us closer to God. At times we need to consider how we nurture and cultivate relationships. We can get caught up in our work and routine tasks and forget the value of smelling the roses with another. Let others know how important they are to your life not only by your actions but by the place you make for them in your life.

Prayers

others may be added

Confident in God's faithfulness, we pray:

◆ Lord, hear our prayer.

For all who seek to become Catholic, we pray: ◆ For catechists, that they do not tire of sharing the Gospel, we pray: ◆ For those who support parish ministry, we pray: ◆ For community leaders, that they be good stewards of their many gifts, we pray: ◆ For the sick, that they be healed, we pray: ◆ For the dying, that they enter eternal life, we pray: ◆

Our Father . . .

Gentle God,
you provided courage
to Korean men and women
to cultivate the faith.
Grant that we join others
in nurturing the faith
within our communities.
May we always use our gifts
to build your reign.
Through our Lord Jesus Christ, your Son,
who lives and reigns with you in the unity
of the Holy Spirit,
one God, for ever and ever.
Amen.

✝ Blessed the poor in spirit, the Kingdom of heaven is theirs!

Saturday, September 21, 2019
Feast of St. Matthew, Apostle and Evangelist

✝ Their message goes out through all the earth.

Psalm 103

page 411

Reading

Matthew 9:9–13

As Jesus passed by, he saw a man named Matthew sitting at the customs post. He said to him, "Follow me." And he got up and followed him. While he was at table in his house, many tax collectors and sinners came and sat with Jesus and his disciples. The Pharisees saw this and said to his disciples, "Why does your teacher eat with tax collectors and sinners?" He heard this and said, "Those who are well do not need a physician, but the sick do. Go and learn the meaning of the words, / *I desire mercy, not sacrifice.* / I did not come to call the righteous but sinners."

Reflection

Tax collectors were not thought of as among the righteous. They were known for adding to their income by charging citizens over the amount due. It may have surprised Matthew that Jesus would call him. By the query made to the disciples, it was obvious that the Pharisees were alarmed that Jesus dined with the likes of Matthew. However, Jesus pointed out that his actions were in accord with God's desires. Have you been surprised by what God has called you to do? Are you sometimes amazed at others he has called? Christ calls us sinners still, to be his humble servants and build up the Reign of God.

Prayers

others may be added

To our merciful Lord, we pray:

◆ Lord, hear our prayer.

For our bishops, that they never shy away from preaching the Gospel, we pray: ◆
For government officials, that they act as instruments of peace, we pray: ◆
For missionaries sharing the Good News in dangerous places, we pray: ◆
For writers and artists as they share their gifts and talents, we pray: ◆
For the sick, that they recover, we pray: ◆
For those who have died, that they be welcomed into heaven, we pray: ◆

Our Father . . .

O God,
you guided St. Matthew
to teach about your Son
and share the Good News of salvation.
Continue our efforts
to be your faithful disciples,
sharing the Word
and living our faith
to bring hope and healing
to a world in need of your love.
Through Christ our Lord.
Amen.

✝ Their message goes out through all the earth.

Sunday, September 22, 2019
Twenty-Fifth Sunday in Ordinary Time

✝ Praise the Lord who lifts up the poor.

Psalm 113

page 412

Reading

Luke 16:9–13

[Jesus said to his disciples:] "I tell you, make friends for yourselves with dishonest wealth, so that when it fails, you will be welcomed into eternal dwellings. The person who is trustworthy in very small matters is also trustworthy in great ones; and the person who is dishonest in very small matters is also dishonest in great ones. If, therefore, you are not trustworthy with dishonest wealth, who will trust you with true wealth? If you are not trustworthy with what belongs to another, who will give you what is yours? No servant can serve two masters. He will either hate one and love the other, or be devoted to one and despise the other. You cannot serve God and mammon."

Reflection

"You cannot serve God and mammon." This is a difficult saying for us, for it is tempting to think that we can be good disciples while also aiming to enjoy riches. Jesus makes the point that we need to be aware of where we focus our thoughts. Is our vision aimed on God or an idol? As we deepen our faith commitment, we devote more of our lives to God's ways. It may take a lifetime to be completely in service to God, but we need to keep that central to our being.

Prayers

others may be added

To our faithful Lord, we pray:

◆ Lord, hear our prayer.

That leaders in the Church inspire the faithful by their service, we pray: ◆
That civic authorities devote their energies to the common good, we pray: ◆
That women and men see their vocation in consecrated/vowed life, we pray: ◆
That those who take part in the coming census be treated respectfully, we pray: ◆
That scientists be supported as they research cures for diseases, we pray: ◆
That the dying be welcomed into the glory of heaven, we pray: ◆

Our Father . . .

Gracious God,
you provide us with all good things.
Grant that we focus our gifts
on serving you and leading others
to your Kingdom.
Through Christ our Lord.
Amen.

✝ Praise the Lord who lifts up the poor.

Monday, September 23, 2019

Memorial of St. Pius of Pietrelcina, Priest

☩ The Lord has done marvels for us.

Psalm 34 *page 401*

Reading *Luke 8:16–18*

Jesus said to the crowd: "No one who lights a lamp conceals it with a vessel or sets it under a bed; rather, he places it on a lampstand so that those who enter may see the light. For there is nothing hidden that will not become visible, and nothing secret that will not be known and come to light. Take care, then, how you hear. To anyone who has, more will be given, and from the one who has not, even what he seems to have will be taken away."

Reflection

At Baptism, the light of faith is symbolized with a candle presented to the newly baptized (or in the case of infants, to a parent or godparent). Through Baptism, Christ has enlightened us, and we are always to walk as children of the light. Reflect on how God has called you to share the gift of your faith. Each of us has benefited from another's faith. How do you continue to pass on the light of faith? When each person hands that light to another, the whole world will be clothed in God's light.

Prayers *others may be added*

To our merciful Lord, we pray:

◆ Lord, hear our prayer.

That religious leaders of all faiths work together for peace, we pray: ◆ That through the intercession of St. Padre Pio, God's mercy and reconciliation may touch others' lives, we pray: ◆ That love will grow in married couples experiencing difficulties, we pray: ◆ That those discerning a future high school or college look to God for guidance, we pray: ◆ That the sick recover, we pray: ◆ That those we miss and mourn experience paradise, we pray: ◆

Our Father . . .

God of light,
you instill in us the light of faith.
Grant that we joyfully pass on that faith
so that your light might shine
in every heart across the world.
Through Christ our Lord.
Amen.

☩ The Lord has done marvels for us.

Tuesday, September 24, 2019
Weekday

☩ Let us go rejoicing to the house of the Lord.

Psalm 34
page 401

Reading
Luke 8:19–21

The mother of Jesus and his brothers came to him but were unable to join him because of the crowd. He was told, "Your mother and your brothers are standing outside and they wish to see you." He said to them in reply, "My mother and my brothers are those who hear the word of God and act on it."

Reflection

Today's Gospel contrasts our limited views with God's broader one. It was natural that one of Jesus' followers told him of his family's appearance in the crowd. Naturally, they would want to get close to him. Jesus' reply showed that he had a larger view of family. He tells those gathered that "all who hear the word of God and act on it" belong to his family. Those we are related to by blood are only a fraction of our family. God calls us into a relationship with a larger family.

Prayers
others may be added

To our loving God, we pray:

◆ Lord, hear our prayer.

That our Church may grow in unity with the Orthodox and other Christian churches, we pray: ◆ That our city officials shed light on the needs of our community, we pray: ◆ That families in crisis find hope and help, we pray: ◆ That parish building projects may come to completion quickly, we pray: ◆ That the sick be strengthened, we pray: ◆ That the dying be welcomed to the glory of heaven, we pray: ◆

Our Father . . .

Almighty God,
you have provided your followers
with a family that spans heaven
and earth.
Grant that we may seek
not only to listen to your Word
but to act on it
to see the glory of your world.
Through Christ our Lord.
Amen.

☩ Let us go rejoicing to the house of the Lord.

Wednesday, September 25, 2019
Weekday

✝ Blessed be God who lives forever.

Psalm 113
page 412

Reading
Luke 9:1–6

Jesus summoned the Twelve and gave them power and authority over all demons and to cure diseases, and he sent them to proclaim the Kingdom of God and to heal the sick. He said to them, "Take nothing for the journey, neither walking stick, nor sack, nor food, nor money, and let no one take a second tunic. Whatever house you enter, stay there and leave from there. And as for those who do not welcome you, when you leave town, shake the dust from your feet in testimony against them." Then they set out and went from village to village proclaiming the good news and curing diseases everywhere.

Reflection
"Take nothing for the journey . . . and let no one take a second tunic." Can we even imagine going somewhere without money or a change of clothes? Jesus had given these followers what they needed —"power and authority over all demons and to cure the sick." They were to trust in what Jesus had instilled in them and that whatever else was needed would be provided. What do you rely on? How far do you trust that God will provide?

Prayers
others may be added

To God, who provides for us, we pray:

◆ Lord, hear our prayer.

That Church leaders continue to welcome and serve those most in need, we pray: ◆ That leaders of nations unite factions in their countries, we pray: ◆ That Bible study leaders look to the Spirit as they break open God's Word, we pray: ◆ That catechetical leaders not lose heart during difficult times, we pray: ◆ That those awaiting an organ donation be patient, we pray: ◆ That the deceased know of our love and appreciation for their living the faith well, we pray: ◆

Our Father . . .

Loving God,
you give us everything we need.
Kindly support our efforts
to use the gifts you have provided us
to relay your power and majesty
as we spread the Good News.
Through Christ our Lord.
Amen.

✝ Blessed be God who lives forever.

Thursday, September 26, 2019

Optional Memorial of Sts. Cosmas and Damian, Martyrs

† The Lord takes delight in his people.

Psalm 34

page 401

Reading

Luke 9:7–9

Herod the tetrarch heard about all that was happening and he was greatly perplexed because some were saying, "John has been raised from the dead"; others were saying, "Elijah has appeared"; still others, "One of the ancient prophets has arisen." But Herod said, "John I beheaded. Who then is this about whom I hear such things?" And he kept trying to see him.

Reflection

Today's Scripture shows the power of jealousy. Herod is relentless in his pursuit of Jesus. He had heard of Jesus' ways and of his followers and desired to know more. As the king, he wanted to be held in the highest esteem, but someone else had captured the attention of the masses. In chapter 13 of Luke, we will read that Herod wants to kill Jesus. In our lives we can give in to doubt and insecurity and let jealousy rupture relationships. When intimidated by another, we should look to God for consolation. Within him is the fullness of life. He will help us seek healthy ways of relating to others.

Prayers

others may be added

To the Lord of our life, we pray:

◆ Lord, hear our prayer.

That our bishops guide us as we seek the way to God, we pray: ◆ That leaders at the United Nations find peaceful solutions, we pray: ◆ That school boards be able to work together to improve education for all children, we pray: ◆ That through the intercession of Sts, Cosmas and Damian, twins find support in their special relationship, we pray: ◆ That the sick may fully recover, we pray: ◆ That twins who have lost their close sibling may be comforted in their mourning, we pray: ◆

Our Father . . .

Dear God,
you gave the world Sts. Cosmas and
Damian as models of faith.
Grant that we may be generous
with our talents and gifts
so that many will know of your love.
Through our Lord Jesus Christ, your Son,
who lives and reigns with you in the unity
of the Holy Spirit,
one God, for ever and ever.
Amen.

† The Lord takes delight in his people.

Friday, September 27, 2019

Memorial of St. Vincent de Paul, Priest

† Hope in God; I will praise my savior and my God.

Psalm 34

page 401

Reading

Luke 9:18–22

Once when Jesus was praying in solitude, and the disciples were with him, he asked them, "Who do the crowds say that I am?" They said in reply, "John the Baptist; others, Elijah; still others, 'One of the ancient prophets has arisen.'" Then he said to them, "But who do you say that I am?" Peter said in reply, "The Christ of God." He rebuked them and directed them not to tell this to anyone.

He said, "The Son of Man must suffer greatly and be rejected by the elders, the chief priests, and the scribes, and be killed and on the third day be raised."

Reflection

Each Sunday we profess the Creed, share in the Eucharist, and go out to serve the world and live our faith. In mission, we bring "the Christ of God" to others. In this Gospel, Peter professes his belief and is told to keep it to himself. The time is not right. Jesus knows that suffering and death are ahead. Once he has risen, people will see his glory. With Jesus' Resurrection, Peter can proclaim that he knows the Messiah. As we serve one another, we also can spread the Good News.

Prayers

others may be added

Trusting in God, we pray:

◆ Lord, hear our prayer.

That pastoral ministers never tire of serving God's people, we pray: ◆ That elected officials renew their efforts to work for the common good, we pray: ◆ That those who serve and work with the poor may continue to be filled with the zeal that enabled St. Vincent to witness the Gospel, we pray: ◆ That the needs of the hungry be met, we pray: ◆ That the sick receive proper health care, we pray: ◆ That the faithfully departed be received into eternal life, we pray: ◆

Our Father . . .

O God of the poor,
you gave St. Vincent the fortitude
to serve the poor.
May we be inspired to see your face
in the poorest of the poor
and to provide their daily bread.
Through our Lord Jesus Christ, your Son,
who lives and reigns with you in the unity
of the Holy Spirit,
one God, for ever and ever.
Amen.

† Hope in God; I will praise my savior and my God.

Saturday, September 28, 2019
Weekday

✝ The Lord will guard us as a shepherd guards the flock.

Psalm 113

page 412

Reading

Luke 9:43b–45

While they were all amazed at his every deed, Jesus said to his disciples, "Pay attention to what I am telling you. The Son of Man is to be handed over to men." But they did not understand this saying; its meaning was hidden from them so that they should not understand it, and they were afraid to ask him about this saying.

Reflection

The Apostles were amazed that Jesus could cure the sick and cast out demons. However, Jesus did not want his followers to think that such acts were the point of his life. He tells them to "pay attention" and then indicates difficulty ahead. We also need to be attuned to specific realities. Our lives have hidden meanings that Jesus can help us understand. Perhaps technology and possessions distract us from being alert to how God is calling us. It is important to find time for quiet prayer so that we can pay attention to the work to which God is calling us.

Prayers

others may be added

To our Shepherd, we pray:

◆ Lord, hear our prayer.

That parishes help the faithful to pay attention to God in their midst, we pray: ◆ That the president and Congress work together for just reforms, we pray: ◆ That affordable housing be found for those in need, we pray: ◆ That prisoners be provided with an opportunity to be rehabilitated, we pray: ◆ That the sick be cured, we pray: ◆ That those we miss and mourn have a place at the banquet feast of heaven, we pray: ◆

Our Father . . .

O Lord,
you guide us with your love.
Grant that we may seek to pay attention
so that we will be aware
of how you are working in our lives.
May we have patience
as we attune our ways to your ways.
Through Christ our Lord.
Amen.

✝ The Lord will guard us as a shepherd guards the flock.

Sunday, September 29, 2019

Twenty-Sixth Sunday in Ordinary Time

✝ Praise the Lord, my soul!

Psalm 146

page 421

Reading

Luke 16:19–25

Jesus said to the Pharisees: "There was a rich man who dressed in purple garments and fine linen and dined sumptuously each day. And lying at his door was a poor man named Lazarus, covered with sores, who would gladly have eaten his fill of the scraps that fell from the rich man's table. Dogs even used to come and lick his sores. When the poor man died, he was carried away by angels to the bosom of Abraham. The rich man also died and was buried, and from the netherworld, where he was in torment, he raised his eyes and saw Abraham far off and Lazarus at his side. And he cried out, 'Father Abraham, have pity on me. Send Lazarus to dip the tip of his finger and water and cool my tongue, for I am suffering torment in these flames.' Abraham replied, 'My child, remember that you received what was good during your lifetime while Lazarus likewise received what was bad; but now he is comforted here, whereas you are tormented.' "

Reflection

Sadly, the chasm between the rich and poor continues today. As we ponder the Gospel, we need to consider whether we have become indifferent to the suffering of others. The Lord hears the cry of the poor. It is up to us to answer their pleas.

Prayers

others may be added

To our God of mercy, we pray:

◆ Lord, hear our prayer.

May church and state partnerships confront the challenges of poverty, we pray: ◆ May the staff at agencies that care for the poor never tire of their ministry, we pray: ◆ May those struggling with choices for daily living find relief and comfort, we pray: ◆ May the celebration of Rosh Hashanah be a blessed one, we pray: ◆ May the sick receive quality care, we pray: ◆ May those who have died be welcomed by Abraham and all the angels, we pray: ◆

Our Father . . .

Good and loving God,
you hear the cries of those most in need.
Help us to be creative
in meeting the needs of the poor
so that all people may be lifted up
and have hope for the future.
Through Christ our Lord.
Amen.

✝ Praise the Lord, my soul!

Monday, September 30, 2019

Memorial of St. Jerome, Priest and Doctor of the Church

☩ The Lord will build up Zion again,
and appear in all his glory.

Psalm 146

page 421

Reading

Luke 9:46–48

An argument arose among the disciples about which of them was the greatest. Jesus realized the intention of their hearts and took a child and placed it by his side and said to them, "Whoever receives this child in my name receives me, and whoever receives me receives the one who sent me. For the one who is least among all of you is the one who is the greatest."

Reflection

As the disciples argue over who is the greatest, they display their egos just as sports figures do when they claim superiority. That bravado may win the hearts of fans but is far from Gospel living. In response to the disciples' argument, Jesus points to a child. He wants his followers to understand that the one considered the least is the greatest. Jesus asks the disciples and us to take on the virtue of humility as we follow him. St. Jerome, whom we honor today, humbly studied and translated Scriptures.

Prayers

others may be added

To the Lord of our life, we pray:

◆ Lord, hear our prayer.

May the pope teach us by his service how to follow Christ, we pray: ◆ May those preparing for the election seek to serve their constituents, we pray: ◆ May translators and Scripture scholars grow in their knowledge and use of God's Word, we pray: ◆ May human trafficking cease, and laws against it be enforced, we pray: ◆ May the ill and their caregivers find strength, we pray: ◆ May peace and tranquility come to those who have died, we pray: ◆

Our Father . . .

God ever faithful and true,
you teach us by your Word.
May we work with others
to serve the needs of the vulnerable.
Guide efforts to build bridges of care.
Through Christ our Lord.
Amen.

☩ The Lord will build up Zion again,
and appear in all his glory.

Tuesday, October 1, 2019

Memorial of St. Thérèse of the Child Jesus, Virgin and Doctor of the Church

✝ God is with us.

Psalm 146

page 421

Reading

Luke 9:51–56

When the days for Jesus to be taken up were fulfilled, he resolutely determined to journey to Jerusalem, and he sent messengers ahead of him. On the way they entered a Samaritan village to prepare for his reception there, but they would not welcome him because the destination of his journey was Jerusalem. When the disciples James and John saw this they asked, "Lord, do you want us to call down fire from heaven to consume them?" Jesus turned and rebuked them, and they journeyed to another village.

Reflection

As the Lord turns toward Jerusalem, he is going forward to his passion, death, and Resurrection. He is resolute in this journey, unlike the disciples who want to call down wrath on those who will not follow Jesus. We might reflect on how we follow Jesus. Do we become distracted at times? St. Thérèse was determined to follow Jesus in little ways. Most of us, too, can make a difference by the little things that we do. What are the small kindnesses that you can do that will impact another?

Prayers

others may be added

To our Lord, who guides us, we pray:

◆ Lord, hear our prayer.

May missionaries be strengthened in spreading the Good News, we pray: ◆ May civic leaders be instruments of peace, we pray: ◆ May young people consider a vocation to serve the Church as a member of a religious order, we pray: ◆ May we seek to act as good stewards of our finances, we pray: ◆ May caregivers receive the support they need, we pray: ◆ May those who have died be greeted by the angels and saints, we pray: ◆

Our Father . . .

Lord God,
you guide your people through trials.
Grant that we be resolute
in our determination
to follow the path laid out for us.
May we look to St. Thérèse
and find the little ways
that can help to bring about
the kingdom of God.
Through our Lord Jesus Christ, your Son,
who lives and reigns with you in the unity
of the Holy Spirit,
One God, for ever and ever.
Amen.

✝ God is with us.

Wednesday, October 2, 2019
Memorial of the Holy Guardian Angels

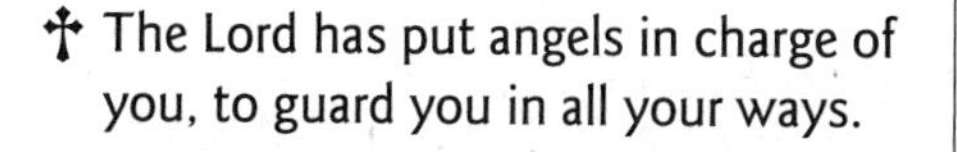

✝ The Lord has put angels in charge of you, to guard you in all your ways.

Psalm 25 *page 399*

Reading *Exodus 23:20–22*

Thus says the Lord: "See, I am sending an angel before you, to guard you on the way and bring you to the place I have prepared. Be attentive to him and heed his voice. Do not rebel against him, for he will not forgive your sin. My authority resides in him. If you heed his voice and carry out all I tell you, I will be an enemy to your enemies and a foe to your foes."

Reflection

When I was a child, Catholic schoolteachers told us to "make room for your guardian angel" and to seek that angel's help when tempted. We were encouraged to name the angel and think of the angel as a friend. From this, we learned that angels are around us, willing to guide us. What a help this was to feel that God sent each of us a heavenly companion. It is important to make room in our thoughts and hearts for the help God provides. Let us keep our lives open to God's messengers who come our way.

Prayers *others may be added*

Trusting in God's guidance, we pray:

◆ Lord, hear our prayer.

May the Church be welcoming to all in need, we pray: ◆ May secretaries and support staff be strengthened as they seek to guide others, we pray: ◆ May firefighters and police offers be kept free from harm, we pray: ◆ May United Nations' peacekeepers be provided the support they need, we pray: ◆ May those who care for and protect the sick be lifted up in God's mercy, we pray: ◆ May the angels guide all who have died to their place at the eternal banquet, we pray: ◆

Our Father . . .

Lord of heaven and earth,
you send your angels
to guide us against the temptations
we confront daily.
Grant that we may always direct our work
toward the splendor of heaven
so that all will know the glory
of the kingdom of God.
Through Christ our Lord.
Amen.

✝ The Lord has put angels in charge of you, to guard you in all your ways.

Thursday, October 3, 2019
Weekday

☩ The precepts of the Lord give joy to the heart.

Psalm 25 *page 399*

Reading *Luke 10:1–3, 8–9*

Jesus appointed seventy-two other disciples whom he sent ahead of him in pairs to every town and place he intended to visit. He said to them, "The harvest is abundant but the laborers are few; so ask the master of the harvest to send out laborers for his harvest. Go on your way; behold, I am sending you like lambs among wolves. Whatever town you enter and they welcome you, eat what they set before you, cure the sick in it and say to them, 'The Kingdom of God is at hand for you.' "

Reflection

During the Dismissal at Mass, we are told, "Go and announce the Gospel of the Lord." This is our sending forth to do God's work in the world. Today's Gospel notes that "the laborers are few." If each of us takes up our call to discipleship, the vineyard will be plentiful with workers. Are you willing to use your talents and heal those who need a warm voice or welcoming touch in their lives? Are you willing to find your work in the vineyard of the Lord?

Prayers *others may be added*

To our Lord, who sends us forth in mission, we pray:

◆ Lord, hear our prayer.

May the Church never tire of preaching the kingdom of God, we pray: ◆ May the United Nations receive the support it needs to continue to build bridges to peace, we pray: ◆ May life be respected from conception on, we pray: ◆ May missionaries be strengthened, especially in dangerous regions, we pray: ◆ May the sick be healed, we pray: ◆ May those who have died rise in glory with the angels and saints, we pray: ◆

Our Father . . .

Loving God,
you have entrusted work to your people.
Grant us assistance as we respond
to your call to serve.
May we live the Gospel
as we share our gifts
and bring peace to those we meet.
Through our Lord Jesus Christ, your Son,
who lives and reigns with you in the unity
of the Holy Spirit,
one God, for ever and ever.
Amen.

☩ The precepts of the Lord give joy to the heart.

Friday, October 4, 2019
Memorial of St. Francis of Assisi

✝ You are my inheritance, O Lord.

Psalm 16

page 396

Reading

Matthew 11:25–30

At that time Jesus exclaimed: "I give praise to you, Father, Lord of heaven and earth, for although you have hidden these things from the wise and the learned you have revealed them to the childlike. Yes, Father, such has been your gracious will. All things have been handed over to me by my Father. No one knows the Son except the Father, and no one knows the Father except the Son and anyone to whom the Son wishes to reveal him."

Reflection

St. Francis changed from living as a son of wealthy parents who indulged in lavish pursuits to a witness of a life of poverty, humility, and charity. Many know of St. Francis by the gentleness with which he treated animals, but that is only one side of his devotion to God. As a penitent, he raised money to restore a chapel and he nursed lepers. Pope Francis began the encyclical *Laudato Si'* with St. Francis' words "Praise be to you, my Lord." Reading that encyclical will help you understand the Church's and the saint's view of how we are called to care for creation.

Prayers

others may be added

Trusting in God, we pray:

◆ Lord, graciously hear us.

May more men and women hear the call to serve in a vocation as a Franciscan religious, we pray: ◆ May world leaders look to St. Francis to be guided in ways of peace, we pray: ◆ May governments work to stem the tide of poverty in developing countries, we pray: ◆ May those seeking employment find a job quickly, we pray: ◆ May the ill be freed from all burdens, we pray: ◆ May all who have died arrive quickly to the banquet feast of heaven, we pray: ◆

Our Father . . .

Gracious God,
you gave St. Francis the openness
to take on a life
that cared for all of creation.
May we, like St. Francis,
give our lives over to you
so that we might present
your love and mercy to all we encounter.
Through Christ our Lord.
Amen.

✝ You are my inheritance, O Lord.

Saturday, October 5, 2019
Weekday

✝ The Lord listens to the poor.

Psalm 34
page 401

Reading
Luke 10:17–24

The seventy-two disciples returned rejoicing and said to Jesus, "Lord, even the demons are subject to us because of your name." Jesus said, "I have observed Satan fall like lightning from the sky. Behold, I have given you the power 'to tread upon serpents' and scorpions and upon the full force of the enemy and nothing will harm you. Nevertheless, do not rejoice because the spirits are subject to you, but rejoice because your names are written in heaven."

At that very moment he rejoiced in the Holy Spirit and said, "I give you praise, Father, Lord of heaven and earth, for although you have hidden these things from the wise and the learned you have revealed them to the childlike. Yes, Father, such has been your gracious will. All things have been handed over to me by my Father. No one knows who the Son is except the Father, and who the Father is except the Son and anyone to whom the Son wishes to reveal him."

Turning to the disciples in private he said, "Blessed are the eyes that see what you see. For I say to you, many prophets and kings desired to see what you see, but did not see it, and to hear what you hear, but did not hear it."

Reflection

When the disciples return after dealing with demons, Jesus praises God. Jesus also cautions the disciples not to rejoice over the wrong things. They should rejoice because God has blessed them, not because of any power they hold. At times that we feel success, we also should look to God and not ourselves. God has given us the ability to do good works. All of our strengths and our talents come from God, so our praise also is directed to him.

Prayers
others may be added

To God, who shines through our works, we pray:

◆ Hear us, Lord.

May parish building projects be directed toward assisting in building the reign of God, we pray: ◆ May civic leaders seek to develop places of peace within neighborhoods, we pray: ◆ May food banks always have enough to serve the poor, we pray: ◆ May those who must work for us on weekends find rest during the week, we pray: ◆ May caregivers be strengthened in their ministry of charity and service, we pray: ◆ May those who are part of a bereavement ministry bring hope to those in their care, we pray: ◆

Our Father . . .

Lord God,
you call us to return to you
to reflect on our vocation and ministry
and give gratitude for our service.
Help us always to take
this time of refreshment and discernment,
confident that it will aid us
in bringing about your kingdom.
Through Christ our Lord.
Amen.

✝ The Lord listens to the poor.

Sunday, October 6, 2019

Twenty-Seventh Sunday in Ordinary Time

☩ If today you hear God's voice,
harden not your hearts.

Psalm 95 *page 408*

Reading *Luke 17:5–10*

The apostles said to the Lord, "Increase our faith." The Lord replied, "If you have faith the size of a mustard seed, you would say to this mulberry tree, 'Be uprooted and planted in the sea,' and it would obey you.

"Who among you would say to your servant who has just come in from plowing or tending sheep in the field, 'Come here immediately and take your place at table'? Would he not rather say to him, 'Prepare something for me to eat. Put on your apron and wait on me while I eat and drink. You may eat and drink when I am finished'? Is he grateful to that servant because he did what was commanded? So should it be with you. When you have done all you have been commanded, say, 'We are unprofitable servants; we have done what we were obliged to do.'"

Reflection

How could faith so small as a mustard seed make a difference? After the Lord tells of what such an amount of faith can do, he relates an account of a master and a servant. It is expected that the servant will wait on the master, no matter how weary the servant is. So, too, we are to continue to follow the Lord, no matter our trials. When we have done so, we do not ask for a reward, for this is what is expected of us. Let us nurture our seed of faith so it grows until we are ready for heaven.

Prayers *others may be added*

Trusting in God, we pray:

◆ Merciful Lord, hear us.

Renew the Church's efforts of formation, we pray: ◆ Bring justice to those exploited by economic practices, we pray: ◆ Strengthen efforts to care for the earth, we pray: ◆ Encourage men and women to be open to their call to serve the Church in a lay ministry, we pray: ◆ Heal the sick, we pray: ◆ Lead those who have died to eternal life, we pray: ◆

Our Father . . .

Lord God,
you give us faith that can do great things.
Grant that we may be supported
as we seek to develop our faith.
May we always serve you
through our discipleship.
Through Christ our Lord.
Amen.

☩ If today you hear God's voice,
harden not your hearts.

Monday, October 7, 2019

Memorial of Our Lady of the Rosary

✝ The Almighty has done great things for me and holy is his Name.

Canticle of Mary

page 423

Reading

Luke 1:26–33

The angel Gabriel was sent from God to a town of Galilee called Nazareth, to a virgin betrothed to a man named Joseph, of the house of David, and the virgin's name was Mary. And coming to her, he said, "Hail, full of grace! The Lord is with you." But she was greatly troubled at what was said and pondered what sort of greeting this might be. Then the angel said to her, "Do not be afraid, Mary, for you have found favor with God. Behold, you will conceive in your womb and bear a son, and you shall name him Jesus. He will be great and will be called Son of the Most High, and the Lord God will give him the throne of David his father, and he will rule over the house of Jacob forever, and of his Kingdom there will be no end."

Reflection

"Hail, full of grace!" the angel exclaims in the greeting to Mary. Praying the Rosary, we address our mother in a similar way. When we say the Hail Mary, we might want to pray for people we love as well as those with whom we have difficulties. In raising up those who trouble us, we are asking that they be put in God's favor. May we receive grace as others are graced with God's love and mercy.

Prayers

others may be added

With Mary, who is full of grace,
we pray:

◆ Lord, hear our prayer.

Inspire pastors to be open to God's plans, we pray: ◆ Aid nations to safely guide refugees and migrants, we pray: ◆ Help women who are pregnant toward a safe delivery, we pray: ◆ Create opportunities for those seeking meaningful work, we pray: ◆ Strengthen those in treatment for addictions, we pray: ◆ Show your face to the dying, we pray: ◆

Our Father . . .

Lord God,
you gave us Mary as our mother.
Grant that we may follow
her model of discipleship
and nurture our love for you.
Help us, by our prayers,
to raise up the lowly
and ease all fears, sadness, and worries.
Through Christ our Lord.
Amen.

✝ The Almighty has done great things for me and holy is his Name.

Tuesday, October 8, 2019
Weekday

✝ If you, O Lord, mark our guilt, who can stand?

Psalm 95

page 408

Reading

Luke 10:38–42

Jesus entered a village where a woman whose name was Martha welcomed him. She had a sister named Mary who sat beside the Lord at his feet listening to him speak. Martha, burdened with much serving, came to him and said, "Lord, do you not care that my sister has left me by myself to do the serving? Tell her to help me." The Lord said to her in reply, "Martha, Martha, you are anxious and worried about many things. There is need of only one thing. Mary has chosen the better part and it will not be taken from her."

Reflection

For many people, this is a perplexing reading. Hospitality is about doing many things well, and Martha is seeking to provide Jesus with a pleasant stay at her home. She would like Jesus to instruct her sister to help her; instead he addresses her anxiety. We might wonder about both Mary's part and Martha's. Jesus calls us to listen and be present. For many of us, this Gospel can help bring our lives into focus. How can we worry less? How can we improve our practice of presence with the Lord?

Prayers

others may be added

Attentive to the needs of those around us, we offer these prayers:

◆ Lord, hear our prayer.

Awaken the hearts of leaders in the Church to listen to the needs of their communities, we pray: ◆ Renew the spirits of civic leaders who find their roles a burden, we pray: ◆ Calm the most anxious in our families, we pray: ◆ Inspire Christians, Jews, and Muslims to meet for interfaith dialogue, we pray: ◆ Heal the brokenhearted, we pray: ◆ Lead the dying to the glory of heaven, we pray: ◆

Our Father . . .

Lord God,
you are always present to us.
Help us hear others' needs
and respond to them with love and mercy
so that all may be relieved
of worries and fears
and know your presence and place in our lives.
Through Christ our Lord.
Amen.

✝ If you, O Lord, mark our guilt, who can stand?

Wednesday, October 9, 2019

Weekday

✝ Lord, you are merciful and gracious.

Psalm 95

page 408

Reading

Luke 11:1–4

Jesus was praying in a certain place, and when he had finished, one of his disciples said to him, "Lord, teach us to pray just as John taught his disciples." He said to them, "When you pray, say: / Father, hallowed be your name, / your Kingdom come. / Give us each day our daily bread / and forgive us our sins / for we ourselves forgive everyone in debt to us, / and do not subject us to the final test."

Reflection

As Jesus teaches the disciples to pray, he shows them that prayer is simple and direct. The prayer that Jesus gives them, first praises God, asking that his name always be held as "holy." From there, God's Kingdom and will are invoked and then our bread and forgiveness are requested. May we not say the words of this prayer quickly but consider their meaning as we pray.

Prayers

others may be added

To the One whose name is holy,
we pray:

◆ Lord, hear our prayer.

May we take to heart the lives of prayer our religious leaders witness, we pray: ◆ Guard those entrusted with protecting lives, we pray: ◆ Aid all who suffer because of violence, we pray: ◆ Call others to serve in lay ecclesial ministry, we pray: ◆ Hear the prayers of those who suffer from depression, we pray: ◆ Bring to the heavenly home the dying who are marked with the sign of faith, we pray: ◆

Our Father . . .

Lord God,
you sent your Son
to draw us closer to you.
Guide us that we may seek
to grow in conversations with you.
May we make our whole lives
a sacrifice of praise to you.
Through Christ our Lord.
Amen.

✝ Lord, you are merciful and gracious.

Thursday, October 10, 2019
Weekday

☩ Blessed are they who hope in the Lord.

Psalm 130

page 418

Reading

Luke 11:9–13

[Jesus said:] "And I tell you, ask and you will receive; seek and you will find; knock and the door will be opened to you. For everyone who asks, receives; and the one who seeks, finds; and to the one who knocks, the door will be opened. What father among you would hand his son a snake when he asks for a fish? Or hand him a scorpion when he asks for an egg? If you then, who are wicked, know how to give good gifts to your children, how much more will the Father in heaven give the Holy Spirit to those who ask him?"

Reflection

Jesus teaches his disciples to trust in prayer. He lets them know that all they need to do is converse with God to receive what they need. Such is God's relationship with humankind that a request begets a response. God is open to listening and supporting us with good things for our journey. Just as Jesus asked the disciples to address God as Father in prayer, he now tells them to think of God as lovingly as a child would a parent. How would a parent respond to a child in need?

Prayers

others may be added

Trusting in God, we pray:

◆ Lord, hear our prayer.

Support the charitable organizations of the Church as they seek to minister to the poor, we pray: ◆ Direct the homeless to shelter, we pray: ◆ Renew indivdiduals who suffer from financial burdens, we pray: ◆ Help those whose homes were destroyed by hurricanes, we pray: ◆ Guide those suffering from anxiety disorders, we pray: ◆ Bring the dying to eternal glory, we pray: ◆

Our Father . . .

Merciful Lord,
you give us all that we need.
Grant that our trust in you will grow
and that we never fail
to seek you in our lives.
Guide our efforts in making your
will known
so that the world may live
in freedom, knowledge, and hope.
Through Christ our Lord.
Amen.

☩ Blessed are they who hope in the Lord.

Friday, October 11, 2019

Optional Memorial of St. John XXIII, Pope

✝ The Lord will judge the world with justice.

Psalm 130 *page 418*

Reading *Luke 11:15–23*

When Jesus had driven out a demon, some of the crowd said: "By the power of Beelzebul, the prince of demons, he drives out demons." Others, to test him, asked him for a sign from heaven. But he knew their thoughts and said to them, "Every kingdom divided against itself will be laid waste and house will fall against house. And if Satan is divided against himself, how will his kingdom stand? For you say that it is by Beelzebul that I drive out demons. If I, then, drive out demons by Beelzebul, by whom do your own people drive them out? Therefore they will be your judges. But if it is by the finger of God that I drive out demons, then the Kingdom of God has come upon you. When a strong man fully armed guards his palace, his possessions are safe. But when one stronger than he attacks and overcomes him, he takes away the armor on which he relied and distributes the spoils. Whoever is not with me is against me, and whoever does not gather with me scatters.

Reflection

On this fifty-seventh anniversary of the convening of the Second Vatican Council, this Gospel brings to mind the words that Pope John XXIII spoke on unity. In his opening address on October 11, 1962, the pope spoke of how the Church works that all may be one, just as Christ prayed on the night before he died. The unity of Catholics, the pope said, must be kept exemplary and firm. Decades after the Second Vatican Council, some still disagree with its teachings. The Church, though, still seeks to gather all who follow Christ.

Prayers *others may be added*

To the Lord who gathers us, we pray:

◆ Lord, hear our prayer.

Bless parish pastoral and finance councils, we pray: ◆ Support the dialogue among members of the Orthodox and Catholic Churches, we pray: ◆ Aid elected officials as they seek to resolve divisions, we pray: ◆ Help families caring for their elders, we pray: ◆ Stay near to those who experience doubt and fear during sickness, we pray: ◆ Bring to the new Jerusalem all who have died, we pray: ◆

Our Father . . .

Lord God,
you provide your Spirit to the Church
to guide her movements.
Move our hearts and minds
to build a communion of love
so that we may gather
those who are scattered
with the promise of hope and renewal.
Through Christ our Lord.
Amen.

✝ The Lord will judge the world with justice.

Saturday, October 12, 2019
Weekday

† Rejoice in the Lord, you just!

Psalm 130 *page 418*

Reading *Luke 11:27–28*

While Jesus was speaking, a woman from the crowd called out and said to him, "Blessed is the womb that carried you and the breasts at which you nursed." He replied, "Rather, blessed are those who hear the word of God and observe it."

Reflection

"Blessed are those who hear the word of God and observe it." Sometimes we may wonder about the decisions in our past and whether we are on the right path in the present. Today, we hear that we are blessed when we hear and observe God's Word. We can be assured that abiding by what we hear in the Scriptures makes a difference in our lives. As we put into practice what Christ teaches, we are placed among the family of God.

Prayers *others may be added*

Confident in the love of God, we pray:

◆ Lord, hear our prayer.

Give strength to leaders in the Church, we pray: ◆ Help state officials as they seek to bring about the common good, we pray: ◆ Protect the unborn, the elderly, and those on death row, we pray: ◆ Heal those recovering from surgery, we pray: ◆ Comfort the dying and those who care for them, we pray: ◆ Lead the deceased to eternal life, we pray: ◆

Our Father . . .

Dear Lord,
you give us your Word
to illumine our hearts.
Renew our resolve
to trust in your guidance
so that all people may know your ways.
Grant that by heeding your Word,
we help bring forth peace and justice.
Through Christ our Lord.
Amen.

† Rejoice in the Lord, you just!

Sunday, October 13, 2019
Twenty-Eighth Sunday in Ordinary Time

☩ The Lord has revealed to the nations his saving power.

Psalm 98
page 410

Reading
Luke 17:11–19

As Jesus continued his journey to Jerusalem, he traveled through Samaria and Galilee. As he was entering a village, ten lepers met him. They stood at a distance from him and raised their voice, saying, "Jesus, Master! Have pity on us!" And when he saw them, he said, "Go show yourselves to the priests." As they were going they were cleansed. And one of them, realizing he had been healed, returned, glorifying God in a loud voice; and he fell at the feet of Jesus and thanked him. He was a Samaritan. Jesus said in reply, "Ten were cleansed, were they not? Where are the other nine? Has none but this foreigner returned to give thanks to God?" Then he said to him, "Stand up and go; your faith has saved you."

Reflection
When he realized that he had been healed, the Samaritan returned, praised God, dropped to the ground, and thanked Jesus. Each Sunday, we return to our parishes to give praise and worship to God as we celebrate the Eucharist. We gather not only to praise God but to offer our sacrifice and to give thanks for all God has provided. The word "Eucharist" means thanksgiving. We not only receive the sacrament but leave the Mass to live a Eucharistic life, or a life of thanksgiving to God. May we keep in mind daily how God has blessed us and give a return of prayers of thanksgiving.

Prayers
others may be added

To our God, who blesses us, we pray:

◆ Lord, hear our prayer.

For the Church, that she extend healing to all who seek it, we pray: ◆ For all people, that they recognize the value of human life, from conception to natural death, we pray: ◆ For all who are lonely, we pray: ◆ For healing for those who are separated or divorced, we pray: ◆ For the suffering, that they find consolation and strength in Christ, we pray: ◆ For the dying, that they be led to the heavenly banquet, we pray: ◆

Our Father . . .

Gracious God of our ancestors,
you lead your people and guide them
to be people of great thanks and praise.
Support us as we renew our efforts
to help others to see your glory
and the blessed world you have created.
Through Christ our Lord.
Amen.

☩ The Lord has revealed to the nations his saving power.

Monday, October, 14, 2019
Weekday

✝ The Lord has made known
his salvation.

Psalm 98 *page 410*

Reading *Romans 1:1–7*

Paul, a slave of Christ Jesus, called to be an Apostle and set apart for the Gospel of God, which he promised previously through his prophets in the holy Scriptures, the Gospel about his Son, descended from David according to the flesh, but established as Son of God in power according to the Spirit of holiness through resurrection from the dead, Jesus Christ our Lord. Through him we have received the grace of apostleship, to bring about the obedience of faith, for the sake of his name, among all the Gentiles, among whom are you also, who are called to belong to Jesus Christ; to all the beloved of God in Rome, called to be holy. Grace to you and peace from God our Father and the Lord Jesus Christ.

Reflection

St. Paul greets the Romans with a description of who he is. He first tells them that he is a "slave of Christ Jesus" and then relates his calling "to be an Apostle." As an Apostle, he has been set apart for the Gospel. His vocation is a grace that has come through Jesus Christ to bring Christians closer to the light of faith. Reading this greeting, we might want to consider how we describe ourselves. As a "slave for Christ," Paul tells us that he serves Christ alone. Are you aware of whether you serve anyone or thing other than Christ? How do you prioritize your mission as a disciple?

Prayers *others may be added*

To the Lord, who gives us all good things, we pray:

◆ Lord, hear our prayer.

For pastors, that they be bold in proclaiming Christ, we pray: ◆ For civic leaders, that they continue to work to end violence in communities, we pray: ◆ For those who are underemployed, we pray: ◆ For hearts to be grateful for the gift of God's bounty, we pray: ◆ For the ill, that they recover quickly, we pray: ◆ For deceased family members, that they be brought to the joy of heaven, we pray: ◆

Our Father . . .

Lord God,
you gave St. Paul the desire
to nurture the faith in your holy ones.
Give us the resolve
to be faithful to the Gospel
so that our lives
might draw others to your grace.
Through our Lord Jesus Christ, your Son,
who lives and reigns with you in the unity
of the Holy Spirit,
one God, for ever and ever.
Amen.

✝ The Lord has made known
his salvation.

Tuesday, October 15, 2019

Memorial of St. Teresa of Jesus, Virgin and Doctor of the Church

✝ The heavens proclaim the glory of God.

Psalm 98

page 410

Reading

Luke 11:37–41

After Jesus had spoken, a Pharisee invited him to dine at his home. He entered and reclined at table to eat. The Pharisee was amazed to see that he did not observe the prescribed washing before the meal. The Lord said to him, "Oh you Pharisees! Although you cleanse the outside of the cup and the dish, inside you are filled with plunder and evil. You fools! Did not the maker of the outside also make the inside? But as to what is within, give alms, and behold, everything will be clean for you."

Reflection

The Pharisee paid close attention to details, such as whether a ritual cleansing occurred before a meal. The Lord, however, is not as concerned about our exterior selves. He asks that we nurture a purity within ourselves. When we do so, our actions will reflect God's holiness. St. Teresa of Avila, whom we honor today, wrote about the interior life in her books on prayer, which include the classic *The Interior Castle*. Based on her writings on mysticism and spirituality, Pope Paul VI named her a doctor of the Church. May she inspire us to work on our interior life to image God in the world.

Prayers

others may be added

To our merciful Lord, we pray:

◆ Lord, hear our prayer.

For the Church, that she shepherd her flock to holiness, we pray: ◆ For elected leaders, that they work for justice, we pray: ◆ For the coming election, that it go smoothly, we pray: ◆ For the environment, that citizens renew efforts to care for it, we pray: ◆ For health and well-being for all who are ill, we pray: ◆ For the glory of God to be revealed to all who have died, we pray: ◆

Our Father . . .

Lord God,
you sent your Son to us
to show us the way to holiness.
Grant that we may seek to cleanse
our interior selves
so that all may see
your image reflected in our lives.
Through Christ our Lord.
Amen.

✝ The heavens proclaim the glory of God.

Wednesday, October 16, 2019
Weekday

☩ Lord, you give back to everyone.

Psalm 23

page 398

Reading

Luke 11:42–46

The Lord said: "Woe to you Pharisees! You pay tithes of mint and of rue and of every garden herb, but you pay no attention to judgment and to love for God. These you should have done, without overlooking the others. Woe to you Pharisees! You love the seat of honor in synagogues and greetings in marketplaces. Woe to you! You are like unseen graves over which people unknowingly walk."

Then one of the scholars of the law said to him in reply, "Teacher, by saying this you are insulting us too." And he said, "Woe also to you scholars of the law! You impose on people burdens hard to carry, but you yourselves do not lift one finger to touch them."

Reflection

With sharp words, Jesus points out to the Pharisees and scholars what they refuse to see. The Pharisees had become enamored with their place in society and the scholars with their ability to interpret the law. Jesus wants them to understand that they have both missed the point of their position. They do not show their love for God and neighbor. How have you allowed laws to get in the way of loving another? What do you need to be able to see more clearly?

Prayers

others may be added

To our faithful God, we pray:

◆ Lord, hear our prayer.

For the Church, that she seek to accompany the faithful through their difficulties, we pray: ◆ For legislators, that they implement just measures for the common good, we pray: ◆ For leaders in workplaces, that they set an example of mercy, we pray: ◆ For those seeking annulments, that they experience healing, we pray: ◆ For the suffering, that they be comforted, we pray: ◆ For the dying, that they join the saints in glory, we pray: ◆

Our Father . . .

Gracious God of all,
you seek to empower us
to grow in holiness.
Grant that we may look humbly
at ourselves
to overcome our blind spots
so that we may serve you
with a pure heart and generous spirit.
Through Christ our Lord.
Amen.

☩ Lord, you give back to everyone.

Thursday, October 17, 2019

Memorial of St. Ignatius of Antioch, Bishop and Martyr

✝ With the Lord there is mercy, and fullness of redemption.

Psalm 98

page 410

Reading

Romans 3:21–26

Brothers and sisters: Now the righteousness of God has been manifested apart from the law, though testified to by the law and the prophets, the righteousness of God through faith in Jesus Christ for all who believe. For there is no distinction; all have sinned and are deprived of the glory of God. They are justified freely by his grace through the redemption in Christ Jesus, whom God set forth as an expiation, through faith, by his Blood, to prove his righteousness because of the forgiveness of sins previously committed, through the forbearance of God—to prove his righteousness in the present time, that he might be righteous and justify the one who has faith in Jesus.

Reflection

Paul guides us to the realization that we belong to God by faith. Christ, shedding his blood for us, redeemed us. No matter our sin, we are saved through the death and Resurrection of Christ. It is humbling to realize that we have done nothing to safeguard our redemption and that God has done everything. May our humble witness lead others to faith.

Prayers

others may be added

To our God of compassion, we pray:

◆ Lord, hear our prayer.

For the Church, that she prepare for the synod in a manner that will bear fruit, we pray: ◆ For peacemakers, that they never lose hope, we pray: ◆ For the end to fear that causes violence, we pray: ◆ For the depressed, that they find comfort that leads to hope, we pray: ◆ For those who care for the sick, that they receive support, we pray: ◆ For the dying, that the angels and saints lead them to paradise, we pray: ◆

Our Father . . .

Ever-faithful God,
you gave St. Ignatius the courage
to give his life as a martyr.
Grant that we may persevere
in speaking out in your name.
May we never lose hope
in the future glory of the kingdom.
Through Christ our Lord.
Amen.

✝ With the Lord there is mercy, and fullness of redemption.

Friday, October 18, 2019

Feast of St. Luke, Evangelist

✝ Your friends make known, O Lord, the glorious splendor of your kingdom.

Psalm 23

page 398

Reading

Luke 10:1–3, 8–9

The Lord Jesus appointed seventy-two disciples whom he sent ahead of him in pairs to every town and place he intended to visit. He said to them, "The harvest is abundant but the laborers are few; so ask the master of the harvest to send out laborers for his harvest. Go on your way; behold, I am sending you like lambs among wolves. Whatever town you enter and they welcome you, eat what they set before you, cure the sick in it and say to them, 'The Kingdom of God is at hand for you.' "

Reflection

Any of us might wonder how we would react if we were among the seventy-two disciples. Jesus sent them "like lambs among wolves" to the towns he would visit. They would enter these places with no guarantee of a bed or meals. Still, they went and in verse 17 of this chapter of Luke, we read that they returned "rejoicing." We may not be sent to distant towns but we are to go forth to spread the Gospel. Living God's will humbly, we may sometimes feel that we are lambs among wolves. Today, we look to St. Luke, whose writings brought many to seek God and whose work as a physician brought physical healing. May we see our gifts as ways to spread the Kingdom of God.

Prayers

others may be added

To the One who shepherds us, we pray:

◆ **Lord, hear our prayer.**

For the Church, that she help the faithful understand the strength that the Sacrament of Anointing of the Sick provides, we pray: ◆ For healthcare workers, that they be present to those they serve, we pray: ◆ For those awaiting a miraculous cure, we pray: ◆ For our planet, that it be treated with care, we pray: ◆ For the homeless, that they find shelter, we pray: ◆ For all who have died, we pray: ◆

Our Father . . .

Lord God,
you gave St. Luke a special gift
for the poor and the sick.
Help all the ill
know of your presence and mercy
so that freed from sin and suffering,
they may enjoy the glory of your reign.
Through Christ our Lord.
Amen.

✝ Your friends make known, O Lord, the glorious splendor of your kingdom.

Saturday, October 19, 2019

Memorial of Sts. John Brébeuf and Isaac Jogues, Priests, and Companions, Martyrs

☩ The Lord remembers his covenant forever.

Psalm 23

page 398

Reading

Luke 12:8–12

Jesus said to his disciples: "I tell you, everyone who acknowledges me before others the Son of Man will acknowledge before the angels of God. But whoever denies me before others will be denied before the angels of God.

"Everyone who speaks a word against the Son of Man will be forgiven, but the one who blasphemes against the Holy Spirit will not be forgiven. When they take you before synagogues and before rulers and authorities, do not worry about how or what your defense will be or about what you are to say. For the Holy Spirit will teach you at that moment what you should say."

Reflection

"The Holy Spirit will teach you at that moment what to say." Jesus explains to his disciples that they do not need to worry what they will say when asked to defend themselves. The Holy Spirit will put words in their mouths. When have you feared that you were not articulate enough to speak up for your faith? Perhaps you need only to put your trust in the Holy Spirit. In their work spreading the faith in North America, today's martyrs relied on guidance from God. Isaac Jogues wrote that giving his life was a return for the life that Jesus gave. Many of these martyrs who died between 1642 and 1649 were priests, save two who were lay missionaries.

Prayers

others may be added

To our Lord, who guides us, we pray:

◆ Graciously hear us, O Lord.

For leaders in the Church, that they trust in the wisdom of the Holy Spirit, we pray: ◆ For our president, that he seek the common good for our nation, we pray: ◆ For missionaries bringing the Gospel to new horizons, we pray: ◆ For vocations to the diaconate, we pray: ◆ For the quick recovery of the sick, we pray: ◆ For the dying, that the angels and saints greet them, we pray: ◆

Our Father . . .

O God,
you gave the martyrs such zeal
that they willingly
gave their lives for the faith.
Guide us by the Spirit,
that we may be your worthy ministers
and seek to care for those in our midst.
Through Christ our Lord.
Amen.

☩ The Lord remembers his covenant forever.

Sunday, October 20, 2019

Twenty-Ninth Sunday in Ordinary Time

☩ Our help is from the Lord who made heaven and earth.

Psalm 121

page 415

Reading

Luke 18:1–8

Jesus told his disciples a parable about the necessity for them to pray always without becoming weary. He said, "There was a judge in a certain town who neither feared God nor respected any human being. And a widow in that town used to come to him and say, 'Render a just decision for me against my adversary.' For a long time the judge was unwilling, but eventually he thought, 'While it is true that I neither fear God nor respect any human being, because this widow keeps bothering me I shall deliver a just decision for her lest she finally come and strike me.'" The Lord said, "Pay attention to what the dishonest judge says. Will not God then secure the rights of his chosen ones who call out to him day and night? Will he be slow to answer them? I tell you, he will see to it that justice is done speedily. But when the Son of Man comes, will he find faith on earth?"

Reflection

"When the Son of Man comes, will he find faith on earth?" The parable that Jesus tells shows how the woman persisted in seeking a judgment. Do we give up on God when we petition him and are not presented with what we desire? Jesus relates that people of faith always seek God.

Prayers

others may be added

Trusting in God, we pray:

◆ Lord, hear our prayer.

That pastoral ministers be filled with zeal for their ministry to the sick, we pray: ◆ That civic leaders guide the community to care for our common home, we pray: ◆ That those who have been wronged find justice and be reconciled, we pray: ◆ That catechumens feel parish support as they make a journey of faith, we pray: ◆ That the sick recover, we pray: ◆ That the dying be brought to eternal life, we pray: ◆

Our Father . . .

Lord God,
you listen to the cries of your people.
Grant that we may never waver
from seeking you.
May we be persistent in our prayer
and guide others to relationship with you.
Through Christ our Lord.
Amen.

☩ Our help is from the Lord who made heaven and earth.

Monday, October 21, 2019
Weekday

✝ Blessed be the Lord, the God of Israel, who has come to the people.

Psalm 121 *page 415*

Reading *Luke 12:16–21*

Then [Jesus] told [the crowd] a parable. "There was a rich man whose land produced a bountiful harvest. He asked himself, 'What shall I do, for I do not have space to store my harvest?' And he said, 'This is what I shall do: I shall tear down my barns and build larger ones. There I shall store all my grain and other goods and I shall say to myself, "Now as for you, you have so many good things stored up for many years, rest, eat, drink, be merry!"' But God said to him, 'You fool, this night your life will be demanded of you; and the things you have prepared, to whom will they belong?' Thus will it be for the one who stores up treasure for himself but is not rich in what matters to God."

Reflection

It is common for many of us to store up material goods to ensure that future needs are met. When we do so, are we putting our faith in things instead of God? We must be careful of our attachments. The man in this parable devoted his time, energy, and money to building larger barns to store possessions. Are we so attached to the things of this world that we forsake what is needed for the next life?

Prayers *others may be added*

Putting our trust in God, we pray:

◆ Lord, hear our prayer.

That dioceses collaborate with parishes for the wise use of resources, we pray: ◆ That citizens carefully discern issues prior to the election, we pray: ◆ That firefighters be kept free from harm, we pray: ◆ That farmers work safely as they make preparations for winter, we pray: ◆ That the sick be strengthened by God's healing presence, we pray: ◆ That the dying experience the glory of the heavenly banquet, we pray: ◆

Our Father . . .

Provident God,
you provide for our every need.
Guide our efforts
to detach from worldly desires
and to devote our lives
to preparing for eternal life,
and fully embracing your love.
Through Christ our Lord.
Amen.

✝ Blessed be the Lord, the God of Israel, who has come to the people.

Tuesday, October 22, 2019

Optional Memorial of St. John Paul II, Pope

✝ Here I am Lord, I come to do your will.

Psalm 121

page 415

Reading

Luke 12:35–38

Jesus said to his disciples: "Gird your loins and light your lamps and be like servants who await their master's return from a wedding, ready to open immediately when he comes and knocks. Blessed are those servants whom the master finds vigilant on his arrival. Amen, I say to you, he will gird himself, have them recline at table, and proceed to wait on them. And should he come in the second or third watch and find them prepared in this way, blessed are those servants."

Reflection

When the master of the house traveled for a wedding or other event, servants had the run of the house to clean, ready, and refresh. Their work was finished and they were ready to greet the master upon his return. Parables usually have a twist. In this parable, the master waits on those servants who are prepared for him. Just like those servants, we do not know exactly when God will appear for us. Will we be focused on him, or will we still have much to do to ready ourselves for his coming? Those who have concentrated on God during this life will be "blessed" in the next life.

Prayers

others may be added

To our generous God, we pray:

◆ Lord, hear our prayer.

That our clergy help us to see
the blessings God provides, we pray: ◆
That elected officials, always consider
the good of the community, we pray: ◆
That human trafficking end, we pray: ◆
That through the intercession of St. John Paul II, all may come to respect human life from conception to natural death, we pray: ◆ That the sick may recover, we pray: ◆ That the dying be welcomed into eternal life, we pray: ◆

Our Father . . .

O God,
you shower us with your love and mercy.
Help us to share these blessings
with our brothers and sisters
until your Son returns in glory
to renew the face of the earth.
Through Christ our Lord.
Amen.

✝ Here I am Lord, I come to do your will.

Wednesday, October 23, 2019
Weekday

✝ Our help is in the name of the Lord.

Psalm 96 *page 409*

Reading *Luke 12:39–40*

Jesus said to his disciples: "Be sure of this: if the master of the house had known the hour when the thief was coming, he would not have let his house be broken into. You also must be prepared, for at an hour you do not expect, the Son of Man will come."

Reflection

During the weeks before Advent, the readings focus on the end-time and urge us to be prepared for the Second Coming. The opportunity to prepare for the next life can be considered a gift. We have been given so much that we can become distracted and focus on the things of this world. These last weeks of the liturgical year turn us to the need to be ready for God, for like a thief, he could come "at an hour you do not expect."

Prayers *others may be added*

To the Lord of our longing, we pray:

◆ Gracious Lord, hear our prayer.

That our pastoral staff help parishioners focus on their spiritual lives, we pray: ◆ That voters study issues and candidates before heading for the polls, we pray: ◆ That those who prepare food in restaurants hear words of gratitude, we pray: ◆ That those who labor and are burdened be treated with respect and dignity, we pray: ◆ That those awaiting transplants may have their burdens relieved quickly, we pray: ◆ That the dying be brought to their eternal glory, we pray: ◆

Our Father . . .

O God,
you provide for us in many ways.
Grant that we may joyfully prepare
for your return through serving
the needs of others.
May we seek to build up your reign
so that the world will be transformed
in your glory.
Through Christ our Lord.
Amen.

✝ Our help is in the name of the Lord.

Thursday, October 24, 2019

Optional Memorial of St. Anthony Mary Claret, Bishop

✝ Blessed are they who hope in the Lord.

Psalm 96

page 409

Reading

Luke 12:49–53

Jesus said to his disciples: "I have come to set the earth on fire, and how I wish it were already blazing! There is a baptism with which I must be baptized, and how great is my anguish until it is accomplished! Do you think that I have come to establish peace on the earth? No, I tell you, but rather division. From now on a household of five will be divided, three against two and two against three; a father will be divided against his son and a son against his father, a mother against her daughter and a daughter against her mother, a mother-in-law against her daughter-in-law and a daughter-in-law against her mother-in-law."

Reflection

Being a disciple of Christ is controversial. We are to nurture a zeal in our hearts that compels us to live out the Gospel. Such a call can be disconcerting to others and instead of ensuring peace in relationships, it may bring turmoil and discord. The fire that Jesus will set will arise from the sparks from the faith of disciples. May our passion for the Gospel set the flame of faith in our friends and family.

Prayers

others may be added

With hearts on fire for Gospel living, we pray:

◆ Lord, hear our prayer.

That the Church may never lose its prophetic voice, we pray: ◆ That communities invest in families, we pray: ◆ That through the intercession of St. Anthony, more men seek to serve God through the Claretians, we pray: ◆ That peace come to war-torn regions, we pray: ◆ That those who care for the sick may find strength in Christ, we pray: ◆ That the saints and angels greet the faithfully departed, we pray: ◆

Our Father . . .

O God,
you enlighten us through the Spirit.
May we faithfully live out our call
and through the fire of our love
bring others to Christ.
Through Christ our Lord.
Amen.

✝ Blessed are they who hope in the Lord.

Friday, October 25, 2019

Weekday

✝ Lord, teach me your statutes.

Psalm 96 *page 409*

Reading *Luke 12:54–59*

Jesus said to the crowds, "When you see a cloud rising in the west you say immediately that it is going to rain—and so it does; and when you notice that the wind is blowing from the south you say that it is going to be hot—and so it is. You hypocrites! You know how to interpret the appearance of the earth and the sky; why do you not know how to interpret the present time?

"Why do you not judge for yourselves what is right? If you are to go with your opponent before a magistrate, make an effort to settle the matter on the way; otherwise your opponent will turn you over to the judge, and the judge hand you over to the constable, and the constable throw you into prison. I say to you, you will not be released until you have paid the last penny."

Reflection

Jesus chastises the crowd, telling them that they can see the obvious but are unable to interpret what is going on around them. What are the signs of the times that we are missing today? Do those signs concern the homeless, the needs of people who are disabled, immigrant populations, or divisions in our community? The Second Vatican Council document *Pastoral Constitution on the Church in the Modern Word (Gaudium et spes)* states, "In every age, the church carries the responsibility of reading the signs of the times and of interpreting them in the light of the Gospel" (4). How do we reflect on the Scriptures to respond to the events of our day?

Prayers *others may be added*

Living authentic Christian lives,
we pray:

◆ Gracious Lord, hear our prayer.

That leaders in the Church inspire humility by how they live, we pray: ◆ That our president and Congress work together for the common good, we pray: ◆ That children who will take part in Halloween celebrations be safe, we pray: ◆ That those who serve in the military be kept free from harm, we pray: ◆ That the sick be comforted, we pray: ◆ That the dying be welcomed to eternal life, we pray: ◆

Our Father . . .

Lord God,
you share in our joys and hopes.
May we try to read the signs of the times
and interpret how you are
at work in our midst.
May our judgments be wise
so that we may obtain
the blessings of heaven.
Through Christ our Lord.
Amen.

✝ Lord, teach me your statutes.

Saturday, October 26, 2019
Weekday

✝ Lord, this is the people that longs to see your face.

Psalm 96 *page 409*

Reading *Luke 13:1–5*

Some people told Jesus about the Galileans whose blood Pilate had mingled with the blood of their sacrifices. He said to them in reply, "Do you think that because these Galileans suffered in this way they were greater sinners than all other Galileans? By no means! But I tell you, if you do not repent, you will all perish as they did! Or those eighteen people who were killed when the tower at Siloam fell on them–do you think they were more guilty than everyone else who lived in Jerusalem? By no means! But I tell you, if you do not repent, you will all perish as they did!"

Reflection

In today's Gospel, the people seem to be blaming what has occurred to a group of people on their sin. Jesus, however, chastises them, telling them that they need to look at their lives and repent. We, too, sometimes spend more time considering another's situation than ours. It is much easier to recognize another's failings. When tempted to focus on someone's wrongdoing, we need to look inside ourselves and realize where we need to repent. If we do not do so, we risk eternal life.

Prayers *others may be added*

With our minds and hearts turning to God, we pray:

◆ Lord, hear our prayer.

That our pastoral staff inspire humility in others, we pray: ◆ That officeholders put others before themselves, we pray: ◆ That those who suffer discrimination may find justice, we pray: ◆ That those in the process of divorce may find healing and strength, we pray: ◆ That the sick recover quickly, we pray: ◆ That the dying be brought to the glory of heaven, we pray: ◆

Our Father . . .

O God of justice,
you shower your people with grace.
Grant that we may seek
to change our lives
to conform to your will
so that we may attain eternal life.
Through Christ our Lord.
Amen.

✝ Lord, this is the people that longs to see your face.

Sunday, October 27, 2019

Thirtieth Sunday in Ordinary Time

✝ The Lord hears the cry of the poor.

Psalm 34 *page 401*

Reading *Luke 18:9–14*

Jesus addressed this parable to those who were convinced of their own righteousness and despised everyone else. "Two people went up to the temple area to pray; one was a Pharisee and the other was a tax collector. The Pharisee took up his position and spoke this prayer to himself, 'O God, I thank you that I am not like the rest of humanity—greedy, dishonest, adulterous—or even like this tax collector. I fast twice a week, and I pay tithes on my whole income.' But the tax collector stood off at a distance and would not even raise his eyes to heaven but beat his breast and prayed, 'O God, be merciful to me a sinner.' I tell you, the latter went home justified, not the former; for everyone who exalts himself will be humbled, and the one who humbles himself will be exalted."

Reflection

How do we sound when we pray? A spiritual director shared with me that she had asked people to record themselves in their prayer. She maintained that the spiritual life could be deepened through listening to one's prayer. For example, if a person found that in prayer, the world was blamed for problems, he or she might move from blame to gratitude and humility. Praying "be merciful to me a sinner," the tax collector stood before God with humility. He knew his place before God.

Prayers *others may be added*

To our God of justice, we pray:

◆ Lord, hear our prayer.

May the Church be known for her mercy, we pray: ◆ May community leaders be mindful of the needs of those who suffer, we pray: ◆ May those recovering from abuse find strength and healing, we pray: ◆ May spiritual directors grow in wisdom and guidance, we pray: ◆ May those awaiting a transplant receive one, we pray: ◆ May those who have died be brought to the heavenly banquet, we pray: ◆

Our Father . . .

Merciful God,
you are always awaiting us.
Help all in need of your care
to know of your deep love and concern
so that we may each
deepen our relationship with you
and grow in holiness and wisdom.
Through Christ our Lord.
Amen.

✝ The Lord hears the cry of the poor.

Monday, October 28, 2019
Feast of Sts. Simon and Jude, Apostles

✝ Their message goes out through all the earth.

Psalm 19
page 397

Reading
Ephesians 2:19–22

Brothers and sisters: You are no longer strangers and sojourners, but you are fellow citizens with the holy ones and members of the household of God, built upon the foundation of the Apostles and prophets, with Christ Jesus himself as the capstone. Through him the whole structure is held together and grows into a temple sacred in the Lord; in him you also are being built together into a dwelling place of God in the Spirit.

Reflection
Each of us builds on the foundation of the last generation. St. Paul reflects that these first Christians came to the faith because of the foundation laid by the Apostles, prophets, and Christ. As we consider our movement toward faith, we can think of the parents and grandparents who taught us prayers and teachers and priests who helped us deepen our faith. The saints we honor today are listed with the Apostles in Luke 6:16. Simon is not Simon Peter but the Simon identified as being called a Zealot. Jude is the Judas who is the son of James. We can look to both Apostles to aid us in continuing to establish the foundation for others to believe.

Prayers
others may be added

To our Lord, the foundation of our lives, we pray:

◆ Lord, hear our prayer.

May our parishioners understand their role in sharing their gift of faith, we pray: ◆ May those preparing for the election be patient with their many tasks, we pray: ◆ May families in crisis or need receive the support they crave, we pray: ◆ May those in prison find strength, we pray: ◆ May caregivers find grace in their ministry to the sick, we pray: ◆ May bereavement ministers assist those who grieve, we pray: ◆

Our Father . . .

O God,
through the intercession
of Sts. Simon and Jude,
may our faith continually grow
and strengthen.
Assist us with your love,
and help us to be
evangelizers of the Good News
to a world in need of your spirit and truth.
Through Christ our Lord.
Amen.

✝ Their message goes out through all the earth.

Tuesday, October 29, 2019
Weekday

† The Lord has done marvels for us.

Psalm 85
page 407

Reading
Luke 13:18–21

Jesus said, "What is the Kingdom of God like? To what can I compare it? It is like a mustard seed that a man took and planted in the garden. When it was fully grown, it became a large bush and 'the birds of the sky dwelt in its branches'."

Again he said, "To what shall I compare the Kingdom of God? It is like yeast that a woman took and mixed in with three measures of wheat flour until the whole batch of dough was leavened."

Reflection

A mustard seed that grows into a large bush and a bit of yeast that provides leavening. Who would have imagined that Jesus would have described the Kingdom of God in such ways? The mustard seed would grow into a bush that would shelter birds and the yeast would make the wheat rise so that a flavorful bread would feed many. The Kingdom of God can permeate every part of our world. It can be like nothing we could imagine. As members of the Kingdom, we can add leavening in God's name to those who need to be lifted up.

Prayers
others may be added

To our God, who does marvelous things, we pray.

◆ Lord, hear our prayer.

May the Church seek to be leavening to those who seek her wisdom, we pray: ◆ May civic leaders find value in dialogue with those in need, we pray: ◆ May farmers find support in their communities of faith, we pray: ◆ May those in need of employment find a job soon, we pray: ◆ May the homebound and sick find comfort and healing, we pray: ◆ May those who have died live in the presence of God forever, we pray: ◆

Our Father . . .

Lord God,
you care for our every need.
Help us be the leavening
that enlivens a torn world
in need of love, compassion, and care.
Through Christ our Lord.
Amen.

† The Lord has done marvels for us.

Wednesday, October 30, 2019
Weekday

☩ My hope, O Lord, is in your mercy.

Psalm 33

page 401

Reading

Luke 13:23–25, 29

Someone asked him, "Lord, will only a few people be saved?" He answered them, "Strive to enter through the narrow gate, for many, I tell you, will attempt to enter but will not be strong enough. After the master of the house has arisen and locked the door, then will you stand outside knocking and saying, 'Lord, open the door for us.' He will say to you in reply, 'I do not know where you are from.' And people will come from the east and the west and from the north and the south and will recline at table in the Kingdom of God."

Reflection

"For many . . . who will attempt to enter will not be strong enough." It is interesting to note that strength is required to enter the narrow gate. But is it our strength or God's strength that opens the gate? Will the gate open because the person of prayer draws strength from dependence on God? Will God open the gate because our bond with the Lord has been strengthened through prayer and the sacraments? The Lord awaits us in the Eucharist. May our eating and drinking his Body and Blood bring us to recline "at table in the Kingdom of God."

Prayers

others may be added

To the Lord, who awaits us, we pray:

◆ Lord, hear our prayer.

May faith leaders work together, we pray: ◆ May nations seek dialogue to end conflict, we pray: ◆ May those who protect us remain safe, we pray: ◆ May service industry workers know of our gratitude and support, we pray: ◆ May the sick recover quickly, we pray: ◆ May the deceased find peace and tranquility in God's care, we pray: ◆

Our Father . . .

O God,
you give us strength
for the journey of faith.
Inspire in us words and deeds
to comfort those who labor and
   are burdened
and so bring your care and love
into a world in need of harmony
   and holiness.
Through Christ our Lord.
Amen.

☩ My hope, O Lord, is in your mercy.

Thursday, October 31, 2019
Weekday

✝ Save me, O Lord, in your mercy.

Psalm 34

page 401

Reading

Luke 13:31–35

Some Pharisees came to Jesus and said, "Go away, leave this area because Herod wants to kill you." He replied, "Go and tell that fox, 'Behold, I cast out demons and I perform healings today and tomorrow, and on the third day I accomplish my purpose. Yet I must continue on my way today, tomorrow, and the following day, for it is impossible that a prophet should die outside of Jerusalem.'

"Jerusalem, Jerusalem, you who kill the prophets and stone those sent to you, how many times I yearned to gather your children together as a hen gathers her brood under her wings, but you were unwilling! Behold, your house will be abandoned. But I tell you, you will not see me until the time comes when you say, / *Blessed is he who comes in the name of the Lord.*"

Reflection

The concerns of the Pharisees and Jesus stand in stark contrast here. The Pharisees seem to be looking out for Jesus as they tell him that Herod is searching for him. Jesus, though, is concentrating on his mission. He will heal now and later accomplish his purpose. Already, the Lord is looking toward the time of his passion, death, and Resurrection. That will not come until after he enters Jerusalem to the greeting of "Blessed is he who comes in the name of the Lord."

Prayers

others may be added

To our healing Lord, we pray:

◆ Lord, hear our prayer.

May our pastor and pastoral staff never tire of bringing the Gospel to others, we pray: ◆ May civic authorities not waver from their mission and vision of public service, we pray: ◆ May all have a safe Halloween, we pray: ◆ May orphans and neglected children find comfort and compassion, we pray: ◆ May those suffering from diseases know healing and strength, we pray: ◆ May the angels lead the dead to eternal life, we pray: ◆

Our Father . . .

Lord God,
you sent your Son to redeem us.
Help us keep our eyes fixed
on the new and eternal Jerusalem.
Lead all your people
to know of your strength
and guide us to devote our lives
to service and contemplation.
Through Christ our Lord.
Amen.

✝ Save me, O Lord, in your mercy.

Friday, November 1, 2019
Solemnity of All Saints

✝ Lord, this is the people that longs to see your face.

Psalm 24

page 398

Reading

Matthew 5:3–12a

"Blessed are the poor in spirit, / for theirs is the Kingdom of heaven. / Blessed are they who mourn, / for they will be comforted. / Blessed are the meek, / for they will inherit the land. / Blessed are they who hunger and thirst for righteousness, / for they will be satisfied. / Blessed are the merciful, / for they will be shown mercy. / Blessed are the clean of heart, / for they will see God. / Blessed are the peacemakers, / for they will be called children of God. / Blessed are they who are persecuted for the sake of righteousness, / for theirs is the Kingdom of heaven. / Blessed are you when they insult you and persecute you / and utter every kind of evil against you falsely because of me. / Rejoice and be glad, / for your reward will be great in heaven."

Reflection

As we celebrate the saints today, we consider how they are blessed to rejoice at the heavenly banquet. The Beatitudes number among the blessed those who are clean of heart, who hunger and thirst for righteousness, and are peacemakers. We are called to live out the mission of Christ each day through our meekness and our work to make this earth a righteous place. As we show God's blessedness to others, we, too, will be blessed.

Prayers

others may be added

To our loving God, we pray:

◆ Lord, hear our prayer.

May the Church always feel called to be the humble face of God in the world, we pray: ◆ May our legislators seek first the welfare of the marginalized, we pray: ◆ May catechists be inspired by the lives of the saints as they teach the Good News, we pray: ◆ May we grow in patience, meekness, and purity of heart, we pray: ◆ May those who are persecuted be given comfort and hope, we pray: ◆ May the dearly departed know the fullness of eternal life, we pray: ◆

Our Father . . .

O God,
you gave your saints the wisdom
to seek you above all things.
We joyfully praise and glorify your name.
Grant that we may one day share
a place in your eternal dwelling.
Through Christ our Lord.
Amen.

✝ Lord, this is the people that longs to see your face.

Saturday, November 2, 2019
Commemoration of All the Faithful Departed

✝ The Lord is my shepherd; there is nothing I shall want.

Psalm 23
page 398

Reading
John 6:37–40

[Jesus said to the crowds,] "Everything that the Father gives me will come to me, and I will not reject anyone who comes to me, because I came down from heaven not to do my own will but the will of the one who sent me. And this is the will of the one who sent me, that I should not lose anything of what he gave me, but that I should raise it on the last day. For this is the will of my Father, that everyone who sees the Son and believes in him may have eternal life, and I shall raise him on the last day."

Reflection

That Christ would not reject anyone who comes to him is comforting. Our Church has set aside this day for those who at their death were not yet opened completely to God's will. We pray that they will be purified, have eternal life, and be raised on the last day.

Prayers
others may be added

Hoping for life everlasting, we pray:

◆ Lord, hear our prayer.

May the Church be a beacon of hope and joy for all those searching for meaning, we pray: ◆ May migrants find welcome homes in new lands, we pray: ◆ May those who work with the elderly and bereaved find comfort, patience, and strength, we pray: ◆ May we continue to share the Good News of salvation in Christ, we pray: ◆ May the sick be healed of their afflictions, we pray: ◆ May the souls of all the faithful departed rest in peace, we pray: ◆

Our Father . . .

Lord God,
trusting in the resurrection,
we pray that you call all souls to yourself.
Raise the dead to life in you,
and deepen the faith
of those who mourn their loss,
that we might grow in faith and strength
and experience your salvation.
Through Christ our Lord.
Amen.

✝ The Lord is my shepherd; there is nothing I shall want.

Sunday, November 3, 2019

Thirty-First Sunday in Ordinary Time

✝ I will praise your name forever, my king and my God.

Psalm 145

page 421

Reading

Luke 19:2–6

Now a man there named Zacchaeus, who was a chief tax collector and also a wealthy man, was seeking to see who Jesus was; but he could not see him because of the crowd, for he was short in stature. So he ran ahead and climbed a sycamore tree in order to see Jesus, who was about to pass that way. When he reached the place, Jesus looked up and said, "Zacchaeus, come down quickly, for today I must stay at your house." And he came down quickly and received him with joy.

Reflection

One can imagine the joy of Zacchaeus, when Jesus sees him. But the story does not end with this tax collector's rejoicing. The next verses tell of the change of heart that Zacchaeus experienced. Not only did he say he would give half his possessions to the poor but he would repay fourfold anyone he had extorted. Upon encountering Jesus, Zacchaeus was able to detach from his possessions. In the Word and the Eucharist we meet Christ. Have those encounters prompted you to detach from any possessions or change in any way?

Prayers

others may be added

To our loving God, we pray:

◆ Lord, hear our prayer.

May communities be inspired by
the Church's witness of compassion,
we pray: ◆ May civic leaders be good
stewards of the resources of their office,
we pray: ◆ May we seek to serve the poor,
we pray: ◆ May the homeless find shelter,
we pray: ◆ May the sick be healed,
we pray: ◆ May those who have died
rejoice at the heavenly banquet,
we pray: ◆

Our Father . . .

God, our loving Father,
you bring us to newness of life.
Guide along the paths of holiness
your people searching for meaning,
so that they may come to rejoice
in their ever deeper relationship
with our Lord Jesus Christ, your Son,
who lives and reigns with you in the unity
of the Holy Spirit,
one God, for ever and ever.
Amen.

✝ I will praise your name forever, my king and my God.

Monday, November 4, 2019

Memorial of St. Charles Borromeo, Bishop

✝ Lord, in your great love, answer me.

Psalm 145 *page 421*

Reading *Luke 14:12–14*

On a sabbath Jesus went to dine at the home of one of the leading Pharisees. He said to the host who invited him, "When you hold a lunch or dinner, do not invite your friends or your brothers or sisters or your relatives or your wealthy neighbors, in case they may invite you back and you have repayment. Rather, when you hold a banquet, invite the poor, the crippled, the lame, the blind; blessed indeed will you be because of their inability to repay you. For you will be repaid at the resurrection of the righteous."

Reflection

Only an extremely gracious person would invite to dinner those who would never repay the kindness in some way. This is exactly what Christ has done in his invitation to us to partake of his Body and Blood in the Eucharist. Christ nurtures us at the Eucharist and then invites us to the heavenly banquet. St. Charles, whom we honor today, shared the Eucharist with the sick and suffering on the street. How do we spread without reserve the grace God has provided us?

Prayers *others may be added*

To our gracious Lord, we pray:

◆ Lord, hear our prayer.

Assist Catholic charitable organizations as they seek to provide for the poor, we pray: ◆ Help men to be open to your invitation to study in the seminary, we pray: ◆ Guide professors who are forming priests, we pray: ◆ Encourage communities to be more open to varied cultures, we pray: ◆ Assist researchers as they seek to develop cures for terminal diseases, we pray: ◆ Welcome to the banquet feast of heaven all who have died, we pray: ◆

Our Father . . .

O God,
you sent your Son
to nurture the world.
Awaken in us
the desire to be attentive
to the cries of your people
so that we may be the face of Christ
in the world.
Through Christ our Lord.
Amen.

✝ Lord, in your great love, answer me.

Tuesday, November 5, 2019
Weekday

✝ In you, O Lord, I have found my peace.

Psalm 145 *page 421*

Reading *Luke 14:16–21*

[Jesus] replied to him, "A man gave a great dinner to which he invited many. When the time for the dinner came, he dispatched his servant to say to those invited, 'Come, everything is now ready.' But one by one, they all began to excuse themselves. The first said to him, 'I have purchased a field and must go to examine it; I ask you, consider me excused.' And another said, 'I have purchased five yoke of oxen and am on my way to evaluate them; I ask you, consider me excused.' And another said, 'I have just married a woman, and therefore I cannot come.' The servant went and reported this to his master. Then the master of the house in a rage commanded his servant, 'Go out quickly into the streets and alleys of the town and bring in here the poor and the crippled, the blind and the lame.' "

Reflection

Each Sunday Catholics gather at Mass to feast on the Word of God and the Eucharist. Sadly, many people pass up this invitation. They may be tired from a long week at work, need to attend to family obligations, or finish chores. Those who are nourished at the liturgy might want to consider who they might invite to pray with the community. Who has your parish overlooked? Who could you tell about the blessing that the Scriptures and the sacraments have been in your life?

Prayers *others may be added*

To the Lord, who provides us with many blessings, we pray:

◆ Lord, hear our prayer.

Help your followers to communicate the joys of the sacraments, we pray: ◆ Assist those who seek to serve the common good, we pray: ◆ Provide patience to those working at the polls, we pray: ◆ Renew the country with zeal for doing God's will, we pray: ◆ Heal the needs of the afflicted, we pray: ◆ Lead those who have died to the glory of the heavenly homeland, we pray: ◆

Our Father . . .

Bountiful God,
you call all people to feast at your table.
Assist us as we renew our efforts
at hospitality
so that others may be drawn to you.
May all know that you unite heaven
and earth
with your mercy and love.
Through Christ our Lord.
Amen.

✝ In you, O Lord, I have found my peace.

Wednesday, November 6, 2019
Weekday

✝ Blessed the one who is gracious and lends to those in need.

Psalm 145

page 421

Reading

Luke 14:25–27

Great crowds were traveling with Jesus, and he turned and addressed them, "If anyone comes to me without hating his father and mother, wife and children, brothers and sisters, and even his own life, he cannot be my disciple. Whoever does not carry his own cross and come after me cannot be my disciple."

Reflection

How can Jesus ask us to hate those who are closest to us and to hate even our life? Our Lord makes the point that anyone, even our own life, can keep us from following Christ as we should. We can become more interested in our pleasures and interests than what God asks of us. When our focus is other than what the Lord seeks, we will refuse to carry our cross and not follow Christ. A disciple constantly examines who or what is being placed before Christ.

Prayers

others may be added

To the Lord, who assists us in taking up our cross, we pray:

◆ Lord, hear our prayer.

Guide our pastor as he seeks to help people put God first in their lives, we pray: ◆ Assist all who are newly elected, we pray: ◆ Help communities as they seek to give hope to the oppressed, we pray: ◆ Assist those in prison as they struggle to find hope, we pray: ◆ Strengthen those awaiting an organ transplant, we pray: ◆ Lead to the joys of heaven all the dearly departed, we pray: ◆

Our Father . . .

O God,
you provide us with all we need.
Grant us the fortitude to put you
above all things, even our own life.
May we renounce those things
that distract from our picking up our cross
to follow you.
Through Christ our Lord.
Amen.

✝ Blessed the one who is gracious and lends to those in need.

Thursday, November 7, 2019
Weekday

✝ I believe that I shall see the good things of the Lord in the land of the living.

Psalm 145 *page 421*

Reading *Romans 14:7–12*

Brothers and sisters: None of us lives for oneself, and no one dies for oneself. For if we live, we live for the Lord, and if we die, we die for the Lord; so then, whether we live or die, we are the Lord's. For this is why Christ died and came to life, that he might be Lord of both the dead and the living. Why then do you judge your brother or your sister? Or you, why do you look down on your brother or sister? For we shall all stand before the judgment seat of God; for it is written: / *As I live, says the Lord, every knee shall bend before me, / and every tongue shall give praise to God.* / So then each of us shall give an account of himself to God.

Reflection

St. Paul began the Letter to the Romans by calling himself "a slave of Christ Jesus." In this passage, he helps the community understand that they do not live or die for themselves but for Christ. With that perspective, why would one judge or look down upon another? If our sights are set on the Lord, we would not be concerned with another's actions. After all, we will give an accounting of our life, not another's, to God.

Prayers *others may be added*

Seeking our Lord, we pray:

◆ Lord, hear our prayer.

Inspire our parishioners to focus their lives on the Lord, we pray: ◆ Help civic leaders working to reconcile people in the community, we pray: ◆ Grant safety to refugees, we pray: ◆ Support teachers and parents as they seek the best for students, we pray: ◆ Comfort those who are sick and need urgent care, we pray: ◆ Shower tenderness on mourners, we pray: ◆

Our Father . . .

Lord God,
you sent your Son to die for our sins.
May we always remember
that we serve you and live for your glory.
Support all who sacrifice each day
to build up your reign
and proclaim your mighty deeds
to all the world.
Through Christ our Lord.
Amen.

✝ I believe that I shall see the good things of the Lord in the land of the living.

Friday, November 8, 2019
Weekday

✝ The Lord has revealed to the nations his saving power.

Psalm 145 *page 421*

Reading *Luke 16:1–8*

Jesus said to his disciples, "A rich man had a steward who was reported to him for squandering his property. He summoned him and said, 'What is this I hear about you? Prepare a full account of your stewardship, because you can no longer be my steward.' The steward said to himself, 'What shall I do, now that my master is taking the position of steward away from me? I am not strong enough to dig and I am ashamed to beg. I know what I shall do so that, when I am removed from the stewardship, they may welcome me into their homes.' He called in his master's debtors one by one. To the first he said, 'How much do you owe my master?' He replied, 'One hundred measures of olive oil.' He said to him, 'Here is your promissory note. Sit down and quickly write one for fifty.' Then to another he said, 'And you, how much do you owe?' He replied, 'One hundred measures of wheat.' He said to him, 'Here is your promissory note; write one for eighty.' And the master commended that dishonest steward for acting prudently."

Reflection

The steward has squandered his master's property until his livelihood is threatened. At that point, he ingratiates himself to those who are in debt to the master by subtracting his commission from the debt owed. Such prudence impresses the master. It is important to pray for prudence, one of the four cardinal virtues, in our lives. The *Catechism of the Catholic Church* states that prudence is used to apply moral principles to particular cases.

Prayers *others may be added*

To our merciful God, we pray:

◆ Gracious Lord, hear our prayer.

Support dioceses awaiting a new bishop, we pray: ◆ Open the hearts of leaders to give generously of their time, we pray: ◆ Secure justice for those awaiting trial, we pray: ◆ Help us to end elements in our culture that do not support life from conception to natural death, we pray: ◆ Give refreshment and peace to the aged and ill, we pray: ◆ Grant eternal rest to those who have died, we pray: ◆

Our Father . . .

Generous God,
you give us many gifts and talents
to be used for the benefit
of building your kingdom.
Teach us to use our skills wisely
and to be honest, trustworthy servants
living always in the light of Christ, who lives and reigns with you in the unity of the Holy Spirit, one God, for ever and ever.
Amen.

✝ The Lord has revealed to the nations his saving power.

Saturday, November 9, 2019

Feast of the Dedication of the Lateran Basilica

† The waters of the river gladden the city of God, the holy dwelling of the Most High.

Psalm 145 *page 421*

Reading *1 Corinthians 3:9c–11, 16–17*

Brothers and sisters: You are God's building. According to the grace of God given to me, like a wise master builder I laid a foundation, and another is building upon it. But each one must be careful how he builds upon it, for no one can lay a foundation other than the one that is there, namely, Jesus Christ.

Do you not know that you are the temple of God, and that the Spirit of God dwells in you? If anyone destroys God's temple, God will destroy that person; for the temple of God, which you are, is holy.

Reflection

Since the Holy Father presides at the Basilica of St. John Lateran, it can be considered the home parish of all Catholics. Today's reading from Corinthians help us consider how the Church is not contained in a building but within the People of God. As St. Paul states, "You are God's building." Within our holy temple, God dwells. At Baptism, we become a member of Christ, who is priest, prophet, and king. As part of Christ's Body, we are to be holy, so that others will be drawn to know Christ.

Prayers *others may be added*

To the Lord, who has made us holy, we pray:

◆ Lord, hear our prayer.

Assist pastoral leaders as they help parishioners renew themselves to witness to the grace of God, we pray: ◆ Assist nations that seek to provide clean water to their people, we pray: ◆ Encourage faith formation leaders as they educate adults, we pray: ◆ Inspire artists as they use their talents increative ways, we pray: ◆ Support researchers who seek cures for diseases, we pray: ◆ Forgive the sins of all who sleep in Christ, we pray: ◆

Our Father . . .

O God,
you build in us a firm foundation of love.
Guide your people to be holy temples
so that they might be a living witness
to justice and peace.
May we continue to grow
in your ways and radiate your love.
Through Christ our Lord.
Amen.

† The waters of the river gladden the city of God, the holy dwelling of the Most High.

Sunday, November 10, 2019

Thirty-Second Sunday in Ordinary Time

☩ Lord, when your glory appears, my joy will be full.

Psalm 17

page 397

Reading

Luke 20:27–36

Some Sadducees, those who deny that there is a resurrection, came forward and put this question to Jesus, saying, "Teacher, Moses wrote for us, *If someone's brother dies leaving a wife but no child, his brother must take the wife and raise up descendants for his brother.* Now there were seven brothers; the first married a woman but died childless. Then the second and the third married her, and likewise all the seven died childless. Finally the woman also died. Now at the resurrection whose wife will that woman be? For all seven had been married to her." Jesus said to them, "The children of this age marry and remarry; but those who are deemed worthy to attain to the coming age and to the resurrection of the dead neither marry nor are given in marriage. They can no longer die, for they are like angels; and they are the children of God because they are the ones who will rise."

Reflection

As the liturgical year nears its end, the readings reflect more on the life to come. In answering the query, Jesus points out that our earthly attachments are not our focus in heaven. When we reach the next life, nothing will be as it is in this world, where people live and die and marry and are given in marriage. There, the focus will be on God.

Prayers

others may be added

Seeking God's ways, we pray:

◆ Lord, hear our prayer.

For pastors, that they may inspire us to aim our sights at the things of heaven, we pray: ◆ For leaders in our community, that they seek justice, we pray: ◆ For renewed efforts to support our planet, we pray: ◆ For food drives and other efforts to end hunger, we pray: ◆ For all who care for the elderly, that they receive support, we pray: ◆ For the dying, that they be welcomed to the heavenly banquet, we pray: ◆

Our Father . . .

O God,
you are always faithful to us.
Guide our ways
and teach us to recognize
that the things of this world are passing
and that you are our true homeland,
where all rest in your love and goodness.
Through Christ our Lord.
Amen.

☩ Lord, when your glory appears, my joy will be full.

Monday, November 11, 2019
Memorial of St. Martin of Tours, Bishop

✝ Guide me, Lord, along the everlasting way.

Psalm 24
page 398

Reading
Luke 17:1–6

Jesus said to his disciples, "Things that cause sin will inevitably occur, but woe to the one through whom they occur. It would be better for him if a millstone were put around his neck and he be thrown into the sea than for him to cause one of these little ones to sin. Be on your guard! If your brother sins, rebuke him; and if he repents, forgive him. And if he wrongs you seven times in one day and returns to you seven times saying, 'I am sorry,' you should forgive him."

And the Apostles said to the Lord, "Increase our faith." The Lord replied, "If you have faith the size of a mustard seed, you would say to this mulberry tree, 'Be uprooted and planted in the sea,' and it would obey you."

Reflection
When I hear this reading, I wish for my faith to increase so that I be able to do more good. I hope to not sin, to forgive, and to be better at saying "I'm sorry." We grow in faith as we seek to forgive and be forgiven. As our lives become more and more rooted in Christian values and virtues, our entire selves are formed more deeply in the faith. St. Martin of Tours was a catechumen when he tore his cloak to clothe a man. As he grew in faith, he brought others to Christianity, including his mother.

Prayers
others may be added

Seeking an increase in faith, we pray:

◆ Lord, hear our prayer.

For our bishop, that he have good health, we pray: ◆ For newly elected officials, that they lead with courage, we pray: ◆ For those, who like Martin of Tours, share their clothes with those in need, we pray: ◆ For veterans, that they be given the assistance they need, we pray: ◆ For the sick, we pray: ◆ For all who died in service to our country, we pray: ◆

Our Father . . .

Lord God,
you gave St. Martin of Tours
such love that he clothed another
with his cloak.
Faithfully guide us to be your witness
of joy, peace, and hope
so that all may come to know
of your steadfast love.
Through Christ our Lord.
Amen.

✝ Guide me, Lord, along the everlasting way.

Tuesday, November 12, 2019

Memorial of St. Josaphat, Bishop and Martyr

☩ I will bless the Lord at all times.

Psalm 24

page 398

Reading

Luke 17:7–10

Jesus said to the Apostles: "Who among you would say to your servant who has just come in from plowing or tending sheep in the field, 'Come here immediately and take your place at table'? Would he not rather say to him, 'Prepare something for me to eat. Put on your apron and wait on me while I eat and drink. You may eat and drink when I am finished'? Is he grateful to that servant because he did what was commanded? So should it be with you. When you have done all you have been commanded, say, 'We are unprofitable servants; we have done what we were obliged to do.'"

Reflection

It is common for human beings to look for praise for the good they have done. Today's reading instructs that following Christ is what is expected of a disciple. St. Josaphat was not afraid of following Christ to his death. He served as an abbot and then a bishop who published a catechism and worked to reform the clergy. His struggle to reunite the Orthodox Church with Rome stirred up passions and he was killed by one of his priests. May we pray that we follow the Lord, no matter his requests.

Prayers

others may be added

To the Lord, who guides us in all we do, we pray:

◆ Lord, hear our prayer.

For Church leaders, that under the patronage of St. Josaphat, they work together for Christian unity, we pray: ◆ For those who suffer for the faith today, jeopardizing their well-being and security, we pray: ◆ For civic leaders, that they care for the needs of the poor, we pray: ◆ For those who work in the ecumenical and interfaith movements, we pray: ◆ For renewal of health for the sick, we pray: ◆ For those who have died, and those who mourn the loss of their loved ones, we pray: ◆

Our Father . . .

Loving God,
you guide us in all that you call us to do.
May we seek to serve you
without counting the cost,
always keeping in mind our gratitude.
Through Christ our Lord.
Amen.

☩ I will bless the Lord at all times.

Wednesday, November 13, 2019
Memorial of St. Frances Cabrini, Virgin

✝ Rise up, O God, bring judgment to the earth.

Psalm 17
page 397

Reading
Luke 17:11–19

As Jesus continued his journey to Jerusalem, he traveled through Samaria and Galilee. As he was entering a village, ten lepers met him. They stood at a distance from him and raised their voice, saying, "Jesus, Master! Have pity on us!" And when he saw them, he said, "Go show yourselves to the priests." As they were going they were cleansed. And one of them, realizing he had been healed, returned, glorifying God in a loud voice; and he fell at the feet of Jesus and thanked him. He was a Samaritan. Jesus said in reply, "Ten were cleansed, were they not? Where are the other nine? Has none but this foreigner returned to give thanks to God?" Then he said to him, "Stand up and go; your faith has saved you."

Reflection
When the lepers see Jesus, they abided by the law and kept a distance. Without even drawing close to them, Jesus heals each leper. Only the Samaritan, a person not respected among the Jews, returns to give thanks. Perhaps the others thought that it was more important to follow Jesus' command to show themselves to the priest. It is apparent here that Jesus places a high priority on giving thanks. How often do you express your thanks to God?

Prayers
others may be added

Opening our hearts to the Lord,
we pray:

◆ Lord, hear our prayer.

For the pope, may he experience good health, we pray: ◆ For world leaders, may they inspire others to share their gifts, we pray: ◆ For those recovering from natural disasters, we pray: ◆ For those who, like Frances Cabrini, work to make migrants and immigrants feel welcome through hospitality, we pray: ◆ For the mentally ill, we pray: ◆ For those who have died, may they be granted eternal rest, we pray: ◆

Our Father . . .

Lord God,
in your kindness you provide for us.
May we be gracious
in accepting your gifts
and tell others of your healing works.
Through Christ our Lord.
Amen.

✝ Rise up, O God, bring judgment to the earth.

Thursday, November 14, 2019
Weekday

✝ Your word is for ever, O Lord.

Psalm 146 *page 421*

Reading *Luke 17:20–25*

Asked by the Pharisees when the Kingdom of God would come, Jesus said in reply, "The coming of the Kingdom of God cannot be observed, and no one will announce, 'Look, here it is,' or, 'There it is.' For behold, the Kingdom of God is among you."

Then he said to his disciples, "The days will come when you will long to see one of the days of the Son of Man, but you will not see it. There will be those who will say to you, 'Look, there he is,' or 'Look, here he is.' Do not go off, do not run in pursuit. For just as lightning flashes and lights up the sky from one side to the other, so will the Son of Man be in his day. But first he must suffer greatly and be rejected by this generation."

Reflection

By nature, humankind looks for what is not apparent to them. In Jesus' time, the Pharisees asked about the coming of the kingdom. Today, people look for signs of the end of the world. Jesus explains that the Kingdom of God is in our midst and still to come. It is hard to understand how the kingdom can be both in the present and the future. When we observe people acting as the face of Christ, we are seeing the Kingdom of God at work.

Prayers *others may be added*

Trusting in God's plan for salvation, we pray:

◆ Lord, hear our prayer.

For renewed holiness for pastoral leaders, we pray: ◆ For physicians, as they seek to strengthen the health of their patients, we pray: ◆ For United Nations' peacekeepers, that their efforts never wane, we pray: ◆ For the patience of those preparing for Thanksgiving, we pray: ◆ For scientists and artists in their quest to explore and show the beauty of God, we pray: ◆ For believers to share in your eternal glory, we pray: ◆

Our Father . . .

God of the living and the dead,
you bring us joy and hope
to know that your reign is now and always present.
Shape our will to bring forth
a kingdom of justice and peace
so that all may be lifted up
by a renewed hope.
Through Christ our Lord.
Amen.

✝ Your word is for ever, O Lord.

Friday, November 15, 2019
Weekday

✝ The heavens proclaim the glory of God.

Psalm 119 *page 414*

Reading *Luke 17:26–30*

Jesus said to his disciples: "As it was in the days of Noah, so it will be in the days of the Son of Man; they were eating and drinking, marrying and giving in marriage up to the day that Noah entered the ark, and the flood came and destroyed them all. Similarly, as it was in the days of Lot: they were eating, drinking, buying, selling, planting, building; on the day when Lot left Sodom, fire and brimstone rained from the sky to destroy them all. So it will be on the day the Son of Man is revealed."

Reflection

Jesus explains that at his Second Coming, people will be just as unaware as they were of other events when many perished. When the flood came, people were carrying on their lives just as they had before. So, too, when fire destroyed Sodom. As we near the end of the liturgical year, today's reading is another call to always be ready for the Master's return. We need to be mindful to be alert, always doing God's will.

Prayers *others may be added*

Turning to our merciful Lord, we pray:

◆ Lord, hear our prayer.

For the Church, may she always act as a beacon of hope, we pray: ◆ For our newly elected officials, may they serve the needs of all, we pray: ◆ For nations seeking better economic values, we pray: ◆ For the lonely, we pray: ◆ For those seeking emergency treatment, we pray: ◆ For our beloved dead, we pray: ◆

Our Father . . .

Merciful Lord,
your justice is for all.
May we always seek your will.
Renew our resolve
to convert to your ways
and keep our eyes fixed on our
heavenly home,
where we will be one with you in glory.
Through Christ our Lord.
Amen.

✝ The heavens proclaim the glory of God.

Saturday, November 16, 2019

Optional Memorial of St. Margaret of Scotland and St. Gertrude, Virgin

✝ Remember the marvels the Lord has done.

Psalm 119

page 414

Reading

Luke 18:1–8

Jesus told his disciples a parable about the necessity for them to pray always without becoming weary. He said, "There was a judge in a certain town who neither feared God nor respected any human being. And a widow in that town used to come to him and say, 'Render a just decision for me against my adversary.' For a long time the judge was unwilling, but eventually he thought, 'While it is true that I neither fear God nor respect any human being, because this widow keeps bothering me I shall deliver a just decision for her lest she finally come and strike me.'" The Lord said, "Pay attention to what the dishonest judge says. Will not God then secure the rights of his chosen ones who call out to him day and night? Will he be slow to answer them? I tell you, he will see to it that justice is done speedily. But when the Son of Man comes, will he find faith on earth?"

Reflection

The widow was persistent with her cause, no matter the time it required to get the judge's attention. God is attentive to our needs but still we sometimes fail to direct ourselves to God in prayer. When we persist in prayer, we fulfill both ours and God's desire for communication. As we pray, our faith will increase as our relationship with God grows.

Prayers

others may be added

To the God of our longing, we pray:

◆ Lord, hear our prayer.

For our pastoral staff, that they continue to seek to be models of prayer, we pray: ◆ For government leaders, that they be open to the workings of God, we pray: ◆ For women inspired by Sts. Margaret and Gertrude, that they continue to deepen their spiritual life, we pray: ◆ For those who are suffering from tragedy and loss, that they find hope, we pray: ◆ For increased efforts to care for the poor, we pray: ◆ For those families who miss and mourn loved ones, we pray: ◆

Our Father . . .

O God,
in your goodness,
you care for your faithful stewards.
Help us always to open our hearts
to experience the joy of prayer
and desire to do your will and work.
Through Christ our Lord.
Amen.

✝ Remember the marvels the Lord has done.

Sunday, November 17, 2019

Thirty-Third Sunday in Ordinary Time

✝ The Lord comes to rule the earth with justice.

Psalm 98

page 410

Reading

Luke 21:12–19

[Jesus said to the crowd:] "They will seize and persecute you, they will hand you over to the synagogues and to prisons, and they will have you led before kings and governors because of my name. It will lead to your giving testimony. Remember, you are not to prepare your defense beforehand, for I myself shall give you a wisdom in speaking that all your adversaries will be powerless to resist or refute. You will even be handed over by parents, brothers, relatives, and friends, and they will put some of you to death. You will be hated by all because of my name, but not a hair on your head will be destroyed. By your perseverance you will secure your lives."

Reflection

Not long before Jesus is handed over to his passion and death, he tells his followers what they will face. They will be betrayed by relatives and will face rulers. They are not to worry about their defense, for God will give them the words. This reading brings to mind the Beatitude in Luke: "Blessed are you when people hate you. . . . Behold, your reward will be great in heaven" (6:27–28).

Prayers

others may be added

With trust in the Lord, we pray:

◆ Lord, hear our prayer.

That the Church be a witness of hope in times of crisis, we pray: ◆ That leaders of nations seek justice and peace, we pray: ◆ That missionaries in troubled lands trust in God's care and support, we pray: ◆ That young women and men discern a call to serve the Church in a vocation of consecrated life or ordained priesthood, we pray: ◆ That all life be kept free from harm, we pray: ◆ That those who have gone before us marked with the sign of faith enjoy their eternal reward, we pray: ◆

Our Father . . .

Faithful Lord,
you promise us eternal life.
Grant that we may always know
that you are at our side
when we speak out in your name.
May we be free from anxiety and fear
as we place our trust in you.
Through Christ our Lord.
Amen.

✝ The Lord comes to rule the earth with justice.

Monday, November 18, 2019

Optional Memorial of St. Rose Philippine Duchesne, Virgin

☩ Give me life, O Lord, and I will do your commands.

Psalm 98

page 410

Reading

Luke 18:35–43

As Jesus approached Jericho a blind man was sitting by the roadside begging, and hearing a crowd going by, he inquired what was happening. They told him, "Jesus of Nazareth is passing by." He shouted, "Jesus, Son of David, have pity on me!" The people walking in front rebuked him, telling him to be silent, but he kept calling out all the more, "Son of David, have pity on me!" Then Jesus stopped and ordered that he be brought to him; and when he came near, Jesus asked him, "What do you want me to do for you?" He replied, "Lord, please let me see." Jesus told him, "Have sight; your faith has saved you." He immediately received his sight and followed him, giving glory to God. When they saw this, all the people gave praise to God.

Reflection

"Lord, please let me see." We may be able to see perfectly well with our eyes. Still, though, we may miss much that is around us. We may overlook those who need our concern. Sometimes our vision is so narrowly focused that we do not see the beauty God has set before us. In our prayer, we might cry out to God to help us to expand our vision to see as he would like us to see. In that way, we will better live the Gospel.

Prayers

others may be added

To our merciful Lord, we pray:

◆ Lord, hear our prayer.

For spiritual renewal and insight from our Church's leaders, we pray: ◆ For openness to peaceful overtures from world leaders, we pray: ◆ For renewed missionary efforts in spreading the Gospel, especially under the patronage of St. Rose, we pray: ◆ For orphans, that they be strengthened through their education, we pray: ◆ For reconciliation and renewal between Native American cultures and those who migrated to this land, we pray: ◆ For our beloved dead who gave their lives to spread the faith, we pray: ◆

Our Father . . .

Gracious God,
you call us to deeper insight.
Help us to see your ways clearly
so that renewed by your healing presence,
we may recognize you in all things.
Through Christ our Lord.
Amen.

☩ Give me life, O Lord, and I will do your commands.

Tuesday, November 19, 2019
Weekday

✝ The Lord upholds me.

Psalm 98

page 410

Reading

Luke 19:2–6

Now a man there named Zacchaeus, who was a chief tax collector and also a wealthy man, was seeking to see who Jesus was; but he could not see him because of the crowd, for he was short in stature. So he ran ahead and climbed a sycamore tree in order to see Jesus, who was about to pass that way. When he reached the place, Jesus looked up and said, "Zacchaeus, come down quickly, for today I must stay at your house." And he came down quickly and received him with joy.

Reflection

Do you ever feel that the smallness of your position keeps you from achieving importance? Do you feel passed over because your talents seem ordinary? Zacchaeus was so small in stature that he needed to climb a tree to see the Lord. The ingenuity of this small man made a difference. Jesus saw him, called out to him, and dined with him. Do not worry about inadequacies. God can see what others do not.

Prayers

others may be added

Trusting in the Lord, we pray:

◆ Lord, hear our prayer.

For the Church, that she always welcome those who seek refuge, we pray: ◆ For governors and state legislators to seek the health and well-being of their people, we pray: ◆ For migrants seeking a safe new home, we pray: ◆ For vocations to the diaconate, we pray: ◆ For the search for a cure for cancer, we pray: ◆ For the dying, that they be welcomed to their eternal home, we pray: ◆

Our Father . . .

Almighty God,
you are aware of all
who occupy our hearts.
Teach us to care for others
with compassion and joy,
lifting their hearts to know and serve you.
Through Christ our Lord.
Amen.

✝ The Lord upholds me.

Wednesday, November 20, 2019
Weekday

✝ Lord, when your glory appears, my joy will be full.

Psalm 150 *page 423*

Reading *Luke 19:11–13, 15–23*

While people were listening to Jesus speak, he proceeded to tell a parable because he was near Jerusalem and they thought that the Kingdom of God would appear there immediately. So he said, "A nobleman went off to a distant country to obtain the kingship for himself and then to return. He called ten of his servants and gave them ten gold coins and told them, 'Engage in trade with these until I return.' But when he returned after obtaining the kingship, he had the servants called, to whom he had given the money, to learn what they had gained by trading. The first came forward and said, 'Sir, your gold coin has earned ten additional ones.' He replied, 'Well done, good servant! You have been faithful in this very small matter; take charge of ten cities.' Then the second came and reported, 'Your gold coin, sir, has earned five more.' And to this servant too he said, 'You, take charge of five cities.' Then the other servant came and said, 'Sir, here is your gold coin; I kept it stored away in a handkerchief, for I was afraid of you, because you are a demanding man; you take up what you did not lay down and you harvest what you did not plant.' He said to him, 'With your own words I shall condemn you, you wicked servant. You knew I was a demanding man, taking up what I did not lay down and harvesting what I did not plant; why did you not put my money in a bank? Then on my return I would have collected it with interest.'"

Reflection

Often we are conflicted over whether to save or spend our gifts and talents. Jesus sends the message that an investment of our gifts enriches the Kingdom. When we show compassion, our love is multiplied as others spread the love that we give. God freely gives love so that we may spend our lives doing the same.

Prayers *others may be added*

Open to God's help, we pray:

◆ Lord, hear our prayer.

For the Church, that she radiate the love God showers on her followers, we pray: ◆ For communities to be good stewards of resources, we pray: ◆ For hearts open to working for justice, we pray: ◆ For patience with each other, we pray: ◆ For the disabled, that theybe supported, we pray: ◆ For the dying, that the angels lead them to paradise, we pray: ◆

Our Father . . .

Heavenly Father,
you build your kingdom with love and justice.
Renew our efforts
to love without measure
as we use our gifts
so that we may bring about the reign
for which you call us to serve.
Through Christ our Lord.
Amen.

✝ Lord, when your glory appears, my joy will be full.

Thursday, November 21, 2019

Memorial of the Presentation of the Blessed Virgin Mary

☩ The Almighty has done great things for me, and holy is his Name.

Canticle of Mary

page 423

Reading

Luke 19:41–44

As Jesus drew near Jerusalem, he saw the city and wept over it, saying, "If this day you only knew what makes for peace—but now it is hidden from your eyes. For the days are coming upon you when your enemies will raise a palisade against you; they will encircle you and hem you in on all sides. They will smash you to the ground and your children within you, and they will not leave one stone upon another within you because you did not recognize the time of your visitation."

Reflection

Jesus is coming close to Jerusalem, which means his passion and death are nearly upon him. He speaks, though, not of himself but of the destruction that the city will face. He wishes that the people would know what would make for peace. In our day, too, violence instills fears for safety. Let us acknowledge that Jesus laments the sadness in our world and the trials before us. May we look to what Jesus taught as we seek the means for peace.

Prayers

others may be added

To our compassionate God, we pray:

◆ Lord, hear our prayer.

For the pope, as he models humility, we pray: ◆ For parents, that under the inspiration of Sts. Anne and Joachim who presented Mary to God, that they may faithfully carry out their duties as Christian parents, we pray: ◆ For those who have lost a child, we pray: ◆ For children who seek a loving home, we pray: ◆ For those desiring asylum, we pray: ◆ For relief for those who hunger, we pray: ◆

Our Father . . .

Peaceful God,
you desire for us to live in a just world.
Guide our words and deeds
to always show your compassion
so that our world may be built up
by a new hope
and renewed in love and justice.
Amen.

☩ The Almighty has done great things for me, and holy is his Name.

Friday, November 22, 2019
Memorial of St. Cecilia, Virgin and Martyr

✝ We praise your glorious name,
O mighty God.

Psalm 150 *page 423*

Reading *Luke 19:45–48*

Jesus entered the temple area and proceeded to drive out those who were selling things, saying to them, "It is written, *My house shall be a house of prayer, but you have made it a den of thieves.*" And every day he was teaching in the temple area. The chief priests, the scribes, and the leaders of the people, meanwhile, were seeking to put him to death, but they could find no way to accomplish their purpose because all the people were hanging on his words.

Reflection

Jesus seeks to cleanse the Temple of anything unpleasing so that the people would be able to hear his teaching. At Baptism, we were cleansed and made temples for the dwelling of the Holy Spirit. How do you keep focus on the temple that is within you? Do you spend quiet time with God to replenish your soul? We need to ensure that our lives do not become frenzied marketplaces but are calm spaces where the Spirit lives.

Prayers *others may be added*

Seeking the Lord's favor, we pray:

◆ Lord, hear our prayer.

For the spiritual growth of the Church, we pray: ◆ For our civic leaders, that they act ethically, we pray: ◆ For children, that their sports organizations respect the Lord's Day, we pray: ◆ For musicians, that with the example of St. Cecilia, they continue their devotion to worship in spirit and truth, we pray: ◆ For those seeking asylum, that they be accorded mercy, we pray: ◆ For all who died at a young age, we pray: ◆

Our Father . . .

Almighty God,
you make your dwelling within us.
Help us see the areas in our life
that need to be freed from business
and drawn to your love and concern.
Through Christ our Lord.
Amen.

✝ We praise your glorious name,
O mighty God.

Saturday, November 23, 2019

Optional Memorial of Bl. Miguel Agustin Pro, Priest and Martyr

☩ I will rejoice in your salvation,
O Lord.

Psalm 98

page 410

Reading

Luke 20:27–36

Some Sadducees, those who deny that there is a resurrection, came forward and put this question to Jesus, saying, "Teacher, Moses wrote for us, *If someone's brother dies leaving a wife but no child, his brother must take the wife and raise up descendants for his brother.* Now there were seven brothers; the first married a woman but died childless. Then the second and the third married her, and likewise all the seven died childless. Finally the woman also died. Now at the resurrection whose wife will that woman be? For all seven had been married to her." Jesus said to them, "The children of this age marry and remarry; but those who are deemed worthy to attain to the coming age and to the resurrection of the dead neither marry nor are given in marriage. They can no longer die, for they are like angels; and they are the children of God because they are the ones who will rise."

Reflection

Concerns about life's laws and boundaries cause us worry; they hold us back from our real purpose. The question of the Sadducees, and Jesus' answer, reminds us that the relationships of earth will not bind us in heaven. Why would we want it to be so? If anything, this reading reminds us of the hope that lies before us. We hope that God and others will see us for who we are around the table at the banquet feast of heaven.

Prayers

others may be added

To our faithful God, we pray:

◆ Lord, hear our prayer.

For the Church, that she act with compassion as she prepares us for the heavenly kingdom, we pray: ◆ For civic laws to support the sanctity of marriage, we pray: ◆ For married couples to be witnesses of love and joy, we pray: ◆ For those couples experiencing marital difficulties, that they may be strengthened, we pray: ◆ For spouses who care for their sick partner, we pray: ◆ For priests, that under the inspiration of Blessed Miguel, they boldly speak the Gospel, we pray: ◆

Our Father . . .

God of the living and the dead,
you will raise us up to the fullness of life
when our pilgrimage is done.
Lead us through life's difficult challenges,
so that we may fully grasp
the meaning and purpose
of our relationships with one another
and build the earthly city of joy.
Amen.

☩ I will rejoice in your salvation,
O Lord.

Sunday, November 24, 2019

Solemnity of Our Lord Jesus Christ, King of the Universe

✝ Let us go rejoicing to the house of the Lord.

Psalm 122

page 416

Reading

Luke 23:35–43

The rulers sneered at Jesus and said, "He saved others, let him save himself if he is the chosen one, the Christ of God." Even the soldiers jeered at him. As they approached to offer him wine they called out, "If you are the King of the Jews, save yourself." Above him there was an inscription that read, "This is the King of the Jews."

Now one of the criminals hanging there reviled Jesus, saying, "Are you not the Christ? Save yourself and us." The other, however, rebuking him, said in reply, "Have you no fear of God, for you are subject to the same condemnation? And indeed, we have been condemned justly, for the sentence we received corresponds to our crimes, but this man has done nothing criminal." Then he said, "Jesus, remember me when you come into your kingdom." He replied to him, "Amen, I say to you, today you will be with me in Paradise."

Reflection

This reading of Christ's passion shows who we are to be as Christians. Just as Christ did not respond to the soldiers who taunted him, we are to turn the other cheek. As the criminal put his faith in Jesus, we are to rely on God. Our lives are gift. We know that God is responsible for all that is good.

Prayers

others may be added

To the God of mercy, we pray:

◆ Lord, hear our prayer.

May the Church be a reconciling force in the world, we pray: ◆ May enemies put behind the past and come together to build relationships, we pray: ◆ May United Nations' peacekeepers be supported in their missions, we pray: ◆ May the ecumenical movement flourish, we pray: ◆ May the sick find comfort and strength, we pray: ◆ May those who have died find eternal joy, we pray: ◆

Our Father . . .

Lord God,
you sent your Son
to die for our sins
and reconcile us with you.
Attune our hearts
to walk faithfully to the call of
our Baptism
to build a kingdom
of reconciliation, justice, and peace.
Through Christ our Lord.
Amen.

✝ Let us go rejoicing to the house of the Lord.

Monday, November 25, 2019
Weekday

✝ Glory and praise for ever!

Psalm 122 *page 416*

Reading *Luke 21:1–4*

When Jesus looked up he saw some wealthy people putting their offerings into the treasury and he noticed a poor widow putting in two small coins. He said, "I tell you truly, this poor widow put in more than all the rest; for those others have all made offerings from their surplus wealth, but she, from her poverty, has offered her whole livelihood."

Reflection

The widow who gives all she has is an example of who Jesus describes as "blessed" in the Beatitudes. Dependent on God, his Kingdom will be hers. All we have, we have received from the Lord and are to give back as a sacrifice of praise. During this week when Thanksgiving occurs, we are especially reminded that we are to use our blessings for others.

Prayers *others may be added*

To the Lord who blesses us, we pray:

◆ Lord, hear our prayer.

May the Church be concerned for all who are poor, we pray: ◆ May our elected officials quickly find shelter for all who are in need of it, we pray: ◆ May those who assist the hungry be fed with the love they share, we pray: ◆ May those parishes seeking staff members to fulfill their mission find appropriate people to fill those positions, we pray: ◆ May the sick find comfort, we pray: ◆ May all who have died rest in God's peace, we pray: ◆

Our Father . . .

Lord God,
you bless us with many gifts.
May we always be open
to the life you set before us,
choosing it freely and serving you
with undivided hearts.
Through Christ our Lord.
Amen.

✝ Glory and praise for ever!

Tuesday, November 26, 2019
Weekday

✝ Give glory and eternal praise to God!

Psalm 96
page 409

Reading
Luke 21:5–9

While some people were speaking about how the temple was adorned with costly stones and votive offerings, Jesus said, "All that you see here—the days will come when there will not be left a stone upon another stone that will not be thrown down."

Then they asked him, "Teacher, when will this happen? And what sign will there be when all these things are about to happen?" He answered, "See that you not be deceived, for many will come in my name, saying, 'I am he,' and 'The time has come.' Do not follow them! When you hear of wars and insurrections, do not be terrified; for such things must happen first, but it will not immediately be the end."

Reflection
It is easy to fixate on the beauty of adornments. Surely the people looking at the stones and votive offerings were proud of the way the area looked. The Lord, however, turns the gaze to the heavenly realm, the place where all is lasting. May we never give in to desires that keep our hearts from seeking God above all.

Prayers
others may be added

Turning our thoughts to the needs of this world, we pray:

◆ Lord, hear our prayer.

May the Church always seek to keep our gaze at heaven, we pray: ◆ May our newly elected officials seek to build the kingdom of God on earth, we pray: ◆ May all travelers reach their destination safely, we pray: ◆ May we come to a new appreciation of the heavenly gifts, we pray: ◆ May those working on cures for cancer receive support, we pray: ◆ May our beloved dead rest in God's peace, we pray: ◆

Our Father . . .

Gracious God,
you call us into a relationship.
Help us to fix our gaze on life with you.
May we never think that the beauty
of things of this earth
rival those of heaven.
Through Christ our Lord.
Amen.

✝ Give glory and eternal praise to God!

Wednesday, November 27, 2019
Weekday

✝ Give glory and eternal praise to God!

Psalm 96

page 409

Reading

Luke 21:12–19

Jesus said to the crowd: "They will seize and persecute you, they will hand you over to the synagogues and to prisons, and they will have you led before kings and governors because of my name. It will lead to your giving testimony. Remember, you are not to prepare your defense beforehand, for I myself shall give you a wisdom in speaking that all your adversaries will be powerless to resist or refute. You will even be handed over by parents, brothers, relatives, and friends, and they will put some of you to death. You will be hated by all because of my name, but not a hair on your head will be destroyed. By your perseverance you will secure your lives."

Reflection

"By your perseverance you will secure your lives." Jesus has just said that some will be put to death after their friends and relatives turn them over to authorities. We may at first think that our mortal lives are secured through perseverance. But eternal life is the one that matters. God leads us to the life that is everlasting. Perseverance in faith will secure that.

Prayers

others may be added

Trusting in the God of all ages, we pray:

◆ Lord, hear our prayer.

May the Church witness the Holy Spirit's wisdom, we pray: ◆ May our civic authorities trust in the wisdom of their constituents, we pray: ◆ May those who suffer persecution trust in God, we pray: ◆ May travelers reach their destination safely, we pray: ◆ May all who protect us be free from harm during this holiday weekend, we pray: ◆ May those we miss and mourn be granted eternal life, we pray: ◆

Our Father . . .

God of the ages past and present,
you guide your people
as they struggle in faith.
Attune our tongues to speak your truth
in loving service to your Word,
who is the Christ for ever and ever.
Amen.

✝ Give glory and eternal praise to God!

Thursday, November 28, 2019
Thanksgiving Day

✝ O God, let all the nations praise you!

Psalm 122

page 416

Reading

Luke 17:11–19

As Jesus continued his journey to Jerusalem, he traveled through Samaria and Galilee. As he was entering a village, ten lepers met him. They stood at a distance from him and raised their voice, saying, "Jesus, Master! Have pity on us!" And when he saw them, he said, "Go show yourselves to the priests." As they were going they were cleansed. And one of them, realizing he had been healed, returned, glorifying God in a loud voice; and he fell at the feet of Jesus and thanked him. He was a Samaritan. Jesus said in reply, "Ten were cleansed, were they not? Where are the other nine? Has none but this foreigner returned to give thanks to God?" Then he said to him, "Stand up and go; your faith has saved you."

Reflection

On this Thanksgiving Day, we recall all that God has provided us, but most especially how he sent his Son so that we would be reconciled with God. Christ continues to nurture us through the Eucharist, a word that means thanksgiving. May we, like the healed Samaritan, express our gratitude to God for his saving love.

Prayers

others may be added

To our Lord, whose love is bountiful,
we pray:

◆ Lord, graciously hear us.

May the Church be a source of gratitude and blessings to all who are lonely, we pray: ◆ May our nation never cease to thank God for the many blessings provided, we pray: ◆ May religious freedom never waver in our land, we pray: ◆ May those who are alone this holiday find comfort in our visits and calls, we pray: ◆ May those who work this holiday know of our gratitude and affection, we pray: ◆ May those who have died be brought to eternal glory, we pray: ◆

Our Father . . .

Abundant God,
you provide to us
the earth and all we reap from it.
Teach us to be grateful
for all of the blessings in our lives.
May we show others the gratitude
that comes from the life you offer.
Through our Lord Jesus Christ, your Son,
who lives and reigns with you in the unity
of the Holy Spirit,
one God, for ever and ever.
Amen.

✝ O God, let all the nations praise you!

Friday, November 29, 2019
Weekday

✝ Give glory and eternal praise to God.

Psalm 122
page 416

Reading
Luke 21:29–33

Jesus told his disciples a parable. "Consider the fig tree and all the other trees. When their buds burst open, you see for yourselves and know that summer is now near; in the same way, when you see these things happening, know that the Kingdom of God is near. Amen, I say to you, this generation will not pass away until all these things have taken place. Heaven and earth will pass away, but my words will not pass away."

Reflection
In the verses prior to today's reading, Jesus spoke of the signs of the coming of God's Kingdom. He tells of the roaring of the sea and people dying of fright in anticipation of what is about to occur. The signs of the coming of the Kingdom will be as obvious as the signs of summer. Todays' reading ends with an assurance for those who adhere to Scripture: Jesus' words will not pass away. Those words were the foundation for Dorothy Day as she sought to shelter and feed the poor through the Catholic Worker Houses. In 2000, the Vatican approved the cause for her sainthood and named her a Servant of God. Day died on November 29, 1980.

Prayers
others may be added

To our faithful Lord, we pray:

◆ Lord, graciously hear us.

May the Church always be hospitable
to the poor, the homeless, the refugee,
we pray: ◆ May countries and their
leaders reflect on the ways they welcome
foreigners, we pray: ◆ May those who
keep the peace be strengthened in
hope, we pray: ◆ May all seeking
meaningful employment secure it,
we pray: ◆ May those who need an
organ transplant find a donor, we pray: ◆
May the angels lead those who have died
into paradise, we pray: ◆

Our Father . . .

You are the temple of glory, Lord God,
and you inspire us to be people of prayer
and holiness.
Sustain our minds and hearts
to stay true to your ways
remain faithful and pure,
always rejoicing in the Spirit.
Through Christ our Lord.
Amen.

✝ Give glory and eternal praise to God.

Saturday, November 30, 2019

Feast of St. Andrew, Apostle

✝ The judgments of the Lord are true and all of them are just.

Psalm 19 *page 397*

Reading *Matthew 4:18–22*

As Jesus was walking by the Sea of Galilee, he saw two brothers, Simon who is called Peter, and his brother Andrew, casting a net into the sea; they were fishermen. He said to them, "Come after me, and I will make you fishers of men." At once they left their nets and followed him. He walked along from there and saw two other brothers, James, the son of Zebedee, and his brother John. They were in a boat, with their father Zebedee, mending their nets. He called them, and immediately they left their boat and their father and followed him.

Reflection

Andrew's call to become a fisher of women and men for Christ can help us reflect on the zeal we possess for our call. Some may be exhausted at this point of life and want to just rest and fish. Rest is important for renewal in our call to follow the Lord and serve others. After refreshment, we can go into the boat anew to evangelize and gather others by our witness. "Come after me" is Christ's continuous call to his disciples.

Prayers *others may be added*

To our Lord, who seeks us, we pray:

◆ Lord, hear us.

May parishes seek to help members understand their vocation as disciples, we pray: ◆ May couples support their children in guiding them to their vocation, we pray: ◆ May husbands and wives discern the call to the diaconate, we pray: ◆ May travelers reach their destination safely during this holiday season, we pray: ◆ May the sick be strengthened, we pray: ◆ May mourners find support and comfort, we pray: ◆

Our Father . . .

Lord God,
you gave St. Andrew
the fortitude to leave all behind
to follow you.
Guide our efforts in reaching out
to build your Kingdom
for the sake of the Gospel
so that all may know your Word
and live it faithfully in their lives.
Through Christ our Lord.
Amen.

✝ The judgments of the Lord are true and all of them are just.

Sunday, December 1, 2019
First Sunday of Advent

✝ Let us go rejoicing to the house of the Lord.

Psalm 122 *page 416*

Reading *Matthew 24:37–42*

Jesus said to his disciples: "As it was in the days of Noah, so will it be at the coming of the Son of Man. In those days before the flood, they were eating and drinking, marrying and giving in marriage, up to the day that Noah entered the ark. They did not know until the flood came and carried them all away. So will it be also at the coming of the Son of Man. Two men will be out in the field; one will be taken, and one will be left. Two women will be grinding at the mill; one will be taken, and one will be left. Therefore, stay awake! For you do not know on which day the Lord will come."

Reflection

What are we awaiting this Advent? Why are we to be alert? Every three years, this reading begins our liturgical year, challenging us to prepare for the coming of Christ. Until the flood came, people continued going about their lives as usual. Only Noah's family was saved. At the Second Coming, those who have been alert to the Lord in their lives will be taken. Those who have fallen asleep to God's desires will be left. With Advent hope, we use this liturgical season to turn our hearts to the Lord.

Prayers *others may be added*

Looking to the Lord with hope,
we pray:

◆ Come, Lord Jesus.

Help the clergy find support to witness hope to their parishioners, we pray: ◆ Awaken civic leaders to the plight of their people in need, we pray: ◆ Assist communities in efforts to eradicate HIV and AIDS as we remember World Aids Day, we pray: ◆ Encourage those seeking funding for social service organizations, we pray: ◆ Heal the brokenhearted, we pray: ◆ Bring to eternal life all who have died, we pray: ◆

Our Father . . .

Gracious God,
you provide the signs of the times
for us to read.
Help us in our efforts
to bring peace
to fearful neighbors and friends,
assuring them of your faithfulness.
Through Christ our Lord.
Amen.

✝ Let us go rejoicing to the house of the Lord.

Monday, December 2, 2019

Advent Weekday

✝ Let us go rejoicing to the house of the Lord.

Psalm 122 *page 416*

Reading *Matthew 8:5–11*

When Jesus entered Capernaum, a centurion approached him and appealed to him, saying, "Lord, my servant is lying at home paralyzed, suffering dreadfully." He said to him, "I will come and cure him." The centurion said in reply, "Lord, I am not worthy to have you enter under my roof; only say the word and my servant will be healed. For I too am a man subject to authority, with soldiers subject to me. And I say to one, 'Go,' and he goes; and to another, 'Come here,' and he comes; and to my slave, 'Do this,' and he does it." When Jesus heard this, he was amazed and said to those following him, "Amen, I say to you, in no one in Israel have I found such faith. I say to you, many will come from the east and the west, and will recline with Abraham, Isaac, and Jacob at the banquet in the Kingdom of heaven."

Reflection

Before receiving Communion, we humbly proclaim our faith with the same words the centurion said. We confess our unworthiness to receive the Body and Blood of Christ in the Eucharist while anticipating Christ's healing presence. This Advent may we ponder these words of faith as we seek to grow closer to our Lord.

Prayers *others may be added*

Looking to the Lord, who heals us, we pray:

◆ Come, Lord Jesus.

Guard the Church from harm, we pray: ◆ Encourage parishioners to support the catechumens, we pray: ◆ Create places of reconciliation and conversations of peace and hope, we pray: ◆ Awaken the faith of those who have stayed away from the liturgy, we pray: ◆ Renew efforts at evangelization, we pray: ◆ Welcome those who have died to eternal life, we pray: ◆

Our Father . . .

Compassionate God,
you heal us spiritually and physically.
Feed our hungers
as we long for you this Advent.
May our journey in faith lead us
to the banquet feast of heaven.
Through our Lord Jesus Christ, your Son,
who lives and reigns with you in the unity of the Holy Spirit,
one God, for ever and ever.
Amen.

✝ Let us go rejoicing to the house of the Lord.

Tuesday, December 3, 2019
Memorial of St. Francis Xavier, Priest

✝ Justice shall flourish in his time,
and fullness of peace for ever.

Psalm 122
page 416

Reading
Luke 10:21–24

Jesus rejoiced in the Holy Spirit and said, "I give you praise, Father, Lord of heaven and earth, for although you have hidden these things from the wise and the learned you have revealed them to the childlike. Yes, Father, such has been your gracious will. All things have been handed over to me by my Father. No one knows who the Son is except the Father, and who the Father is except the Son and anyone to whom the Son wishes to reveal him."

Turning to the disciples in private he said, "Blessed are the eyes that see what you see. For I say to you, many prophets and kings desired to see what you see, but did not see it, and to hear what you hear, but did not hear it."

Reflection
During Advent, we can seek to see the world with childlike eyes, so that our vision might take in the kingdom of God in our midst. To change how you look and listen to the sounds and sights around you, pray to God, praising him and asking to be blessed with a pure heart that is open to see the world as he sees.

Prayers
others may be added

Turning to the One who blesses us,
we pray:

◆ Come, Lord Jesus.

Renew the spirit of our bishops, as they seek to awaken the faithful to God's grace, we pray: ◆ Guide women and men into a vocation of service to the Church, we pray: ◆ Turn the hearts of those who would terrorize others, we pray: ◆ Support farmers in their care of the earth, we pray: ◆ Heal the sick, we pray: ◆ Bring to the pathway of heaven those who have died, we pray: ◆

Our Father . . .

Lord God,
through all ages,
you guide your people to grace.
With hearts open to the Spirit,
may a childlike faith
be enkindled in them
so that they may count themselves
among those who are blessed.
Through Christ our Lord.
Amen.

✝ Justice shall flourish in his time,
and fullness of peace for ever.

Wednesday, December 4, 2019

Advent Weekday

✝ I shall live in the house of the Lord
all the days of my life.

Psalm 23 *page 398*

Reading *Matthew 15:29–37*

At that time: Jesus walked by the Sea of Galilee, went up the mountain, and sat down there. Great crowds came to him, having with them the lame, the blind, the deformed, the mute, and many others. They placed them at his feet, and he cured them. The crowds were amazed when they saw the mute speaking, the deformed made whole, the lame walking, and the blind able to see, and they glorified the God of Israel.

Jesus summoned his disciples and said, "My heart is moved with pity for the crowd, for they have been with me now for three days and have nothing to eat. I do not want to send them away hungry, for fear they may collapse along the way." The disciples said to him, "Where could we ever get enough bread in this deserted place to satisfy such a crowd?" Jesus said to them, "How many loaves do you have?" "Seven," they replied, "and a few fish." He ordered the crowd to sit down on the ground. Then he took the seven loaves and the fish, gave thanks, broke the loaves, and gave them to the disciples, who in turn gave them to the crowds. They all ate and were satisfied. They picked up the fragments left over—seven baskets full.

Reflection

This Gospel account portrays the many ways that Jesus tends to the needs of his followers. Not only did he heal and teach, he provided food for all assembled. Our Lord's compassion reaches out to us spiritually, physically, and emotionally, desiring that we be whole. His love is bountiful, as is evident by the leftover baskets of food.

Prayers *others may be added*

To the One who sustains us, we pray:

◆ Come, Lord Jesus.

Prepare the hearts of catechists to be open to all as they share God's Word, we pray: ◆ Provide a gentle spirit to Communion ministers who visit the sick, we pray: ◆ Renew efforts at peace and justice in war-torn areas, we pray: ◆ Give courage to young people to live their faith boldly, we pray: ◆ Break down the barriers that keep the sick from good health care, we pray: ◆ Bring those who have died to eternal glory, we pray: ◆

Our Father . . .

Dear Lord,
you sent your Son,
to heal, teach, and feed your people.
Increase compassion in our hearts
so that we may regularly be moved
to act on behalf of others
and strengthen the Body of Christ.
Through Christ our Lord.
Amen.

✝ I shall live in the house of the Lord
all the days of my life.

Thursday, December 5, 2019
Advent Weekday

✝ Blessed is he who comes in the name of the Lord.

Psalm 23 *page 398*

Reading *Matthew 7:21, 24–27*

Jesus said to his disciples: "Not everyone who says to me, 'Lord, Lord,' will enter the Kingdom of heaven, but only the one who does the will of my Father in heaven.

"Everyone who listens to these words of mine and acts on them will be like a wise man who built his house on rock. The rain fell, the floods came, and the winds blew and buffeted the house. But it did not collapse; it had been set solidly on rock. And everyone who listens to these words of mine but does not act on them will be like a fool who built his house on sand. The rains fell, the floods came, and the winds blew and buffeted the house. And it collapsed and was completely ruined."

Reflection

Jesus draws a distinction here between those who listen to the Word of the Lord and those who make it part of their lives by doing God's will. If we give lip service to the Lord but fail to reform our lives, we do not honor him. During this Advent, we can look at what we need to change in our lives to prepare ourselves for Christ.

Prayers *others may be added*

Preparing for the Lord's return,
we pray:

◆ Come, Lord Jesus.

Reinvigorate the hearts of pastors as they share the Gospel, we pray: ◆ Aid those seeking to implement just laws to build the common good, we pray: ◆ Encourage leaders trying to build a culture of respect for all life, we pray: ◆ Assist those who look to deepen their faith through study, we pray: ◆ Support healthcare workers in their ministry, we pray: ◆ Help the dying trust in God, we pray: ◆

Our Father . . .

O God,
you guide us to renew our efforts
to know and please you.
Help us to grow in faithfulness
so that we will be drawn
to support the values of the Gospel
and aid in the building
of the kingdom of God.
Through Christ our Lord.
Amen.

✝ Blessed is he who comes in the name of the Lord.

Friday, December 6, 2019

Optional Memorial of St. Nicholas, Bishop

✝ The Lord is my light and my salvation.

Psalm 27

page 399

Reading

Matthew 9:27–31

As Jesus passed by, two blind men followed him, crying out, "Son of David, have pity on us!" When he entered the house, the blind men approached him and Jesus said to them, "Do you believe that I can do this?" "Yes, Lord," they said to him. Then he touched their eyes and said, "Let it be done for you according to your faith." And their eyes were opened. Jesus warned them sternly, "See that no one knows about this." But they went out and spread word of him through all that land.

Reflection

What is it we need to see this Advent? Even when we are faithful to prayer and receiving the sacraments, it is easy to overlook places in our lives where change is needed. It is wise to ask a trusted friend to help us see into our dark corners. Let us trust in another to help us recover sight in areas where we are blind. Pray for openness to this discussion.

Prayers

others may be added

With humble hearts, open to growing with Christ, we pray:

◆ Come, Lord Jesus.

Strengthen your clergy as they seek to open the eyes of their assemblies, we pray: ◆ Enlighten elected officials to seek better ways of seeing the needs of their people, we pray: ◆ Protect the unborn and the elders so that all may have abundant life, we pray: ◆ Help us look to St. Nicholas for creative ways of ministering to needs, we pray: ◆ Give refreshment and support to those who are lonely, we pray: ◆ Console families who grieve a loss, we pray: ◆

Our Father . . .

Gentle God,
you raise up the lowly
and help those truly in need.
Open our eyes
to the concerns of your people
so that we may always
spread your compassion
and grow in holiness of heart.
Through Christ our Lord.
Amen.

✝ The Lord is my light and my salvation.

Saturday, December 7, 2019

Memorial of St. Ambrose, Bishop and Doctor of the Church

☩ Blessed are all who wait for the Lord.

Psalm 122 *page 416*

Reading *Matthew 9:35–36, 10:1, 5a, 7*

Jesus went around to all the towns and villages, teaching in their synagogues, proclaiming the Gospel of the Kingdom, and curing every disease and illness. At the sight of the crowds, his heart was moved with pity for them because they were troubled and abandoned, like sheep without a shepherd.

Then he summoned his Twelve disciples and gave them authority over unclean spirits to drive them out and to cure every disease and every illness.

Jesus sent out these twelve after instructing them, "As you go, make this proclamation: 'The Kingdom of heaven is at hand.'"

Reflection

After Jesus notices that the people are like sheep without a shepherd, he sends out the Twelve to heal. As disciples, we are called to minister to those we meet. Do we know people for whom anxiety is a demon and need a calm voice in their lives? Are there people in your life who need kind guidance? Who seems to be without a shepherd to lead them?

Prayers *others may be added*

To our healing Shepherd, we pray:

◆ Lord, hear our prayer.

Assist clergy in their role of preaching and healing, we pray: ◆ Awaken newly elected leaders to their call to work for justice and peace, we pray: ◆ Call young women and men to be sisters, brothers, deacons, and priests, we pray: ◆ Support healthcare workers in their patience and kindness, we pray: ◆ Heal all who are sick and suffering, we pray: ◆ Raise the dead to life in the Spirit, we pray: ◆

Our Father . . .

Compassionate and loving God,
you heal the pain and suffering in
our lives
and call us to reach out in mercy
to others.
Help us bring your touch of grace
to lift up those who are suffering
and unburden their load.
Through Christ our Lord.
Amen.

☩ Blessed are all who wait for the Lord.

Sunday, December 8, 2019

Second Sunday of Advent

✝ Justice shall flourish in his time, and fullness of peace forever.

Psalm 72

page 406

Reading

Matthew 3:1–4

John the Baptist appeared, preaching in the desert of Judea and saying, "Repent, for the kingdom of heaven is at hand!" It was of him that the prophet Isaiah had spoken when he said: / *A voice of one crying out in the desert, / Prepare the way of the Lord, / make straight his paths. /* John wore clothing made of camel's hair and had a leather belt around his waist. His food was locusts and wild honey. At the time Jerusalem, all Judea, and the whole region around the Jordan were going out to him and were being baptized by him in the Jordan River as they acknowledged their sins.

Reflection

In today's Gospel, we hear that we are to be active in reforming our lives. The reading calls us to "repent," "prepare the way of the Lord," and "make straight his paths." These verbs help us realize that we need to strive continually to renew ourselves in the Lord. In repenting, we are to bring about God's ways and turn to God so that the kingdom may come. We can look inward and ask ourselves what we need to change or turn from at this time. Preparing for new growth means learning to release old patterns. By confessing our sins and making changes in our lives, we ready ourselves to make a place within the "inn" of our lives for Jesus.

Prayers

others may be added

Turning to God, who can help us change, we pray:

◆ Lord, hear our prayer.

For continued conversion and renewal for our pastoral leaders as they read the signs of the times, we pray: ◆ For adequate housing, water, and food and nutrition for all who toil in our world, we pray: ◆ For all families, especially couples who are experiencing crises now, we pray: ◆ For children suffering from cancer, we pray: ◆ For ongoing peace talks in regions of conflict, we pray: ◆ For those who have died, we pray: ◆

Our Father . . .

God of renewal and hope,
you sent your prophet John the Baptist
to call us to change our lives
so that we might serve you in fullness.
Give us courage
to mend our ways
so that we may faithfully live out
our baptismal call.
Through Christ our Lord.
Amen.

✝ Justice shall flourish in his time, and fullness of peace forever.

Monday, December 9, 2019

Solemnity of the Immaculate Conception of the Blessed Virgin Mary

✝ Sing to the Lord a new song, for God has done marvelous deeds.

Canticle of Mary *page 423*

Reading *Luke 1:26–35*

The angel Gabriel was sent from God to a town of Galilee called Nazareth, to a virgin betrothed to a man named Joseph, of the house of David, and the virgin's name was Mary. And coming to her, he said, "Hail, full of grace! The Lord is with you." But she was greatly troubled at what was said and pondered what sort of greeting this might be. Then the angel said to her, "Do not be afraid, Mary, for you have found favor with God. Behold, you will conceive in your womb and bear a son, and you shall name him Jesus. He will be great and will be called Son of the Most High, and the Lord God will give him the throne of David his father, and he will rule over the house of Jacob forever, and of his Kingdom there will be no end." But Mary said to the angel, "How can this be, since I have no relations with a man?" And the angel said to her in reply, "The Holy Spirit will come upon you, and the power of the Most High will overshadow you. Therefore the child to be born will be called holy, the Son of God.

Reflection

"How can this be?" In humility, Mary might have wondered how God could have chosen her. We also might wonder why God would choose us for a task, ministry, or vocation. Sometimes people feel that it is impossible for them to accomplish what God has set before them. Nothing, however, is impossible with God. It is important to trust, as Mary did, that God will be close to you in your vocation.

Prayers *others may be added*

Listening to God's Word, we offer our prayers:

◆ Come, Lord Jesus.

For the Church, that she reach out to single mothers, guiding them in their vocation, we pray: ◆ For social service agencies, that they receive the support required to assist families in need, we pray: ◆ For those seeking a child through adoption, we pray: ◆ For the building of trust between cultures, we pray: ◆ For healing for those who have lost a child, we pray: ◆ For children who have died unexpectedly and the healing of their parents, we pray: ◆

Our Father . . .

Gracious God,
you sent Gabriel
to announce your plan to Mary.
Through your loving kindness,
help us to be open and trusting
of your ways
so that we may serve you in holiness.
Through Christ our Lord.
Amen.

✝ Sing to the Lord a new song, for God has done marvelous deeds.

Tuesday, December 10, 2019
Advent Weekday

✝ The Lord our God comes with power.

Psalm 96
page 409

Reading
Matthew 18:12–14

Jesus said to his disciples: "What is your opinion? If a man has a hundred sheep and one of them goes astray, will he not leave the ninety-nine in the hills and go in search of the stray? And if he finds it, amen, I say to you, he rejoices more over it than over the ninety-nine that did not stray. In just the same way, it is not the will of your heavenly Father that one of these little ones be lost."

Reflection
If shepherds would search for a member of the flock who wandered off, wouldn't those who care for God's flock do the same? Even if a single person is lost, God awaits the return. God searches us out, and we should search out and minister to those who stray. How could we leave anyone behind? As disciples, we should have the same concern as God for those Jesus gently calls "these little ones."

Prayers
others may be added

To the Shepherd, who seeks us out, we pray:

◆ Lord, hear our prayer.

For the Church, that her doors be always open to wanderers, we pray: ◆ For refugees and migrants seeking a new home and country of safety, we pray: ◆ For efforts to provide safe water, we pray: ◆ For the movement of economies to support renewable energies, we pray: ◆ For those in hospice, that they have a restful day, we pray: ◆ For those who have died, that they be welcomed to eternal life, we pray: ◆

Our Father . . .

Ever loving God,
you seek the lowly and lost
and bring them into your friendship.
May we always be as open
and welcoming
in our efforts to reach out
with compassion,
especially to those who are most in need.
Through Christ our Lord.
Amen.

✝ The Lord our God comes with power.

Wednesday, December 11, 2019
Advent Weekday

✝ O bless the Lord, my soul!

Psalm 96

page 409

Reading

Matthew 11:28–30

Jesus said to the crowds: "Come to me, all you who labor and are burdened, and I will give you rest. Take my yoke upon you and learn from me, for I am meek and humble of heart; and you will find rest for yourselves. For my yoke is easy, and my burden light."

Reflection

In sending Jesus, God provided a place for us to find rest. The yoke that we take is obedience to God. Considering that our obedience is to the one who loves and provides for us, the yoke is light and the burden easy. Advent is a good time to meditate on how we might learn humility from Jesus.

Prayers

others may be added

Resting in Christ's yoke, we pray:

◆ Lord, hear our prayer.

For the Church, that she reach out to those who are burdened from their labors, we pray: ◆ For those who are seeking a better life in a new country, we pray: ◆ For those burdened with debt, that financial counseling be made available to them, we pray: ◆ For all who are lonely after a divorce, we pray: ◆ For the sick, may they be strengthened through the Sacrament of Anointing of the Sick, we pray: ◆ For support for all who mourn the loss of a life partner, we pray: ◆

Our Father . . .

Compassionate God,
you provide refuge for our burdens.
Sustain us through life's challenges
and raise up the downtrodden.
Grant that we may know
the words to comfort
those who are burdened
during this Advent.
Through Christ our Lord.
Amen.

✝ O bless the Lord, my soul!

Thursday, December 12, 2019

Feast of Our Lady of Guadalupe

✝ You are the highest honor of our race.

Canticle of Mary

page 423

Reading

Luke 1:39–47

Mary set out in those days and traveled to the hill country in haste to a town of Judah, where she entered the house of Zechariah and greeted Elizabeth. When Elizabeth heard Mary's greeting, the infant leaped in her womb, and Elizabeth, filled with the Holy Spirit, cried out in a loud voice and said, "Most blessed are you among women, and blessed is the fruit of your womb. And how does this happen to me, that the mother of my Lord should come to me? For at the moment the sound of your greeting reached my ears, the infant in my womb leaped for joy. Blessed are you who believed that what was spoken to you by the Lord would be fulfilled."

And Mary said: / "My soul proclaims the greatness of the Lord; / my spirit rejoices in God my savior."

Reflection

An aspect of Mary's mission is taking hospitality to those most in need. Mary appears as a pregnant mother to show her care for all God's people. God uses faithful servants, like Mary and us, to be instruments of hospitality and wholeness. We are to meet people where they are and lift them up so that they might understand the grace that God has given them. Mary, whom Pope John Paul II named Mother of the Americas, witnessed the love of God to Juan Diego and the people of Tepeyac. We are to provide like witness to those we meet.

Prayers

others may be added

Inspired by the witness of faith by Mary, we pray:

◆ **Lord, hear our prayer.**

For the Church, that she reach out to people of all nationalities, we pray: ◆ For civic leaders, that they work toward affordable health care for all, we pray: ◆ For midwives and all who assist in giving birth, we pray: ◆ For couples hoping to conceive or adopt a child, we pray: ◆ For families who have lost a child, we pray: ◆ For those who suffer from addictions, we pray: ◆

Our Father . . .

God of all nations and peoples,
you led your servant Mary
to reach out to the people
of the Americas at Guadalupe.
Guide your disciples
to radiate your joy and love
to those who need to be uplifted.
Through Christ our Lord.
Amen.

✝ You are the highest honor of our race.

Friday, December 13, 2019
Memorial of St. Lucy, Virgin and Martyr

✝ Those who follow you, Lord, will have the light of life.

Psalm 72 *page 406*

Reading *Matthew 11:16–19*

Jesus said to the crowds: "To what shall I compare this generation? It is like children who sit in marketplaces and call to one another, 'We played the flute for you, but you did not dance, we sang a dirge but you did not mourn.' For John came neither eating nor drinking, and they said, 'He is possessed by a demon.' The Son of Man came eating and drinking and they said, 'Look, he is a glutton and a drunkard, a friend of tax collectors and sinners.' But wisdom is vindicated by her works."

Reflection

"But wisdom is vindicated by her works." John the Baptist lived an ascetic lifestyle, wearing camel's hair and eating locusts and honey. He pointed the way to the Lord, but people criticized his ways. Jesus dined with the wealthy, as well as prostitutes, and he was taken to task for that. The wisdom of men can be acknowledged by the work that they have done. We must be careful not to pay attention to petty and hurtful comments people make about us or others who are helping prepare for the Lord's return.

Prayers *others may be added*

Confident that God guides us, we pray:

◆ Lord, hear our prayer.

For Catholic charitable organizations as they serve those most in need, we pray: ◆ For those who suffer from diseases in their eyes, that through the intercession of St. Lucy, they may be cured, we pray: ◆ For those who suffer from mental illness, may they receive proper health care, we pray: ◆ For postal workers as they extend themselves during the weeks before Christmas, we pray: ◆ For the critically wounded, that they heal quickly, we pray: ◆ For those who have died, that they be welcomed to eternal life, we pray: ◆

Our Father . . .

Gracious God
you gave John the wisdom
to point people to Jesus.
Encourage us as we seek
to help people find their
path to Christ.
May we not be concerned
what others say but only
seek to please you with our life.
Through our Lord Jesus Christ, your Son,
who lives and reigns with you in the unity
of the Holy Spirit,
one God, for ever and ever.
Amen.

✝ Those who follow you, Lord, will have the light of life.

Saturday, December 14, 2019

Memorial of St. John of the Cross, Priest and Doctor of the Church

✝ Lord, make us turn to you; let us see your face and we shall be saved.

Psalm 72 *page 406*

Reading *Matthew 17:9a, 10–13*

As they were coming down from the mountain, the disciples asked Jesus, "Why do the scribes say that Elijah must come first?" He said in reply, "Elijah will indeed come and restore all things; but I tell you that Elijah has already come, and they did not recognize him but did to him whatever they pleased. So also will the Son of Man suffer at their hands." Then the disciples understood that he was speaking to them of John the Baptist.

Reflection

No matter how great Elijah was, Jesus explains to the disciples, he went unrecognized upon his return and was put to death. Jesus also foretells his own death, saying that the Son of Man will not be recognized and will suffer. As the Third Sunday of Advent approaches, let us pray that we be granted the vision to see the Lord in our midst. St. John of the Cross, whom we honor today, depicted his seeking of union with God through poems of love. His writings, which include the poem "The Dark Night of the Soul" and the treatise *The Ascent of Mount Carmel*, detail the four phases of the path to God.

Prayers *others may be added*

To our Lord, who suffered for us, we pray:

◆ Lord, hear our prayer.

For vocations to the Carmelite Order, we pray: ◆ For citizens, that they take an active part in civic life, we pray: ◆ For our parishioners, that through the intercession of St. John of the Cross, they renew their efforts at deepening their spiritual life, we pray: ◆ For the continued healing of those who have been abused, we pray: ◆ For nurses and doctors, that they be strengthened as they seek to heal patients, we pray: ◆ For our beloved dead, we pray: ◆

Our Father . . .

Loving God,
you grace the life of your followers
in many ways.
Grant that we may always
give glory and praise to you
so that all may know
the joy and hope that your disciples share.
Through Christ our Lord.
Amen.

✝ Lord, make us turn to you; let us see your face and we shall be saved.

Sunday, December 15, 2019

Third Sunday of Advent

✝ Lord, come and save us.

Psalm 146

page 421

Reading

Matthew 11:7–11

As they were going off, Jesus began to speak to the crowds about John, "What did you go out to the desert to see? A reed swayed by the wind? Then what did you go out to see? Someone dressed in fine clothing." Those who wear fine clothing are in royal palaces. Then why did you go out? To see a prophet? Yes, I tell you, and more than a prophet. This is the one about whom it is written: / *Behold, I am sending my messenger ahead of you; / he will prepare your way before you.* / Amen, I say to you, among those born of women there has been none greater than John the Baptist; yet the least in the kingdom of heaven is greater than he."

Reflection

Today's readings and prayers help us focus on the joy that is within the Advent season. Christians are called to embody the joy that comes from encountering Christ. Pope Francis writes in *The Joy of the Gospel* that "the Gospel, radiant with the glory of Christ's cross, constantly invites us to rejoice." After all, the pope writes in the exhortation, even amid persecution, the disciples were filled with joy. "Why should we not also enter into this great stream of joy?" the Holy Father asks.

Prayers

others may be added

To our Lord, who gives us reason for joy, we pray:

◆ Lord, hear our prayer.

That those who feel little hope may find comfort in the Church, we pray: ◆ That communities provide job counseling to those who are underemployed, we pray: ◆ That the homeless be provided shelter, we pray: ◆ That those preparing to become Catholic find a welcoming community, we pray: ◆ That those who are depressed find counseling, we pray: ◆ That the souls in purgatory be received into heaven, we pray: ◆

Our Father . . .

Lord God,
you sent John the Baptist
to remind us
to prepare our hearts for you.
Awaken in us the desire
to change our lives
and help others experience the joy
of a relationship with you.
Through Christ our Lord.
Amen.

✝ Lord, come and save us.

Monday, December 16, 2019
Advent Weekday

✝ Teach me your ways, O Lord.

Psalm 25 *page 399*

Reading *Numbers 24:15–17a*

Then Balaam gave voice to his oracle:
The utterance of Balaam, son of Beor,
the utterance of the man whose
eye is true,
The utterance of one who hears
what God says,
and knows what the Most
High knows,
Of one who sees what the
Almighty sees,
enraptured, and with eyes unveiled.
I see him, though not now;
I behold him, though not near:
A star shall advance from Jacob,
and a staff shall rise from Israel.

Reflection

An angel who has embodied Balaam's donkey provides the words for this vision. Balaam is able to foretell the coming of the Messiah through the line of Jacob. Balaam was a seer, but he relied on the angel for this vision. It is easy to think of angels as beings that visited earth during another time. Perhaps this Advent, you might want to be open to messengers from God. Are there people and events that are pointing you toward God?

Prayers *others may be added*

To the Lord, who sent the Messiah to us, we pray:

◆ Lord, hear our prayer.

That the Church may be an instrument of God's hope for those seeking refuge, we pray: ◆ That nations may work together to care for the environment, we pray: ◆ That individuals who struggle with addictions may be freed, we pray: ◆ That all may have religious freedom, we pray: ◆ That all who are sick recover quickly, we pray: ◆ That those who walk in the valley of death may come to Christ's light, we pray: ◆

Our Father . . .

God of all ages,
you provide messengers
with visions to guide your people.
Help us to see you more clearly
so that we may come to know
and serve with joy
Jesus Christ our Lord, your Son,
who lives and reigns with you in the unity
of the Holy Spirit,
one God, for ever and ever.
Amen.

✝ Teach me your ways, O Lord.

Tuesday, December 17, 2019
Advent Weekday

✝ Justice shall flourish in his time,
and fullness of peace forever.

Psalm 72

page 406

Reading

Matthew 1:17

Thus the total number of generations from Abraham to David is fourteen generations; from David to the Babylonian exile, fourteen generations; from the Babylonian exile to the Christ, fourteen generations.

Reflection

Family trees are marvelous reminders of our heritage. They recall that we stand on the shoulders of those who have gone before us. The verse we read today is the last of seventeen verses that chronicles Jesus' roots. The names in the ancestral line reveal that not all were of pristine character just as is evident in our family trees. Still, each generation shapes the next to live the faith. We can give thanks for those who imparted the faith to us. May we take care as we teach the faith to the next generation through our words and actions.

Prayers

others may be added

To our Lord, who sent his Son, so that we might have life, we pray:

◆ Lord, hear our prayer.

That the Church continue to seek to make Christ known to all nations, we pray: ◆ That political parties respect the dignity of all people, we pray: ◆ That families be reconciled during this season, we pray: ◆ That young people researching a college to attend may be open to God's help, we pray: ◆ That the sick not lose faith, we pray: ◆ That the angels bring all who have died to paradise, we pray: ◆

Our Father . . .

Lord God,
from one generation to the next,
you are faithful and kind.
Support our efforts
to sustain your vision
of justice and love
so that others may learn
the ways they should walk
in faithfulness and service.
Through Christ our Lord.
Amen.

✝ Justice shall flourish in his time,
and fullness of peace forever.

Wednesday, December 18, 2019
Advent Weekday

✝ Justice shall flourish in his time,
and fullness of peace for ever.

Psalm 72 *page 406*

Reading *Matthew 1:18–21*

This is how the birth of Jesus Christ came about. When his mother Mary was betrothed to Joseph, but before they lived together, she was found with child through the Holy Spirit. Joseph her husband, since he was a righteous man, yet unwilling to expose her to shame, decided to divorce her quietly. Such was his intention when, behold, the angel of the Lord appeared to him in a dream and said, "Joseph, son of David, do not be afraid to take Mary your wife into your home. For it is through the Holy Spirit that this child has been conceived in her. She will bear a son and you are to name him Jesus, because he will save his people from their sins."

Reflection

A common storytelling device is to provide flashbacks that provide the backstory that shows why characters behave the way as they do. We know the story that Matthew's account provides of Christ's birth. Still, periodically we need to return to it and seek to read it with fresh eyes. Joseph is told not to be afraid. He needed great trust in God to believe what the angel told him. What do you fear in your life? Where do you need to place more trust in God? We have heard that nothing is impossible with God. Try to rely on the Holy Spirit in your difficulties.

Prayers *others may be added*

To our Lord, through whom all things are made possible, we pray:

◆ Lord, hear our prayer.

That the Church witness to all people God's loving care, we pray: ◆ That world leaders demonstrate concern for the poor, we pray: ◆ That those who protect us be kept free from harm, we pray: ◆ That holiday preparations be free from anxiety, we pray: ◆ That those awaiting surgery be calmed by our prayers and concern, we pray: ◆ That eternal life be granted to our deceased loved ones, we pray: ◆

Our Father . . .

Almighty God,
you gave Joseph the wisdom
to trust in you.
Continue to empower us
to support your will
and work to fulfill your mission
to make all things new in Christ,
who lives and reigns with you in the unity
of the Holy Spirit,
one God, for ever and ever.
Amen.

✝ Justice shall flourish in his time,
and fullness of peace for ever.

Thursday, December 19, 2019
Advent Weekday

✝ My mouth shall be filled with your praise, and I will sing your glory!

Psalm 98

page 410

Reading

Luke 1:13–18

But the angel said to him, "Do not be afraid, Zechariah, because your prayer has been heard. Your wife Elizabeth will bear you a son, and you shall name him John. And you will have joy and gladness, and many will rejoice at his birth, for he will be great in the sight of the Lord. He will drink neither wine nor strong drink. He will be filled with the Holy Spirit even from his mother's womb, and he will turn many of the children of Israel to the Lord their God. He will go before him in the spirit and power of Elijah to turn the hearts of fathers toward children and the disobedient to the understanding of the righteous, to prepare a people fit for the Lord."

Then Zechariah said to the angel, "How shall I know this? For I am an old man, and my wife is advanced in years."

Reflection

Like Zechariah, we can be slow to accept what we are told and even to acknowledge God's goodness. Zechariah had a hard time believing that an elderly couple would be parents. However, God makes the barren fertile and is merciful toward those who please him. As we come close to Christmas, seek to find God's grace around you.

Prayers

others may be added

To our God of surprises, we pray:

◆ Lord, hear our prayer.

That the Church reach out to all who doubt, we pray: ◆ That the lowly be lifted up, we pray: ◆ That travelers reach their destination safely, we pray: ◆ That more men dedicate their lives to the ordained priesthood, we pray: ◆ That those who are ill find hope in the prayers of their friends and family, we pray: ◆ That those who have died be welcomed to eternal life, we pray: ◆

Our Father . . .

O God,
you blessed Elizabeth and Zechariah
with a son who would prepare
the people for the Messiah.
Help us to see the many ways
that you enter our lives
and guide us to point others to you.
Through our Lord Jesus Christ.
Amen.

✝ My mouth shall be filled with your praise, and I will sing your glory!

Friday, December 20, 2019

Advent Weekday

✝ Let the Lord enter; he is the king of glory.

Psalm 96

page 409

Reading

Luke 1:26–33

The angel Gabriel was sent from God to a town of Galilee called Nazareth, to a virgin betrothed to a man named Joseph, of the house of David, and the virgin's name was Mary. And coming to her, he said, "Hail, full of grace! The Lord is with you." But she was greatly troubled at what was said and pondered what sort of greeting this might be. Then the angel said to her, "Do not be afraid, Mary, for you have found favor with God. Behold, you will conceive in your womb and bear a son, and you shall name him Jesus. He will be great and will be called Son of the Most High, and the Lord God will give him the throne of David his father, and he will rule over the house of Jacob forever, and of his Kingdom there will be no end."

Reflection

In the midst of the chaos and joy of this season of preparing, we hear the words of an angel greeting Mary. Can you imagine the angel addressing you with "The Lord be with you"? Having also found favor with us, God expects us to bear the life of Jesus to others. Do you let others in on the joy that knowing Christ brings to your life? The Holy Spirit has come down upon us in the midst of the chaos to guide us in showing Christ, the main gift, to others.

Prayers

others may be added

Confident that the Lord is present with us, we pray:

◆ Lord, hear our prayer.

That our priests recognize the grace given to them to share the Good News, we pray: ◆ That our nation's leaders bear witness to justice and peace, we pray: ◆ That couples challenged by conflict, heal and grow in reconciliation, we pray: ◆ That travelers reach their destinations safely, we pray: ◆ That those awaiting major surgery find healing, we pray: ◆ That the angels lead those who have died into paradise, we pray: ◆

Our Father . . .

Lord God,
you lifted up a woman
of humble upbringing
to bear your Son to the world.
Grant that we may always
seek to fulfill your call to us
to tell of your love to all we meet.
Through Christ our Lord.
Amen.

✝ Let the Lord enter; he is the king of glory.

Saturday, December 21, 2019
Advent Weekday

✝ Let the Lord enter; he is the king of glory.

Psalm 96
page 409

Reading
Luke 1:39–45

Mary set out in those days and traveled to the hill country in haste to a town of Judah, where she entered the house of Zechariah and greeted Elizabeth. When Elizabeth heard Mary's greeting, the infant leaped in her womb, and Elizabeth, filled with the Holy Spirit, cried out in a loud voice and said, "Blessed are you among women, and blessed is the fruit of your womb. And how does this happen to me, that the mother of my Lord should come to me? For at the moment the sound of your greeting reached my ears, the infant in my womb leaped for joy. Blessed are you who believed that what was spoken to you by the Lord would be fulfilled."

Reflection
Three times Elizabeth uses the word "blessed." Elizabeth states that Mary is blessed among women and then that the fruit of her womb is blessed. Finally, she addresses her faith, saying, "Blessed are you who believed what was spoken to you by the Lord would be fulfilled." In chapter 12 of Matthew's account, Jesus says, "Whoever does the will of my heavenly Father is my brother, and sister, and mother." Mary has believed in the promise. Open yourself to the fulfillment of God's promise in Jesus Christ.

Prayers
others may be added

Acknowledging our trust in God, we pray:

◆ Lord, hear our prayer.

That the pope continue his steadfast trust in God, we pray: ◆ That those who work for peace never lose heart, we pray: ◆ That those who protect us be safe during the holidays, we pray: ◆ That travelers reach their destination with ease, we pray: ◆ That those who care for people in hospice know of the appreciation of families, we pray: ◆ That those we miss and mourn be brought to heaven, we pray: ◆

Our Father . . .

O God of all fulfillment,
you blessed Mary
with the grace
to believe what was spoken
and bear the Son of God.
Grant that we may
be attentive to the words
you speak to us in Scripture.
May we proclaim your message
to all we encounter.
Through Christ our Lord.
Amen.

✝ Let the Lord enter; he is the king of glory.

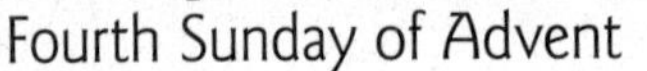

Sunday, December 22, 2019

Fourth Sunday of Advent

✝ Let the Lord enter; he is king of glory.

Psalm 25

page 399

Reading

Matthew 1:18–24

This is how the birth of Jesus Christ came about. When his mother Mary was betrothed to Joseph, but before they lived together, she was found with child through the Holy Spirit. Joseph her husband, since he was a righteous man, yet unwilling to expose her to shame, decided to divorce her quietly. Such was his intention when, behold, the angel of the Lord appeared to him in a dream and said, "Joseph, son of David, do not be afraid to take Mary your wife into your home. For it is through the Holy Spirit that this child has been conceived in her. She will bear a son and you are to name him Jesus, because he will save his people from their sins." All this took place to fulfill what the Lord had said through the prophet: / *Behold, the virgin shall conceive and bear a son, / and they shall name him Emmanuel,* / which means "God is with us." When Joseph awoke, he did as the angel of the Lord had commanded him and took his wife into his home.

Reflection

In this reading, we see that Joseph is a "righteous" man. He trusts the angel and follows through with what is asked of him. He takes Mary into his home and cares for her because he trusts in what the prophets foretold and knows that "God is with us."

Prayers

others may be added

Trusting in the will of God, we pray:

◆ Come, Lord Jesus.

May the pope and bishops work toward building trust with other institutions, we pray: ◆ May churches work together to build the ecumenical dialogue necessary to repair Christ's vine, we pray: ◆ May women and men faithfully serve God as lay associates to a religious order, we pray: ◆ May all treasure the blessings of the Christmas season, we pray: ◆ May those suffering depression find comfort and relief, we pray: ◆ May those who have died be welcomed into paradise, we pray: ◆

Our Father . . .

Lord God,
you gave Joseph the courage
to trust in the word of an angel.
Guide our steps today
and lead us along the paths
you have chosen for us
so that we may welcome your Son
into the world anew.
Through Christ our Lord.
Amen.

✝ Let the Lord enter; he is king of glory.

Monday, December 23, 2019
Advent Weekday

✝ Lift up your heads and see; your redemption is near at hand.

Psalm 25

page 399

Reading

Luke 1:57–66

When the time arrived for Elizabeth to have her child she gave birth to a son. Her neighbors and relatives heard that the Lord had shown his great mercy toward her, and they rejoiced with her. When they came on the eighth day to circumcise the child, they were going to call him Zechariah after his father, but his mother said in reply, "No. He will be called John." But they answered her, "There is no one among your relatives who has this name." So they made signs, asking his father what he wished him to be called. He asked for a tablet and wrote, "John is his name," and all were amazed.

Reflection

In the lineage of Jesus, no name is used a second time. Just so with the herald John: only he was given the mission of preparing the way of the Lord. Each of us has a unique mission in witnessing to the Son of God. May we, like Zechariah, put our trust in God and submit to his work in our lives.

Prayers

others may be added

With confidence in God's plan,
we pray:

◆ Come, Lord Jesus.

May the leaders of the Church inspire us to share God's Word, we pray: ◆ May our government serve the needs of all for the common good, we pray: ◆ May citizens support life from conception to natural death, we pray: ◆ May expectant parents look forward to a safe delivery of their child, free from complications, we pray: ◆ May those who find the holidays difficult be lifted up by our support, we pray: ◆ May parents who have lost a child be comforted, we pray: ◆

Our Father . . .

O God,
you surprise your people
and choose the barren to bring forth life.
Increase our efforts at serving your will
and support our zeal
to promote your reign.
Through Christ our Lord.
Amen.

✝ Lift up your heads and see; your redemption is near at hand.

Tuesday, December 24, 2019

Advent Weekday

✝ Forever I will sing the goodness of the Lord.

Psalm 89

page 407

Reading

Luke 1:67–68, 73–79

Zechariah his father, filled with the Holy Spirit, prophesied, saying: . . . / "This was the oath he swore to our father Abraham: / to set us free from the hand of our enemies, / free to worship him without fear, / holy and righteous in his sight all the days of our life. / You, my child, shall be called the prophet of the Most High, / for you will go before the Lord to prepare his way, / to give his people knowledge of salvation / by the forgiveness of their sins. / In the tender compassion of our God / the dawn from on high shall break upon us, / to shine on those who dwell in darkness and the shadow of death, / and to guide our feet into the way of peace."

Reflection

The verses in today's reading from Luke make up the Canticle of Zechariah, which the Church prays at Morning Prayer. In his song of praise, Zechariah recalls God's faithfulness. God pledged to Abraham that his descendants would be able to worship without fear. In the child Jesus, the prayers of a people are answered. Today, we recognize how blessed we are to follow in the footsteps of those who trusted in God's will and we proclaim anew God's wondrous works.

Prayers

others may be added

To our faithful Lord, we pray:

◆ Come, Lord Jesus.

May the Church, in its ministry to prisoners, continue to bring hope and Christ's love, we pray: ◆ May our national leaders recognize the power present in their service, we pray: ◆ May interfaith dialogue strengthen efforts for peace, we pray: ◆ May all children receive food and shelter, we pray: ◆ May those awaiting medical treatment be comfortable as they await surgery, we pray: ◆ May the angels lead all who have died into paradise, we pray: ◆

Our Father . . .

O God,
you raise up the lowly
and bring hope to our fallen world.
As we await the dawn of our Savior
and celebrate his birth,
may we be renewed in his glory
and go forth bringing his hope and love
to the lonely and downtrodden.
Through Christ our Lord.
Amen.

✝ Forever I will sing the goodness of the Lord.

Wednesday, December 25, 2019

Solemnity of the Nativity of the Lord (Christmas)

✝ All the ends of the earth have seen the saving power of God.

Psalm 98

page 410

Reading

John 1:1–5, 14

In the beginning was the Word, / and the Word was with God, and the Word was God. / He was in the beginning with God. / All things came to be through him, / and without him nothing came to be. / What came to be through him was life, / and this life was the light of the human race; / the light shines in the darkness, / and the darkness has not overcome it.

And the Word became flesh / and made his dwelling among us, / and we saw his glory, / the glory as of the Father's only Son, / full of grace and truth. /

Reflection

When I hear this reading, I often recall the Cameroon song "He Came Down," which has been transcribed and arranged by John Bell. The Word just had to come to be with us. All the love and energy of the Trinity broke into our world to remind us of the communion that is ours. From a birth at Bethlehem to a cross at Calvary, the mystery of the Word, God's living flesh, is here among us. We have new life forever. Let us be that Word, that flesh today, to show others why the Word came down to us.

Prayers

others may be added

To our Lord, who sent his Son,
we pray:

◆ Lord, hear our prayer.

May our Church show forth the Father's love, we pray: ◆ May world leaders demonstrate God's peace, we pray: ◆ May families grow closer in God's joy, we pray: ◆ May those who find Christmas difficult experience the Father's hope, we pray: ◆ May those who are ill and in the hospital experience Christ's healing, we pray: ◆ May the dead come to the beauty of heavenly glory, we pray: ◆

Our Father . . .

O God,
you sent your Son
to dwell among us.
Awaken in us the call
you have given us to serve others.
Throughout the coming year,
may we show loving kindness and
hospitality to all we meet
so that all may see your glory
and know that Emmanuel is here.
Through Christ our Lord.
Amen.

✝ All the ends of the earth have seen the saving power of God.

Thursday, December 26, 2019
Feast of St. Stephen, the First Martyr

✝ Into your hands, O Lord, I commend my spirit.

Psalm 31
page 400

Reading
Matthew 10:17–22

Jesus said to his disciples, "Beware of men, for they will hand you over to the courts and scourge you in their synagogues, and you will be led before governors and kings for my sake as a witness before them and the pagans. When they hand you over, do not worry about how you are to speak or what you are to say. You will be given at that moment what you are to say. For it will not be you who speak but the Spirit of your Father speaking through you. Brother will hand over brother to death, and the father his child; children will rise up against parents and have them put to death. You will be hated by all because of my name, but whoever endures to the end will be saved."

Reflection
St. Stephen allowed the will of God to shape his life, not worrying about who would hate him or hand him over to authorities. The Acts of the Apostles notes that Stephen worked "wonders and signs among the people" and spoke with "wisdom and spirit" when debated (6:8, 10). At his trial for blasphemy, he gave an account of salvation history from Abraham through Solomon (Acts 7), finally chastising his accusers for not observing the law. When we trust and allow the will of God, the Spirit shapes and molds us.

Prayers
others may be added

Trusting in the will of God, we pray:

◆ Lord, hear our prayer.

May the Spirit guide us to speak and witness the beauty of our faith in ways that move others to seek to become part of the Body of Christ, we pray: ◆ May the Spirit fill parishioners who seek to support the catechumens, we pray: ◆ May catechists never lose hope as they witness and teach the faith, we pray: ◆ May couples preparing for the Sacrament of Matrimony continue to grow in love, we pray: ◆ May those awaiting a transplant feel support and peace, we pray: ◆ May those who have died, especially those martyred for the faith, meet St. Stephen in the heavenly kingdom, we pray: ◆

Our Father . . .

O God,
you gave St. Stephen the courage
to be steadfast in his faith.
May we continue to be strong
in our resolve to follow the Gospel
and bring its message to others.
Support our efforts at revealing your truth
and allow your message
to touch the hearts
of those who question your presence.
Through Christ our Lord.
Amen.

✝ Into your hands, O Lord, I commend my spirit.

Friday, December 27, 2019

Feast of St. John, Apostle and Evangelist

✝ Rejoice in the Lord, you just!

Psalm 98

page 410

Reading

John 20:1a, 2–4, 6–8

On the first day of the week, Mary of Magdala came to the tomb early in the morning, while it was still dark, and saw the stone removed from the tomb. So she ran and went to Simon Peter and to the other disciple whom Jesus loved, and told them, "They have taken the Lord from the tomb, and we don't know where they put him." So Peter and the other disciple went out and came to the tomb. . . . When Simon Peter arrived after him, he went into the tomb and saw the burial cloths there, and the cloth that had covered his head, not with the burial cloths but rolled up in a separate place. Then the other disciple also went in, the one who had arrived at the tomb first, and he saw and believed.

Reflection

Our faith is a gift given at Baptism. We need to continue to open ourselves to our faith so that it will live within us and permeate others. Today's reading provides us a chance to see where we need to roll away the stone so that we can believe more fully. We are called, as Mary of Magdala was, to profess the Gospel and help others see a reason to believe.

Prayers

others may be added

To the God of the covenant, we pray:

◆ Lord, hear our prayer.

May members of the Body of Christ witness the Resurrection of Christ through deeds of love and service, we pray: ◆ May all world leaders bring God's peace and justice, we pray: ◆ May teachers and catechists be refreshed during the Christmas season so they will continue to share the faith, we pray: ◆ May more women and men serve as volunteers in parish ministries of the church, we pray: ◆ May the sick quickly recover from their illnesses, we pray: ◆ May the angels lead all who have died into paradise, we pray: ◆

Our Father . . .

O God,
you gave the Apostle John
the ability to witness the glory
of your Word made flesh,
Support our ways of sharing
the wisdom and faith of your Son
so that others may come to know
and believe
in the one who delivers us from sin
and evil
and transforms our lives in love
and peace.
Through Christ our Lord.
Amen.

✝ Rejoice in the Lord, you just!

Saturday, December 28, 2019

Feast of the Holy Innocents, Martyrs

✝ Our soul has been rescued like a bird from the fowler's snare.

Psalm 124

page 417

Reading

Matthew 2:13–15

When the magi had departed, behold, the angel of the Lord appeared to Joseph in a dream and said, "Rise, take the child and his mother, flee to Egypt, and stay there until I tell you. Herod is going to search for the child to destroy him." Joseph rose and took the child and his mother by night and departed for Egypt. He stayed there until the death of Herod, that what the Lord had said through the prophet might be fulfilled, / *Out of Egypt I called my son.*

Reflection

In Matthew's Gospel account, we hear of a king who feels so threatened by a child that he searches him out. Nations across the world still need to do much to protect innocent children. Even in the United States, some children cannot pay attention in school because they do not have a home or the assurance of three meals. In some neighborhoods, children are killed from random gunshots. Children in many families do not have adequate health care. We need to work to protect the young. One of the first steps to do this may be to stay alert to signs of racism and discrimination.

Prayers

others may be added

To our loving God, we pray:

◆ Lord, hear our prayer.

May leaders in the Church continue to speak out against the evils in our world, we pray: ◆ May governments work to enact legislation that respects all life, from conception until natural death, we pray: ◆ May families who have been affected by the death of innocents feel comfort and our support, we pray: ◆ May all religions work together to protect human life, we pray: ◆ May those who work in health care support the dignity of the sick and suffering, we pray: ◆ May the grieving find strength and support from our prayers, we pray: ◆

Our Father . . .

O God,
you awaken in us the concern
of the holy gifts
in the life of all your people.
Support our efforts to protect humanity
from the evils of hatred, anger,
and jealously
that lead to destruction.
Through Christ our Lord.
Amen.

✝ Our soul has been rescued like a bird from the fowler's snare.

Sunday, December 29, 2019

Feast of the Holy Family of Jesus, Mary, and Joseph

☩ Happy are those who fear the Lord.

Psalm 96

page 409

Reading

Matthew 2:19–23

When Herod had died, behold, the angel of the Lord appeared in a dream to Joseph in Egypt and said, "Rise, take the child and his mother and go to the land of Israel, for those who sought the child's life are dead." He rose, took the child and his mother, and went to the land of Israel. But when he heard that Archelaus was ruling over Judea in place of his father Herod, he was afraid to go back there. And because he had been warned in a dream, he departed for the region of Galilee. He went and dwelt in a town called Nazareth, so that what had been spoken through the prophets might be fulfilled, *He shall be called a Nazorean.*

Reflection

Dreams, warnings, travel and movement dominate Matthew's account of the infancy narrative. Sadly, the horrific tragedy of infanticide and destruction still takes place in the world. Joseph was attentive to the signs and followed God's paths for his family. We also have a role in allowing God's ways to be fulfilled. May we be alert to ways that life is crushed in our society.

Prayers

others may be added

To the God of providence, we pray:

◆ Lord, hear our prayer.

Unite the members of the Church
in deeds of service, we pray: ◆
Assist those who work against prejudices
that cause harm to God's family,
we pray: ◆ Help leaders as they seek to
end divisions among nations, we pray: ◆
Aid communities as they try to keep
families together, we pray: ◆ Free the
world of violence and hatred, we pray: ◆
Bring all who have died to the joys of
heaven, we pray: ◆

Our Father . . .

O God,
you provided the Holy Family
with strength to face adversity.
Grant our families the fortitude
to resolve problems
and become a witness
of your love.
Help all in need
to know your kindness and compassion.
Through Christ our Lord.
Amen.

☩ Happy are those who fear the Lord.

Monday, December 30, 2019
Sixth Day within the Octave of Christmas

✝ Let the heavens be glad and the earth rejoice!

Psalm 96 *page 409*

Reading *Luke 2:36–38*

There was a prophetess, Anna, the daughter of Phanuel, of the tribe of Asher. She was advanced in years, having lived seven years with her husband after her marriage, and then as a widow until she was eighty-four. She never left the temple, but worshiped night and day with fasting and prayer. And coming forward at that very time, she gave thanks to God and spoke about the child to all who were awaiting the redemption of Jerusalem.

Reflection

We may know people in the parish who, like Anna, spend much time praying, fasting, and being open to God. Our prayers, fasting, and regular presence to the Lord bear witness to the glory of God. Our challenge is never to lose hope that God is working in our midst today. When we observe God's presence, we should point it out to others. Where do you see Christ working in your community?

Prayers *others may be added*

To our ever present Lord, we pray:

◆ Lord, hear our prayer.

Help parishes find ways to keep their doors open for prayer in safe conditions, we pray: ◆ Assist nations that have committed resources to protect the environment, we pray: ◆ Encourage communities that seek to end abuse against the most vulnerable, we pray: ◆ Challenge young people to stay faithful to God's call for them through worship and service, we pray: ◆ Heal those who suffer from chronic illnesses, we pray: ◆ Bring those who have died to glory in your Kingdom, we pray: ◆

Our Father . . .

Heavenly God,
you gave the prophetess Anna
a steadfast faith
to witness to your presence.
Stir up in us a desire
to worship and serve you.
Through Christ our Lord.
Amen.

✝ Let the heavens be glad and the earth rejoice!

Tuesday, December 31, 2019
Seventh Day within the Octave of Christmas

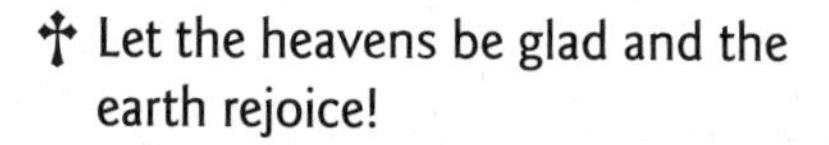

✝ Let the heavens be glad and the earth rejoice!

Psalm 96

page 409

Reading

John 1:10–13, 15

He was in the world, / and the world came to be through him, / but the world did not know him. / He came to what was his own, / but his own people did not accept him.

But to those who did accept him he gave power to become children of God, to those who believe in his name, who were born not by natural generation nor by human choice nor by a man's decision but of God.

John testified to him and cried out, saying, "This was he of whom I said, 'The one who is coming after me ranks ahead of me because he existed before me.' "

Reflection

Reading the Prologue of John's account of the Gospel is a wonderful way to end this year. These verses bring us to the heart of our faith. Through the Word of God, we have been given the possibility of becoming children of God. It is up to each baptized person to nurture the faith that is God's gift to us. Our light of faith supports the true light of Christ, showing others that Christ dwells among us. Let us prepare for a new year of living the faith, testifying to the truth, and shining the brightness of Christ.

Prayers

others may be added

To our Lord, who sent the Word to show us the way, we pray:

◆ Lord, hear our prayer.

Attune Church leaders to their special gifts, we pray: ◆ Renew civic leaders who strive for the common good, we pray: ◆ Aid communities that welcome the stranger, we pray: ◆ Help those falsely imprisoned to secure justice, we pray: ◆ Encourage those who suffer seasonal depression, we pray: ◆ Awaken all who have died to the joys of heaven, we pray: ◆

Our Father . . .

As you dwell among us, O God,
you bring your Word
to enlighten our hearts and minds
and grow in your likeness.
Support our new year's dreams
with your truth and hope
so that we may fulfill your will
and bring the Good News
to all those who await a great light.
Through Christ our Lord.
Amen.

✝ Let the heavens be glad and the earth rejoice!

Psalter

Psalm 8:4–5, 6–7, 8–9

When I behold your heavens, the work of your fingers,
the moon and the stars which you set in place —
What is man that you should be mindful of him,
or the son of man that you should care for him?

You have made him little less than the angels,
and crowned him with glory and honor.
You have given him rule over the works of your hands,
putting all things under his feet.

All sheep and oxen,
yes, and the beasts of the field,
The birds of the air, the fishes of the sea,
and whatever swims the paths of the sea.

Psalm 16:5, 8, 9–10, 11

O Lord, my allotted portion and my cup,
you it is who hold fast my lot.

I set the Lord ever before me;
with him at my right hand I shall not be disturbed.
Therefore my heart is glad and my soul rejoices,
my body, too, abides in confidence;
Because you will not abandon my soul to the nether world,
nor will you suffer your faithful one to undergo corruption.
You will show me the path to life,
fullness of joys in your presence,
the delights at your right hand forever.

Psalm 17:1, 2–3, 6–7, 8, 15

Hear O LORD, a just suit;
attend to my outcry;
hearken to my prayer from lips without deceit.

From you let my judgment come;
your eyes behold what is right.
Though you test my heart, searching it in the night,
though you try me with fire, you shall find no malice in me.

I call upon you, for you will answer me, O God;
incline your ear to me; hear my word.
Show your wondrous kindness,
O savior of those who flee.

Hold me in the shadow of your wings.
I in justice shall behold your face;
On waking, I shall be content in your presence.

Psalm 19:8, 9, 10, 11

The law of the LORD is perfect,
refreshing the soul,
The decree of the LORD is trustworthy,
giving wisdom to the simple.

The precepts of the LORD are right,
rejoicing the heart.
The command of the LORD is clear,
enlightening the eye.

The fear of the LORD is pure,
enduring forever.
The ordinances of the LORD are true,
all of them just.

Psalm 23:1–3a, 3b–4, 5, 6

The LORD is my shepherd; I shall not want.
In verdant pastures he gives me repose;
Beside restful waters he leads me;
he refreshes my soul.

He guides me in right paths
for his name's sake.
Even though I walk in the dark valley
I fear no evil; for you are at my side
With your rod and your staff
that give me courage.

You spread the table before me
In the sight of my foes;
You anoint my head with oil;
my cup overflows.

Only goodness and kindness follow me
all the days of my life;
And I shall dwell in the house of the LORD
for years to come.

Psalm 24:1–2, 3–4, 5–6

The LORD's are the earth and its fullness;
the world and those who dwell in it.
For he founded it upon the seas
and established it upon the rivers.

Who can ascend the mountain of the LORD?
or who may stand in his holy place?
One whose hands are sinless, whose heart is clean,
who desires not what is vain.

He shall receive a blessing from the LORD,
a reward from God his savior.
Such is the race that seeks for him,
that seeks the face of the God of Jacob.

Psalm 25:2–3, 4–5ab, 6 and 7bc

In you I trust; let me not be put to shame,
let not my enemies exult over me.
No one who waits for you shall be put to shame;
those shall be put to shame who heedlessly break faith.

Your ways, O LORD, make known to me;
teach me your paths,
Guide me in your truth and teach me,
for you are God my savior.

Remember that your compassion, O LORD,
and your kindness are from of old.
In your kindness remember me,
because of your goodness, O LORD.

Psalm 27:7–8a, 8b–9abc, 13–14

Hear, O LORD, the sound of my call;
have pity on me, and answer me.
Of you my heart speaks; you my glance seeks.

Your presence, O LORD, I seek.
Hide not your face from me;
do not in anger repel your servant.
You are my helper; cast me not off.

I believe that I shall see the bounty of the LORD
in the land of the living.
Wait for the LORD with courage;
be stouthearted, and wait for the LORD.

Psalm 30

I will praise you, Lord, you have rescued me
and have not let enemies rejoice over me.

O Lord, I cried to you for help
and you, my God, have healed me.
O Lord, you have raised my soul from the dead,
restored me to life from those who sink into the grave.

The Lord listened and had pity.
The Lord came to my help.
For me you have changed my mourning into dancing,
you removed my sackcloth and clothed me with joy.
So my soul sings psalms to you unceasingly.
O Lord my God, I will thank you for ever.

Psalm 31:2, 6, 12–13, 15–16, 17, 25

In you, O LORD, I take refuge;
  let me never be put to shame.
In your justice rescue me.
Into your hands I commend my spirit;
  you will redeem me, O LORD, O faithful God.

For all my foes I am an object of reproach,
  a laughingstock to my neighbors, and a dread to my friends;
  they who see me abroad flee from me.
I am forgotten like the unremembered dead;
  I am like a dish that is broken.

But my trust is in you, O LORD;
  I say, "You are my God.
In your hands is my destiny; rescue me
  from the clutches of my enemies and my persecutors."

Let your face shine upon your servant;
  save me in your kindness.
Take courage and be stouthearted,
  all you who hope in the LORD.

Psalm 33:10–11, 12–13, 14–15

The LORD brings to nought the plans of the nations;
he foils the designs of peoples.
But the plan of the LORD stands forever;
the design of his heart, through all generations.

Blessed the nation whose God is the LORD,
the people he has chosen for his own inheritance.
From heaven the LORD looks down;
he sees all mankind.

From his fixed throne he beholds
all who dwell on the earth,
He who fashioned the heart of each,
he who knows all their works.

Psalm 34:2–3, 4–5, 6–7

I will bless the LORD at all times;
his praise shall be ever in my mouth.
Let my soul glory in the LORD;
the lowly will hear me and be glad.

Glorify the LORD with me,
let us together extol his name.
I sought the LORD, and he answered me
and delivered me from all my fears.

Look to him that you may be radiant with joy,
and your faces may not blush with shame.
When the afflicted man called out, the LORD heard,
and from all his distress he saved him.

Psalm 40:2, 4, 7–8, 8–9, 10

I have waited, waited for the LORD
and he stooped toward me and heard my cry.
And he put a new song into my mouth,
a hymn to our God.

Sacrifice or oblation you wished not,
but ears open to obedience you gave me.
Holocausts or sin-offerings you sought not;
then said I, "Behold, I come."

"In the written scroll it is prescribed for me,
to do your will, O my God, is my delight,
and your law is within my heart!"

I announced your justice in the vast assembly;
I did not restrain my lips, as you, O LORD, know.

Psalm 51:3–4, 5–6a, 6b–7

Have mercy on me, O God, in your goodness;
in the greatness of your compassion wipe out my offense.
Thoroughly wash me from my guilt
and of my sin cleanse me.

For I acknowledge my offense,
and my sin is before me always:
"Against you only have I sinned,
and done what is evil in your sight"—

That you may be justified in your sentence,
vindicated when you condemn.
Indeed, in guilt was I born,
and in sin my mother conceived me.

Psalm 63:2, 3–4, 5–6, 8–9

O God, you are my God, whom I seek;
  for you my flesh pines and my soul thirsts.

Thus have I gazed toward you in the sanctuary
  to see your power and your glory,
For your kindness is a greater good than life;
  my lips shall glorify you.

Thus I will bless you as I live;
  lifting up my hands, I will call upon your name.
As with the riches of the banquet shall my soul be satisfied,
  and with exultant lips my mouth shall praise you.

You are my help,
  and in the shadow of your wings I shout for joy.
My soul clings fast to you;
  your right hand upholds me.

Psalm 66:1–3a, 5 and 8, 16–17

Shout joyfully to God, all the earth;
  sing praise to the glory of his name;
  proclaim his glorious praise.
Say to God: "How tremendous are your deeds!"

Come and see the works of God,
  his tremendous deeds among the children of Adam.
Bless our God, you peoples;
  loudly sound his praise.

Hear now, all you who fear God, while I declare
  what he has done for me.
When I appealed to him in words,
  praise was on the tip of my tongue.

Psalm 67:2–3, 5, 6, 8

May God have pity on us and bless us;
may he let his face shine upon us.
So may your way be known upon the earth;
among all nations, your salvation.

May the nations be glad and exult
because you rule the people in equity;
the nations on the earth you guide.

May the people praise you, O God;
may all the peoples praise you!
May God bless us,
and may all the ends of the earth fear him!

Psalm 68:10–11, 20–21

A bountiful rain you showered down, O God,
upon your inheritance;
you restored the land when it languished;
Your flock settled in it;
in your goodness, O God, you provided it for the needy,

Blessed day by day be the Lord,
who bears our burdens; God who is our salvation.
God is a saving God for us;
the LORD, my Lord, controls the passageways of death.

Psalm 71:1–2, 3–4a, 5–6, 15, 17

In you, O LORD, I take refuge;
let me never be put to shame.
In your justice rescue me, and deliver me;
incline your ear to me, and save me.

Be my rock of refuge,
a stronghold to give me safety,
for you are my rock and my fortress.
O my God, rescue me from the hand of the wicked.

For you are my hope, O LORD;
my trust, O God, from my youth.
On you I depend from birth;
from my mother's womb you are my strength.

My mouth shall declare your justice,
day by day your salvation.
O God, you have taught me from my youth,
and till the present I proclaim your wondrous deeds.

Psalm 72:1–2, 7–8, 12–13, 17

O God, with your judgment endow the king,
 and with your justice, the king's son;
He shall govern your people with justice
 and your afflicted ones with judgment.

Justice shall flower in his days,
 and profound peace, till the moon be no more.
May he rule from sea to sea,
 and from the River to the ends of the earth.

He shall rescue the poor man when he cries out,
 and the afflicted when he has no one to help him.
He shall have pity for the lowly and the poor;
 the lives of the poor he shall save.

May his name be blessed forever;
 as long as the sun his name shall remain.
In him shall all the tribes of the earth be blessed;
 all the nations shall proclaim his happiness.

Psalm 84

How lovely is your dwelling place,
  O LORD of hosts!
 My soul yearns and pines
  for the courts of the LORD.
My heart and my flesh
  cry out for the living God.

Happy they who dwell in your house!
 continually they praise you.
Happy the men whose strength you are!
 their hearts are set upon the pilgrimage.

O LORD of hosts, hear my prayer;
 hearken, O God of Jacob!
O God, behold our shield,
 and look upon the face of your anointed.

Psalm 85:8 and 10, 11–12, 13–14

Show us, O LORD, your mercy,
and grant us your salvation.
Near indeed is his salvation to those who fear him,
glory dwelling in our land.

Kindness and truth shall meet;
justice and peace shall kiss.
Truth shall spring out of the earth,
and justice shall look down from heaven.

The LORD himself will give his benefits;
our land shall yield its increase.
Justice shall walk before him,
and salvation, along the way of his steps.

Psalm 89:2–3, 4–5, 27 and 29

The promises of the LORD I will sing forever;
through all generations my mouth shall proclaim your faithfulness.
For you have said, "My kindness is established forever";
in heaven you have confirmed your faithfulness.

"I have made a covenant with my chosen one,
I have sworn to David my servant:
Forever will I confirm your posterity
and establish your throne for all generations."

"He shall say of me, 'You are my father,
my God, the Rock, my savior.'
Forever I will maintain my kindness toward him,
and my covenant with him stands firm."

Psalm 90:3–4, 5–6, 12–13, 14, 17

You turn man back to dust,
saying, "Return, O children of men."
For a thousand years in your sight
are as yesterday, now that it is past,
or as a watch of the night.

You make an end of them in their sleep;
the next morning they are like the changing grass,
Which at dawn springs up anew,
but by evening wilts and fades.

Teach us to number our days aright,
that we may gain wisdom of heart.
Return, O LORD! How long?
Have pity on your servants!

Fill us at daybreak with your kindness,
that we may shout for joy and gladness all our days.
And may the gracious care of the Lord our God be ours;
prosper the work of our hands for us!
Prosper the work of our hands!

Psalm 95:1–2, 6–7, 8–9

Come, let us sing joyfully to the LORD;
let us acclaim the Rock of our salvation.
Let us come into his presence with thanksgiving;
let us joyfully sing psalms to him.

Come, let us bow down in worship;
let us kneel before the LORD who made us.
For he is our God,
and we are the people he shepherds, the flock he guides.

Oh, that today you would hear his voice:
"Harden not your hearts as at Meribah,
as in the day of Massah in the desert,
where your fathers tempted me;
they tested me though they had seen my works."

Psalm 96:1–2, 2–3, 11–12, 13

Sing to the LORD a new song;
  sing to the LORD, all you lands.
Sing to the LORD; bless his name.

Announce his salvation, day after day.
  Tell his glory among the nations;
  among all peoples, his wondrous deeds.

Let the heavens be glad and the earth rejoice;
  let the sea and what fills it resound;
  let the plains be joyful and all that is in them!
Then shall all the trees of the forest exult.

They shall exult before the LORD, for he comes;
  for he comes to rule the earth.
He shall rule the world with justice
  and the peoples with his constancy.

Psalm 97:1, 6, 11–12

The LORD is king; let earth rejoice;
  let the many isles be glad.
The heavens proclaim his justice,
  and all peoples see his glory.

Light dawns for the just;
  and gladness, for the upright of heart.
Be glad in the LORD, you just,
  and give thanks to his holy name.

Psalm 98:1, 2–3, 3–4, 5–6

Sing to the LORD a new song,
for he has done wondrous deeds;
his right hand has won victory for him,
his holy arm.

The LORD has made his salvation known:
in the sight of the nations he has revealed his justice.
He has remembered his kindness and his faithfulness
toward the house of Israel.

All the ends of the earth have seen
the salvation by our God.
Sing joyfully to the LORD, all you lands:
break into song; sing praise.

Sing praise to the LORD with the harp,
with the harp and melodious song.
With trumpets and the sound of the horn
sing joyfully before the King, the LORD.

Psalm 100:2, 3, 4

Sing joyfully to the LORD, all you lands;
serve the LORD with gladness;
come before him with joyful song.

Know that the LORD is God;
he made us, his we are;
his people, the flock he tends.

Enter his gates with thanksgiving,
his courts with praise;
Give thanks to him; bless his name.

Psalm 103:1–2, 3–4, 9–10, 11–12

Bless the LORD, O my soul;
  and all my being, bless his holy name.
Bless the LORD, O my soul,
  and forget not all his benefits.

He pardons all your iniquities,
  he heals all your ills.
He redeems your life from destruction,
  he crowns you with kindness and compassion.

He will not always chide,
  nor does he keep his wrath forever.
Not according to our sins does he deal with us,
  nor does he requite us according to our crimes.

For as the heavens are high above the earth,
  so surpassing is his kindness toward those who fear him.
As far as the east is from the west,
  so far has he put our transgressions from us.

Psalm 104:1, 24ac, 29–30, 31, 34

Bless the LORD, O my soul!
  O LORD, my God, you are great indeed!
How manifold are your works, O LORD!
  The earth is full of your creatures.

If you take away their breath, they perish
  and return to their dust.
When you send forth your spirit, they are created,
  and you renew the face of the earth.

May the glory of the LORD endure forever;
  may the LORD be glad in his works!
Pleasing to him be my theme;
  I will be glad in the LORD.

Psalm 112:1–2, 3–4, 5–6

Blessed the man who fears the LORD,
  who greatly delights in his commands.
His posterity will be mighty upon the earth;
  the upright generation shall be blessed.

Wealth and riches are in his house;
  his generosity shall endure forever.
Light shines through the darkness for the upright;
  he is gracious and merciful and just.

Well for the man who is gracious and lends,
  who conducts his affairs with justice;
He shall never be moved;
  the just man shall be in everlasting remembrance.

Psalm 113

Praise, you servants of the LORD,
  praise the name of the LORD!
Blessed be the name of the LORD
  both now and forever.

High above all nations is the LORD;
  above the heavens his glory.
Who is like the LORD, our God, who is enthroned on high
  and looks upon the heavens and the earth below?

He raises up the lowly from the dust;
  from the dunghill he lifts up the poor
to seat them with princes,
  with the princes of his own people.

Psalm 116:12–13, 15–16bc, 17–18

How shall I make a return to the LORD
for all the good he has done for me?
The cup of salvation I will take up,
and I will call upon the name of the LORD.

Precious in the eyes of the LORD
is the death of his faithful ones,
I am your servant, the son of your handmaid;
you have loosed my bonds.

To you will I offer sacrifice of thanksgiving,
and I will call upon the name of the LORD.
My vows to the LORD I will pay
in the presence of all his people.

Psalm 117:1bc, 2

Praise the LORD, all you nations;
glorify him, all you peoples!
For steadfast is his kindness toward us,
and the fidelity of the LORD endures forever.

Psalm 118:1–2, 16–17, 22–23

Give thanks to the LORD, for he is good,
for his mercy endures forever.
Let the house of Israel say,
"His mercy endures forever."

"The right hand of the LORD has struck with power;
the right hand of the LORD is exalted.
I shall not die, but live,
and declare the works of the LORD."

The stone which the builders rejected
has become the cornerstone.
By the LORD has this been done;
it is wonderful in our eyes.

Psalm 119:1–2, 4–5

Blessed are they whose way is blameless,
who walk in the way of the LORD.
Blessed are they who observe his decrees,
who seek him with all their heart.

You have commanded that your precepts
be diligently kept.
Oh, that I might be firm in the ways
of keeping your statutes!

Psalm 121:1bc–2, 3–4, 5–6, 7–8

I lift up my eyes toward the mountains;
whence shall help come to me?
My help is from the LORD,
who made heaven and earth.

May he not suffer your foot to slip;
may he slumber not who guards you:
Indeed he neither slumbers nor sleeps,
the guardian of Israel.

The LORD is your guardian; the LORD is your shade;
he is beside you at your right hand.
The sun shall not harm you by day,
nor the moon by night.

The LORD will guard you from all evil;
he will guard your life.
The LORD will guard your coming and your going,
both now and forever.

Psalm 122:1–2, 3–4, 4–5, 6–7, 8–9

I rejoiced because they said to me,
"We will go up to the house of the LORD,"
And now we have set foot
within your gates, O Jerusalem.

Jerusalem, built as a city
with compact unity.
To it the tribes go up,
the tribes of the LORD.

According to the decree for Israel,
to give thanks to the name of the LORD.
In it are set up judgment seats,
seats for the house of David.

Pray for the peace of Jerusalem!
May those who love you prosper!
May peace be within your walls,
prosperity in your buildings.

Because of my relatives and friends
I will say, "Peace be within you!"
Because of the house of the LORD, our God,
I will pray for your good.

Psalm 124:2–3, 4–5, 7cd–8

Had not the LORD been with us—
when men rose up against us,
Then would they have swallowed us alive
when their fury was inflamed against us.

Then would the waters have overwhelmed us;
The torrent would have swept over us;
over us then would have swept
the raging waters.

Broken was the snare,
and we were freed.
Our help is in the name of the LORD,
who made heaven and earth.

Psalm 126:1–2, 2–3, 4–5, 6

When the LORD brought back the captives of Zion,
we were like men dreaming.
Then our mouth was filled with laughter,
and our tongue with rejoicing.

Then they said among the nations,
"The LORD has done great things for them."
The LORD has done great things for us;
we are glad indeed.

Restore our fortunes, O LORD,
like the torrents in the southern desert.
Those that sow in tears
shall reap rejoicing.

Although they go forth weeping,
carrying the seed to be sown,
they shall come back rejoicing,
carrying their sheaves.

Psalm 130:1–2, 3–4, 5b and 7a, 7bc

Out of the depths I cry to you, O LORD;
  Lord, hear my voice!
Let your ears be attentive
  to my voice in supplication.

If you, O LORD, mark our iniquities,
  LORD, who can stand?
But with you is forgiveness,
  that you may be revered.

I trust in the LORD;
  my soul trusts in his word.
My soul waits for the LORD
  more than sentinels wait for the dawn.
Let Israel wait for the LORD.

For with the LORD is kindness,
  and with him is plenteous redemption.

Psalm 132

LORD, remember David
and all his anxious care:
How he swore to the LORD
vowed to the mighty one of Jacob.

"I will not enter the house where I live,
nor lie on the couch where I sleep;
I will give my eyes no sleep
my eyelids no rest,
Till I find a place for the LORD,
a dwelling for the Mighty One of Jacob."

The LORD swore to David
a firm promise from which he will not withdraw:
"Your own offspring
I will set upon your throne."

For the LORD has chosen Zion;
he prefers her for his dwelling.
"Zion is my resting place forever;
In her will I dwell, for I prefer her."

Psalm 136:1–3, 4–6, 7–9

Give thanks to the LORD, for he is good,
for his mercy endures forever;
Give thanks to the God of gods,
for his mercy endures forever.
Give thanks to the Lord of lords,
for his mercy endures forever;

Who alone does great wonders,
for his mercy endures forever;
Who made the heavens in wisdom,
for his mercy endures forever;
Who spread out the earth upon the waters,
for his mercy endures forever.

Who made the great lights,
for his mercy endures forever,
The sun to rule in the day,
for his mercy endures forever,
The moon and stars to rule over the night,
for his mercy endures forever.

Psalm 138:1–2ab, 2cde–3, 7c–8

I will give thanks to you, O LORD, with all my heart,
for you have heard the words of my mouth;
in the presence of the angels I will sing your praise;
I will worship at your holy temple
and give thanks to your name.

Because of your kindness and your truth;
for you have made great above all things
your name and your promise.
When I called, you answered me;
you built up strength within me.

Your right hand saves me.
The LORD will complete what he has done for me;
your kindness, O LORD, endures forever;
forsake not the work of your hands.

Psalm 145:1–2, 8–9, 10–11, 13b–14

I will extol you, O my God and King,
 and I will bless your name for ever and ever.
Every day will I bless you,
 and I will praise your name for ever and ever.

The LORD is gracious and merciful,
 slow to anger and of great kindness.
The LORD is good to all
 and compassionate toward all his works.

Let all your works give you thanks, O LORD,
 and let your faithful ones bless you.
Let them discourse of the glory of your kingdom
 and speak of your might.

The LORD is faithful in all his words
 and holy in all his works.
The LORD lifts up all who are falling
 and raises up all who are bowed down.

Psalm 146:6c–7, 8–9a, 9bc–10

The LORD keeps faith forever,
 secures justice for the oppressed,
 gives food to the hungry.
The LORD sets captives free.

The LORD gives sight to the blind;
 the LORD raises up those who are bowed down.
The LORD loves the just;
 the LORD protects strangers.

The fatherless and the widow he sustains,
 but the way of the wicked he thwarts
The LORD shall reign forever,
 your God, O Zion, through all generations. Alleluia.

Psalm 147:1–2, 3–4, 5–6

Praise the LORD, for he is good;
sing praise to our God, for he is gracious;
it is fitting to praise him.
The LORD rebuilds Jerusalem;
the dispersed of Israel he gathers.

He heals the brokenhearted
and binds up their wounds.
He tells the number of the stars;
he calls each by name

Great is our LORD and mighty in power;
to his wisdom there is no limit.
The LORD sustains the lowly;
the wicked he casts to the ground.

Psalm 148:1–2, 11–12, 13, 14

Praise the LORD from the heavens,
praise him in the heights;
Praise him, all you his angels,
praise him, all you his hosts.

Let the kings of the earth and all peoples,
the princes and all the judges of the earth,
Young men too, and maidens,
old men and boys.

Praise the name of the LORD,
for his name alone is exalted;
His majesty is above earth and heaven.

He has lifted up the horn of his people.
Be this his praise from all his faithful ones,
from the children of Israel, the people close to him. Alleluia.

Psalm 150:1b–2, 3–4, 5–6

Praise the LORD in his sanctuary,
  praise him in the firmament of his strength.
Praise him for his mighty deeds,
  praise him for his sovereign majesty.

Praise him with the blast of the trumpet,
  praise him with lyre and harp,
Praise him with timbrel and dance,
  praise him with strings and pipes.

Praise him with sounding cymbals,
  praise him with clanging cymbals.
Let everything that has breath
  praise the LORD! Alleluia!

The Canticle of Mary

My soul proclaims the greatness of the Lord,
my spirit rejoices in God my savior
for he has looked with favor on his lowly servant.

From this day all generations will call me blessed:
the Almighty has done great things for me,
and holy is his Name.

He has mercy on those who fear him
in every generation.
He has shown the strength of his arm,
he has scattered the proud in their conceit.

He has cast down the mighty from their thrones,
and has lifted up the lowly.
He has filled the hungry with good things,
and the rich he has sent away empty.

He has come to the help of his servant Israel
for he has remembered his promise of mercy,
the promise he made to our fathers,
to Abraham and his children for ever.

Victimae Paschali Laudes

Christians, to the Paschal Victim
 Offer your thankful praises!
A Lamb the sheep redeems;
 Christ, who only is sinless,
 Reconciles sinners to the Father.
Death and life have contended in that combat stupendous:
 The Prince of life, who died, reigns immortal.
Speak, Mary, declaring
 What you saw, wayfaring.
"The tomb of Christ, who is living,
 The glory of Jesus' resurrection;
Bright angels attesting,
 The shroud and napkin resting.
Yes, Christ my hope is arisen;
 To Galilee he goes before you."
Christ indeed from death is risen, our new life obtaining.
 Have mercy, victor King, ever reigning!
 Amen. Alleluia.